Good, Reliable, White Men

THE WORKING CLASS IN AMERICAN HISTORY

Good, Reliable, White Men

Railroad Brotherhoods, 1877–1917

PAUL MICHEL TAILLON

UNIVERSITY OF ILLINOIS PRESS
Urbana and Chicago

Manufactured in the United States of America
1 2 3 4 5 C P 5 4 3 2 1

∞ This book is printed on acid-free paper.

Library of Congress Cataloging-in-Publication Data
Taillon, Paul Michel, 1962–
Good, reliable, White men : railroad brotherhoods, 1877–1917 /
Paul Michel Taillon.
p. cm. — (The working class in American history)
Includes bibliographical references and index.
ISBN 978-0-252-03485-5 (cloth : alk. paper) —
ISBN 978-0-252-07678-7 (paper : alk. paper)
1. Railroads—Employees—Labor unions—United States—History—19th century. 2. Railroads—Employees—Labor unions—United States—History—20th century. 3. Fraternal organizations—United States—History—19th century.
4. Fraternal organizations—United States—History—20th century.
5. Working class—United States—History—19th century.
6. Working class—United States—History—20th century.
7. United States—Economic conditions—1865–1918.
8. United States—Social conditions—1865–1918. I. Title.
HD6515.R1T35 2009
331.88'11385097309034—dc22 2009009430

For Jennifer

Contents

Acknowledgments

Good, Reliable, White Men would never have come to light had it not been for the assistance and support of many people and institutions. It is a pleasure to acknowledge them.

This book began as a PhD dissertation at the University of Wisconsin–Madison. Research for that study was made possible by travel grants from the University of Wisconsin, an Albert J. Beveridge Research Grant from the American Historical Association, and a Short-Term Resident Fellowship from the Newberry Library. A Charlotte W. Newcombe Doctoral Dissertation Fellowship from the Woodrow Wilson National Fellowship Foundation facilitated the writing. A New Staff Research Grant and a Research and Study Leave Grant-in-Aid from the University of Auckland, as well as a Grant-in-Aid from the Hagley Museum and Library, underwrote research necessary to reshaping the dissertation into a book. The University of Auckland provided support at a crucial moment in the form of a University Research Fellowship, which provided a semester away from teaching duties to complete revisions to the manuscript. I thank all these institutions for their generosity.

The many people who have taken an interest in my research not only made this book possible but also made the process of writing it more enjoyable. My first debts of gratitude go to Nathan Godfried and David Roediger, the historians who, knowingly or not, awakened my interest in the study of history and who have become and remained friends over the years. At the University of Wisconsin–Madison, Colleen Dunlavy, Herbert Hill, Jonathan Zeitlin, and David Zonderman helped me form the early ideas that I have, with any luck, elaborated into persuasive arguments. In the drafting of the dissertation and its transformation into a book, a community of scholars and friends offered encouragement and criticism: Ava Baron, Patricia Cooper, Roger Horowitz, Marla Hughes, Jon Huibregste, Joseph McCartin, David Roediger, and Nick Salvatore. Special thanks go to friends who read various drafts and portions of the manuscript: Bruce Fehn, David Myers, David Roediger, and Thomas Winter. (I am extremely fortunate to have had Thomas's friendship and support; his work on manhood and the YMCA served as a model for me, and his advice and commentary shaped important aspects of this book. I, along with his many friends and family, continue to miss him.) I am especially grateful to Jennifer Frost, Grey Osterud, and Barry Reay for reading the manuscript in its entirety and suggesting many improvements. The reviewers who read the manuscript for the University of Illinois Press—Colin Davis and Stephen Norwood—pushed me to clarify and improve many aspects of the book, as did James Barrett in his capacity as coeditor of the Working Class in American History series. I am also grateful to Laurie Matheson, senior acquisitions editor at the University of Illinois Press, who supported the project all along. Nicholas Taylor, who copyedited the manuscript, made the book much more readable. At the University of Auckland, I have enjoyed the friendship and support of my colleagues in the Department of History.

Without archivists and librarians, it would be impossible for the historian to research and write history. I would like to thank Roger Horowitz, associate director of the Hagley Museum and Library's Center for the History of Business, Technology, and Society; Richard Strassberg and Barb Morley at the Kheel Center for Labor-Management Documentation and Archives, Cornell University; and James Cassedy at the National Archives and Records Administration. Thanks also to staff at the New York Public Library, the Newberry Library, the Southern Labor Archives at Georgia State University, and the State Historical Society of Wisconsin for the time and assistance that they gave me during the long research for this book.

Portions of chapters 1, 2, 3, and 5 appeared in different form in three previously published essays: "'To Make Men out of Crude Material': Work Culture, Manhood, and Unionism in the Railroad Running Trades, c. 1870–1900," in Roger Horowitz, ed., *Boys and Their Toys: Masculinity, Technology, and Class* (New York: Routledge, 2001), 33–54; "'What We Want Is Good, Sober Men': Masculinity, Respectability, and Temperance in the Railroad Brotherhoods, c. 1870–1910," *Journal of Social History* 36 (Winter 2002): 319–38; and "Americanism, Racism, and 'Progressive' Unionism: The Railroad Brotherhoods, 1898–1916," *Australasian Journal of American Studies* 20 (July 2001): 55–65. I thank Routledge, the *Journal of Social History*, and the *Australasian Journal of American Studies* for permission to reprint this material.

I would like to close by thanking my family, beginning with my parents. To my children, Cealagh and Luc, I thank you for your love and unconditional belief in me. Completing this book with you two around has been more interesting, but it has also been that much more worthwhile. Finally, to Jennifer Frost. Without her this book would not exist. She saw the significance in this project before I did, and remained steadfast in her conviction that it was worth doing. Her insight, perception, judgment, time away from her own research and writing, and love have been crucial to what this study has become. I cannot imagine having done it without her.

Abbreviations

AFL	American Federation of Labor
ARU	American Railway Union
BLE	Brotherhood of Locomotive Engineers
BLF	Brotherhood of Locomotive Firemen
BLFE	Brotherhood of Locomotive Firemen and Enginemen
BLFLS	Brotherhood of Locomotive Firemen Ladies' Society
CB&Q	Chicago, Burlington & Quincy Railroad
FM	*Firemen's Magazine*
GMA	General Managers' Association
ICC	Interstate Commerce Commission
ISR	*International Socialist Review*
KoL	Knights of Labor
LEJ	*Locomotive Engineers' Journal*
LEMJ	*Locomotive Engineers' Monthly Journal*
LFEM	*Locomotive Firemen and Enginemen's Magazine*
LFM	*Locomotive Firemen's Magazine*
NAM	National Association of Manufacturers
NCF	National Civic Federation
ORC	Order of Railway Conductors
RAG	*Railway Age Gazette*
RT	*Railroad Trainman*
RTJ	*Railroad Trainmen's Journal*
YMCA	Young Men's Christian Association

Good, Reliable, White Men

INTRODUCTION

Reconsidering the Railroad Brotherhoods

On September 7, 1902, president Theodore Roosevelt traveled to Chattanooga, Tennessee, for a speaking engagement at the twenty-first biennial convention of the Brotherhood of Locomotive Firemen (BLF). The occasion of Roosevelt's appearance was the usual stuff of politics, for he had recently nominated the Firemen's former grand master Frank P. Sargent the new U.S. commissioner of immigration. With his visit, Roosevelt paid public tribute to Sargent and the organization that he had led for over fifteen years. (In true Roosevelt fashion, he also paid tribute to his own wisdom in appointing a capable man to an important governmental office.) On another level, however, Roosevelt's journey to Chattanooga was highly symbolic and historically significant. As with most public presidential appearances, and certainly in the case of a "spin-conscious" president like Theodore Roosevelt, the Firemen's convention afforded the opportunity to send a larger message to the American people. Likely the first time that a sitting U.S. president addressed a body of union men in convention, the occasion was noteworthy for the timing of Roosevelt's appearance and the content of his remarks.[1]

The date of Roosevelt's speech marked almost exactly the anniversary of the event that had thrust him into the presidency: the assassination of William McKinley on September 6, 1901. That history-changing incident had come at the hands of Leon Czolgosz, a native-born Polish American worker who had suffered unemployment and hardship during the long economic depression of the 1890s. Like a number of other individuals in similar circumstances, Czolgosz came into contact with anarchist teachings and concluded that only the overthrow of capitalism through violence could bring justice to working people. Most Americans and public commentators saw McKinley's assassination as an act of irrational violence and the anarchism behind it as an insane ideology. The governmental inquest into the affair concluded that Czolgosz was deranged. Yet Czolgosz was not deranged, and Roosevelt was one of the few politicians who recognized that the changing social conditions of the industrial age had fostered the assassin's actions. Since the 1870s, economic dislocation and rising labor conflict had plagued the United States, coming to a climax in the strike-wracked 1890s. Growing inequalities of wealth seemed to have created an almost unbridgeable divide between rich and poor; immigrants arriving daily in the nation's ports and border towns were transforming the nation's population; conditions of industrial labor were increasingly dangerous and unhealthy; women and children were being forced to work in degrading factories and sweatshops; and, emerging out of this brew, a growing radicalism threatened Americans' safety. Thus, in his first annual message as president on December 3, 1901, Roosevelt denounced anarchist terrorism, praised labor unions, and promised to address the great social problems and antagonisms of the day by trimming the excesses of unfettered capitalism and calling on Americans to engage in national self-examination and self-improvement.[2]

Yet the problems of class conflict and social disruption increased as the new century got under way. In May 1902, over 140,000 miners in the anthracite coalfields of northeastern Pennsylvania went on strike for higher wages, shorter hours, and recognition of their union, the United Mine Workers. The mine owners refused to bargain. Coming amid the economic expansion following the 1890s depression, the strike threatened to disrupt the nation's basic source of domestic heat and looked to be the most disruptive work stoppage among the soaring number of stoppages that occurred in the early years of the twentieth century. As summer came to an end, rising coal prices, sporadic violence, and growing public concern pressured Roosevelt to avert the impending crisis. In late September, the president moved to mediate the conflict, arranging an unprecedented conference of coal operators and union leaders. The outcome was a presidential commission that ended the strike and awarded a 10 percent wage increase to anthracite workers. Roosevelt's skillful handling of the crisis won him international acclaim and pointed the way to a new means of handling labor conflict when the "public interest" was at stake: mediation and arbitration, under government auspices, of disputes between organized bodies of workers and employers.[3]

Roosevelt doubtless had the anthracite crisis and McKinley's assassination in mind when he took the podium at the Firemen's convention that day in early September. Outlining the circumstances facing the nation as a result of industrial capitalism, he reminded his audience that "we . . . as a people . . . find set before us for solution during the coming century problems which need the best thought of all of us." The American people had cause for hope, he continued, for in facing those problems they could be comforted by the achievements of unions like the Brotherhood of Locomotive Firemen, which had been led with "courage," "skill," "wisdom," "the spirit of fair dealing as between man and man," and "wise self-restraint." These were themes that Roosevelt had sounded in his first presidential address, and he returned to them in his Chattanooga speech. In the age of the large-scale corporation, workers had to organize in unions, yet the BLF was also a positive good in its emphasis on self-improvement. "We need good laws," insisted Roosevelt, "but back of it all lies the need for that which nothing else can supply—the need for a higher average of individual citizenship." And the BLF stood as nothing less than "an object lesson in good American citizenship." With unions like the Firemen fostering good citizenship and acting responsibly in labor relations, Roosevelt envisioned a coming reconciliation among the nation's estranged social classes.[4] In Chattanooga that day, the president spoke to one of the central challenges of the twentieth century, one that preoccupied a generation of Americans, and suggested responsible trade unionism as a key element in meeting that challenge.[5]

This book is a study of four trade unions that embodied Theodore Roosevelt's vision of responsible unionism: the Brotherhood of Locomotive Engineers, the Order of Railway Conductors, the Brotherhood of Locomotive Firemen, and the Brotherhood of Railroad Trainmen. These unions—collectively known as the "Big Four" railroad brotherhoods—had their origins in the Civil War years; between 1877 and 1917, they became among the most powerful set of unions in the United States. In that process, the brotherhoods developed a style of unionism that at the time (and since) has been variously characterized as "conservative," "business," "voluntarist," "prudential," "uplift," "benefit-oriented," and "responsible." These unions had their admirers and detractors, yet by the early years of the twentieth century they accumulated and wielded a great deal of power, challenging the authority of the great railroad corporations, commanding the attention of U.S. presidents, and influencing public policy. So strong had they become that in the summer of 1916, when they jointly threatened a national rail strike to win the eight-hour workday, they forced the intervention of president Woodrow Wilson and an unprecedented act of Congress granting their demands. The Adamson Act, as it came to be known, marked a milestone in Progressive Era politics and the development of the modern liberal state. As "responsible" unions, the railroad brotherhoods appeared unlikely to initiate dramatic action, yet they did so with great success.[6]

The brotherhoods did indeed have histories of conservatism, fraternalism, and craft exclusiveness. Admitting only the highly skilled, very specialized, and well-paid workers of the railroad running trades—engineers, conductors, firemen, and brakemen—the brotherhoods represented less than one-fifth of all railroad workers and were composed more conspicuously of white men of American and rural parentage than any other major North American labor union. They steeped themselves in quasi-Masonic fraternalism and hewed to rigid craft lines, avoiding broader class agendas, eschewing alliances with other labor organizations, and disavowing strikes as a way to resolve labor disputes. With these proclivities, the brotherhoods remained aloof from the American Federation of Labor (AFL), becoming the largest and longest-running group of independent unions. Lastly, the railroad brotherhoods earned dubious distinction as perhaps the most racist unions, noted for their antipathy toward people they regarded as nonwhite. Whereas trade unions in the United States customarily limited their membership to white men, in the early twentieth century the brotherhoods went a step further and attempted to eliminate black workers from the running trades entirely.[7]

Many historians have regarded the railroad brotherhoods as embodying the worst tendencies of a generally conservative American working class. Existing accounts of the brotherhoods and other trade unions explain their character and portray their success as the result of a narrow business unionism focused on delivering "bread-and-butter" services to their membership. The brotherhoods' focus strictly on the economic interests of their crafts, and the avoidance of disruptive social, political, and religious issues—so the argument goes—allowed them to escape distracting, chimerical visions of social reform; they also avoided potential repression from employers and the state. Indeed, the brotherhoods' narrow organizational focus enabled them to concentrate their energies on the problems that really concerned their members: the control of jobs and wages. Like other craft unions, their approach to unionism succeeded because brotherhood members were principally "job-conscious" and apolitical. At the same time, the brotherhoods' success in maintaining the loyalty of their members has been taken as proof of the underlying conservatism of the rank and file.[8]

This view of the railroad brotherhoods—and of trade unionism and American workers generally—has its origins in the work of the "old," institutionally oriented labor history of John R. Commons, and has been reinforced in the "new" labor history as well. Studying the labor movement during the first decades of the twentieth century, the same years that trade unionism came to prominence, Commons and his students arrived at their interpretations in large part by sympathetic observation of the contemporary labor movement and by taking at face value AFL president Samuel Gompers's definition of unions as simply "the business organizations of the wage-earners." In this line of thought, trade unions succeeded because they "delivered the goods" to workers more interested in pork chops than social reform or revolution, as Howard Kimeldorf has put it.[9] The "new" labor historians of the 1970s and 1980s adopted much the same view, but they dismissed the brotherhoods, and trade unions generally, as conservative, backward-looking organizations devoted merely to the self-interest and material welfare of a privileged segment of the labor force. With the new labor history's emphasis on culture over institutions; its mission to uncover workers' experience in the family, workplace, and community; and its tendency to focus on moments of radicalism and militancy, moderate workers' movements have gone largely ignored. Indeed, regarded by most historians as conservative and relatively elite institutions, the railroad brotherhoods could not seem to be more irrelevant.[10] Even in the best study of railroad labor conflict and unionism, Shelton Stromquist's *A Generation of Boomers*, the brotherhoods figure as the weary counterpoint to the vibrancy of industrial organization.[11] Both the old and new labor history contributed to an image of the railroad brotherhoods as the epitome of conservative trade unionism.[12] Yet such a view distorts our understanding of the ways in which ordinary Americans responded to the profound changes wrought by the development of industrial capitalism, and it misrepresents the nature and role of unions in that process.

Through a thematic and analytic narrative, drawing on and speaking to a range of literatures, this book provides an account of the railroad brotherhoods from the period of their formation in the 1860s and 1870s to the consolidation of their power on the eve of U.S. entry into World War I. It argues that the railroad brotherhoods played an important role in these events and became a potent force in a key economic sector and in national-level politics by the early years of the twentieth century. It suggests that the unionism of the railroad brotherhoods was successful and influential for three interrelated reasons. First, it commanded the loyalties of thousands of strategically placed railwaymen. Second, it capably navigated the treacherous waters of the late nineteenth century, a period that witnessed the demise of other, "less-prudential" unions; crucially, in the Erdman Act of 1898, the brotherhoods helped bring about a system of state-sanctioned collective bargaining, which guaranteed brotherhood survival. Third, brotherhood unionism flourished under this system of collective bargaining, pushing the system in directions not anticipated by its framers and forcing its revision and expansion. The federal policy that helped create the conditions for the brotherhoods' success did so unexpectedly, for it had merely aimed to contain labor conflict in the nation's most important industrial sector. The received wisdom of the old and new labor histories, however, does little to explain the story of these unions, the loyalties that they inspired, and their impact on early twentieth-century politics and society.

To properly understand the railroad brotherhoods and the successes and failures of the labor movement in the United States, we must pay attention to the agency of working people, the collective identities they constructed, and the institutions they built. The first of these tasks requires parting with preconceived assumptions about skilled workers and the nature of class in the United States. On the face of it, skilled workers like engineers and conductors appear as "labor aristocrats."[13] But this idea obscures as much as it illuminates, for skilled railroad workers occupied a contradictory class position; to borrow from sociologist Eric Olin Wright, they stood "in-between" non-skilled workers and lower-level managers at the permeable, ambiguous border between the working and middle classes. They were semiautonomous workers who labored within a highly bureaucratic environment. They possessed a high degree of technical and cognitive skill, exercised a relatively high degree of control over their immediate labor processes, supervised one or more helpers, and earned wages that put them within the lower reaches of the middle class. Yet their control over their labor power was circumscribed by the highly rule-bound nature of running-trades work; further, the rhythms and the difficult, dirty, and dangerous nature of their jobs were incontestably working class, not middle class.[14]

Given their class location, it should not be surprising that railroaders did not always behave in a class-conscious manner, at least in a Marxian sense.[15] Simply put, skilled workers did not have to think much about the "choice" before them, as Eugene V. Debs put it, between capitalism and socialism. They chose capitalism, as well as trade unionism, in overwhelming numbers. Brotherhood members were not socialists, but neither were they simply job-conscious and apolitical. They sought to advance within a social and economic system that by the end of the nineteenth century had become stacked against them as individuals. Although skilled workers built unions that operated within the capitalist system, these were also organizations that contested managerial power for control of the workplace. Understanding skilled workers and taking seriously the actions of unions like the railroad brotherhoods allows us to focus on what they *did* accomplish rather than what they *should* have accomplished.[16]

Taking the brotherhoods seriously also opens the door to understanding the influences of gender and race on union organization and action, the second necessary task. Over the past decade and a half, new approaches to the study of gender and race have transformed historical scholarship. The use of gender as a category of analysis is now commonplace. Labor historians have uncovered the myriad ways in which gender has shaped the work process, the wage form, workplace conflicts, class relations, and gender relations.[17] With a few notable exceptions, compared with studies focusing on the middle class, however, understanding of working-class masculinity and manhood remains rather weakly developed in labor history.[18] More controversial have been engagements over "whiteness," which have centered on the integrity of the concept as an analytical category.[19]

As the title implies, *Good, Reliable, White Men* finds utility in the concepts of gender and race as analytical categories. It is based in the premise, to quote Gail Bederman, that gender "is a *historical* and *ideological* process" in which individuals position themselves, and are positioned, as women or men. As Bederman argues, men claim certain kinds of authority based on their particular types of bodies.[20] Analogously, to adapt the ideas of Barbara J. Fields and Evelyn Brooks Higginbotham, race also is an ideological process and a historical product by which groups recognize and signify difference and hierarchy vis-à-vis one another. With the historical legacy of slavery in the United States, as well as the decades of legal, economic, and political segregation and subordination, whites have claimed certain kinds of authority and advantages based on skin color over African Americans and other racial minorities.[21] The two processes, together with class, are inextricably and simultaneously interlinked systems of privilege and oppression. In other words, manhood and whiteness figure both as categories of identity and exercises in power, inseparable from the phenomena of sexism and racism.[22] In their capacity to signify relations of power, gender and race have shaped the class experience. Class, as a concept describing productive and reproductive relationships, can be lived through gender and race, and working-class solidarity can be reinforced by solidarities of race and gender.[23] This dynamic was certainly the case in the railroad brotherhoods. Attention to this dynamic can illuminate unions like the brotherhoods, shedding light on their fraternal cultures, labor relations strategies, and political languages, not to mention their drive to evict black railwaymen from their workplace.

The railroad brotherhoods' campaigns to drive black firemen and brakemen from the railroads have featured prominently in scholarly debate over the American labor movement's institutional racism. Critics have documented the importance of unions in the historical construction and maintenance of job structures that benefited white workers at the expense of black workers (as well as other minorities and women). They have also debated the relative importance of employers, the state, and white workers in this process.[24] In the railroad industry, racial hierarchies had their origins in the segmented nature of the workplace, which was determined by employers. Overlaid by hiring practices that determined which jobs would be for whites or blacks, these job structures virtually guaranteed competition and racial tensions. Nevertheless, white railroaders chose to act on those structures. They did so collectively through their unions, and they exploited the Erdman Act labor relations machinery, even though it had not been intended for that purpose.[25] Collective identity and perceptions of collective interest shaped "what workers could do and dream in their lifetimes," as David Roediger has written. But shaped by race and gender, and institutionalized in unions like the brotherhoods, the consequences of what white workers could do were dire.[26]

The importance of institutions highlights the third task: to take unions seriously, but from an "un-Commons" perspective. In its focus on the railroad brotherhoods as the organizational expression of skilled railroad workers' power, this book builds on the "new institutionalism." New institutionalist approaches to the study of American labor have combined the new labor history's emphasis on culture and community with analysis of the labor movement both in the context of the larger political economy and in relation to other institutions. Such an approach focuses on unions because they mattered; trade unions as institutions had a greater impact historically than did workers individually or even as groups of individuals. Moreover, institutional forces shaped the relationships among workers, as well as between and among workers, unions, employers, and the state.[27]

The new institutional perspective highlights the fact that the fate of workers' movements was often beyond their control, and that they constructed their collective identities and institutional ideologies and strategies under conditions not of their own choosing. For instance, brotherhood leaders and activists drew on the republican legacy of the American Revolution and the cultural form of fraternalism as organizing frames, but these choices were shaped in an arena of conflict, in the face of employer and, for much of the period under study, state opposition. Union builders were often idealists but also pragmatists, and their overriding goals were effective unionism and institutional survival. If the railroad brotherhoods adopted a "conservative" posture, they did so not because of some essential conservatism on the part of their membership. Union leaders recognized that working people, both individually and collectively, were not always the makers of their own destinies. They needed allies, or at least a national state that was not overtly hostile to their aspirations. In the nineteenth century, a staunchly laissez-faire political economy, combined with a legal-political order opposed to collective action, encouraged unions to avoid inclusive organization, shun broad reform efforts, and be wary of political engagement. Yet over time, the relationships among unions, employers, and the state changed. Unions continuously and creatively tested the limits of the established order through industrial action and ongoing efforts to influence the centers of public power and state policy. Labor and state dialectically shaped each other, producing the distinctive twentieth-century American labor movement and liberal state.[28] Railroad workers and their unions played a prominent role in that process and so demand investigation and understanding.

Scholarship on railroad workers and railroad unionism provides a necessary starting point for investigation. Walter Licht's *Working for the Railroad* (1983) and Shelton Stromquist's *A Generation of Boomers* (1987) deserve special mention as studies that have contributed mightily to our understanding. Licht's study of the pioneering American railwaymen in the nineteenth century was a groundbreaking work. Combining a range of quantitative data with qualitative sources, it is a social history that, in its synthesis of labor and business history, has become indispensable for any study of railroads and railroaders. Unions, however, feature only peripherally. Stromquist covers about half the time period under study in this book and discusses the railroad brotherhoods' strategies. Based in an analysis bringing together the railroad labor market, national political economy, and local communities, the book persuasively explains the pattern of railroad labor conflict and union organization during the 1880s and early 1890s.[29] I am deeply indebted to Stromquist's account, and I view my book as building on his scholarship, extending the implications of his arguments into the twentieth century. Nevertheless, I also depart from him in my view of the railroad brotherhoods as an important union tradition. *Good, Reliable, White Men* investigates more deeply the brotherhoods' cultural worlds, especially regarding gender and race; refigures the relationship of the brotherhoods to the state; suggests that they offer a useful window onto processes of social, cultural, and political change over the late nineteenth and early twentieth centuries; and argues for their historical role in helping to propel those changes on the railroads.

The greatest industrial enterprise of the nineteenth century, the railroads were central to many facets of American economic, social, cultural, and political development. Breaking down physical space and connecting the nation, the railroads created the transportation arteries of domestic and international markets, provided the means for establishing networks of urban settlement, supplied outlets for durable goods, offered a model for large-scale corporate organization and managerial practice, shaped the instruments of capital formation, and propelled government to infuse massive public resources into private business. Along the way, they provided an important site for conflicts over gender, race, class, and rights, and prompted momentous debates and epic contests about the proper relationships among government, private enterprise, labor, and management.[30] Railwaymen stood at the center of these developments. Their work was vital for national life, and they knew it. Railwaymen achieved a degree of notoriety and public standing unknown among other tradesmen, and with their mobility they developed a worldview tied to their local communities yet also national in perspective. And because they were comparatively well educated and often had time on their hands, they read and debated issues of the day. At the same time, railwaymen worked with their hands, negotiated a unique form of industrial discipline, and contended with harrowing risks during the course of their labor.

Accelerating industrialization during and after the Civil War prompted railwaymen to organize unions. Engineers in Detroit, Michigan, founded the Brotherhood of Locomotive Engineers (BLE) in 1863, followed by the Order of Railway Conductors (ORC), the Brotherhood of Locomotive Firemen (BLF), and the Brotherhood of Railroad Brakemen between the late 1860s and early 1880s. The railroad brotherhoods, however, were not the only expression of unionism on the railroads during the Gilded Age. A number of labor organizations like the Knights of Labor (KoL) and the American Railway Union (ARU), which were more industrial in character, rose and fell.[31] Still, as important as these unions were, the brotherhoods were among the first to organize nationally, and they outlasted their competitors to play leading roles in the labor movement and national politics by the early twentieth century. At the same time, they demonstrated some of the shortcomings of craft-based unionism, and their institutional racism helped propel some of the era's worst tendencies.

During these years, industrial capitalism underwent its full development, and matters of class became the central axis of conflict in American society. The Civil War catalyzed this process by destroying slavery, guaranteeing the Union's permanence, shifting power into the hands of northern capitalists, and initiating the modern American state. The war cleared the way for the development of a national railroad system and stepped up the cycle of expansion and collapse that characterized nineteenth century economic growth. Combined with battles between workers and capitalists for the workplace, this pattern of growth generated much of the class conflict of these years. The 1890s marked a turning point as the combined forces of capital and the state destroyed the nascent industrial unionism of the ARU, shaping labor relations well into the twentieth century. The early years of the twentieth century also were transitional, marking the consolidation of corporate capitalism and the expanded capacities of the national state. By the time of World War I, these developments had propelled important shifts in the nation's culture and politics as Americans came to question a nineteenth-century legal-political order grounded in laissez-faire liberalism.[32] The brotherhoods both contributed to these historical developments and provide a window onto a crucial period in American history.

This book proceeds in both thematic and chronological fashion. Chapter 1 surveys the experience of running-trades work, its impact on the household, and the ways in which it shaped the culture of the men who operated the trains in the late nineteenth and early twentieth centuries. The next two chapters explore the social and cultural worlds of the railroad brotherhoods in the 1880s. Chapter 2 interrogates the brotherhoods' fraternal cultures, emphasizing the ways that their fraternalism reflected a tradition of working-class mutualism within the context of a Victorian moral order. Chapter 3 engages with the brotherhoods' approach to labor-capital relations, linking it to their fraternal culture, as well as to the larger laissez-faire legal and political order of the late nineteenth century. Chapter 4 focuses on the "crisis" decade of the 1890s and the ways in which the brotherhoods both responded and contributed to its resolution, especially through their role in the passage of the Erdman Act of 1898. The Erdman Act marked a transition point from nineteenth-century liberalism of the free market to the "new" liberalism of the twentieth century, characterized by state intervention and collective bargaining. Chapter 5 considers the cultural and institutional changes resulting from these events, as well as their legacies, particularly the apparent waning of fraternal culture and the rise of a new Americanist discourse in the brotherhoods. The last two chapters examine the brotherhoods' widening pattern of industrial and political action within the Erdman Act industrial relations regime and the "new" politics of the Progressive Era. Chapter 6 examines the brotherhoods' "craft industrialism" and the ways that it both proceeded from and challenged the Erdman Act arbitration system, bringing it to a crisis point by 1915. Chapter 7 weaves a number of strands together as it explains the role of the brotherhoods in the events of 1916 and the passage of the Adamson Act. The conclusion connects the history of the railroad brotherhoods during these years to the history of the interwar period and the larger story of American unionism's successes and failures. In the end, this book argues for the relevance of unions like the railroad brotherhoods, for their history is a part of the broader history of American labor in all of its complexity.

This group of railwaymen worked on the Santa Fe Railroad between Streator and Pekin, Illinois, 1918. The photograph captures the mix of respectability, roughness, pride, and skill characteristic of the running trades. Kheel Center for Labor-Management Documentation and Archives, Cornell University.

These two individuals, probably a fireman and a brakeman, worked on the Chicago & Northwestern Railroad on the Wisconsin Division in 1917. The photograph suggests their sense of themselves as good, reliable, white men. Kheel Center for Labor-Management Documentation and Archives, Cornell University.

"Benevolence, Sobriety, Industry" were the fraternal values central to the Brotherhood of Railroad Trainmen. Brotherhood of Locomotive Trainmen Chart, ca. 1920s. Kheel Center for Labor-Management Documentation and Archives, Cornell University.

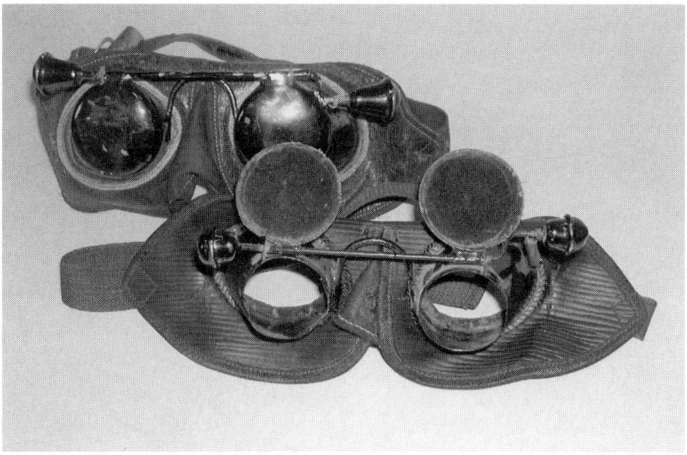

Items used in brotherhood initiation rituals. Above, this wagon was used in Order of Railway Conductors initiations. The candidate had to remain standing while pulled, blindfolded, around the lodge room. Below, hoodwinks worn by candidates to the Switchmen's Union of North America and Brotherhood of Railroad Trainmen during initiation rituals. As meaningful images were displayed on a screen, the eye flaps were lifted, permitting the candidate to see. Kheel Center for Labor-Management Documentation and Archives, Cornell University.

Peter M. Arthur, grand master, Brotherhood of Locomotive Engineers, and Eugene V. Debs, grand secretary and treasurer of the Brotherhood of Locomotive Firemen, were principal architects of the brotherhoods' unionism of the 1880s. Drawing from Souvenir of Brotherhood of Locomotive Firemen Fourteenth Annual Convention, 1888. Kheel Center for Labor-Management Documentation and Archives, Cornell University.

While the trade unions and the Knights of Labor go at it, Peter M. Arthur guides the brotherhood train of progress into the future. After the Pullman boycott of 1894, the brotherhoods' conservative unionism in the 1880s persuaded reformers and governmental figures that these unions could be relied on as partners in stable railroad labor relations. Drawing by Joseph Keppler, *Puck* (August 25, 1886). American Social History Project.

The brotherhoods' women's auxiliaries were indicative of the all-female organizing of the Progressive Era. They institutionalized women's social networks for self-education and support of the unions. Above, executive officers of the Brotherhood of Locomotive Firemen and Enginemen Ladies Society. Illustration from *The Brotherhood of Locomotive Firemen and Enginemen 35th Anniversary and 11th Biennial Convention, Columbus 1908, Souvenir.* Kheel Center for Labor-Management Documentation and Archives, Cornell University.

In the first decade of the twentieth century, larger locomotives and longer trains meant poorer working conditions for railroaders. This cartoon appeared in the *Railroad Trainman* (February 1912, 106).

The arbitration ending the 1912 standoff between the Brotherhood of Locomotive Engineers and the eastern railroads proved a turning point in the industrial relations regime established by the Erdman Act of 1898. Newspaper clipping, *Washington Evening Star* (April 23, 1912), National Mediation Board, Record Group 13, National Archives and Records Administration.

The Adamson Act of 1916 drew the brotherhoods into both electoral politics and a historic alliance with the Democratic Party, which paid large dividends for the Democrats in the 1916 election. In the cartoon at right, reprinted in the *Locomotive Firemen and Enginemen's Magazine* (November 1916, 509), the railroads train Republican candidate Charles Evans Hughes to oppose the Adamson eight-hour law.

1

Workplace and Household Life in the Running Trades

"A railroad conductor, or an engineer, had about as much prestige, and about the same amount of public attention, as a crack air-mail pilot of today," recalled Harry French in his 1938 memoir, *Railroadman*. The occasion of French's reminiscence was his promotion to freight conductor in the late 1880s, an event that advanced his and his wife Molly's social standing in the small town of Ottawa, Kansas. The measure of his success came when the town's barber placed French's shaving mug in the front window: "In this swanky shop an ornate rack . . . displayed the shaving mugs and razors of its patrons. Each mug and razor bore the name of its owner in shining gilt Germanic lettering. Those aspiring to real fame could press their noses against the somewhat wavy glass window and ascertain that Conductor Harry French of the L., L. & G. was shaved at that shop." This event marked a milestone in French's railroading career and signaled his respectable community standing. Yet French's behavior was not always respectable. He used coarse language, chewed and spat tobacco, frequented saloons, and drank heavily. His behavior, combined with unpredictable work hours and frequent geographical moves, took its toll on his family. A few years after his promotion, Molly left him and took their children with her.[1]

Harry French's story illustrates the disruptive impact of railroad work on family life and reflects the dual—even contradictory—standing of railwaymen in American society and culture. On the one hand, the railroader as hero figured prominently in popular culture. By the early twentieth century, the noble engineer, embodied by John Luther "Casey" Jones, stood in the same pantheon of American heroes as Davy Crockett and Buffalo Bill, fixed in the American imagination as the embodiment of bravery, duty, and self-sacrifice. Occupying a strategic place in a prominent industry, the men who ran the trains stood as self-made, self-directing skilled workers contributing to national progress through their labor. In the towns and cities where they lived, railroad men and their wives and families often stood as examples of working-class achievement and respectability. Little wonder that they developed a fierce craft pride. Yet for all the glamour, running-trades workers were really little more than machine operators, working within a distinctive environment that was nonetheless disciplined and highly bureaucratized. Grime, irregular work rhythms, physical hardships, arduousness, risk, and boredom defined the work of operating trains and undermined the respectable standing of the railwayman's family. In these circumstances, railroaders engaged in less respectable conduct, using foul language or "toughly" confronting the harsher conditions of work, while their wives struggled to negotiate the disconnect between dominant gender norms and the material reality of their lives. These features of running-trades life produced a work culture that in certain aspects was unique to railroads in the United States.

Railwaymen and the Running Trades

The railroad industry in the United States dated from the 1820s and went through its initial phases of development over the decades before the Civil War. The war, with its sundering of the nation, interruption of the labor supply, and inflationary economy, disrupted the railroad industry and the lives of its workers. Yet it also marked a point of departure for the growth and consolidation of the railroads over the following three decades. Over this period of time, railroad work (as well as the geographically dispersed and bureaucratically structured environments in which it occurred) emerged in its modern form, and many of the issues that animated the organization of the railroad brotherhoods arose out of this era of accelerating industrialization.

The creation of a national railroad network in the United States occurred in roughly three phases between the Civil War and the end of the nineteenth century. Between 1863, the year in which a Republican-controlled Congress passed the Pacific Railroad Act, and the onset of economic depression in 1873, the railroad industry completed the first transcontinental railroad across the western United States and filled in the pre-Civil War railroad network in the East. Following economic recovery in 1878, the railroads laid the greatest amount of new mileage of any single period of expansion, pushing additional transcontinental routes to completion. After a brief downturn in the economy from 1883 to 1886, the railroads pushed their lines beyond their established territories, creating multiple regional and transcontinental routes, only to be stopped in their tracks by the severe depression of the 1890s. At the start of the twentieth century, following the depression-induced consolidation of the railroads into large systems, the outline of the national rail network stood completed with close to 200,000 miles of track in operation, a figure that rose to over 259,000 miles by 1916.[2]

The growth and profits of America's "leading sector" rested on the labor of hundreds of thousands of men and women. From an estimated 7,000 railroad workers in 1840, the number of railroad employees reached nearly 750,000 by 1890, about 4 percent of the nation's workforce. By 1910, the industry's total had risen to 1,699,000. As the nation's largest employers, the railroads accounted for a little over half the total employment in the transportation and public utilities sector in the last third of the nineteenth century. In numbers alone, the size of the railroad labor force outpaced other industries.[3] Across the nation, most railwaymen worked in large, bureaucratically complex work organizations. By 1873, the Pennsylvania Railroad reigned as the largest of the nineteenth-century railroads, capitalized at $398 million and controlling over 6,600 miles of track. It employed approximately 20,000 workers, a figure that rose to 65,000 by 1890. Toward the turn of century, increasing numbers of railroaders worked for fewer, but larger, corporations as mergers and consolidation of trunk lines integrated more short-line railroads into national and international systems. In 1877, the majority of railwaymen worked for fifty corporations, yet by 1889, when railroad employment stood at 750,000, nearly half of them worked for the sixteen largest companies.[4]

Like their European counterparts, American railroads responded to challenges associated with size, geographic scale, and intricacy of operation—hallmarks of the new industrial order—and pioneered modern, bureaucratic organizational techniques. As the first businesses whose transactions and property holdings extended over vast distances, railroads depended on the synchronized operation of sophisticated equipment and the activities of thousands of employees. By the Civil War era, the industry had developed hierarchies staffed by professional managers and had embraced a decentralized, line-and-staff organizational model (in contrast to the more centralized structure of European railroads). In both Europe and the United States, the railroads' distinctive functional arrangement of operations into separate departments, one looking after the construction and maintenance of rails and roadbeds and another maintaining rolling stock and coordinating traffic, resulted from these organizational innovations.[5]

American railroads organized their labor force into a complex job hierarchy segmented by multiple gradations of skill, prestige, and arduousness. But unlike railroads in Europe, matters of ethnicity, race, and region unique to the United States shaped the American railroad labor force.[6] In the road department, young men drawn from the lower echelons of a racially stratified labor market predominated in the industry's unskilled construction and maintenance sectors. In the South, these men tended to be African American; in the Southwest, Mexican laborers predominated. In the West, Chinese and Japanese immigrants formed the majority; and in the Northeast and Midwest, immigrants from southern and eastern Europe prevailed. Accounting for the plurality of the overall railroad labor force (roughly 30 percent), these men performed the labor-intensive work necessary to the upkeep of roadbeds and track.[7] In the roundhouses and repair shops, a complicated array of crafts—machinists, boilermakers, blacksmiths, carpenters, car repairmen, painters, and upholsterers—performed a wide variety of tasks necessary in the maintenance of engines and rolling stock. Skilled metal- and woodworkers, approximately one-fifth of the workforce, tended to be native-born and of European parentage, whereas the shops' semiskilled and unskilled labor force often were foreign-born ethnic and native-born black workers. In and around the stations and offices, nearly 17 percent of the workforce performed clerical tasks and facilitated the transfer of freight and passengers. The remainder of the railroad labor force worked as telegraphers, signal operators, and in other assorted capacities. White men typically made up the clerical and miscellaneous grades, but after the turn of the century railroads began to hire lower-paid, high school–educated women to work in offices equipped with laborsaving machines.[8]

American running-trades workers—the engineers, conductors, firemen, and brakemen who operated the trains—shared common features with European railwaymen, although factors unique to the United States—geographical dispersion and the nation's ethnic and racial makeup—set them apart. They accounted for about 20 percent of the total workforce and presented a much more homogenous profile. Like Harry French, born and raised in the midwestern town of St. Charles, Missouri, they were white men from native-born, old-immigrant stock. As with English railwaymen, given the railroad's abrupt arrival in the countryside they disproportionately came from rural backgrounds. Like their English and French counterparts, American railwaymen, at least those who won promotion to engineer or conductor, tended to come from "respectable" agrarian or skilled working-class backgrounds.[9] In the South, the racial division of labor diverged from other parts of the country. Since the period of slavery, southern railways had engaged the labor of black men as brakemen and firemen, paying them less than white men for the same work. This practice, however, did not extend to the engineer or conductor categories. Popular and managerial assumptions about the relative worth and ability of "white" and "dark" races, as well as the benefits to the company of paying black workers artificially low wages, informed the construction of this racially segmented labor force. On the other hand, whereas the racial hierarchy of railroad work required some justification, its gender composition occasioned little debate, for it appeared self-evident. Customary notions of what constituted men's work dictated that only men would be hired for railroad construction, maintenance, and operation in the years before World War I. Like many industrial and craft workplaces during these years, the locomotive footboard and caboose were homosocial environments inhabited predominantly by white men.[10]

Age and generational experience marked American running-trades workers. In the late 1870s and 1880s, passenger engineers and conductors were older men, having reached their career destinations in these positions by their mid-thirties on average, as Walter Licht has found. Firemen and brakemen typically were young men in their late teens and early twenties, having already worked a few years as laborers. This generation of railroaders enjoyed relatively rapid promotion as a result of industry expansion in the post-1870s depression years. For the succeeding generation, however, promotion would come more slowly, as the 1890s depression halted new construction and the railroads concentrated on consolidating existing lines after 1900.[11] The engineers and conductors of the 1880s, moreover, would have lived through the Civil War years as young men. The data on railroaders' rate of military participation in the Civil War is incomplete and not easily obtained; to the extent that Civil War veterans found their way into the postwar railroad labor force, however, they carried their experience as soldiers with them into their careers as railroad workers. As Russell L. Johnson has put it, military service gave soldiers "their first taste of industrial work relations and working conditions." Military discipline and organization may have prepared these men for railroad work and at the same time contributed to the bureaucratic organization of that work.[12] The generation that replaced these workers from the 1890s through the 1910s, however, coming of age in the postwar years, would have grown up not with the experience of the war, but rather with its memory.

The Civil War and the vagaries of the railroad labor market distinguished the experiences of American running-trades workers, but train operation in Europe and the United States did share many commonalities. The work was demanding and required skills different from those of most other industrial occupations. On the "head-end" of the train, engineers operated the steam locomotive, monitoring steam pressure, boiler water level, and other mechanical workings. The engineer had to be able to read and interpret operating rules, timetables, and running orders. He needed good eyesight, stamina, and knowledge of the track to run his train safely and on time. On the road, he listened to his engine, interpreting its sounds and rhythms. In event of breakdown, he had to be able to diagnose the problem and make repairs. After the introduction of air brakes in the 1890s, he needed fine judgment and an exquisite touch to stop the train smoothly and in the proper place. Lastly, the engineer exercised a high degree of control over the execution of his work. From the time that he received his orders until he delivered his engine to the roundhouse, he was relatively independent.[13]

Firemen worked under the engineer's supervision shoveling coal into the locomotive's firebox, a dirty, dangerous, and backbreaking job. Although the position cannot be regarded as skilled, firing a locomotive demanded a combination of intelligence and physical ability. The fireman's basic task was to pitch coal through a small opening into the firebox from a swaying deck, arranging it properly to achieve greatest combustion. Providing steam when the engineer wanted it, however, meant feeding the fire to meet *future* demands, because steam engines were not quickly responsive sources of power. In addition, the fireman monitored the firebox crown sheet, making sure that it was always covered with water to prevent an explosion, and assisted the engineer in observing signals. The relationship between firemen and engineers was hierarchical, yet they worked together as a team. As engineers-in-training they labored in anticipation of advancing to the other side of the cab, a promotional practice that had developed by the 1850s. This practice came with built-in tensions, however, for firemen formed a potential pool in the labor supply, threatening to undercut experienced and higher-paid engineers.[14]

Technically in charge of the train, the conductor handled train orders, oversaw the crew, and made sure that his train arrived at its destination on time. On passenger trains he collected fares and assisted passengers, whereas on freight runs he was responsible for the cargo manifest. Before departing, he walked the length of the train, inspecting each car and its couplings, made sure that the train had proper supplies, and saw that the crew read their train orders and understood the run. As "captain" of the train, the conductor rode in the caboose, sitting in its cupola, where he could observe the train's conduct. Conductors needed to be literate as well as have practical judgment and record-keeping ability. For passenger runs they had to be courteous but also ready to manage volatile situations. The conductor's duties made him a combination of supervisor, traveling clerk, public relations representative, and sometimes peacemaker. Although conductors' earnings did not quite compare with those of engineers, they enjoyed considerable independence in their work and in fact exercised more general authority than their counterparts on the head-end of the train.[15]

Working under the conductor's direction, brakemen operated the brakes, opened and closed switches, acted as flagmen when necessary, and on passenger runs announced the next station. Before the spread of air brakes, the process of stopping a moving train required brakemen to pick their way along the tops of cars, setting and releasing brakes. Brakes had to be set in such a way as to slow down the train without sliding the wheels or bringing the train to a halt too abruptly. Stopping or slowing a train took more than just nimbleness to stay on top of the cars or the brute strength to turn a brake wheel; it took teamwork among all members of the train crew. Brakemen also coupled and uncoupled cars, tasks that required them to step in between the cars and remove or insert an iron pin into the connecting links as the engineer eased the two cars together or gently pulled them apart. Such procedures, and the skills necessary to them, persisted well into the twentieth century (as the installation of automatic couplers and air brakes remained uneven).[16] In the yards, switchmen (essentially brakemen) performed the work of breaking apart and making up trains.

For the work they performed, running-trades workers earned high rates of pay. Railroad wages corresponded to the industry's occupational hierarchy: train crews enjoyed the highest wages, section laborers the least. Engineers and conductors earned roughly twice that of firemen and brakemen. Regionally, railwaymen in the West, where railroad expansion placed greatest pressure on the labor market, earned more than their eastern counterparts, followed by those in the South. Overall, running-trades remuneration compared favorably with the rest of the nation's industrial labor force, "wages which fairly placed them among the lower professional groups in society," according to Selig Perlman.[17] Such wages enabled the better paid among the running trades to enjoy a level of real comfort in their lives. Engineers and conductors could obtain mortgages and become home owners while still setting aside enough for a few luxuries. High wages combined with unique skills and work experiences to set the running trades apart from the rest of the industrial labor force and contributed to the reputation of engineers and conductors for identifying with management. In terms of regularity of earnings, the differential between their wages and those of railroad laborers, the prestige that they enjoyed, their conditions of living, and the prospects for their children's advancement, senior engineers had much in common with their English counterparts as "labor aristocrats."[18]

If high pay rates defined running-trades work, so too did its "burdens." Long hours of labor and unpredictable work rhythms combined to make the work of operating trains arduous and actual take-home pay uneven. The nature of train operation demanded that train crews put in extended hours—twelve to twenty-four hours, and sometimes more, at a stretch—and absent themselves from home for days or weeks at a time. "It is no uncommon thing for an engineer to go for nearly a week without sleep except in snatches on the road or waiting on a branch or engine house," commented a Brotherhood of Locomotive Engineers member in 1869.[19] The hours of work were as variable as they were long. A railroader could work flat-out or not at all, depending on the condition of the economy or time of year. Agricultural harvest rushes, inclement weather, and cyclical economic patterns produced irregular employment and uneven work hours.[20]

These destabilizing factors affected methods and rates of pay in both the United States and Europe. From the 1850s through the 1870s, American running-trades workers were paid by the day. In the years after the Civil War, railroads defined "a day" as a certain length of elapsed time and the duties performed during the course of that time, usually a run or series of short runs and the attendant maintenance to locomotives and cars. But because running-trades work was so uneven in intensity and hours, the basis for pay varied widely. Workers wanted standardized payment that reflected compensation for extra work, such as freight volume and the length of runs (which increased after the Civil War). Management favored flexibility and a payment scheme that did not itemize work performed. By the mid-1880s, the industry arrived at what would become the formula for railroad wages into the twentieth century, which combined the number of miles run with hours worked to arrive at set daily rates of pay with overtime compensation. Nevertheless, the determination of wages remained an ongoing point of contention between railroad workers and employers over the last third of the nineteenth century.[21]

Even when the work and pay were steady, what really set railroad work apart was its own uniquely chaotic brand of industrial time. After the Civil War, as railroad mileage expanded and the volume of freight increased, more and more running-trades workers operated freight trains, which could run twenty-four hours a day on irregular schedules according to season and weather. Train crews could be called at any hour of the day or night for a run, particularly if they were on the "extra board"—a list of those running-trades workers, usually low in seniority, who did not have regular runs and were available on call. Once en route, there was no quitting time; work was finished when the train arrived at its destination. And a common feature of work life for all train crews involved waiting—waiting to be called, and waiting in their trains in yards or on sidings for their orders to go.[22] English historian and former railwayman Frank McKenna termed these hours "peculiar." Surveying the conditions of U.S. railwaymen in his 1900 report to the Industrial Commission, Samuel McCune Lindsay characterized railroad service as "a life in itself, somewhat apart from that of the ordinary man . . . in an occupation that follows the conventional hours of work."[23] Combined with the need to remain alert and maintain control over machines weighing thousands of tons traveling at rapid rates of speed, such working conditions took their toll on the nerves and health of running-trades workers, especially engineers.[24]

In addition to enduring long and unpredictable hours, harsh weather conditions, and physical and mental stress, American running-trades workers toiled under the constant threat of crippling injury or death. Boiler explosions, derailments, and, above all, the primitive hand braking and "link and pin" coupling systems made railroading one of the riskiest occupations of the nineteenth century.[25] Despite significant underreporting of accidents, figures from the Interstate Commerce Commission (ICC) showed that railroaders outpaced almost every other occupation in terms of injury. From 1889, the year that the ICC began collecting data on accidents, to 1892, the fatality rate of the overall railroad workforce was 3.14 per 1,000 workers, roughly equal to bituminous coal mining. That was a high figure, but it paled in comparison to running-trades workers' death rate of 9 per 1,000, which in turn was dwarfed by the figure that Mark Aldrich has extrapolated for brakemen of 17.4 per 1,000. The only industry to approach the railroads in industrial deaths was eastern anthracite coal mining, in which 7.10 miners per 1,000 died annually over the 1860s and 1870s, and western hard-rock mining, in which 7.8 per 1,000 workers died annually over the same period.[26] State-level injury statistics also paint a graphic picture: in 1908, the Illinois Bureau of Labor Statistics found that in workplace accidents, railroaders accounted for 56 percent of broken ribs, 50 percent of broken arms, 41 percent of broken legs, 54 percent of all hand injuries, 30 percent of lost fingers, 71 percent of severed arms, and all legs amputated.[27] Despite such accident rates, the United States was among the last of the industrialized nations to install safety devices. Thus in

1907 alone, 87,644 railroad workers were injured, and a 1910 study concluded that U.S. railroads had 3 times the annual death rate and 5 times the injury rate of British railroads, and 2.5 and 5 times the rates of Germany.[28]

These accidents claimed brakemen as principal victims. Although they made up no more than 10 percent of the total workforce before 1880, they accounted for 35 to 50 percent of all injuries and fatalities. Whereas engine crews were more likely to meet their demise as a result of spectacular but relatively infrequent accidents like boiler explosion, derailment, or collision, brakemen contended with a greater number of more routine mishaps. Scrambling atop moving cars to set brake wheels, or stepping between cars during coupling to insert a link, made their occupation one of the deadliest in the industrial era.[29] The perils of coupling multiplied in the yards. Making up and breaking apart trains meant that switchmen were constantly climbing on and off of cars, inserting themselves between cars, and running alongside them while in motion. When Harry French found a job in the yards of the Hannibal & St. Joe Railroad in the 1880s, his older sister expected him to be killed: "It is an actual fact that all through my employment as a switchman she kept one clean sheet for the express purpose of wrapping up my mangled remains."[30]

Already by the 1850s, railroad safety had become an issue of public concern as improvements in roadways and rolling stock failed to keep pace with industry growth, thereby producing rising accident and mortality rates.[31] But it was during the Civil War and the ensuing period of national railroad expansion that matters of working hours, workplace safety, rates and manner of pay, and questions over the supply of labor prompted running-trades workers to organize unions. In the meantime, the burdens and rewards of the railroad workplace shaped the domestic lives of nineteenth-century railroaders.

The Running Trades and the Household

Given the nature of train operation, the very functioning of American, like European, railroads required a particular configuration of gender relations in running-trades workers' households. As with all industrial workers, railwaymen required reproductive maintenance, and this they found most typically within the traditional nuclear household. Most running-trades workers married and became sole wage earners, while their wives provided the unpaid domestic labor that kept the men functioning in the workplace. At the same time, running-trades work rhythms had a profound effect on family life, making their households different from those of most other industrial workers. And it was wives who kept the household running and experienced most acutely the dislocations of running-trades life. Nevertheless, to paraphrase Elizabeth Jameson, like other working-class households, two key assumptions about work and intimacy framed gender relations in running-trades families: railroading was men's work, and "good, decent homes" sheltered patriarchal families. Men and women who succeeded in living these assumptions came closest to achieving working-class standards of achievement and respectability.[32]

Railroaders married and had families in proportion to the adult population at large, but their marriage and family patterns changed as they advanced through the running-trades hierarchy.[33] Brakemen and firemen, who tended to be younger and earn less, were less likely to be married than conductors and engineers. Figures from the Kansas Bureau of Labor and Industrial Statistics indicate that in the years 1890 to 1900, between 70 and 80 percent of brakemen and firemen had wives, while 90 to 95 percent of engineers and conductors were married. Brakemen and firemen typically had two to three children, whereas conductors and engineers were likely to have three or more.[34] Early promotion encouraged marriage and children at a relatively early age, and, with the wages that engineers could expect to earn, they could keep their children in school and their wives at home. As with women in society generally, the domestic circumstances and class status of women in railroading families were largely shaped by their husbands' or fathers' earning capacity and place in the relations of production.[35]

A running-trades worker's ability to support a family corresponded with his place in the railroad occupational hierarchy. As a group, railwaymen demonstrated a rate of breadwinning consistent with skilled workers generally (about 75 percent), according to an 1884 study by the Illinois Bureau of Labor Statistics.[36] But as with their marriage and family patterns, running-trades workers' ability to earn a family wage increased as they advanced up the job ladder. Almost all engineers and conductors were the sole breadwinners for their families and demonstrated the largest surplus income at the end of the year compared to others in running trades, which they either saved or invested in insurance. By contrast, firemen and brakemen were more likely to need assistance from wives and children. Brakemen had the most difficult time, for as a whole they were unable to meet all their families' expenses. Still, running-trades families compared favorably with other working families; about 12 percent of railroad families found themselves in debt at the end of the year, but that figure was only about half the percentage for the Illinois labor force as a whole.[37]

Earnings and living standards in the running trades were in fact less secure than aggregate figures might suggest. Railroaders' actual income could vary considerably. Engineers who ran regular freight or passenger runs could expect high and steady earnings, for instance, but the earnings of recently promoted engineers with little seniority fluctuated with the ebb and flow of business and assignments to irregular runs. In general, regularity of employment—determined by the season, state of business, and seniority—and method of remuneration governed running-trades workers' income. And the latter was shaped by a host of factors such as overtime, apprenticeship, delayed time, deadheading, special service, extra mileage rates, and "arbitrary" allowances. Moreover, any number of events—illness, injury, layoff, suspension—could cut into earnings and deplete resources and savings. Like the rest of the working class, "aristocratic" engineers and conductors, not to mention firemen and brakemen, faced uncertainty and insecurity every day.[38]

In these circumstances, women's physical labor in the home and management of husbands' incomes enabled railroad families to get by on the family wage. In keeping with the patriarchal ideology of the late nineteenth and early twentieth centuries, the wives of train-service workers retired from the wage labor force upon marriage, taking up responsibility for unpaid domestic labor. Wives augmented income by boarding single railroaders or taking in washing, planting vegetable gardens, keeping hens, and manufacturing items that would otherwise have to be purchased with cash.[39] This arrangement allowed the majority of working-class families to get by on the threshold of existence, but it likely allowed the families of running-trades workers to enjoy a standard of living and a level of respectability otherwise unobtainable, demonstrating Jeanne Boydston's point that, "by supplying for free the cooking, cleaning, and laundry services that must otherwise be purchased with cash, a wife stretched a man's income and improved his security against the market." In a society that assessed the respectability of a household as a measure of a husband's income, a skilled wife could cover up a marginal income by keeping up appearances.[40] Wives of running-trades workers thus faced situations similar to those of most working-class wives of the late nineteenth century. They were responsible for all aspects of domestic labor necessary to the maintenance of the household and to their spouse's participation in the industrial labor force. And like other working-class wives, their husbands' work rhythms affected their domestic labor.[41]

As Mark Rosenfeld has found in his study of Barrie, Ontario, running-trades work schedules *necessitated* wives' roles as full-time domestic workers, especially where children were concerned. Long hours and extended separations from husbands meant that the primary responsibility for care of children and financial management of the household fell to the wives. Like the wives of fishermen and sailors, railroaders' wives learned not only how to be self-reliant in their husbands' absences, but they also exercised a real degree of control and autonomy. Indeed, many enjoyed their independence and found that household life was actually easier to manage with husbands away on the road. When husbands returned, families had to readjust household schedules and wives had to deal again with patriarchal authority. Wives had to be tension managers as well, coping with spouses' work-related pressures and inability to participate consistently in family affairs.[42]

The capricious work schedules of the running trades also shaped housewives' domestic routines. They not only had to organize their own domestic schedules, but they also had to juggle those schedules to meet the unpredictable work routines of their husbands. Getting up at odd hours to prepare meals for husbands complicated the ordinary tasks of cooking, cleaning, and mending and washing clothes. The ordinary routine of housework, already physically demanding in the context of nineteenth-century household technology, was compounded by spouses' erratic schedules. "Lulu June," the wife of a Canadian locomotive foreman, emphasized the disruption and exhaustion caused by her husband being called in the middle of the night in 1909: "Unable to sleep again I lay and meditate on the work of the coming day until it is time to get up and do what my tired brain has been planning all night." In addition, "Lulu June" found that unpredictable work schedules interfered with "normal" family life and got in the way of the family's participation in community events, producing "the spoiled evenings and interrupted family gatherings and lonely walks to the church caused by engine No. something getting stuck."[43]

Together with irregular work schedules, the residential patterns of railway families tended to separate them from the larger communities in which they lived. In railroad towns like Emporia, Kansas, the families of railwaymen became increasingly segregated into one particular ward over the 1880s and 1890s, a pattern resulting in part from their irregular work rhythms. In the days before the spread of telephone service to working-class homes, the calling system meant that train crews had to live almost within earshot of the yards, a fact especially true for the younger men who fired and braked the trains. By 1897, the *Emporia Gazette* found that the town had divided "into three castes—the school and resident folk, the railroaders, and the 'niggers.' An incoming stranger may ask the Santa Fe conductor who lives here, about [the president of the Normal School], and this blue-coated official will answer, 'never heard of him.' Equally the northenders profess the utmost ignorance of any 'doings' in the south end of town, where the railroad boys live." Railwaymen and their families, for their part, objected to their ranking. "One feels the cold shoulder ever since he or she has been a brother, or sister, wife or mother of a railroad man," lamented an "Engineer's Wife." As was true in Europe, the larger community viewed the "abnormal" lives of American railway families with suspicion.[44]

Frequent geographical moves necessitated by work assignment or promotion compounded these problems. As "Lulu June" related, "We have been moved from place to place until I can pack my household effects in the dark, and even the family dog knows the use of a packing box and hunts up his collar and chain from force of habit." When the transfer order came, "perhaps twenty-five miles or perhaps half way across the continent," she wrote, "by the next train he goes and his wife has the packing to do and the family to look after until her long-suffering 'hubby' gets settled in his new sphere and hunts up a house." Combined with the social isolation that tended to accompany full-time domestic labor, frequent moves only made worse "that feeling of utter loneliness and depression that comes to the stranger in a strange home."[45] Particularly in the more sparsely populated West, railwaymen's wives complained of the isolation and challenges of running households.[46] When the pressures became overwhelming, or the rewards insufficient, wives took matters into their own hands; some even abandoned their families. Sam Speas recalled his father, an engineer on the Denver & Rio Grande Railroad at the turn of the century, telling the story of a section boss who came home to find his house dark, his children crying, and his wife a few hours' distant on an eastbound train. Unable to care for his children alone, he wired his unmarried sister to "come immediately" from Denver to keep the household together.[47]

Yet most running-trades workers' wives coped with the burdens of railway life by building networks of support and depending on one another in their husbands' absences. In railroad division towns, where wives were more likely to come from railroading families, they based these networks on kinship. But in the absence of immediate family, women reached out to friends and neighbors, particularly the wives of other railroad workers. Women also elaborated informal networks into formal all-female societies, such as auxiliaries connected with the church and the union. These contacts provided railway women with sources of emotional support and companionship, as well as information, goods, and services necessary to survival. From family members or friends, women gained the knowledge of railway operations required to juggle household schedules and understand husbands' work-related burdens. In times of tragedy, such support networks enabled women to cope. "Lulu June" related an incident in which a machinist arrived in their town and suddenly died of heart failure, "leaving his family of six children among strangers and with hardly enough food in the house to see them over the day." The young widow was grief-stricken and bereft of emotional or material support until the women came to her rescue: "With the help of the neighbors I did all I could until the suddenness of the blow had worn off and the affairs of the poor man were settled."[48]

Wives' roles as full-time homemakers were important to gender identity in running-trades households. They constructed their sense of femininity at the interstices of the railway workplace, household, community, and larger societal assumptions about the proper place and role of women. Over the late nineteenth century, dominant ideas held that women were frail but nevertheless superior to men, and that their domain was the home. Railway women and men largely shared assumptions about marriage and full-time housewifery. This way of thinking did not reflect a simple imposition of patriarchal ideas, however, for many women viewed these goals as positive and desirable. As Jameson has pointed out, only a minority of American women could achieve the ideal of "true womanhood" in its strict formulation. Rather, domesticity was a flexible ideology, and it helped working-class women and men make sense of their lives. Women were keenly aware of their importance to their families' welfare, and they took pride in their roles as household managers, often under trying circumstances.[49] Wives were also central to husbands' images of themselves as breadwinners and as men. For running-trades workers, and workingmen generally, breadwinning held great cultural significance, despite the economic necessity that made them breadwinners. In the workplace, breadwinning represented the reward of skill, hard work, and the ability to endure harsh working conditions. In the household, breadwinning confirmed their masculinity and supported their patriarchal authority. As a Canadian engineer's son recalled, "Back in those days the women didn't work. If a woman had to go out to work her husband was kinda looked down upon because he was supposed to keep her."[50]

Both running-trades workers and their wives worked to meet cultural expectations for proper gender conduct, even as they modified dominant ideals to suit the material circumstances of their lives. Most railroad families conformed to the traditional patriarchal model with the husband as head of household. Wives' catering to male needs, however, did not necessarily mean deference or submission to male authority. Not only did the conditions of railroad work require wives to be strong, but they could also be aggressive when it came to defending their families' interests. Gender relations were the result of negotiation, both among family members and between dominant ideologies and material realities. Railway wives accepted key aspects of dominant gender norms while refashioning others to reflect their everyday circumstances. These women wanted to enjoy the rewards of housewifery, motherhood, and respectable status in their communities, and so matters of economic security, family stability, and respect and love from their partners mattered a great deal to them.[51] For their husbands, public demonstration of masculinity as head of household and family wage earner also mattered a great deal, but it was intimately connected to the workplace. As in many other nineteenth-century trades, manhood was understood in terms of skill, strength, sexuality, and breadwinning. A "true" railroad man possessed the skill necessary to work efficiently and fearlessly in a dangerous environment, and his earning capacity demonstrated his fitness to marry and head a household.[52] Threats to the ability of railroaders and their wives to perform these roles—wage and workforce reductions during economic downturns, workplace hazards that could cost a man a limb and therefore earning potential—figured as motivating factors in the origin of the railroad brotherhoods, but so too did their workplace culture.

The Culture of the Running Trades

Like the disciplined ethical code that David Montgomery has described among nineteenth-century metal-trades workers, the work culture created by railwaymen as a relatively autonomous sphere of action on the job contained elements of independence, craft pride, and mutualism. In part an organic culture arising from the workplace—a "realm of informal, customary values and rules that mediate the formal authority structure of the workplace," in Susan Porter Benson's words—work culture elaborated workers' understandings of what constituted a good day's work and how work should be executed. It celebrated the individual self-assertion of the skilled worker, but in line with the collective good. Running-trades work culture had its historical origins, on the head-end of the train at least, in the antebellum machine shops and factories that produced the first locomotives. Early engineers came from among the machinists that produced these machines; even as the supply of engineers shifted to the fireman's side of the cab and they solidified their place atop the railroad labor force, they retained elements of machinists' sense of their skill as embodied capital underpinning their standing as independent men and virtuous citizens. These latter elements stood in a tradition of American working-class republicanism and white supremacy that based demands for fair wages, job security, predictable promotion, and the right to organize on workers' rights as white, male citizens. Combined with the unique features of running-trades work, this sense of skill produced a distinct operating craft identity by the middle of the nineteenth century in which egalitarianism, independence, and respectability warred with hierarchy, discipline, and roughness.[53] Work culture, at bottom, is a product of the central struggle between worker and capitalist; in the unique circumstances of railroad work, the struggle for control of the workplace shaped running-trades work culture.

From the railroad industry's beginnings, a central point of contention between officers and employees involved the proper execution of work. From management's viewpoint, efficient and safe railroad operation and company profits depended on the synchronized actions of employees. In contrast to the mass-production industries, where managers and scientific-management experts began to succeed in separating conception from execution by the early twentieth century, in railroading, managers had to rely on what sociologist Andy Friedman has termed "responsible autonomy." Managers in both Europe and the United States responded to the challenge of directing running-trades workers' autonomy in keeping with the firm's priorities by developing an elaborate set of rules governing the conduct of work, enforced by a quasi-military style of discipline.[54] Before promotion, every railwayman had to pass an examination given by a rules examiner and pledge to carry a rule book when on duty. The penalty for violating "the rules" typically involved a hearing before the division manager in which the guilty worker might be suspended without pay or dismissed.[55] Yet even with such penalties, managers depended on the cooperation and trust of their employees, for running-trades workers' adherence to the rules remained at their own discretion on the road. Because it was impossible to mandate absolute guidelines for every possible exigency that might arise, train crews had to be flexible. A good measure of running-trades workers' autonomy, particularly that which engineers and conductors enjoyed, resided in their application of railroad rules, for they had to judge, select, and interrelate the appropriate rules in the course of their work.[56]

In the gap between official protocols and actual performance of work, the experience, collectively held knowledge, and ethical code that guided running-trades workers in their work developed over the nineteenth century.[57] As applied, the rules might bear little resemblance to their written form. Within a hierarchical and disciplined industrial environment, railroaders worked according to, with, and around the exacting set of rules that governed their work. Perhaps influenced by Civil War veterans' encounters with military rules and procedures, the mark of "good railroading" in the late nineteenth century was the ability not to follow the rules exactly but to interpret and apply them with common "railroad" sense, taking risks when necessary to complete the task. As Harry French recalled, "In the early [eighteen] nineties the train crews made their own rules to fit various occasions." Such attitudes often conflicted with managerial opinions as to what constituted "good railroading." But for French, "The general idea was to keep trains moving. Any man's ability to do just that determined, to a large extent, how highly he was rated as a railroadman."[58] French's comments suggest how craft pride and independence mingled with a certain conception of masculine conduct in the ethical code of the running trades. Demanding a "manly" bearing toward the boss as well as fellow workers, as Montgomery has described it, this code involved elements of "dignity, respectability, defiant egalitarianism, and patriarchal male supremacy." These elements came together in the concept of "manliness."[59]

Notions of proper masculine conduct, shaped by the economic and cultural transformations of the market revolution, had become well established by the time of the Civil War in the United States. The "manly" standards to which many skilled workers held themselves derived from a model based in the social relations and cultural ideals of the antebellum artisanal workshop. Such a model, according to sociologist Michael Kimmel, demanded formal manners with women and loyalty to male comrades. It represented the honest toiler; extolled the principles of hard work, craftsmanship, and self-reliance; asserted the right to full citizenship of the man whose independence resided in his ownership of skill; and emphasized civic engagement balanced with workplace solidarity.[60] By mid-century, though, the artisan largely had become a figure of the past, and the ideal that he represented was reforged within a factory setting, the wage relationship, and the disciplined and hierarchical Civil War Union army.[61]

Late nineteenth-century railroad workers had an indirect connection to the artisan workshop. Nevertheless, they drew on prevailing ideals of manliness to fashion ideas about teamwork and mutualism unique to the running trades. The contemporary research of anthropologist Frederick Gamst may shed some light onto their ethical codes. A "'rail' is a self-assured and reliable *man*, who does not resort to an 'alibi' for not performing properly on the job or for unsociable job behavior. A 'good rail' is operationally skilled, knowledgeable, and efficient—he saves time and effort for all on the crew. And the 'rail' is reasonably careful with personal safety, but much more with the protection of fellow employees." A rail was a team player; he did not turn "stool-pigeon" on another rail bending the rules. Indeed, railroaders had to look out for and rely on one another. Improvisation and cooperation were essential to getting a train over the road and to minimizing workplace hazards. Combined with the extensive time that railroaders spent with one another, the teamwork necessary to complete the job fostered a sense of brotherhood.[62]

A hierarchy made of skill, age, and gender overlaid the camaraderie of running-trades work culture. With proud, respectable engineers and conductors at the top, the running-trades hierarchy could be as conflictual as it was cooperative. A masculine style of interaction informed the legendary tensions that developed within the running trades. The conflict between engineers and conductors over control of the train—the engineer controlled the locomotive but by the rules it was the conductor who was in charge—revealed differing conceptions of skill and style of manhood. Engineers, who found their sense of manhood in their mastery of complicated machinery and steadiness in the face of danger, viewed conductors as posturing dandies in kid gloves. Engineers referred to conductors as "messenger boys," "brass buttons," "dudes," "silk gloves," and "smart alecks." Indeed, conductors, who derived their professional identity more from their clerical responsibilities for passengers and freight, cultivated a style of manhood emphasizing distinctive dress (top coats and silk hats early on, and uniforms by century's end), dignity, and responsibility. For their part, they judged engineers to be coarse, uncultured, and dirty; they were "grunts," "hogs," "pounders," "rawhiders," and "stack busters."[63]

Tensions also developed between the senior and junior crafts of the running trades. Progressing through entry-level positions, young brakemen and firemen learned about the technology, techniques, and procedures from their older supervisors. Among engine crews, close relations often developed. The paternalism that characterized these relationships reflected strong bonds as well as the deference and respect that the older men demanded. Older men may well have watched younger men carefully, however, for as they aged they knew that the newcomers represented a source of competition and eventual replacement.[64] Firemen were dependent on engineers for training and promotion, but the latter could be parsimonious with their knowledge or abusive in their stations. On the Minneapolis, St. Paul & Sault Ste. Marie Railway, for instance, the engineer reportedly "owned" the fireman. "No matter how much they may differ, the fireman has no redress," wrote a fireman to the *Locomotive Firemen's Magazine* in 1897. "He is the engineer's slave and all the freedom he has is to quit if he don't like it."[65] Still, engineers and firemen shared their social worlds away from work. Conductors, however, did not admit brakemen to theirs. Infatuated with their sense of status, they believed themselves too respectable to associate with brakemen, whose youth and reputation for rowdiness set them apart.[66]

If the culture of the running trades was inegalitarian but close-knit, it produced an almost unbridgeable social divide when it came to the rest of the railroad workforce. Like their European counterparts, American railwaymen nurtured a sense of theirs as elite crafts. English engine crews did not regard station men or the clerical force as "really" railwaymen, as they had nothing to do with the actual movement of trains, and guards came in for a particularly bad rap: "A guard gets his living like a prostitute, lying on his back." American engineers and conductors had equally strong opinions. Roundhouse machinists were "chambermaids" or "greaseballs"; according to Sal Costa, son of a Canadian shop laborer born in 1908, "Those engineers, they'd look at an ashpit man or a yardman as if he was shit." The sense of superiority running through these views resulted from the running trades' position at the apex of the railroad labor hierarchy and demonstrated a common gender component: lesser-skilled workers had neither the training nor the manhood worthy of respect.[67]

Within the running trades in the United States, racial hierarchy complicated the already-fractious relationships between engineers and firemen and between conductors and brakemen in ways that distinguished the experience of American running-trades workers from their English counterparts. Like most white Americans, railroaders thought in terms of race. The historical formation of this thinking, set in place over the first half of the nineteenth century as working-class formation in the North dovetailed with the rise the slave system in the South, produced an especially pronounced racialized class consciousness. As David Roediger has argued, the white working class saw in black slaves the "Other," whose economic dependency indicated moral degeneracy. "Whiteness," in Roediger's view, served as a "wage," compensating the emerging industrial working class for its loss of autonomy and the alienation of wage labor. The Civil War heightened this tendency, even as it remade the meanings and boundaries of freedom, in northern white workingmen's fears of labor market competition with emancipated slaves.[68]

In the South, the end of slavery and the rise of the Jim Crow system of race relations held particular significance for engineers and conductors who worked with black firemen and brakemen; they insisted on not just deference from blacks but also on a greater range of labor than they could exact from whites. "My information," wrote an 1887 correspondent to the *Locomotive Firemen's Magazine*, "is that there are members of the [Brotherhood of Locomotive Engineers] who prefer a colored fireman to a white man for the reason that the negro fireman does all their dirty work, such as oiling, packing, wiping and many other things."[69] Such everyday instances of dominance over black workers informed the consciousness of white railwaymen, racializing their class/craft consciousness. The fact that black men performed the labor-intensive work of firing and braking made that work "nigger work," and in the process made the work of engineers and conductors both "white" and "respectable."[70]

This distinction encouraged southern white firemen and brakemen to resent the presence of black men in these job categories. In addition to the issue of job competition, black workers undermined white claims to the respectability of firing and braking. As with engineers and conductors, white firemen and brakemen distinguished between "nigger work" and respectable labor. They connected heavy, unskilled manual labor with degradation, dependency, and servility. "Nigger heaven" referred to a boxcar's roof, and "nigger locals" were burdensome short runs. With these understandings and the labor-intensive nature of their work, white firemen no doubt were aware of the double meanings behind such nicknames as "blackie" and "big smoke." The existence of black firemen and brakemen gave credence to whites' fears that firing and braking was indeed "nigger work" and that they might in fact be "slaving like niggers."[71]

The fears of white brakemen and firemen suggest that there was another side to the culture of the running trades, one at odds with the somewhat "prissy" image of labor aristocrats. For all their vaunted craft pride and sense of elitism, running-trades workers were just that—workers. Even the engineers and conductors were not free of the disdain with which nineteenth-century Victorian society held manual labor. Brakemen and firemen, in their liminal position in the railroad job hierarchy, may have stood out as particular objects of suspicion.[72] Awareness of these attitudes may have led these workers to distance themselves from the "roughness" of the unskilled working class by embracing the trappings of bourgeois respectability and demanding respect for their skills as a signifier of manhood.[73]

Yet at the same time, perhaps making a virtue of necessity or emerging from "manly" confrontation with their working conditions, railroaders also celebrated the more elemental aspects of running-trades work as badges of manhood. The same sense of mastering railroading technology and conditions of work that informed their sense of themselves as men also informed a sense of themselves as possessing the bravery, endurance, and strength in the more physical and dangerous aspects of their jobs.[74] In his memoir, Herbert Hamblen conveyed running-trades workers' "tougher" sense of masculine identity through his contempt for the industry's nonmanual workers in his description of a train workers' strike: "The clerks in the offices were hustled out into the yard, and made to sweat and lacerate their delicate hands, tear and soil their clothes, and injure their tender feelings, by pulling spikes from switches, clawing the green coal out of the fireboxes, dragging heavy and 'nasty' hoses to the engines, and forming bucket and cordwood brigades."[75] Like working-class Civil War soldiers—who drew "on a form of rough democratic manhood that rejected emotional display and social refinement in favor of physical courage and endurance," in Frances Clarke's words—Hamblen and other railroaders constructed identities in opposition to dominant forms of masculinity associated with the developing middle class. The camp and field life of the Civil War, which rewarded toughness and punished squeamishness, not to mention the experience of combat that many soldiers viewed as a test of courage, may have contributed to this kind of sensibility among the railroaders of the 1870s–80s generation.[76]

This kind of masculine posture influenced railroaders' attitudes toward the dangers of their work. Railroaders dealt with workplace hazards in a variety of ways, but all were expected to confront the possibility of injury or death "manfully." Writing to the *Railroad Brakemen's Journal* in February 1886 from Bowling Green, Kentucky, a brakeman laconically reported, "It is rough on the boys to have to ride out on top. We have had two or three little collisions lately, but no one hurt as jumping seems to be a kind of preventative and it has been indulged in of late." Like workers in other hazardous industries, running-trades workers viewed the risks as part and parcel of railroading. And like miners, lumbermen, longshoremen, and sailors, they did not accept unnecessary risks, but they did believe in approaching their work with a combination of coolness, courage, and skill. As John Williams-Searle has found, veteran rails viewed fearlessness and sensible, successful risk taking as indicators of professionalism and manliness.[77]

Railroaders' attitudes toward risk were also shaped by prevailing understandings about manhood and suffering generated by the Civil War, only a decade or two distant in the 1870s and 1880s. The war itself profoundly shook Americans with its unprecedented scale of death and destruction. The war also reinforced certain aspects of nineteenth-century white manhood, particularly the view that manhood resided not in the body's physical attributes but rather in its disciplining and mastering. For Union soldiers who escaped death but suffered maiming injuries, a disciplined response to injury held the potential to inspire and redeem the nation for which they had fought. As Americans and disabled veterans memorialized the conflict, individual dismemberment, or the "Empty Sleeve," came to be equated with national unity and white manhood. At the same time, the ability to endure the pain and hardship of traumatic injury—demonstrated in stories of soldiers, mainly from working-class backgrounds, laughing at the sight of their wounds or whistling on the way to hospital—stood as proof of manhood in a more rugged way. In such a context, railwaymen could hardly complain about mere workplace hazards. On the contrary, a railroader's injury in the service of the railroad and the traveling public could be seen in a similar light to that of the soldier sacrificing life and limb on the battlefield for God and country. As with demonstration of courage in battle, bravery in the face of workplace danger (and the display of scars afterward) could be taken as a sign of manhood earned.[78]

Rather less nobly, running-trades workers' masculine assertiveness and workplace autonomy could take on distinctly "rough" aspects, particularly in connection with the consumption of alcohol. Nineteenth-century working-class alcohol use occurred within the historical context of an antebellum drinking culture in which men of all classes consumed large amounts of alcohol. Railroaders earned reputations for drinking whiskey, brandy, and beer on and off the job, as did workers in a host of other working-class occupations.[79] Some observers attributed alcohol consumption to the dangers and the irregular hours of running-trades work. Certainly, the saloon often was one of the few places to eat, sleep, or kill time. In 1902, an officer of the Chicago, Burlington & Quincy Railroad (CB&Q) complained that in Alliance, Nebraska, there was "absolutely no place for a single man to go and be entertained, except the saloons."[80] In places like Salida, Colorado, a Santa Fe Railroad division point on the high plains, the options may have been worse. Clinton M. Graham, who began work there as a callboy in 1917, recalled Salida as a "wide-open" town: "There were thirteen saloons and about twenty houses of prostitution." He regularly had to look for train crews in "the whorehouses and saloons."[81] Away from home and the watchful eyes of their communities, the temptation to booze, gamble, and frequent houses of prostitution may have been difficult to resist.

At the same time, communal drinking formed an important element of running-trades work culture, fostering emotional bonds and a sense of solidarity. When Harry French began drinking as a teenager in the 1880s (because "all railroad men drank"), he socialized into the masculine world of railroading. Communal drinking helped railwaymen to make sense of their shared work experiences and served to mark out an oppositional space against management—"to soothe their grievances and demonstrate mutual sympathy; drink evil and bad luck to some obnoxious official and drink long life and continued prosperity to themselves."[82] When management attempted to control their alcohol intake, railwaymen could react with manly defiance. Harry French related an incident in 1890s Oregon when a supervisor employed a spy to photograph train crews patronizing saloons. French's crew appointed two brakemen "to notify [the spy] that his presence was desired east of the Rocky Mountains" and dunked him in the frozen Willamette River until he agreed to leave. "I would not call them hard boiled," recalled French. "That term would leave their characteristic in a definite pansy stage."[83]

The railroad workplace, a homosocial space apart from the world of the Victorian middle class, fostered a masculine style that combined elements of both manual- and craft-work cultures. Railroaders shared as much in common with the manual working class and its aggressive celebration of physical strength, pugnacity, and consumption of alcohol as badges of masculine identity, as they did with the craftsmen who demanded respect for their skills as a signifier of manhood. The rough aspects of running-trades culture, however, could be dysfunctional in their conflict with the imperatives of railroad discipline and their overlap with the household. During a six-month period in 1900, for instance, the Southern Pacific Railroad dismissed 212 employees, of which 77 were sacked for "intemperance," the largest single category. For Harry French, the combination of railroad life and boozing destroyed his marriage. Unhappy with his job-hopping, frequent absences, smoking, and drinking, his wife demanded a divorce and left French for a merchant. "At least he's a gentleman. He doesn't smoke or drink," she declared. "He doesn't chew or use vile language, either." "She was choosing between a railwayman and a gentleman of exemplary habits," French commented ruefully.[84]

* * *

Harry French's stories reveal the complex, and in certain aspects unique, masculine style of running-trades work culture. To be sure, railroading work culture shared many features with the cultures of other skilled workers. Yet it was also distinctive, arising out of a unique work environment and developing its own argot, customs, and pronounced exclusiveness. This exclusiveness undermined the possibility of broader multigrade solidarity with the larger railroad workforce. Still, running-trades work culture, in all its complexity, challenged managerial prerogative. From the industry's beginnings, American railroaders tested and resisted managerial authority informally in the execution of their work and in their propensity to drink. Even their exclusivist attitudes reflected another aspect of control struggles on the railroads. Sensitive to the ease with which junior counterparts could replace established engineers and conductors, the latter developed occupational cultures that both vaunted and tried to ensure their status by limiting access to the profession. Firemen and brakemen adopted similar postures regarding the rest of the railroad labor force. Ultimately, though, culture was of limited value in controlling labor markets. Some sort of institutional presence was necessary, and running-trades work culture provided the raw material for building formal organizations. The result of this institution building—the railroad brotherhoods—reflected the complexities of both running-trades work and work culture.

In the mid-1850s, engineers on eastern railroads translated their sense of occupational identity and work culture into an institutional form when they organized the first running-trades union, the National Protective Association of the Brotherhood of Locomotive Engineers of the United States, in response to management attempts to flood the labor market with inexperienced men. The union was short-lived, killed off by the economic crash of 1857, but it displayed central features of what would become brotherhood-style organizing: struggle for control of the workplace and the railroad labor market, and a desire to promote the respectable craft identity of running-trades workers. With the economic recovery brought on by the Civil War, as well as the inflationary consumer prices and pressure on the railroad labor market also produced by the war, engineers formed the first of the permanent railroad brotherhoods, the Brotherhood of Locomotive Engineers (BLE), in 1863. The issues animating the BLE's founding reflected both wartime circumstances and factors associated with railroad-industry growth extending into the postwar period: the propensity of employers to hire cheaper, inexperience engineers; the disconnect between unpredictable hours of work with rates and methods of pay; the lack of predictable lines and procedures for promotion; and the lack of any means for engineers to formally express their concerns about these issues.[85]

As the Civil War propelled the railroads into a new phase of expansion, these issues intersected with the effects of growth and increasing trunk-line competition in the late 1860s and early 1870s. Pushed to the wall in the depression of the 1870s, railroad officers responded with wage reductions and job cuts. Workers perceived management's response as an effort to wrest away control over the conditions of their work, which they regarded as their "rights" as workingmen. The ensuing struggle culminated in the Great Strike of 1877, a showdown between a generation of railroad workers and officers over basic issues concerning control of the workplace and labor market. The Brotherhood of Locomotive Engineers had engaged in a series of strikes since its inception, but after defeats on the Boston & Maine and Reading railroads in early 1877, it moved decisively away from support of industrial action.[86] Thereafter, over the next decade, the BLE and the rest of the brotherhoods would emphasize another aspect of their unionism: fraternally based mutual aid that responded to the hazards of railroad work and aimed at maintaining the professional and respectable standing of the running-trades worker and his family. This orientation allowed the brotherhoods to present themselves as organizations that could step into the gap in managerial authority in the workplace. In return for recognition as the representatives and suppliers of skilled railroad labor, the brotherhoods promised to deliver good, reliable, white men.

2

Victorian America and the Brotherhoods' Fraternal Culture

The scene might have gone like this: the hooded candidate knelt before an altar in a darkened room, illuminated only by candlelight. In his left hand he held a leaf of the Bible, and in his right hand a ticket punch. The lodge members, in formal attire and regalia, formed two straight lines along the sides of the room facing the altar. A man calling himself the chief conductor advanced to the altar, and the two lines formed a circle around him and the candidate, clasping hands. The conductor then administered the oath to the candidate, who swore "without evasion or reservation and may I live shunned by all, friendless and forsaken, may I die alone, unmourned, unblest and unshriven, and may my name and my memory be accurst should I ever violate any portion of this or any obligation to the Order, so help me God." After administering this oath and instructing the candidate in the secret work, the conductor gave a series of raps with his gavel and the members filed past the candidate, giving him the secret grip. The candidate was now a full-fledged member of the order.[1] Such an event could have easily taken place in any number of the all-male fraternal associations that dotted the United States at the turn of the twentieth century. Yet the organization practicing this initiation ritual was neither the Freemasons, nor the Odd Fellows, nor any other quasi-Masonic association, but rather the Order of Railway Conductors.

Unions like the railroad brotherhoods were as much all-male fraternal associations as they were labor organizations. Fraternalism was one of the most widespread social and cultural phenomena of Victorian America, manifested in the widespread Masonic fraternal order movement and the massive Grand Army of the Republic. For early union leaders, fraternalism served as a readily available organizing frame. Like the Masons and the Odd Fellows, unions like the brotherhoods organized as collectively governed communities, emphasized masculine identity, employed a language of fraternity and brotherhood, adhered to the values of morality and respectability, and practiced self-improvement. And like many unionists of the late nineteenth century, brotherhood men also sought fellowship in the lodge hall. For the many drawn to it, Masonic fraternalism ameliorated the competition and hierarchies of the industrial age by offering a vision of kinship based on the ideals of the preindustrial artisanal workshop and a ritualized order in which all members could become masters. Unlike the Masons, though, the brotherhoods and many other trade unions practiced a distinctive brand of *labor* fraternalism that drew on the antebellum legacy of artisanal producerism and suffused it with meaning derived from their work experience. Their vision of kinship was based more explicitly in class and reflected an implicit criticism of class hierarchies. Gaining admission to a union like one of the railroad brotherhoods involved more than simply signing a union card. Symbolically expressed in fraternal ritual, it meant joining a band of fellow workers as brothers, pledging allegiance to those brothers, and swearing to abide by and uphold a mutualistic ethical code.[2]

The railroad brotherhoods belonged to a hardy tradition of working-class mutualism. In the pre–welfare state era, voluntary associations providing health and life insurance represented the principal means by which Americans protected themselves against sickness and death. Often religiously affiliated or ethnically based, these societies were fraternal in character.[3] British and American trade unions like the brotherhoods also provided these kinds of services, along with a range of social benefits. At the same time, like the miners' unions, brotherhood insurance arose out of the practice of workplace self-help, for railroaders worked in an industry so hazardous that fraternal insurance societies and companies typically refused them membership.[4] The logic of mutual aid animated brotherhood unionism and embodied the concept of the union as an extended family whose members had multiple obligations to one another. This kind of logic prompted Progressive Era labor economist Robert Franklin Hoxie to describe the railroad brotherhoods as "friendly" or "uplift" unions.[5]

The brotherhoods' fraternal culture and practice of mutual aid both derived from and responded to the historical developments defining Victorian America in the years after the Civil War. Directly and indirectly, the war stimulated the enormous growth in fraternalism's popularity by accelerating the pace of industrialization; altering prevailing ideas about manhood, independence, and respectability; and affecting popular attitudes toward disability and death.

Brotherhood men shared with other Americans the values of morality, respectability, and a commitment to personal independence, often expressed in the concept of "manhood" and the character-based sense of selfhood that it reflected. Such beliefs arose from a Victorian culture rooted in the principles of laissez-faire and the material circumstances of the self-regulating market. During the middle years of the nineteenth century, this order produced a close enough approximation of a democratized, commercialized republic in its egalitarian social forms to make these ideals plausibly meaningful. But by the 1870s, cyclical economic expansion, concentration of economic power, and unprecedented social conflict began to make clear that self-reliance and personal rectitude did not lead to independence.[6] Workplace accidents that undercut the corporeal bases of railroaders' independence reinforced this lesson, and Civil War–era attitudes toward honorable injury reinforced justifications for collective assistance. As employees of the corporations driving the economy's leading sector, the men of the running trades both won and lost from these developments. In responding to the new hierarchies of power and privilege created by post–Civil War economic development, the brotherhoods captured this ambivalence, deriving meaning from the Victorian ethos of acquisitive individualism and proprietary capitalism even as they challenged that ethos and its consequences.

Brotherhood culture reflected these tensions, for these unions had to contend with the nineteenth-century idea that, in Melvyn Dubofsky's words, "neither trade unionists nor capitalists should have the power to restrain free choice among individual workers."[7] Accordingly, brotherhood leaders articulated a concept of respectable manhood as an ideal and code of behavior that acknowledged free choice and individual agency but remained firmly ensconced in a collective and mutualistic craft identity. At the same time, brotherhood men and their wives adapted the dominant ideology of separate spheres and "true womanhood" to the realities of railway family life and their collective needs. Elaborated through women's participation in the ladies' auxiliaries, womanhood and domesticity complemented manhood and breadwinning as powerful categories for the organization of collective identity and the mobilization of collective interest.[8]

The Logic and Practice of Mutual Aid

Over the last third of the nineteenth century, a cooperative insurance movement arose in the United States and became the leading form of compensation against accidental disability and death by the 1890s. Fraternal in character and oriented to the needs of workingmen, this movement belonged to a long tradition of mutual assistance dating back to eighteenth-century England. Over the first half of the nineteenth century, mutual insurance societies sprang up in the United States and western Europe offering protection against hazards ranging from fire to maritime loss. After the Civil War, the spread of industrial wage labor and the restructuring of the family around the family wage stimulated the development of associations protecting workers against the loss of income and the cost of medical care caused by disability or death. In addition to cooperative insurance societies, trade unions figured as one of the most important and most successful expressions of this movement.[9]

The railroad brotherhoods had their origins in this post–Civil War period of experimentation, when dangerous working conditions and the difficulty of obtaining individual insurance policies provided railwaymen with a powerful impetus for the organization of mutual aid. The Brotherhood of Locomotive Engineers dedicated itself to the provision of mutual aid with the establishment of a "Widows', Orphans', and Disabled Members' Fund" in 1866 and the "Locomotive Engineers' Mutual Life Insurance Association" in 1867. The former was a charity fund, but the latter provided life and permanent disability insurance for its members, making the BLE the first North American union to sponsor a formal life-insurance program. Conductors, firemen, and brakemen followed the engineers' examples, establishing themselves as benefit-oriented fraternal orders in 1868, 1873, and 1883, respectively. From the late 1870s through the 1890s, switchmen and members of a number of nonoperating crafts, including the telegraphers and maintenance-of-way employees, also organized on the brotherhood model.[10] Experiencing rapid, if uneven, growth, the brotherhoods' insurance programs had a combined membership of nearly eighty-five thousand by century's end, and between 1867 and 1927 they had paid out over $208,226,400 to members or their families in death and disability claims.[11]

The Civil War also played an important role in the development of fraternally based insurance, for its unprecedented carnage transformed Americans' relationship with death, as Drew Gilpin Faust has argued. In its scale, brutality, and seeming endlessness, the Civil War marked a new departure as battlefield slaughter and mortality touched nearly every family, making death the war's most widely shared experience. So widespread was this suffering that it overrode "persisting differences about the meanings of race, citizenship, and nationhood to establish sacrifice and its memorialization as the ground on which North and South would ultimately reunite." Americans were hardly unfamiliar with death before the war, but the war's shift in both the incidence and experience of death pushed citizens to reconstruct conventional emotional and material means of handling it in a drastically altered world. The fraternal insurance movement did not originate with the Civil War, but that cataclysmic event propelled it forward as Americans developed on a new scale the means for attending to the burial of the dead and the provision of those left behind. By the 1880s, the size and reach of the federal government's Civil War pension system had established a precedent for the provision of assistance. And the ready analogy of injured worker to wounded soldier, whose honorable sacrifice proved his worthiness for public benefit, reinforced the view that care went to those who had earned it.[12]

The idea that death or disability honorably incurred in the course of service to nation, corporation, or the traveling public earned the worker some kind of aid merged with fraternal values to guide brotherhood insurance programs. These dynamics reflected both a larger nineteenth-century trend toward the adoption of life insurance and a deeper Victorian cultural ambivalence about that trend's financial costing of human life. Brotherhood insurance programs grew out of the running-trades' work culture, taking the informal mutual aid practiced by railwaymen in their workplaces and communities and institutionalizing it within their fraternal culture. The brotherhoods substituted fraternal obligation for "paid protection" of contractual, market-based commercial life insurance. They defined fraternal insurance as a system of mutual aid among brothers motivated by "spontaneous love and duty." Brotherhood men viewed insurance as part of a larger web of mutual aid that included informal assistance, emotional support, and acts of charity or "benevolence." At the same time, insurance represented an investment against future misfortune and possible pauperism; it was an act of prudent planning or self-help. Most important, benefits delivered as a result of injury in the course of manfully executing a risky task enabled brotherhood men to think about mutual aid and even benevolence in ways that avoided associations of assistance with dependency.[13]

Brotherhood insurance and informal mutual aid aimed to keep members and their families independent and free of charity, a commitment that received expression in brotherhood mission statements and constitutions. "To unite the Railroad Brakemen; to promote their general welfare and advance their interests . . . to protect their families by the exercise of a systematic benevolence, very needful in a calling so hazardous as ours, this fraternity has been organized," stated the constitution of the Brotherhood of Railroad Brakemen.[14] Similar statements guided the practices of the Engineers, Firemen, and Conductors. The purpose of fraternal insurance, pronounced grand master William R. Worth at the BLF's third annual convention in 1876, "is to provide a reliable fund for the widows and children in the event of the death of those on whom they rely for support, as well as to provide for brothers who may be so unfortunate as to become disabled for life." Brotherhood spokesmen emphasized that fraternal insurance involved more than simply the provision of money. When a brotherhood man invested in an insurance policy, he could rest assured that his brothers would be there for him and his family in the event of tragedy. "He is providing a guarantee note, signed by thousands of his brothers, that in case of his death or disability those he loves and cherishes will be cared for," declared the *Locomotive Firemen's Magazine* in 1897. "The brothers who are united with you in bonds of fellowship will see that you and yours receive that to which you are entitled."[15]

A defining feature of the brotherhoods' insurance programs was the distinction they made between life and disability insurance, and illness and accident insurance.[16] As a rule, the national unions administered the former and the local lodges oversaw the latter. Life and disability insurance plans made lump-sum payments to totally disabled members or, if killed, to their widows and families, whereas illness and accident insurance provided weekly benefits to those temporarily incapacitated. Local lodges acted as intermediaries between recipients and national offices. If a departed member had carried life insurance with the brotherhood, the local lodge saw to it that the beneficiaries received payment. If a disabled or deceased member in good standing had not carried insurance, the lodge did its best to assist him charitably out of its mutual aid fund, if it had one. If the member was only temporarily incapacitated through accident or illness, it was up to the local lodge to assist him.

The brotherhoods' national constitutions obliged local lodges to care for members in distress but left to them the specific manner in which they did so.[17] The particular form and amount of benefit provided ranged from formally organized mutual aid associations to informal assistance of members in need. The records of Brotherhood of Railroad Trainmen Division No. 191, of Fort Howard, Wisconsin, provide a window onto the practice of mutual aid on the local level. In 1886, the lodge voted to pay an indemnity to sick or disabled members of $7 per week for ten weeks and then $3.50 per week for another ten weeks. To fund the payments, the lodge assessed each member $0.50 per month in addition to regular dues. In April 1887, the lodge acted on this provision when J. Alexander fell off a box car at Depere, Wisconsin, and broke his wrist, approving his benefit for the time that he was laid up, an amount that came to $31. Over the next thirty years the lodge tinkered with its benefit arrangements. In 1891 it lowered sick benefits to $5 per week for ten weeks, and in 1892 it voted to do away with benefits, opting to assist sick or injured members on an ad hoc basis. In 1916, the lodge formalized its beneficiary system when it voted to draw up "by Laws to a sick benefit fund."[18]

Like the Fort Howard Trainmen's lodge, many lodges organized formal mutual aid associations. As chief engineer Peter M. Arthur testified in 1892 before the Interstate Commerce Commission, "A majority of the [BLE's] subdivisions have also a health association which pays $10 per week to its members who may be sick for one week or more."[19] Benefit payments generally amounted to one-third to one-half of lost wages. In view of the fact that loss of income, not medical expenses, rendered incapacitated railroaders destitute, such payments were essential. In addition to covering lost income, brotherhood lodges also furnished nonmonetary financial assistance, paying the rent or heating bills of laid-up brothers.[20] Local benefits varied in form and could take up a large share of lodges' financial resources. Union dues and assessments financed disability and sickness benefits; if the local had organized a separate mutual aid association, separate dues and assessments provided the funds.[21] Local lodges attempted to build up sufficient surpluses to survive periods of increased claims or when unemployment depleted the ability of members to contribute. Otherwise, the lodge would have to host a fundraiser, liquidate its treasury, or depend on the generosity of individual members.[22] Larger lodges donated money out of their general funds to families of disabled men, whereas smaller ones made special assessments on members or sought contributions.

In addition to monetary assistance, brotherhood lodges coordinated visits to sick brothers and saw to the welfare of their families. National union constitutions required local lodges to appoint relief committees, "who shall, when a member is reported sick or disabled, visit him without delay, and extend to the suffering member such assistance as he may require."[23] Visiting committees aided disabled members and their families in tangible ways. In addition to distributing benefit payments, relief committees saw to it that bedridden members received material sustenance.[24] Visiting delivered not just material assistance but also human contact, providing essential emotional support and speeding recovery. Writing to the *Railroad Trainmen's Journal* in 1891, an Arkansas brakeman revealed the psychological effect of mutual aid. If a brotherhood man was "overtaken by sickness or some other misfortune . . . the brothers [would] come to his rescue and enable him to maintain himself and family until the clouds of adversity [had] passed away."[25]

National brotherhood insurance kicked in at the point of disabling injury or death. The paid claim usually arrived in the widow's or disabled member's hands within a month's time, delivered by the local lodge secretary or treasurer. The size of policies varied among the brotherhoods; the Engineers, whose members enjoyed the highest wages in the running trades, offered policies of up to $4,500 in 1897, whereas the Trainmen, at the lower end of the scale, only offered up to $1,200.[26] The brotherhoods' journals devoted entire sections to letters from grateful members and their families. Brakeman William Meekly of Columbia, Pennsylvania, thanked the Brotherhood of Railroad Trainmen for his 1895 disability payment: "It was indeed a welcome Valentine, although I would prefer my limb instead." Widows of deceased members regularly wrote to the brotherhood journals expressing their gratitude, and the editors, eager to advertise their unions' benevolence, gave them prominent coverage. Mrs. Jeanette Costello, writing in 1895, thanked the BRT for payment of her deceased husband's policy and expressed her gratitude "to the members of Bay State lodge No. 88 for their sympathy, kind words and beautiful flowers."[27] In these expressions of gratitude, brotherhood men and their families revealed the personal nature of fraternal insurance as well as the profound material difference that it made, enabling families to live in respectable circumstances.

When a brotherhood man's injuries or illness proved fatal, brotherhood mutualism escorted him to the hereafter, seeing to it that he be properly buried. When J. Alexander was killed in Fon du Lac, Wisconsin, in June 1892 "while making coupling," the Fort Howard lodge convened a special meeting "to make arrangements" for his funeral, delegating tasks, appointing committees, and drawing up detailed plans for the conduct of ceremonies. The lodge levied an assessment to pay for expenses and held the funeral at the lodge's hall with the entire membership in attendance.[28] Brotherhood funerals, which could be impressive public affairs, offered an opportunity for brothers to symbolically express their grief and publicly reaffirm fraternal values. Lodges draped their charters in black, extended sympathy to the dead man's family, and eulogized their departed brother.[29] A letter to the *Locomotive Firemen's Magazine* from Lodge No. 264 in Anaconda, Montana, notifying readers of the death of a member, emphasized honor, worthiness, and manliness: "He was sober, industrious and ever generous to a fault. His sterling integrity, careful industry and jovial good humor ever made for him friends among his fellow workers, and gained him the respect and confidence of his superiors in position as to employment, but he had no superiors as to manhood."[30]

Brotherhood mutual aid served a variety of purposes. It helped to maintain decent living standards for railwaymen and their families in times of calamity and, in terms of gender roles and relations, helped to maintain men and women in respectability. Moreover, as John Fabian Witt has observed, mutual insurance reflected an attempt to adapt the Civil War ideal of masculine free-labor citizenship to an industrializing republic: workingmen collectively defending their masculine independence against the vagaries of the workplace. The practice of mutual aid also reflected the reality of workplace risk and the understanding that accidents occurred in the service of corporations that drew profits from railroaders' labor but did not take responsibility for hazardous conditions. More broadly, mutual aid and the value system of which it was part helped build a sense of community and solidarity; it aided families in making sense of the commonplace tragedies of working-class life.[31]

Fraternal Ritual and Fraternal Values

Complementing the practice of mutual aid, fraternal ritual stood at the center of brotherhood culture in the nineteenth century. A wide variety of nineteenth-century unions, including the railroad brotherhoods and the assorted unions representing the industry's nonoperating employees, practiced fraternal ritual. As with any organization, ritual was important to the very "being" of these unions, for, as David Kertzer writes, they could only be "seen" by members symbolically.[32] Borrowing from Freemasonry, Protestant religion, and the culture of the workplace, early brotherhood leaders constituted their unions as fraternal orders. Permeated with a sense of sacredness, brotherhood rituals emphasized mutualism, harmony, and respectability. These values, expressed in the overlapping ideals of "brotherhood" and "manhood," defined strict lines of personal behavior, dictated how members interacted with each other, and directed how they dealt with the outside world.

Ritual defined the railroad brotherhoods' organizational structures and governing procedures. Their chapters were organized into a hierarchy of national and regional "supreme lodges" and local "subordinate lodges." Officers were invested with august titles, such as "Grand Chief Engineer" or "Grand Master." Local lodge officialdom was similarly composed of chief officers and assistants, guides, chaplains, and guards.[33] Both local- and national-level officers adorned themselves with symbolic paraphernalia. Officers of the Conductor's Grand Division wore regalia of "black silk velvet scarves worn on the right shoulder, bound with gold lace, gold fringe on the lower side, a pair of clasped hands at the intersection, [and] the letters 'P. F.,' enclosed in a wreath."

Local lodge officers similarly festooned themselves with finery of "purple and white metal or silver."[34] Rank-and-file members, too, involved themselves in the pageantry by wearing more modest regalia at meetings; they also wore buttons, pins, charms, and rings as part of their everyday clothing.[35]

Brotherhood meetings were also ritualistic. They were arranged according to prescribed formats involving opening and closing ceremonies, elaborate speeches, prayers, and hymns, preset agendas, and formalized modes of interaction. As prescribed in the ORC's ritual, an altar with a copy of the Bible on it stood at the center of the brotherhood lodge room. At the far end of the room sat the lodge master, at his "station," on a raised platform with a table and gavel. On either side of the master resided the secretary and assistant masters. Ideally, the room had some sort of anteroom, attended by an outer guard, for examining visitors' credentials, and a door manned by an inner guard.[36] The opening and closing ceremonies of Brotherhood of Locomotive Firemen lodges required the warden to "qualify" himself by approaching the master, giving the "grip"—grasping the two first fingers of the master's right hand with his first two fingers, allowing the thumb to touch the ends of his fingers around the fingers of the master's with the right hand, while placing his left hand on the master's right shoulder, signifying, "We are linked together"—and whispering the secret word in his left ear. The warden then examined each brother in the same manner, proceeding from the master's right around the room. After a prayer by the chaplain, the warden retired to the anteroom to examine visitors. After these preliminaries, the meeting began. The meeting closed with a final prayer by the chaplain, the collecting of the ritual books for safekeeping by the secretary, and the brothers rising together and giving the "retiring sign"—the right hand extended straight outward toward the altar, fingers closed, palm upward, then opening the hand, palm still upward, and placing the hand over the heart, which meant, "No malice do I hold, none do I carry with me, my secrets I shall keep."[37] For brotherhood men, the lodge was a sanctuary, a shelter from the outside world and a place where they could conduct their business in private.

Outside the lodge, passwords and signs enabled brotherhood men to identify one another. The Engineers' Sign of Recognition involved raising one's open hands above the head in a semicircle, with the points of the fingers meeting between and just above the eyes. Both hands then were brought down over the eyes and to the sides with a quick movement, representing the penalty of having one's eyes torn from their sockets in case of disloyalty. The BLE's password for the year 1877 was the word "Michigan." To use it, two brothers gave the grip—shaking the right hand while giving the side of the other's hand four quick taps with the little finger—and, with each placing the left side of the toe of the right foot against the left side of the instep of the other's right foot, the visiting brother bent forward, whispering the first syllable in the other's ear, "Mich"; the other brother whispered back, "I"; and the stranger finished with, "Gan."[38] Small wonder that from the 1870s onward, the non-railroading public thought of the railroad brotherhoods as secret societies.

The most important brotherhood ritual was the initiation ceremony. A mélange of Masonic motifs and meanings derived from railwaymen's experiences, initiation rituals functioned as secular conversion ceremonies (involving metaphors of birth, life, death, and rebirth) that tested the candidate, instructed him in the mysteries of the order, and involved an oath, or "obligation," binding the initiate to the group. Brotherhood officers pressed the candidate with challenging questions, gave "emblematic" lectures, and in general impressed on him the seriousness of the brotherhood's mission and his obligation to the order. Brotherhood ritual was as practical as it was entertaining and emotionally compelling; ritual confirmed and strengthened members' sense of group identity and served as an important means through which they experienced the community of brotherhood. Like those of other fraternal societies, brotherhood initiations strove to demonstrate the uniqueness of the group, separating members from the outside world, and binding the applicant to the organization by the strongest possible ties.[39]

The Brotherhood of Locomotive Engineers' initiation ritual of the 1870s combined solemnity, quasi-religiousness, and theatricality to produce these outcomes. The chaplain questioned the applicant in the lodge anteroom, ascertaining his motives for joining the union. The applicant was then blindfolded and conducted into the lodge room, which was darkened and silent. The members then rose with "a great rush and racket," followed by the singing of a dirgelike ode while the guide twice marched the candidate around the room. The candidate was then led to the chief engineer, who portentously inquired, "Who approaches?" The guide stated that he had a friend who wished to become a member of the brotherhood. The chief engineer questioned the candidate and ordered the guide to conduct him to the second engineer, who challenged him in the same manner. Satisfied, the second engineer ordered the candidate to an altar draped with ceremonial regalia, where he placed his left hand on the Bible and repeated an oath given by the chief engineer. The initiate swore to uphold the honor and secrecy of the lodge and to recommend only brotherhood men for employment, concluding, "To all of which I do pledge my most sacred honor, binding myself to a rigid execution of every promise, in spirit and in letter, to the uttermost, under no less a penalty than to have my eyes torn from their sockets, and to myself be forever damned and disgraced by all members of this Brotherhood of Locomotive Engineers. So help me God!" With this oath, the lights came on, the blindfold was removed, and the newly admitted member was further instructed on his duties as a brotherhood man.[40]

Bending Masonic rites to working-class purposes, brotherhood initiation rituals tested not only the candidate's sincerity but also his ability as a skilled running tradesman.[41] The Conductors, for instance, used a small wooden wagon, the letters "ORC" emblazoned on its sides, to pull the blindfolded candidate—standing—into the lodge room. As if the challenge of remaining upright was not enough, the wagon was equipped with a sliding bed to simulate the action of a railway car in motion. If the candidate completed a circuit of the lodge room successfully, he demonstrated his competence as a conductor. Other unions employed similar tests. The Brotherhood of Railway Carmen, a shop-craft union, blindfolded the candidate, dressed him in overalls, and required him to work on a platform. When the platform gave way beneath him, he was "saved" by fellow workmen. The ritual tested the initiate's competency and demonstrated the importance of mutualism.[42] Ritualized testing aimed to disorient and awe the candidate and propel him on a symbolic journey from nonmember to member.[43] Initiated into the Brotherhood of Locomotive Firemen in 1875 on the Vandalia Railroad, Eugene V. Debs wistfully recalled the experience as a turning point in his life: "I am one of that circle of twenty-one, in the center of the room, repeating in solemn voice the obligation that is to bind me to my fellow-firemen to the end of my days. It is a solemn moment and an impressive scene. The hour is striking for an eventful change in my life. The boy vanishes; the man appears." Although Debs recorded his reminiscence thirty years after the fact as a heroic conversion saga more consistent with his later image as a Socialist spokesman, it nevertheless suggests the power of ritual as a rite of passage to bind the neophyte to the order and its values.[44]

In addition to testing the candidate, a principle purpose of the initiation ritual was instruction of the candidate in the "mysteries" and values of the order. In the Brotherhood of Locomotive Firemen, the initiate was seated before a screen in the darkened lodge room wearing a hoodwink (essentially a blindfold with eye flaps that could be opened and closed) over his head. The lodge chaplain began by explaining the benevolent purposes of the union: "To protect its members from injustice; to bestow upon them and their loved ones charitable donations that will make life's burden lighter at a time when death has robbed the helpless and afflicted of all means of support." At this point the lodge members slowly pronounced the BLF's motto of "Protection, Charity, Sobriety, Industry." The rest of the lecture followed, as a stereopticon projected a series of scenes on the screen: a fireman leaving his home and family "for the last time"; a train with an engine crew as they "faithfully perform their duty"; a train wreck; a funeral with brotherhood men in attendance, "tenderly and affectionately" laying their brother to rest; and a lodge representative presenting a paid-up insurance policy to the fireman's widow. At each scene, a lodge member lifted the hoodwink's eye flaps as the chaplain explained the scene's significance. The lecture reached an emotional and symbolic climax as the chaplain emphasized the brotherhood's duty to the deceased member and his family.[45] The candidate, having witnessed his own metaphoric death, could rest assured that his family would be taken care of, and he knew that it was his duty to do the same for the families of his brothers.

Stilted and formalized as these rituals may appear, they were of practical value to nineteenth-century railwaymen. Distinguishing brotherhood fraternalism from its middle-class cousin (even as it borrowed from it) was its working-class content and central concern with improving the condition of its members through collective self-help. Brotherhood icons, symbols, regalia, and initiation rituals, for instance, derived from and referred to railwaymen's work experiences and identities.[46] The rituals of periodic meeting ensured that lodge proceedings were orderly, remained confidential, demarcated meeting time from real time, separated the "sacred" inner workings of the lodge from the "profane" outside world, and gave the event the proper aura of seriousness.[47] Inside the lodge, a brotherhood man might involve himself by participating in ceremony. When he left the lodge room and its rituals, the secret work helped to carry the member's sense of belonging to a larger collectivity and reminded him of its mutualism, whereas secret handshakes and passwords served the practical function of protecting brotherhood activities from hostile employers and an unsympathetic public. These rituals made membership an interactive, intimate affair, requiring members to memorize and use ritual on an everyday basis.[48] Ritualism and secrecy heightened the class purpose of the brotherhoods by fostering élan, shared identity, and group cohesiveness; impressive initiation ceremonies and elaborate leadership hierarchies conferred dignity and importance on the group's activities.[49] With its sacredness and morality, ritual also contributed to male bonding and a masculine construction of solidarity.[50]

Only Good, Reliable, White Men

The masculine solidarity of brotherhood men figured as part of a broader movement language of manliness and manhood that permeated and animated the railroad brotherhoods over the late nineteenth century. A language of manliness had characterized the organized labor movement since the late 1820s. The railroad brotherhoods carried on this tradition into the 1890s, articulating their vision of manhood within the discursive communities set by their national conventions, lodge meetings, and, above all, union journals. Rich and diverse in content, the brotherhoods' monthly journals served as principal points of contact between the individual member and the national union. In addition to containing news of interest to railroaders, they reported on internal union matters, wage negotiations, and national union conventions. They also featured editorials on union policy, national political affairs, or social matters, as well as poetry, serialized fiction, and instructional and uplifting literature. Lastly, and perhaps most important, they contained correspondence sections featuring the letters of individual members to the journal editor. In these missives, brotherhood men expressed their opinions on events of the day, brotherhood policy and action, and the views of other members. Indeed, debates and exchanges among members appeared across several issues of the journals at a time, sometimes running hot when the issue under debate was contentious. The discursive communities fostered by the monthly journals knit together geographically dispersed memberships; they also served as forums for refining and disseminating collective subjectivities defined by a particular kind of manhood.

In their language of manliness, brotherhood men and their leaders echoed and adapted the widespread concept of manhood as embodied in the dominant culture of the Victorian middle class. The ideal of white manhood, as it came into focus in the antebellum North from the 1820s through the 1860s, took form in relation to the ideals of domesticity and true womanhood. In its popular expression, womanhood and manhood prescribed guidelines for behavior that fitted with an age of laissez-faire industrial-capitalist expansion. Women were to be keepers of the household, making it a retreat from the competitive world; in that private bastion, they were to exert an uplifting and rejuvenating influence on the men, who sallied forth into the world. Men were to be competitive, aggressive, and acquisitive, traits deemed necessary for success in the marketplace. "Manhood," though, stood less as a reflection of masculine identity than as an expression of what masculine conduct ideally should be. Prior to the moral relativism of the modern era, Victorian

Americans believed that individual conduct remained subject to broad, yet precise, standards. For men who came of age during the years stretching from the 1860s through the 1870s, values like courage, honor, godliness, and self-discipline guided their thoughts and actions.[51]

Understood in these terms, hegemonic manhood aligned with the concept of "character." A central feature of Victorian culture and articulations of middle-class masculinity, character, writes Thomas Winter, "balanced notions of hard work and individual acquisitiveness with a sense of duty, service, self-restraint, and civilized morality." In setting up this tension between acquisitive individualism and individual responsibility, the ideal sought to sanction market performance while reigning in the worst features of unbridled competition. In so doing, it posited men as independent moral agents, free to put their individual talents to work for self-advancement, though not necessarily at the expense of the larger community. For antebellum northerners, these ideas dovetailed with the widespread assumption that democratic self-government depended on a virtuous male citizenry capable of exercising independence, self-control, and civic responsibility.[52]

Yet the nineteenth-century preoccupation with character and manhood reflected concepts of gender identity in flux. On the one hand, the Civil War experience both challenged and reinforced central aspects of character-based definitions of manhood. As Anne C. Rose has written, white Victorian Americans viewed the war as a struggle over profound issues, and therefore as a chance to find meaning in secular pursuits, recast ideals, and convince themselves of the importance of human effort. As citizen-soldiers, men viewed the war as a test of courage, honor, sacrifice, and manhood. The actual experience of camp life and combat disillusioned many soldiers. Nevertheless, the prospects of personal glory and shared idealism, together with the influence of sentimentalism in Victorian culture and the view that suffering and sacrifice were necessary for national redemption, dominated postwar remembrance. Out of the conflict, Victorians emerged with a sense of optimism and manhood conceived in the sentimental terms of bravery, sacrifice, and mastery of self and circumstance. By the 1880s, aging veterans came to share a kind of "culture of character," writes David W. Blight, in which they viewed themselves as "preservers of an older, more wholesome society, uncorrupted by materialism and rooted in individual honor."[53] In fact, antebellum character-based definitions of manhood were ambivalent, reflecting, in Winter's words, "the attempt of American Victorians to culturally connect an emergent marketplace to a vision of a socially and economically more stable communal past." The expanding marketplace that gave rise to this definition also narrowed and refined it. By the time of the Gilded Age, it seemed that dominant definitions of manhood focused less on ideals like duty and self-restraint than on entrepreneurship and moneymaking.[54]

By the late nineteenth century, hegemonic definitions of manhood were unattainable to working-class men. In bourgeois thinking, wage labor rendered men dependent; in the buffeting currents of economic and social change, mastery of circumstance probably seemed inconceivable. Nevertheless, brotherhood definitions of manhood did not jettison individual agency but rather hitched it to understandings of citizenship embedded in the changing meaning of wage labor. At the core of brotherhood articulations of manhood resided a belief in manly autonomy based in self-directing, productive labor. For many skilled workers during the middle decades of the nineteenth century, a citizenry could be independent only to the extent that it controlled the means of production and remained free from relationships of dependence, which would corrupt virtuous self-government. Membership in a trade and ownership of a skill provided sufficient economic independence within the wage-labor employment relationship and enabled workers like railwaymen to think of themselves as virtuous citizens and manly, autonomous beings. In 1879, Brotherhood of Locomotive Firemen leader and secretary William Sayre argued that skill and exercise of judgment in labor formed the basis of individual good character, a virtuous citizenry, and a healthy republic: "the government . . . [was] the fruit of labor" and the laborer was the "lord of the realm."[55] A good deal of this was certainly consistent with dominant ideals of manliness. Brotherhood notions of manhood posited individual accountability, clearheadedness, and hard work as necessary for individual social advancement. Consistent with the character ideal and economic mobility, brotherhood men believed that a man established his self-esteem and earned the respect of his fellow workers, superiors, and community through industry, sobriety, and responsibility—ideals enshrined in the brotherhoods' mottos.

At the same time, brotherhood definitions of manhood adapted middle-class norms to working-class ends, viewing productive labor as virtuous, criticizing the exploitative potential of the market, and directing workingmen's respectable free agency toward their own "deliverance from oppression and abasement," in the words of Gregory Kaster. As Nick Salvatore has shown, Eugene V. Debs, as editor of the *Locomotive Firemen's Magazine* through the 1880s and the early 1890s, probably did more than any other trade unionist to elaborate this definition of manhood. In an 1885 editorial entitled "Art Thou a Man?" Debs observed that it was possible to be masculine in gender but not be a "man." For him, "manhood" and "manliness" referred less to identity than to a code of conduct defined by values such as courage, high-mindedness, duty, and honor, values that the Civil War's memory had reinforced in American culture by the 1880s. A "man" was "true to wife and home, to obligation and trust"; a man judged other men "by character rather than cash or coat," eschewed "profit by the misfortune of others," despised "prevarication," disdained "the arts of the cheat," avoided "hypocrisy," and acted according to "conscience and judgment." Most important, a man was one "who knows his rights" and had the "moral and physical courage" to "dare maintain them." A few years later, Debs spelled out the meanings of "manliness," "manly," and "manfulness" as synonyms "of bravery, courage, heroism, firmness, resolution, nobleness—of all qualities becoming a man." Despite the cross-class moral connotations of these qualities, Debs routinely praised the "manly spirit" of brotherhood men who remained loyal to their unions and true to their brothers in defense of their rights and well-being.[56]

Prescribing values and behavior by calling to mind their evil opposites, Debs also scorned workers who lacked manliness, "the mean," "the weak, the spineless, the white-livered and chicken-hearted." The "opposite of manliness," meanness smacked of cowardliness, selfishness, baseness, and "human degradation." "Mean" men included lower-level officials who abused their "little brief authority" and made life difficult for loyal union men. Certainly mean and lacking in manhood was the "sucker," the "man who sells his manhood for the sake of currying favor with his superiors." Similarly, the "'dead beat' [was] a contemptible creature" that preyed on fellow workers. Debs expressed disgust at such men.[57] Pinkerton agents, reviled among unionists for breaking strikes, were "hired assassins—things bearing the form of men." But above all, the meanest was the "scab," a figure "beneath a 'Pinkerton cut-throat' . . . worse than some afflicted cur, wallowing in a filthy gully, and gasping his last breath." Why did this writer and others hold the scab in such contempt? "Because," wrote an 1891 correspondent to the *Magazine*, "it takes a man of good grit and nerve to stand and defend himself, and this grit and nerve a genuine scab has not got—he is a coward, deprived of manhood and honor." The scab stood for everything *un*manly; in taking the "bread out of the mouths of the wives and children of his associates," he threatened union men's efforts to be "manly husbands and fathers."[58]

The concept of manliness had mutualistic overtones, linking manly backbone with labor solidarity and prescribing brotherly conduct toward one's fellow unionists. At one level, the ideal of "brotherhood" expressed the bonding of men in fictive-kin and gender-specific relations as "brothers."[59] Longtime Brotherhood of Locomotive Engineers member A. R. Cavner put it this way in 1876: "My idea of the term Brotherhood is a compact of men associated together for some specific or general result, and any association in order to succeed must combine the essential elements of unity and strength."[60] "Brotherhood" also referred to collective self-help. Although they were not opposed to industrial capitalism per se, and although they looked favorably on individual advancement, brotherhood men also recognized the inequality of industrial-capital development.[61] In an unforgiving and rapidly changing world, and in a vocation as dangerous and unpredictable as railroading, a man had to depend on the assistance of his brothers for his and his family's welfare. The concept of "brotherly love" captured this mutualistic spirit. "True brotherly love," wrote fireman J. M. Sheire in 1898, "we understand to be, first a desire on our part to be helpful whenever we see that such help is necessary to a brother."[62] To be "manly" was to be "brotherly," and vice versa.

The ideals of brotherhood and brotherly love implied sacred obligations among brotherhood men, a duty to one another and their unions. Closely related to the concept of honor, and one of the defining imperatives of character, "duty" animated the moralistic rhetoric of brotherhood manliness. One of the markers of adult manhood for the Victorian middle class, duty was also a mobilizing, disciplining, and legitimating concept for organized workingmen. For them, like the middle class, the idea implied a man's breadwinning responsibilities to family. "Our duties to our families consist in our best efforts to provide food for our homes and little ones," wrote an 1886 correspondent to the *Locomotive Engineers' Monthly Journal*. But it also marked out railwaymen's heavy responsibilities in the workplace. The "duty of running a train," Peter M. Arthur insisted in 1890, "depends upon one man, and he is the man at the front. The lives of hundreds and happiness of many more are at his mercy." And, of course, duty denoted a workingman's commitment to his union. The brotherhoods' constitutions, laws, and rituals spelled out the duties of subordinate lodges, and individual members and officers continually reminded brotherhood men of their duties. "We have for years been instilling in the minds of men the duty of being men in the broadest sense of the term, that it is character that makes the man," Arthur explained.[63] Most broadly, duty called on workingmen to exercise their agency in the cause of both labor and the republic. Thus, duty linked the gender identity of manhood as virtuous citizenship with the trade- and class-specific need for solidarity, as well as the collective manly agency that made solidarity possible.[64]

Brotherhood leaders believed that not all men possessed the "manly resolve" to follow through on these fundamental moral obligations, and so they took care in whom they admitted to their unions. In constructing labor solidarity as masculine, explains Kaster, "invocations of duty" worked to exclude those "who fell outside the full republican citizenship [that] duty implied." Moreover, the brotherhoods' claims to representing skilled, respectable labor rested on their standing as exclusive, hierarchical societies of men. The fraternal solidarity underpinning this project, as Mary Ann Clawson has written "was based as much upon a process of exclusion as it was a ritual of unification."[65] Thus, the Brotherhood of Locomotive Firemen stipulated that only men "white born, of good moral character, sober and industrious, sound in body and limb" would be eligible for membership.[66] These membership policies produced a homogenous membership, mirroring the male and overwhelmingly white, native-born character of the running-trades workforce. Neither women nor recently arrived (and unskilled) immigrants nor African Americans qualified for membership, and the issue usually went without comment. Like most other trade unions, the brotherhoods functioned as institutions for the privileging of white men's access to jobs and the celebrating of their racial superiority.[67]

On the few occasions when questions over race and membership did arise, as when the question of affiliating with the American Federation of Labor came up for debate in the Brotherhood of Locomotive Firemen in 1896–97, brotherhood men rejected any deviation from their membership policy. For some years, AFL president Samuel Gompers had been courting the brotherhoods, encouraging them to join the federation. But when it became clear that the AFL required the removal of the "white only" clause from their constitutions, an explosion of protest ripped through the pages of the *Locomotive Firemen's Magazine*. Despite Gompers's assurances that the requirement would not compel the BLF to admit black workers, most white firemen were unwilling to part with the explicit statement against it.[68] Southern members voiced the loudest and most vehement objections. J. S. Boyd, writing from Springfield, Missouri, remained unconvinced "that negroes will make good Brotherhood men." Reflecting on the issue in 1902, fireman Ernest Martin wondered, "Why lower the standard of labor by injecting into the union one so lazy and indolent, who has no ambition to raise himself above the condition he is now in?" A fireman writing from McComb City, Mississippi, stated his view bluntly: blacks were "in no way qualified to sit in our council rooms."[69]

The debate over the race bar involved intertwined matters of race, gender, respectability, identity, region, and memory. On one level, brotherhood men balked on the grounds that union membership, or even striking the "white" clause, implied social equality with African Americans.[70] Lyle Johnston, of Chattanooga, Tennessee, vowed, "When it comes to a lot of nigger lovers putting me down equal with the negro I am forever done with the B. L. F. or any other order that favors negro equality." It was not so much that these men feared black railroaders in their lodge rooms as much as they demanded that the union they belonged to declare itself in favor of white supremacy. Indeed, matters of whiteness and brotherhood were connected; as a BLF man from Meridian, Mississippi, wrote in 1902, "The boys of the South are too white to shake hands with a 'burr-head' and call him brother."[71] The vehemence of the southern membership's feelings no doubt derived in part from the reassertion of white supremacy in the South in the 1880s and 1890s. The lack of engagement and numerous expressions of support on the part of northern members likely reflected shared assumptions of white superiority, as well as an uncritical memory of the Civil War as fought not over fundamental moral issues involving human freedom but as a "nonideological" conflict between brothers whose causes were equally honest and just. Such a memory, of course, played into national reconciliation, reunion, and the construction of national identity and common white manhood, but it was also necessary to the Firemen to build southern membership and maintain national organizational harmony.[72]

Feelings ran deep, for to even countenance the possibility of admitting African Americans amounted to an unthinkable break with the internal dynamics of the Firemen's fraternal culture. For most brotherhood men, "equality" was more than an abstract concept. In the context of fraternal bonding, it implied black and white as "brothers," a sacred relationship. "I, for one, and I think I voice the sentiments of every B. of L. F. man where there are negro firemen, could not and would not 'brother' the negro under any circumstances," declared W. E. White. "I am satisfied his place is not where white men are expected to take him by the hand and call him brother and take him to the bosoms of their families and introduce him to their wives and daughters as Bro. ______." As White's statement hinted, matters of masculine pride also were at stake, an issue that a fireman from Mer Rouge, Louisiana, made explicit: "My wife and child would not own me if I should go out and attend a meeting of any order, the membership of which was partly composed of the . . . 'burr-head.'"[73] The membership's racist outpouring revealed the racial coding of fraternal values and respectability. In cultural-political terms, the shutting out and denigrating of African Americans placed the railroad brotherhoods well within the culture of what Robert Wiebe has called American "lodge democracy."[74]

This racist discourse also revealed the racial coding of manhood. Whiteness was central to brotherhood men's ideal of manhood, and manhood contributed to their ideas about what was "white." To be "manly" was to be "brotherly," both of which were "white" characteristics. By the same token, manhood involved traits associated with whiteness: honor, independence, trustworthiness, and self-respect. The term "white man," or simply "white," signified nothing less than respectable, honorable conduct. In contrast, black railwaymen came in for a lengthy list of negative, unmanly, unwhite attributes. They were "degraded, without honor, principle, pride or fair intelligence," of "slothful habits and dense ignorance," prone to "immorality, drunkenness, and vice of every description," and "worthless, in fact, dangerous to the service."[75] In denouncing African American men in such terms, brotherhood members constructed a negative counterimage to their own collective identity as manly, white men.[76]

Perhaps brotherhood men were projecting, given the nastiness of their racist discourse. Their denunciations of black railroaders, and of unmanly and un-brotherly conduct in general, may have revealed doubts about their own standing as men, and even possibly fears that their oppression at the hands of other men—employers and supervisors—had to do less with the powers arrayed against them than with their own interior state.[77] For example, pity, outrage, disgust, and self-loathing mingled in the responses of brotherhood men to the Philadelphia & Reading Railroad's 1889 demand that firemen leave the BLF or be fired. Writing under the name "Independence" in the *Locomotive Firemen's Magazine*, a correspondent castigated the Reading but also condemned the men who chose to remain in the company's service: "The employes of the Reading are now in its grasp and wear their collars, like so many dogs. Their independence is knocked clean out of them, they have the appearance of slaves. I see them frequently, but they no longer have the appearance of men." The following year, when the company issued an order compelling baggage masters and brakemen to shave their beards, the humiliation and unmanning of Reading employees seemed complete; they had become "whiskerless serfs." Lest readers missed the connection between race and manhood, Debs spelled it out for them, contrasting "serf" and "slave" with "freedom," "liberty," and "independence."[78]

If the Reading employees lacked the courage to stand up for their manhood by resigning, brotherhood leaders also understood that ordinary men needed a good deal of encouragement and support to assert their manhood under such trying circumstances. They knew that railwaymen, even brotherhood members, were likely to succumb to unmanly temptations (e.g., alcohol) without sufficient guidance. Indeed, the rougher aspects of running-trades work culture, as well as some railroaders' reputation for drinking and recklessness, did cast doubt on the respectability of railroad men. Thus, at the same time that the brotherhoods condemned and excluded men who did not meet their standards for manhood, they also devoted considerable effort to ensuring that brotherhood members conducted themselves honorably and respectably as men. Pervaded by an emphasis on moral uplift of the craft, much of the manliness rhetoric was prescriptive in thrust. The railroad brotherhoods employed the high-minded rhetoric of fraternal manhood as a framing device that justified, dignified, and animated collective action.[79]

Women and the Railroad Brotherhoods

Brotherhood men were concerned about issues of manhood, but so too were their wives. Like the Masonic fraternal associations, the railroad brotherhoods believed that they could make railroaders better men. Their gender exclusivity and portrayal of men as morally self-sufficient, however, put these organizations into conflict with some of the age's strongest social currents, particularly the widespread Victorian belief that only through the agency of women could men attain virtue. In the years after the Civil War, women began to organize in the public sphere around issues like temperance and suffrage, translating the antebellum cult of domesticity's portrayal of women as uniquely virtuous and compassionate into a degree of public authority and power. In so doing, these women not only challenged the male monopoly of political power in American society, but they also questioned the legitimacy of all-male secret societies as bastions of male difference, privilege, and power. Beginning in the 1850s, Masonic fraternalists began to accommodate the demands of women for participation in their orders by instituting ladies' auxiliaries.[80]

These developments also animated the formation of trade union ladies' auxiliaries, but with one important difference. Like their middle-class sisters and counterparts in Europe, the wives and daughters of union men organized in the public sphere to establish social networks among themselves and so gain a degree of institutional power. Unlike the challenge to the Masonic orders, the female relatives of union men did not challenge the union as a bastion of male power but rather organized to support it as a *class* institution operating in their interests. The wives of brotherhood workers led the way in organizing ladies' auxiliaries in the mid-1880s, followed in the 1890s by wives of railroad machinists in the Knights of Labor, who wished to maintain their connection to the labor movement as that organization declined. These women understood that husbands' assertions of manliness and respectable manhood enabled wives to lay claim to respectability and the right to treatment as "ladies." These norms were undeniably middle class in the emphasis placed on domesticity, separate spheres, and the ideal of ladyhood. Because such values had limited scope in the working class, wives adapted and refined them in the knowledge that their husbands' earnings, especially if they were engineers or conductors, made these values plausible. These women also knew that the union helped maintain the family income that enabled these aspirations.[81] The wives of brotherhood men had a vested interest in their husbands' unions, prompting them to organize auxiliaries to help the brotherhoods in their manly missions; these organizations also helped wives assert their ladyhood, a dimension of brotherhood and wider trade union life that conventional labor histories have largely ignored.[82]

The organizers of the brotherhoods' ladies' auxiliaries believed that their feminine influence could assist the railroad brotherhoods in making better men. According to reminiscences published in the *Locomotive Firemen's Magazine*, the wives of locomotive firemen in Tucson, Arizona, had become concerned about the lack of "wholesome" after-work activities for unmarried firemen. Patterning themselves on the "Eastern Star" ladies' auxiliaries of the Free Masons, ten wives of BLF members organized themselves into a "ladies society" in April 1884 in the adobe home of Georgia M. Sargent. The group lasted only two years, but during its existence it hosted monthly socials and edited a paper, the *Nondescript*. The *Arizona Citizen* praised the society for bringing "the firemen and their associates into pleasant social circles" and making "their home and lodge-room surroundings more attractive than the public resorts to which men naturally drift when not surrounded by such influence." Looking back on its brief existence, Sargent asserted that those "pioneer women" "firmly believed that they could exert a home influence among the brothers." As for the brothers, they "were not a bad lot . . . all they needed to bring to the surface their sterling qualities was the refining influence which is exerted by association with pure womanhood and home surroundings."[83] Echoing the sentiment, Mary E. Cassell, an energizing presence in the BLE's Ladies Auxiliary, wrote in the *Engineers' Journal*, "I think if we can make *good* 'Brotherhood' women, we will have *better* Brotherhood men."[84]

Propelled by the belief that the relationship between the union lodge and the railwayman's home needed to be institutionalized, women married to BLF members organized additional Ladies Society lodges across North America. By the end of the 1880s, the Ladies' Society (BLFLS) had grown to a dozen lodges nationally; by the turn of the century, it boasted a membership of over 1,500. Wives of engineers, conductors, and brakemen also followed the BLFLS example, founding ladies' auxiliaries in 1887, 1888, and 1889, respectively. The Engineers' Ladies' Auxiliary, which began in Chicago with 10 members, grew to a membership of over 5,000 thousand by 1898 (a figure that increased to

25,000 in 500 "divisions" by 1910). And by century's end, the Conductors and Trainmen's auxiliaries had grown to almost 3,000 and over 2,200 members, respectively. Membership in most local auxiliaries numbered in the teens, but some city-based locals rose to over one hundred.[85] Patterning themselves on the fraternal structure and culture of the brotherhoods, the auxiliaries had officers with elaborate titles, rituals, regalia, and passwords; members addressed each other as "sister."[86]

The stated missions of the ladies auxiliaries reflected their commitment to community building among the women and families of brotherhood men.[87] In addition to hosting socials for brotherhood men and their families, as well as fundraisers for the local brotherhood lodge, the ladies' auxiliaries visited fellow members and wives in times of need.[88] Auxiliary constitutions stipulated charity and mutual assistance as goals. "The great object of the Auxiliary to the Brotherhood of Locomotive Engineers," wrote Mrs. James Haley, a member of the St. Paul, Minnesota, local, in the *Engineers' Journal*, "is to promote sociability and strengthen the bond of friendship among the families of its members, and to give consolation and assistance in time of affliction. Who can sympathize more fully with a bereaved Sister than the wife of the engineer?"[89] "Leah," writing from Florence, South Carolina, in 1892, expressed her gratitude to the wives of fellow engineers, "who were willing to lend me a helping hand and encouraging words" when illness struck her family: "Then when the Angel of Death claimed our darling boy, they came with sympathetic hearts, and never will I forget their kindness."[90]

Despite their avowed purpose in assisting the brotherhoods, brotherhood men initially greeted the ladies' auxiliaries with ambivalence. Not one of the brotherhoods actually initiated the creation of an auxiliary. Rather, the issue seems to have been how to respond to women's organizing efforts. In the case of the Firemen, despite the fact that women began organizing local Ladies Societies in the mid-1880s, it was not until the 1890 national convention that the union drew up a constitution for the auxiliary and officially recognized it. (It appears that grand master Frank Sargent, husband to Georgia Sargent, played a key role in these events.)[91] In this process, the Firemen and the other brotherhoods institutionalized the subordinate relationship of the auxiliaries to local lodges and the national union. The BLF grand master appointed the Ladies Society's national president, and the Trainmen had "councilmen" sit on local auxiliary executive boards. Local auxiliaries often had to ask the lodge for permission to use its hall.[92]

Practices like these have led some labor historians to view auxiliaries as symptomatic of the unequal gender relations between auxiliary and union underlying women's exclusion from union governance and power.[93] Nevertheless, as Susan Levine and others have observed, auxiliaries like the brotherhoods' became established vehicles through which women educated themselves, supported the union, developed their own insurance plans, debated issues of the day, exercised some real autonomy, and gained important organizational experience. As was the case in the brotherhoods, housewives who felt some security in their homes, and who looked to their husbands' incomes to support the family, gave the auxiliaries its strongest support. Generally, trade unions in industries that employed few women sponsored auxiliaries, and the women who did join looked to the auxiliaries for educational, political, and social contacts. Women found these connections at monthly meetings, but the brotherhoods' monthly journals also functioned as vehicles for the building of women's community within the union.[94]

With the growth of the auxiliaries in the 1890s, women's voices began to appear in the journals with increasing regularity as they instituted special women's sections, written and edited by women. Variously titled "ladies" or "women's" departments, these sections contained editorials on such matters as marriage, motherhood, womanhood, and manhood in addition to poetry, fiction, and educational and fashion features. The women's sections also printed letters in which women exchanged opinions and advice on such topics as household management, child care, cooking, and dealing with the vagaries of railroad life. Sharing personal difficulties with one another, women asked for assistance on family and personal matters. Women like "Annie" reported in 1891 that the *Locomotive Firemen's Magazine* kept her company. Gertrude R. Ohlsten admitted to leaving her "'stews'" and "'broils'" "to peep over 'hubby's' shoulder" when the *Locomotive Engineers' Journal* arrived at her house: "The *Journal* is a strong social tie, bringing together, as it does, the East and the West, the North and the South, and making friends and acquaintances of those who would otherwise be strangers."[95] The women's sections provided women a forum for creating a discursive sphere that broadened their community beyond the bounds of geography.

Among the early and persisting topics of editorial and exchange in the women's sections, issues of womanhood and domesticity featured prominently. In their emphasis on women's virtuousness and concern for domestic responsibilities, editorials and correspondence reflected a prescriptive vision of womanhood that paralleled the brotherhoods' version of respectable manhood and echoed the nineteenth-century middle-class gender ideology of domesticity and separate spheres. "A woman's worth is to be estimated by the real goodness of heart, the greatness of her soul, and the purity and sweetness of her character, and a woman with a kindly disposition and well balanced temper is both lovely and attractive," wrote Ella U., a "fireman's sister" from Kansas City, Missouri, in a letter to the *Locomotive Firemen's Magazine* in November 1889. "She makes the best of wives and truest of mothers, and has a higher purpose of living." In 1897, editor Birdie St. Clair Dorsey emphasized women's regenerative qualities emanating from the home: "If all mothers endeavored to make home what it should be, me thinks the whole world would be made to feel the divine nod of approval. Man would soon be placed on a higher pedestal of perfection and be more in harmony with the laws of the eternal."[96] Unlike the labor feminism of the Knights of Labor, which insisted on full equality with men in the workplace and within the labor organization, brotherhood women and men placed women firmly in the household, where they were to play an essential supporting role to men in the public sphere.[97]

Brotherhood men fully agreed with this vision of womanhood and the home. In correspondence, editorials, poetry, and fiction, their vision of womanhood complemented the idealized "manly" image that they constructed for themselves, echoing the ideology of domesticity and separate spheres. The home often figured as a "sanctuary" or "fortress," shielding brotherhood men and their families from the selfishness, competition, risk, and degradation of the outside world.[98] They tended to refer to women in idealized terms as morally and spiritually superior beings, "natural" keepers of the home and redeemers of society. For one BLF member, "A Cheerful Wife" was "a woman [who], in the darkest hours, brightens the hours like a piece of sunshiny weather." Such a wife literally made it possible for the husband, whatever his calling, to succeed in the atavistic struggle of the workplace: "The husband goes into the world in a conqueror's spirit. No matter how people annoy and worry him through the day, far off her presence shines, and he whispers to himself, 'At home I shall find rest!' So day by day she literally renews his strength and energy." In an 1885 letter to the Brotherhood of Locomotive Engineers, Illinois Central Railroad president James C. Clarke revealed that corporation officials approved of railwaymen who had their domestic lives in order: "Men should always seek to make the domestic circle the most attractive to themselves, their wives and their children, for it is there the rest, comfort and happiness in life must be found." He added that, of course, it was the "duty" of men to live prudently and provide for their families.[99]

Women editors and correspondents did not completely or uncritically accept or agree, however, on nineteenth-century ideals of womanhood and domesticity. Their organization in auxiliaries alone challenged the notion that class interests and unionism should operate solely on the initiative of men. And if, according to correspondents like Gertrude Ohlsten, "woman's chief ambition (deny it though it she may) is to please a man," others like "Minnie" in 1891 pointed out that wives and mothers seldom, if ever, enjoyed a day off from household duties: "My ideas on waiting on a man don't go very far," she admitted bluntly. Women like Minnie argued for the reciprocal and complementary relations traditional to laboring households but also implicit in the doctrine of separate spheres: "Husbands speak kind words to your wives . . . come home with a smile on your face. It always takes two to make a bargain. A wife cannot make a home happy if her husband don't help her."[100] Suggesting that domesticity could be mobilized in the service of women's interests, other correspondents agreed, adding that husbands' responsibilities began with earning a family wage.[101]

When it came to neglectful or abusive husbands, women were of a single mind. An 1890 letter from "May" to the *Locomotive Firemen's Magazine* described a husband who did not talk to his wife after work, who left after meals to play cards and spend money not to return until the next day, and who opined that anything she bought or made was "horrible": "He has never come or gone without a kiss. I am perfectly heart sick, at having a husband and never seeing him more than two hours out of twenty four, if there is a remedy in this world for such a husband I should like to have it."[102] Sisters expressed their sympathy, scolded the negligent husband, and offered advice. Many, like "Anna, a Fireman's Friend," assuming the best of the husband, encouraged May to try harder to "bring him back to his former self."[103] May's situation hinted at some of the recurring facts of life for brotherhood wives and mothers: railroad work's disruption of "normal" family life, economic insecurity, dependence on men as family breadwinners, and vulnerability to potentially abusive spouses.

The brotherhoods and the women's auxiliaries zeroed in on inappropriate conduct ranging from alcohol consumption to gambling, complementing the rhetoric of manliness and moral uplift of the craft with incentives for good conduct and sanctions for bad behavior. By organizing "wholesome" entertainments like dances, picnics, concerts, ice cream socials, and train excursions, auxiliary wives encouraged husbands to spend their recreational time with their families. At the same time, the brotherhoods made behaviors affecting members and family grounds for censure or expulsion. In 1886, for example, the Brotherhood of Railroad Trainmen expelled eighty-three members for "non-payment of dues" (the most common offense), "drunkenness," "dead-beat," "defrauding lodge," "general principles," "unbecoming conduct," "contempt of lodge," "engaging in liquor business," "stealing," and "deserting family." If intemperance affected the household, brotherhood men considered it their responsibility to enforce proper conduct there, investigating instances of alcohol and domestic abuse. At an 1887 meeting of Brotherhood of Railroad Trainmen Lodge 191, in Fon du Lac, Wisconsin, "Bro. Lynch reported Bro. Kiper as being Drunk and abusing his Wife most shamefully." Lynch requested that the lodge appoint a committee to look into the matter, and at the next meeting Kiper was expelled.[104]

Despite brotherhood efforts, the record suggests that they fought an ongoing battle against improper conduct. Whether they were successful, however, is not as important as their *claim* that they were doing something about the "problem" of alcohol consumption and disreputable conduct among running-trades workers. Viewed this way, craft uplift and temperance work stood as a cultural expression of brotherhood men's yearning for independence and respectability through a process of distancing from the roughness and dysfunction of the unskilled working class.[105] "Twenty years ago locomotive enginemen were, as a class, a reckless, roystering, intemperate, and uneducated set of men, social outcasts, shunned and ignored by self-respecting persons. To-day they are sober, industrious, self-respecting, and respected," declared Wilfred P. Borland, author of a serialized advice column in the *Locomotive Firemen's Magazine* in 1893. Grateful wives, too, wrote to the journals expressing their appreciation of the unions' uplifting influence, as did "A Fireman's Wife" in 1876: "My good husband though given to associations not in accordance with my feminine views of life, has been, through the Brotherhood of Locomotive Firemen, made a better man."[106] Craft uplift and temperance also embodied brotherhood men and women's claims to moral authority. For the brotherhoods as trade unions, such claims became central to their efforts to win legitimacy in the eyes of railroad managers.

* * *

Labor fraternalism defined the railroad brotherhoods and their functioning as trade unions. At the heart of brotherhood culture stood the collective identities of manhood and womanhood, as well as the concepts of brotherhood and brotherly love. The fraternal logic underlying brotherhood unionism presented union and auxiliary as an extended family whose members had multiple obligations and shared a collective responsibility for the well-being of their "brothers" and "sisters." This logic encouraged "deep" involvement in the organization not simply as a material-economic matter, but also in terms of morality and identity. Fostered by the practices of ritual and mutual aid, deep and open-ended commitment helped the brotherhoods survive in the hostile political and economic climate of the late nineteenth century. Fraternalism also helped railwaymen reconcile Victorian ideals with the need for collective action as they, like other Americans, began to lose faith in the capacity of the market to deliver opportunity and justice. This dynamic, and the tensions within it, emerged throughout the 1880s in the elaboration of union work rules and in bargaining with employers. Viewing their ability to certify the competence, safety, and manliness of railroad workers as a principal bargaining asset, the brotherhoods sought to make good on the claim that they were societies of skilled workers and morally upstanding, respectable men. They attempted to facilitate the individual agency of the railroader in his own personal advancement, merging personal ambition with fidelity to the employer. At the same time, they couched this effort within a mutualistic understanding of advancement and loyalty to the union—workers pulling "themselves upward by their collective bootstraps," in David Montgomery's words.[107]

3

Free-Labor Ideology and Labor Relations in the Gilded Age

In March 1886, the *Railroad Brakemen's Journal* published an illustration of the scenes in the Brotherhood of Railroad Brakemen's banner. Illustrative of the significant events in a brotherhood brakeman's life, one scene in particular stood out: "the meeting between Employer and Employee. . . . A Brakeman has just left his caboose to meet the Manager in the office. He is received with the consideration due a man. Complaints are heard, wrongs are righted, and the Brakeman returns to his post." As the *Journal* explained, the scene was a harbinger of "the coming era of compromise and good feeling" between railroad workers and management toward which the union was working. If employers and workers could meet as men, the *Brakemen's Journal* suggested, there should be no labor conflict.[1] What was noteworthy about the scene was its conveyance of free-labor ideology and social harmony.

In their approach to labor-capital relations during the 1880s, the railroad brotherhoods had a complicated relationship with free-labor ideology and the ideal of social harmony. Like most Americans living in towns and smaller cities in the mid- to late nineteenth century, brotherhood men found it difficult to completely discard their faith in the principle of individual opportunity through the capitalist marketplace. During the Civil War era, free-labor ideology celebrated this classical liberal belief, holding that individual success depended on personal habits and abilities, along with a corresponding absence of constraints on the individual. As a cultural orthodoxy, free-labor ideology fostered a political-legal climate lauding natural law and the sanctity of private property while opposing anything that interfered with free markets and individual rights and action. At the same time, free-labor ideology held that because everyone should benefit from economic expansion, according to individual ambition and industriousness, class divisions were merely temporary states of affair, and that a mutuality of interests should prevail among members of the community. In this line of thought, labor and capital worked together as part of an economic process that produced prosperity and social harmony for the whole nation. Yet economic concentration and eroding conditions of work in the railroad industry after the Civil War forced railwaymen to reconsider their orthodoxies. In organizing the brotherhoods, they adapted their beliefs in individual autonomy and agency to the notion that they were due rights as members of the community, and that the only way to secure those rights was to act collectively.[2]

The railroad brotherhoods and other trade unions nevertheless ran afoul of a core free-labor doctrine. The employment relationship was a private concern with no room for collective interests. During the 1870s and 1880s, the brotherhoods responded to this challenge by emphasizing the common identity held to exist among managers and workers as men, as well as their common interests in the smooth running of industrial enterprise. As brotherhood leaders liked to think of it, the relationship between employer and employee was not one of conflict, but rather one of mutual service and shared commitment to social harmony. If it was not exactly an equal relationship, the brotherhoods contended that a railroader's standing as a man counted for more than the remuneration that he received or the work authority that he exercised.[3]

Brotherhood leaders attempted to elide the free-labor order, even as they reaffirmed and challenged it, by recasting the employment relationship as among "men," one in which brotherhood leaders "as men" met with railroad executives "as men" on behalf of "the men." Rooted in their fraternal culture and responding to the prevailing legal-cultural values of Victorian America, their approach acknowledged the private, common-law definition of the employment relationship while also creating a space for collective representation by presenting the union as a voluntarist affair of independent and free men. Such an approach made sense in the post–*Commonwealth v. Hunt* (1842) era in which trade unions enjoyed status as voluntary associations of individuals but little clear right of action as representative bodies.[4] Brotherhood leaders also emphasized the character of their unions as mutual benefit associations dedicated to raising the moral and intellectual standing of their members through collective self-improvement, thus assuring their dependability as employees. With a rhetoric and strategy that resembled the efforts of British trade unions, the brotherhoods worked to win the acceptance of the public and railroad management in Gilded Age America.[5]

At bottom, though, the railroad brotherhoods' ability to garner the attention, let alone the respect, of corporate management depended on their ability to control the market for running-trades labor. Like other craft unions in Europe and the United States, the brotherhoods worked to restrict access to jobs, standardize wages and working conditions, and establish work rules. From the late 1870s onward, the brotherhoods worked to enforce institutional control over jobs through noncoercive means. Whereas other unions, particularly in industries with lower fixed costs, attempted to regulate the competitive labor market through hiring halls, union labels, and licensing arrangements, the brotherhoods relied on the scarcity of their members' skills and the inducements of fraternal unionism to organize running-trades workers so thoroughly as to achieve "virtual" closed shops.[6] The brotherhoods downplayed, but never completely denied, the disruptive potential of their strategically located members, whose relatively small numbers and centrality in railroad operations facilitated organization and collective action. Unlike their counterparts in the stations, offices, maintenance-of-way sectors, and repair shops and roundhouses, the strike action of running-trades workers could bring a railroad to an immediate halt. After the traumatic experiences of the Great Strike of 1877, the carrot of promising to discipline railwaymen and the stick of implied disruption was enough to bring a number of railroad corporations to the bargaining table. Yet, by the end of the 1880s, the brotherhoods' reliance on labor market scarcity, as well as the inter-brotherhood tensions born of craft exclusiveness, would prove their undoing.

Free-Labor Ideology and the Brotherhoods' Approach to Labor Relations

Free-labor ideology and steadily increasing labor conflict from the 1870s to the 1890s set the context for management and the brotherhoods to explore ways to guarantee stable labor relations on the railroads. With the triumph of the North, the consolidation of the national state, and the ratification of the Thirteenth Amendment in 1865, the Civil War sanctified the ideal of free labor in American culture and politics at the same time that it unleashed an era of labor organizing and conflict. Sharply rising income inequality produced by the railroad boom–induced economic expansion of the postwar years, combined with the wrenching crash of the economy in 1873, challenged labor's understanding of free-labor ideology as a commitment to citizen–wage earners' independence. Spurred by rapid changes in industrial workplaces and the spread of wage labor, a wide range of labor organizations formed, and the ensuing battles between labor and capital defined the next three decades.

The Great Strike of 1877 inaugurated this era of conflict. With the nation in the grip of depression, and unemployment and hunger stalking the nation's wage earners, the Baltimore & Ohio Railroad's 10 percent wage cut of July 1 touched off an explosion. The ensuing walkouts of railroad workers spread into a national rail strike, accompanied by riots in Baltimore, Pittsburgh, and Chicago, and a general strike in St. Louis. With its violence and scale, the strike went down as one of the most spectacular episodes of mass conflict in U.S. history.[7] Over the following years, labor conflict escalated across the nation. Including the railroads and all other industries, the total number of strikes increased from 471 with 101,000 workers walking out in 1881 to 1,432 with over 407,000 participating in 1886. Labor conflict peaked in the 1890s; in 1894 alone, 505,000 workers across all industrial sectors participated in 1,349 strikes.[8] Through the end of the century, the repercussions of the Great Strike continued to be felt.

On the railroads, the Great Strike of 1877 set the tone for labor-capital relations. The pressures of competition and economic depression in the years leading up to and including the 1870s had led the major trunk lines to pursue wage cuts and various cost-saving measures; these actions violated railroaders' sense of their "rights as workingmen." The brotherhoods emerged during this period, as did a countertendency in railroad unionism. These industrially oriented "strikers' unions," principally composed of shop-craft workers and junior members of the running trades, formed amid strikes to achieve immediate objectives. In the 1870s, the Brakemen's Brotherhood stood as the principle embodiment of this strain; in the 1880s, it was the Knights of Labor; and in the 1890s, the American Railway Union (ARU) carried the banner of industrial unionism. These organizations, and the veterans of the Civil War era who organized and joined them, played leading roles in the Great Strike of 1877, as well as the majority of railroad strikes through the 1890s. Before 1885, railroad strikes were episodic, but large, as symbolized by the events of 1877. From 1886 to 1894, the number of strikes increased dramatically. In the ARU, railroaders added to the crescendo of nineteenth-century industrial conflict with the Pullman strike and boycott of 1894.[9]

Rapid but cyclical growth, a free-swinging approach to freight rates, and capital intensity shaped the pattern of railroad labor conflict. With the return to prosperity following the 1870s depression, railroad construction generated a tremendous demand for labor, particularly in the trans-Mississippi

West. Labor scarcity pushed managers into an ongoing quest to lower wages and lessen their dependence on skilled labor, a quest deepened both by the industry's capital intensity and the slowdown in railroad expansion caused by the economic recession of the mid-1880s. With vast amounts of capital tied up in machinery, roadbeds, and superstructure, the railroad's fixed costs accounted for a far higher proportion of total unit costs than in other nineteenth-century industries. The railroads' cost efficiency depended on scale economies—the volume of traffic and the distance traveled—which, in turn, generated incentives for continuous operation and rate discrimination. In addition to fostering virulent competitive behavior and chaotic growth, high fixed costs also affected the balance of power between labor and management, making railroads vulnerable to work stoppages.[10]

Matters of corporate organization and training also influenced labor-capital relations. Even though most of them had university education or experience in the military, American railroad managers (in contrast to their European counterparts) did not rely on theory so much as practical experience. This orientation dovetailed with the decentralized nature of railroad administration, in which companies were organized into semiautonomous units with divisional and local officials wielding a great deal of discretion and authority. Such a setup allowed for flexibility and the shining of individual ability on the part of administrative staff, as well as for a relatively personal degree of contact between manager and worker. Charles Elliot Perkins, vice president and then president of the Chicago, Burlington & Quincy Railroad (CB&Q) in the 1870s and 1880s, encouraged "personal acquaintance," believing that it promoted "good understanding" between officials and employees.[11]

This approach grew out of managerial understanding of free labor in its connection with classical liberalism and the principles of laissez-faire. Given that free labor implied consensual relations among autonomous private actors institutionalized by the labor market, managers held that market forces should set wages and that the employment relationship was strictly between the employee and the firm. The employee owed his unquestioning allegiance and obedience to the company, and in turn would be rewarded with wages and promotion according to his performance. Such a perspective, of course, left no room for collective worker organization, and managers tended to regard unionism as a threat to managerial authority and worker loyalty. On this point American executives stood in agreement with their European counterparts. Nevertheless, the American railroad system of organization and management also fostered paternalism, nepotism, and inconsistency in matters of discipline. This tendency combined with conflicts over wages to breed employee discontent, one outcome of which was unionism.[12]

Postdepression railroad expansion in the early 1880s created propitious conditions for craft-style unionism. Still, labor conflict from 1877 to 1894, the adverse political climate of the Gilded Age, and the disproportionate power wielded by corporations forced unions like the railroad brotherhoods to proceed carefully or risk destruction. The brotherhoods faced a situation similar to that of railway unions in Europe, where labor segmentation and employer hostility channeled unionism in a conservative, craft-oriented direction. In early nineteenth-century England, to evade legal repression skilled workers organized trade unions disguised as friendly societies. The English Amalgamated Society of Railway Servants, founded in 1871, remained a cautious, benefit-oriented organization well into the 1890s. The Associated Society of Locomotive Engineers and Firemen, founded in 1880, also faced unfriendly management; by focusing on enginemen's scarce skills and doggedly working for better wages and working conditions, however, it became the premier, albeit exclusive, running-trades union in England. From the mid-1880s, when memories of the Paris Commune were still alive, to the turn of the century, French engineers and firemen organized a number of craft-oriented unions emphasizing exclusivity, worker self-improvement, and moderation in relations with management. Like these unions, the brotherhoods avoided strikes and deployed respectability as a tactic. They presented themselves to hostile railroad corporations and an unsympathetic public as organizations dedicated to ameliorating railwaymen's difficult working conditions and curbing some of the arbitrary authority of managers over workers.[13]

From the end of the Civil War until the depression of the 1870s, the railroad brotherhoods focused on establishing themselves as permanent institutions and gaining public and employer acceptance. During these years, they fleshed out their fraternal cultures, built up their mutual aid programs, elaborated guidelines for the conduct of members, and set up traveling systems to regulate members' movements. During this early period, mutual aid was about the only thing that these unions could offer their members; especially in the lean years of the 1870s, the brotherhoods used cooperative insurance to ensure member loyalty and discipline.[14] Although the Engineers adopted a conciliatory stance, the organization never lost sight of the problems that had led to its formation in the 1860s: the arbitrary authority of division-level supervisors, inequitable methods of payment, overly long and unpredictable hours, insecurity in tenure of employment, and the efforts of management to flood the market for engineers. From the beginning, by negotiating written agreements the Engineers worked toward establishing some sort of control over the hiring of engineers, the manner in which they were paid, and their job security. Prior to the 1880s, local unions in a number of trades unilaterally adopted working rules governing wages and working conditions, and depended on their members to enforce them. On the railroads, however, early unions were never in a position to enforce such "legislation."[15]

Railroad management had to be persuaded of the brotherhoods' legitimacy. Nineteenth-century railroad managers typically brooked no interference in what they regarded as their common-law rights to administer operations as they saw fit. Before the 1870s, management established railroad wages and work rules either through verbal agreement or by fiat in the form of posted schedules. This practice often led both to abuse of local authority on the part of division superintendents or master mechanics and disparities in working conditions.[16] Writing in 1903, D. J. Brown, a longtime BLE member, recalled the "prejudice on the part of railroad officials." In the 1860s, "It was quite a rare occurrence for employees, either individually or in committee, to visit the office of the manager or president, and such visits when made were not always profitable to the visitors."[17] In the Engineers' first-ever strike, against the Galena and Chicago Union Railroad in March 1864, the railroad's officers declared, "No railway management can recognize as a right, any dictation as to wages they shall pay, the rules and regulations they shall adopt, or whom they shall or shall not employ." The ensuing backlash against the union was so intense that it led to both a change of leadership, making Charles Wilson grand chief engineer in August 1864, and the adoption of a more nonconfrontational course.[18]

In these circumstances, brotherhood leaders pushed for harmonious relations with railroad employers. As would leaders of the United Mine Workers later in the century, brotherhood leaders publicly argued that an essential harmony characterized the interests of labor and capital. "There is nothing so essential to the success of both classes—the employers and employed—living and working in peace and harmony," declared Peter M. Arthur, who presided as grand chief engineer from 1874 to 1903. *Firemen's Magazine* editor Eugene V. Debs drew on the image of fraternity to describe the ideal relationship between labor and capital: "One of our fundamental doctrines is that labor and capital are brothers." In free-labor terms, the two needed each other: "Money capital is useless without the assistance of labor capital, skill capital, muscle capital, and this fact ought to, and must eventually, bring money capital and labor capital into harmonious alliance." Joshua Leach, founder and first grand master of the Brotherhood of Locomotive Firemen, made the same point in 1876: "The interests of labor and capital . . . are mutually dependent one upon the other. Let us show to the capitalist that instead of arraying ourselves against him we join with him hand in hand, and with a proper recognition of his sphere of operation and his peculiar interests, are earnestly endeavoring to do that which will benefit both classes."[19] In this line of thinking, working-class organizing, a logical counterpart to concentrated capital, spelled not an era of conflict but one of cooperation, with labor and capital working together for economic progress. Labor committed itself to respecting managerial prerogative, abiding by written contracts, and heeding the social order. In return, management recognized the brotherhoods' right to exist and to negotiate for respectful treatment of their members.[20]

The brotherhoods' belief in harmonious relations between labor and capital was pragmatic, but it also rested on a free-labor vision of economic growth as an evolutionary process resulting from individual entrepreneurial effort. This vision presented industrial development as proceeding logically, fairly, and progressively, resulting in the greatest good for all—even if that growth resulted in industrial concentration. As Nick Salvatore has shown, brotherhood men like Debs viewed the railroad corporation as an inevitable feature of economic development. Reacting to the Great Strike of 1877 and restating his faith in social harmony, Debs described the corporation as "the architect of progress"; through its "magic power the uncultivated inhabitant is lifted from the shades of ignorance and idleness." The key to Debs's viewpoint was William Riley McKeen, president of the Vandalia Railroad, whom Debs regarded as a friend. For Debs, McKeen personally embodied these positive aspects of the corporation, an understanding that suggests the relatively small-scale, if not intimate, nature of some railroad companies during the 1870s. As late as 1877, despite the year's epic strikes, it was still possible for a brotherhood lodge secretary and a railroad president to see themselves as members of a socially harmonious community. This view fostered the development of a cultural script playing out the relations between labor and capital. For Debs and other brotherhood men, all men were citizens and equal in principle. Through talent and hard work, though, some men had proved their worth and merit above the majority. Those who had risen to eminence in government and business therefore stood as examples to be emulated. Railroad executives figured as role models and their corporations as examples of advancement.[21]

Brotherhood men nevertheless recognized the corporation as an imperfect engine of progress. Individual railwaymen were anything but equal to it, and in its power the corporation loomed as a potential threat to the community. The same vision of manhood and social harmony that led men like Debs to equate the interests of workers and employers could also inform an understanding of harmony coequal, in Salvatore's words, "with a concept of justice that demanded active community control of the more avaricious aspects of one's personality." With its historical roots in the eighteenth century, this understanding reflected a vision of the United States as a classless society of citizen-producers working for individual and community advancement while opposing those who wished only to selfishly extract wealth from the community. This producerist ethos found fullest expression in the labor republicanism of the Knights of Labor (KoL) during the 1870s and 1880s. The railroad brotherhoods also partook of the republican tradition. They emphasized its more conservative legacies, however, joining it with a conception of the United States not as an egalitarian society, but rather as a moral hierarchy of individuals, with the best men at the top. If the corporation threatened railwaymen's standing as individual men and as members of a community, it was not for them to rise collectively against it, but for the "better" railwaymen to show the way. The brotherhoods also differed from the Knights in embracing a tradition of republican rights that granted moral force to the individual and the market. Where they differed from the entrepreneurial expression of this tradition was in the view that individual freedom had to be collectively protected and monitored.[22]

Together with the prerogatives of skill, this understanding of harmony informed the brotherhoods' respectable approach to unionism; as did their rhetoric of manliness, it prescribed restrained, consensual, and collective opposition to injustice. Respectable railroad men defended their rights and interests, but they did so lawfully, orderly, and honorably. They did not seek unfair advantage over their employers, and they certainly did not pursue class warfare. This vision of collective action pervaded labor movements in the United States and Great Britain across the middle decades of the nineteenth century, "a kind of manly, moral middle ground between passion and submission," in the words of Gregory Kaster.[23] In the 1870s and 1880s, brotherhood leaders took this line of thinking and deployed it in the service of harmonious class relations. "We want to be friendly with our employers, and serve them faithfully," stated Debs. "We want to become intelligent and respectable enough to merit their sympathy and confidence. We want to have it so that if any difference or difficulty exists between us, we can stand before them upon a perfect social equality, and state our grievances like men." Brotherhood rhetoric held that problems could be solved if worker and employer met as men, as the *Railroad Brakemen's Journal* suggested in

1886: "The meeting between Employer and Employee . . . suggestive of the coming era of compromise and good feeling."[24]

Statements like these reflected the convictions of true believers but may also be read as rhetoric intended for public consumption, as attempts to mobilize and discipline the rank and file while winning public and managerial support. Anticipating the "prudential unionism" of the American Federation of Labor, brotherhood leaders presented themselves as leaders of respectable men who could be trusted to negotiate peacefully and in good faith. They promised to recognize managerial prerogative, and guaranteed that their followers would adhere to negotiated agreements. Moreover, when they did have grievances, they would use restrained and dignified means to express them.[25]

Carrying off the rhetoric of class harmony and restrained collective action, and gaining management's trust, required steady, sober union officers. As Debs put it, brotherhood men wished to merit the confidence of their employers. Thus, brotherhood leaders were men who had distinguished themselves not only in service to the union but also by their skill as railroaders and as respectable men. Moreover, these individuals had risen from the ranks of railwaymen, demonstrating a capacity for social mobility and, presumably, the character and ability necessary for meeting with railroad officials as equals. They needed to be able to negotiate with management, deal with workers' grievances, and speak publicly. They had to defend brotherhood interests yet avoid calamitous breaks with employers, and they maintained public images of probity and respectability. In public, at union gatherings, and in negotiations with management, brotherhood leaders portrayed themselves as honorable, responsible men who balanced both employers' and employees' interests. Mindful that elites associated order with respectable behavior, brotherhood leaders scrupulously observed proper decorum in public and promised that their followers would do likewise. As the brotherhoods grew, they required permanent and salaried union officials who were chosen for their professional abilities as much as their character.[26]

From the 1860s into the 1880s at the committee level, where the bulk of negotiations occurred and where the relatively intimate quality lent some plausibility to the idea of "man-to-man" labor relations, brotherhood men approached railroad management in a respectful, often deferential manner. As Debs stated in 1879, "The Brotherhood of Locomotive Firemen shall act only as becomes gentlemen when they attempt to enhance their interests as laborers."[27] Accordingly, a committee of engineers on the Chicago, Burlington & Quincy Railroad began their 1881 petition for a wage increase with the following words: "We the undersigned Passenger Engineers running on the Chicago Division ask this favor of you thinking it no more than justice our selves." The committee explicitly framed the petition as a "request" and closed by reiterating their loyalty to the firm: "We are very Respectfully your Obedient Servants." Similarly, a committee of switch engineers working in the Pennsylvania Railroad's Chicago yards carefully phrased their petition to management, circa late 1880s, "respectfully" requesting a wage increase.[28] Working railwaymen had good reason to approach their bosses cautiously. Especially in the early days of brotherhood unionism, committeemen knew that they risked losing their jobs as a result of their activity. Consequently, committee members tended to be older, established employees with good work records. Respectful language minimized the chances of management's displeasure while increasing the chances of favorable response. Managers, for their part, met with committees but often insisted that they represented only an assemblage of workers, not the union. If they granted a committee's petition, managers often responded only with a verbal agreement or a posted schedule revision.[29]

A centralized process of handling grievances enhanced the brotherhoods' ability to maintain labor peace. In the late 1860s, grand chief engineer Charles Wilson moved to formalize BLE grievance procedures and restrict the autonomy of local divisions.[30] At its second convention in 1875, the Brotherhood of Locomotive Firemen adopted formal grievance machinery. If a member presented a grievance to his local lodge, the lodge was to decide whether "under the existing circumstances the management is justified in its action." If not, a committee formed for the occasion would meet with the officials of the company. If that failed, the Grand Lodge would review the issue and visit the company if necessary. If this also failed, the Grand Lodge would retire to secret session "and determine upon future action." Such a complicated procedure located the power to call strikes solely with the national officers.[31]

As a rule, the brotherhoods disavowed strikes. In his push for harmonious relations with employers in the late 1860s and early 1870s, Charles Wilson so downplayed the use of the strike, and moved so vigorously to quash any local division that attempted an unauthorized strike, that the BLE appeared to be nothing more than a benevolent organization, even though it never officially declared itself against strikes. Even after the pragmatic Peter Arthur replaced the conservative Wilson as grand chief in 1874, the union retained its reputation for avoiding open conflict with management.[32] For their part, the Conductors, Firemen, and Brakemen all went on record as officially against strikes. "We deprecate strikes," affirmed George W. Heidenthal at the

Brotherhood of Locomotive Firemen's 1876 convention, "and lament that a necessity exists for ever uniting in any manner against the wishes of those for whom we labor." Brotherhood of Railroad Brakemen grand master Stephen Wilkinson forcefully stated in 1886 that his union "has never been regarded as in any way opposed to the companies, and has NEVER TAKEN PART IN any strikes, nor is it a part of their creed to participate in any such transactions." As evidence of his union's benign intentions, Wilkinson emphasized its dedication to mutual aid and self-help: "The simple Simon Pure of the order is to help each other. . . . The advantage of such assistance is of far more importance to the brakemen, who are constantly being injured, disabled and killed from accidents, than it would be to many other classes. BESIDES CONFERRING THESE BENEFITS, the brotherhood seeks to elevate the social and moral status of the brakemen as a class."[33] This kind of image helped the brotherhoods to defuse the hostility of employers and the public, especially in their early years, when they were weak and vulnerable.[34]

"To Make Men out of Crude Material"

The railroad brotherhoods' claims to credibility with railroad management in the 1870s and 1880s had much to do with their promises to respect managerial prerogative and discipline railwaymen. Nevertheless, the brotherhoods considered their basic selling point the assertion that they, and they alone, could certify the competence of railroad workers. Presenting themselves as brokers of reliable railway labor, the brotherhoods addressed those aspects of railroad work and workers' conduct that concerned managers and undercut railroaders' public reputations: their workplace autonomy, their inclination to bend or break the rules, the consumption of alcohol among some, and the fact of their manual labor and irregular work schedules. In place of the rougher styles of workplace masculinity, the brotherhoods publicly announced their intentions to instill a conception of manhood that balanced manly independence, commitment to the union, and loyalty to the employer.

In an era when labor unions' public standing was dubious at best, claiming to uplift workingmen could provide an avenue to acceptance by both the public and railroad management. If railroad corporations were unable to ensure that their employees conducted themselves responsibly on the job, perhaps the unions representing those workers could. If the public harbored doubts about railwaymen, perhaps the brotherhoods could convince them otherwise. Beginning with Charles Wilson's leadership of the BLE in the mid-1860s, brotherhood leaders saw their mission as ensuring that their members had the necessary skills and appropriate habits, and were sufficiently sober, to make them professional and safe railroad workers. The brotherhoods committed themselves to the self-improvement of their members through technical instruction and moral uplift. This, brotherhood leaders believed, would convince railroad managers and the larger community of the validity of their unions and efficacy of their leadership. "The object of our institution is to make men out of crude material," Eugene V. Debs stated in 1881. "When we have succeeded in that . . . when we are fully qualified to receive our rights, they will be accorded us."[35]

In their rhetoric of moral uplift, Debs and other brotherhood leaders revealed a conception of class relations in which workers figured as junior partners to capital. In the early 1880s, Debs placed responsibility for social discord on the shoulders of working people. Just as he regarded the corporation as "the architect of progress," he looked to employers as both personal and social models of the qualities of manhood and citizenship necessary for harmonious labor relations and railwaymen's advancement. In Debs's early estimation, because railway managers had already demonstrated their virtue and ability by rising to their eminent stations, and because workers themselves were responsible for social disorder, the union should emulate corporations' success and focus on making their members responsible citizens and workers.[36] Rhetorically, brotherhood leaders proclaimed the equality of railroad men and corporate managers, but in practice they believed that the rank and file needed guidance and leadership. As leaders, brotherhood officers like Wilson, Arthur, and Debs regarded themselves both as the equals of corporation executives as well as stewards of railwaymen. It was their duty to bring into harmony the interests of the two, but the burden lay with the latter to prove their worth.

As a public discourse, the railroad brotherhoods' rhetoric sought to win managerial sympathy, but it also fit with the larger nineteenth-century free-labor ideology and belief in mobility through self-improvement. In part, this view rested on a faith in the capacity of men for self-improvement and the idea that independence and social mobility came to those who applied themselves. Poverty, dependence, and social disorder, after all, were the antithesis of hard work, the result of laziness and moral laxity.[37] As the *Engineers Monthly Journal* moralized in 1874, "In our land every avenue is open to all, with the same chance of success . . . entirely upon himself rests success or failure . . . the stepping stone to wealth and success is economy in all things." If a man were "willing to practice those principles of self denial and economy that lead to a better and higher sphere of existence," he would be assured of "gigantic monuments of honor."[38] Those monuments were not pecuniary, but rather the cultivation of manly character. Eugene V. Debs elaborated in an 1882 editorial entitled "The Square Man": "The square man everybody honors. Riches and social position may belong to the [sneaky man], but they will not bring him that mead of self-respect, that full measure of love from his fellows, which the square man enjoys as a result of his grandeur of character."[39]

As Debs implied, railroading demanded not just technical skills, but also "good character." The brotherhood leaders of the 1870s and 1880s expected railwaymen to follow orders and perform their work-related tasks cheerfully and without expectation of special reward. Placing the employer's interests above his own, an employee should be reliable and indispensable, and should recognize that what was best for his employer was also good for him. In the course of such behavior, the thinking went, railwaymen would take their employers as models of conduct and qualify for advancement within the bureaucratic structure of the railroads. "Every fireman should be faithful and conscientious in the discharge of his calling," exhorted George W. Heidenthal at the Brotherhood of Locomotive Firemen's 1876 convention, "and those who labor rightly will, in due time, be rewarded." As the worker bettered his material condition, so he would become a better man. Ultimately, not only would the railwayman advance, but he would also qualify himself for respectful treatment from his employer and set the grounds for labor and management to meet "man-to-man."[40]

The brotherhoods' self-improvement work involved the provision of educational programs that ran the gamut of railroading. Individual lodges, for instance, often set aside a portion of the monthly meeting for technical and industrial education, and the brotherhoods' journals provided special sections devoted to these topics. The *Locomotive Engineers Monthly Journal*'s "Technical Department" featured articles addressing issues such as "Freight Train Handling" and "Running Problems to Answer."[41] And the *Locomotive Firemen's Magazine* included a "Mechanical Department" containing items like "Primary Lessons in Steam Engineering," "Scientific Firing," and "What Should a Young Fireman Know?"[42] The *Magazine* encouraged members to study chemistry to understand the "underlying . . . reactions that change coal into carbon monoxide and carbon dioxide, and the heat changes that accompany this transformation."[43] Technical drawings of locomotive and train-car mechanical systems abounded, as well as articles and illustrations on new railroad technologies. These essays, and similar offerings in the *Railway Conductor* and *Railroad Brakemen's Journal*, expounded on the technical aspects of railroading.[44]

At the same time, brotherhood educational work attempted to ensure that brotherhood men took on the habits necessary for the demands and responsibilities of railroad labor—that is, to "be faithful and conscientious in the discharge of [one's] calling."[45] This effort included "prescriptive" journal essays on proper work habits, as well as exhortations at union meetings promoting punctuality, tidiness, alertness on the job, and the avoidance of alcohol.[46] "Look at the men who have been promoted the last few years and compare them with the men who have been discharged or kept where they never get any thing better," admonished the *Railroad Brakemen's Journal* in 1886. "You will find the former had a reputation for neatness and watchfulness while on duty, while the latter are tossed here and there, first on one car and then on another, and finally no one wants him and he is discharged." A series of articles entitled "Practical Talks To Young Engineers," appearing in the *Locomotive Firemen's Magazine* in 1893, stressed adherence to company rules while acknowledging the necessity for on-the-job decision making: "When you receive your train order, read it thoroughly and give it to the fireman . . . *never read an order the second time* . . . have it thoroughly impressed on your mind at the first reading. . . . Imagine any contingency that is liable to occur to prevent the successful completion of your trip; disaster overtakes the person who is not looking for it." In similar fashion, hoping to persuade its members to comply with company rules, the Order of Railway Conductors launched a campaign for "perfect service" in the late 1880s.[47]

Brotherhood educational work emphasized the concept of "duty" in the multiple arenas of men's lives: union lodge, workplace, and household. Brotherhood leaders called on their followers to be true to their brothers as union men, to dedicate themselves to their crafts and conduct themselves as dependable employees at work, and to earn a family wage as a result of productive labor to support their households as breadwinners.[48] In the words of BLF member H. J. Facke, the brotherhood was based on "fidelity to obligations, honorable ambitions [and the] building of a good, pure manly character." For one brotherhood official, this process amounted to nothing less than "successful man-building."[49] Brotherhood leaders presented workplace responsibility, employer loyalty, and commitment to self-improvement as manly virtues. "The most sacred and binding seal known by civilized men is the pledge of honor," Debs lectured in 1882. "No man, with any moral scruple, would be able to contemplate, without a keen feeling of shame, the record of a broken pledge. It is our aim to impress this fact upon the minds of our members . . . the obligation they take to support the rules and principles of our Order is as binding upon a man as a bond backed by millions, and anyone who violates that obligation strikes down his very manhood with his own hand."[50] It did not matter whether a pledge was made to one's union or to one's employer; it was a contract to be honored. In the brotherhoods' construction, manliness involved the rejection of erratic, irregular behavior and the embracing of steadiness, service, and commitment to the work ethic.

Brotherhood leaders knew, however, that exhortations to duty and good habits were not enough. They were competing against the less reputable workplace and leisure practices that informed the rougher styles of masculinity among railwaymen. Thus, brotherhood leaders worked to construct a masculine identity that did not simply repudiate the masculinity of the workplace, but rather incorporated and transcended it. Brotherhood leaders attempted to translate the virtues that they preached into "heroic," "manly" qualities. Debs's "Square Man" represented self-restraint, courage, and dedication to duty: "If the square man grasps the throttle of an engine there will be no sleeping at that post. Lives are entrusted to him; all his faculties are on the alert for danger. . . . Clear-brained, keen-eyed, strong-armed he stands at his post, and if the hour of danger overtakes him while there, he will never desert it. Duty does not call to him in vain. All the time while his engine is skimming along the rail . . . he stands there silent, watchful, fearless." In this vision, Debs emphasized responsibility, control over the body, coolness in the face of danger, and self-sacrifice to save others. But if railroading demanded bodily control in the best Victorian fashion, Debs nevertheless acknowledged the physically taxing aspects of the job. In an 1884 essay, he painted a portrait of manhood based in corporeal ability and practical mental aptitude: "[Railroaders] are remarkable for common sense. They are bronze-browed, hard-fisted, noble-natured men. They are forever dealing with problems which demand and command serious thought. A locomotive fireman cannot, in the nature of things be a dude."[51]

It was a glorified vision, but Debs connected his understanding of manhood to the skilled work of railroading. For Debs and others, control and restraint of the body, a notion firmly grounded in the railroad work process, had distinctly working-class meanings. In contrasting railwaymen to "dudes," Debs ridiculed the "unmanly" conduct of leisure-class men who did not work with their hands. By contrast, respectable *working-class* manhood celebrated the risks and rewards of physical labor, emphasizing its ennobling effects and stressing the superiority of "authentic experience." "The cultured and refined with their silks and laces and arrogant pride, sweep by in majestic disdain when meeting this class of workers, little dreaming that beneath that blouse beats a heart as brave and chivalrous as ever distinguished knights of old," wrote A. J. Schmidt, a fireman from Cleburne, Texas, in 1891. "What matters the rough exterior, the soiled over clothes and the grease and coal dust? 'A man's a man for a that.'"[52] Regardless of their appearance, brotherhood railroaders insisted that their character and the content of their work made them respectable, heroic men.

To be sure, brotherhood leaders were asking railroad men to sacrifice some of the romance, adventure, and spontaneity of running-trades work, and to forgo some of the more "earthy" pleasures of leisure. In so doing, they understood these men must part with, at least to a degree, the more unrefined styles of workplace masculinity. In exchange, brotherhood leaders offered mutual benefit, self-improvement, respectful treatment at work, and occupational security and advancement.

As brotherhood leaders sought to win over railwaymen, they also worked to position themselves with railroad management. In return for recognition, as Debs put it, the brotherhoods promised "to give to railway corporations a class of sober and industrious men." Indeed, they argued that it was in the interests of the railroads to encourage the brotherhoods in this enterprise. By 1889, as Peter Arthur believed, "the [Brotherhood of Locomotive Engineers] had been instrumental in giving the railway companies a better class of men than they would otherwise have had."[53]

Such promises required expression at a more practical and meaningful level than mere public pronouncements. The traveling card encapsulated the brotherhoods' view of themselves as brokers of skilled labor. The Engineers' card, for instance, indicated how long the engineer in question had been running a locomotive and whether he had served in yard or road service. The Firemen's card stated what railroad the job-seeking fireman had worked for, for how long, and in what capacity. In both cases, an officer of the lodge verified the accuracy of the information and attested to it with a signature, and so guaranteed the member's competency and good character. The BLE made this policy explicit, holding itself "responsible for the good conduct and character of all members whom they report out of work or to whom they issue traveling cards."[54] Central to the brotherhoods' moral stewardship (and, by extension, their claims to respectability and legitimacy) was their ability to guarantee that their members indeed were competent, safe, sober, and trustworthy—in short, that they had the right kind of manhood.

Ultimately, though, the test came in the brotherhoods' policies and actions in specific work situations.[55] Brotherhood officers stood ready to relay managerial concerns to the rank and file. In 1901, for instance, J. I. Whiddon, the Engineers' general chairman in Macon, Georgia, wrote to lodge officers about "irregularities complained of by general officers of the [Southern Railroad] and traveling public, which reflect very much on the engineers." These "irregularities" included "black smoke," "not sounding [the] whistles according to the rules," and "passenger trains . . . badly jerked."[56] When it came to violating the employer's trust, the brotherhoods followed strict disciplinary procedures. The Brotherhood of Locomotive Engineers made it an offense to conduct oneself as anything other than an exemplary employee. "Should any Brother neglect his duty or injure the property of his employer, or endanger the lives of persons," he was to be brought up on charges. Such was the case in 1893 when the secretary of Brotherhood of Railroad Trainmen Lodge No. 93, in Moosic, Massachusetts, "preferred charges against Frank A. Green for stealing goods from the F. R. R. Co. and recommended that he be expelled for same." Indeed, brotherhood officers willingly reported members to management. Eugene V. Debs himself informed the Vandalia Railroad about the poor medical condition of a member who had applied for a job as engineer. Upon learning that the individual in question had a poor heart, the road declined to hire him and thanked Debs for his action.[57]

If a member's work conduct was affected by alcohol, the brotherhoods were especially severe. Self-policing, as Peter Arthur reported to the Interstate Commerce Commission in 1889, was a measure of the brotherhoods' seriousness in delivering sober and safe men: "Their laws are very rigid as to drinking, they having expelled during the last year three hundred and seventy-five members for intoxication; and whenever a man is detected dissipating he is punished and the officers of the road are notified of the same."[58] The year in question may well have been exceptional with such a large number expelled, and the situation on the ground was undoubtedly more complex, for the brotherhoods fought an ongoing and never entirely successful battle against alcohol use and improper conduct. Nevertheless, as public rhetoric, Arthur's comments achieved their aim in promoting the reputation of the brotherhoods as officially committed to producing reliable men.

Indeed, brotherhood leaders claimed success in their mission. "Our employers are not slow in discovering this marked advance in morality, as is evidenced on every hand by the frequent advancements and promotions, and the seeking in our ranks, as is often done, for good, trustworthy, sober men," maintained grand master Frank W. Arnold at the Brotherhood of Locomotive Firemen's 1882 convention. "The Brotherhood of Railroad Brakemen are doing a great deal of good here," agreed a brakeman in 1886. "They have been the means of reforming a great many men. A man who belongs to this order must be upright, sober and industrious. Railroad officials are beginning to see the good of the order and are giving brotherhood men the preference." Likewise, a contributor to the *Locomotive Firemen's Magazine* argued in 1891 that the BLF had educated "the membership up to a high standard." Railroad officials, he conceded, used to oppose organized labor, but the "wise" ones no longer did, for "the train service has attained to such a degree of perfection a high order of skill and training is essential on the part of the men in charge." "Railroad managers have discovered this," he added, "and have accepted the inevitable."[59]

By the 1880s, a number of railroad managers understood the importance of fostering a suitable type of manhood among the men in their employ. It "is very much the business of the company to make sober, moral men of their employees," asserted Theodore Vorhees, vice president of the Philadelphia & Reading Railroad. Like the brotherhoods, a number of managers viewed developing character-based manhood among their workers as the key to industrial peace, a belief expressed in their support of the Young Men's Christian Association's (YMCA) work among railwaymen. Charles L. Colby, president of the Wisconsin Central Railroad, argued that "the main object [of the YMCA] is to afford [the workers] . . . the opportunities for elevating social pleasures, for moral and religious growth and cultivation . . . and, above all else, for the acquirement of sterling Christian character." Although only a minority of railroad managers actively supported the YMCA's work (and, like other forms of welfare capitalism, did so with a view to it as a bulwark against unionism), the sentiment that animated that support enjoyed wider currency among the men running the nation's railroads.[60]

A small number of railroad executives began to the view the railroad brotherhoods as viable partners in labor relations. Together with their antistrike rhetoric and declarations of respectability, the brotherhoods' promises to deliver workers of high manly character met a real need and must have seemed an antidote to labor radicalism in the aftermath of the Great Strike of 1877.[61] Into the 1880s, managers corresponded with brotherhood leaders and spoke of their organizations, as Debs described it, "in the kindliest terms." William H. Vanderbilt of the New York Central Railroad was pleased at the rapid development of the Brotherhood of Locomotive Firemen, the *Firemen's Magazine* reported in 1880.[62] New York Central president Chauncey Depew, known for his tolerant view of organized labor, spoke to the Engineers in 1886, lauding them as "a model for trades union. You are not only the most successful of labor organizations, but you have the respect of and confidence of those whom you so admirably serve—the people and the corporations." James C. Clarke, Illinois Central Railroad president (and not known for his labor-friendly views), echoed the brotherhoods' rhetoric of class harmony: "The interests of employes and employers are mutual and when properly appreciated and understood—the success of the one is the benefit of the other."[63] And Santa Fe railroaders reported officials' preference for brotherhood men, citing the brotherhoods' ability to develop more efficient, dependable employees.[64] Annual passes for brotherhood officers, free transportation to conventions, and a willingness to meet with them in person—as demonstrated by officials of the Wabash, Illinois Central, and other railroads—revealed a growing rapprochement between union and management by the middle of the decade.[65]

With the Brotherhood of Locomotive Engineers in the lead, the brotherhoods set their sights on the establishment of bargained and contractual relations with employers. The BLE became the first union in the railroad industry to win a written agreement when it signed a contract with the forward-looking Vanderbilt in 1875. Over the next two decades, with the Engineers leading the way, the brotherhoods entered into formal agreements detailing such issues as wages, rest periods, overtime, seniority rights, and grievance and disciplinary procedures. Written agreements provided favorable wages and working conditions while protecting railwaymen against the vagaries of railroad work and arbitrary management. They also reflected railroad management's growing acceptance of the wisdom of dealing with workers collectively, but only after brotherhood rhetoric in the aftermath of the Great Strike of 1877 convinced them so.[66]

The Breakdown of the Brotherhood Approach

With favorable treatment from railroad managers, it seemed by the mid-1880s that the railroad brotherhoods were on their way to redefining the employment relationship and establishing a system of "industrial legality."[67] The brotherhoods' conviction that their success resided in the prerogatives of skill reinforced their commitment to protect their interests alone. The Engineers and the Conductors ignored the struggles of other railroad workers, particularly the shop crafts, and in some cases assisted in the breaking of their strikes, earning them reputations for arrogance, aloofness, and class collaboration.[68] Nevertheless, the brotherhoods' vision of harmonious labor relations required more than promises of good intentions. Without material incentive, railroad managers were unlikely to grant the brotherhoods any recognition or concede any power, no matter how benign the putative intentions. At bottom, the brotherhoods' successes and their vision of labor-capital relations depended on their ability to control the market for skilled railroad labor. In effect, what the brotherhoods pursued in the 1880s amounted to an effort to regulate the competitive labor market in a way that would later be associated with the "new unionism" of the 1890s and early twentieth century. The success of the railroad brotherhoods' approach to labor-management relations depended on two key conditions—scarcity in the market for running-trades labor and the relatively intimate nature of labor relations. As Shelton Stromquist has shown, the brotherhoods' success during the 1880s resulted as much from expansion-induced labor scarcity as their conservative postures. By the second half of the 1880s, however, the railroad industry was changing in ways that spelled trouble for these proud unions.[69]

Labor scarcity was a problem for railroad management. With intensifying competition among railroads in the early 1880s, and an economic downturn lasting from 1883 to 1886, management searched for ways to reduce wages. In the shop crafts, management succeeded in introducing laborsaving technology and imposing wage reductions. In the running trades, which were less conducive to such technology, railroad managers in the more-settled regions of the upper Midwest and the Great Plains began introducing policies designed to increase the supply of running-trades labor through active and systematic recruitment, rapid promotion, revision of work rules to permit fuller utilization of existing labor, and disciplinary procedures. These policies resulted in deteriorating working conditions; a more rationalized, bureaucratic, and impersonal work environment; and a climate less hospitable to the growth of unionism. Inevitably, workers and managers clashed over the determination of wages, promotion, and seniority, particularly in the West, where demand for labor was greatest. The ensuing conflict set the tone for labor organization and strategy during the second half of the 1880s.[70]

In the shop crafts, the engagements came early, in the wake of the business downturn of 1883–85. The most notable of these strikes occurred on Jay Gould's southwestern system in 1885–86, as shopmen—and smaller numbers of trackmen and even some running-trades workers—angered by the company's cost-cutting measures, went out under the auspices of the Knights of Labor in a multigrade labor show of strength. The Knights' success in that 1885 strike against Gould's Wabash Railroad marked the first time that a labor organization had defeated a large corporation, and it sparked a surge of membership in the KoL. The Knights' meteoric growth revealed a shedding of apathy and deference on the part of industrial workers across the nation, which fed directly into the "Great Upheaval" of the 1880s.[71] It also demonstrated that non–running trades workers—and some firemen, engineers, and brakemen—were less interested in the social harmony of brotherhood-style unionism than in organizational forms that would defend their interests through collective action. In the running trades, the brotherhoods succeeded in holding at bay management's attempts to manipulate the labor supply. But as railroad construction began to ebb during the mid-1880s economic downturn, the brotherhoods found their ability to command management's attention waning and their relations with one another fraying.[72]

The first indication of the turning tide came not in brotherhood-employer conflict, but rather in intra-brotherhood conflict. Management attempts to manipulate the labor supply and lower wage costs, particularly the practices of promoting engineers from within the company and paying newly promoted engineers at a lower rate (called "classification"), soured relations between the Brotherhood of Locomotive Engineers and the Brotherhood of Locomotive Firemen. The Engineers had watched the younger union, expecting firemen promoted to engineer to drop their BLF memberships and join the BLE. But as the Firemen grew stronger and more comprehensive in the early 1880s, many newly promoted engineers retained membership in their original organization, even as they became members of the Engineers. The dynamics of seniority, promotion, and classification exacerbated the situation. When a fireman was promoted to engineer, he went from the top of the firemen's seniority list to the bottom of the engineers' list, where he found himself again working irregular freights and earning low pay. For a newly promoted engineer struggling to survive this "starving time," retaining lower-cost membership and insurance coverage in the Firemen made sense. By the mid-1880s, the BLF loomed as a potential dual union. In 1885, the Engineers moved to preempt jurisdictional competition by unilaterally amending its constitution to prohibit membership in more than one union.[73]

BLF firemen were outraged, believing that the Engineers' action relegated their union to the status of a junior and inferior partner, thereby replicating at an institutional level the hierarchical relationship between engineer and fireman. Debs regarded it as "an insult and a menace," an attack on a substantial portion of the Firemen's membership, and an undermining of what had appeared to be a growing fraternal feeling between the two organizations.[74] Earlier developments within the Firemen shaped its response. By the mid-1880s, some firemen began dissenting from the idea that skill defined the man; they felt that, as apprentice engineers, they had more in common with engineers and their employers than with other segments of railroad labor. Particularly in the western United States, firemen witnessed management mistreatment of workers and repression of their unions, and they came to doubt the brotherhood vision of harmony based in common manhood and free-labor ideology. Some of these men argued that firemen *were* skilled workers and ought to be paid and respected as such. By decade's end, others even argued that skill was irrelevant and that a man should be judged according to his character, regardless of his job category or social station.[75]

Eugene V. Debs, who was beginning his own transformation from labor conservative to labor radical, became the leading brotherhood exponent of a view that exalted producers' rights, as well as the principles of justice and the common equality of all. Expanding on the implications of producer theory over 1885 and 1886, Debs adopted an increasingly critical tone toward the corporation and monopoly, which he saw as threats to the legacy of the American Revolution, and began denouncing blacklisting, predatory wealth, and corporate paternalism. As a result of his extensive organizing trips across the nation, Debs was alerted to the changing conditions of work and the impatience of many railwaymen; consequently, he had begun to reexamine his understandings of harmony and manhood. Debs's 1885 "Art Thou a Man?" editorial, in which he contrasted manhood and monopoly for the first time, signaled a shift to a more strident conception of manhood.[76] "American workingmen are not serfs," he wrote in another essay. "They are not cringing, fawning, lickspittles, who approach railway superintendents on their bellies in the dust." Still, Debs did not experience an instant conversion; over the second half of the 1880s he continued to uphold workers' obligations to their employers, but as matters of honor rather than deference and social hierarchy: "Be faithful to the company in whose service you may be employed for the reason that justice demands it; but to be faithful to your employers doesn't carry with it the demand that you must surrender your manhood."[77]

The shifting views of Debs and others took the Brotherhood of Locomotive Firemen in a new, more militant direction. At the union's 1885 convention, delegates—led by firemen who had experience with the Knights of Labor on the Gould system and who had seen his reprisals against that organization—replaced the conservative Frank W. Arnold with the more aggressive yet pragmatic Frank P. Sargent as grand master. As secretary treasurer, Debs stood as the sole national officer returned to office. The magnitude of these developments became clear when the convention rescinded the union's 1879 pledge abjuring strikes and directed Debs to approach the Engineers with a plan for cooperating with them in the handling of grievances. But when Debs visited the Engineers' convention the following month, his proposal was ignored and he witnessed the delegates pass the amendment barring dual union membership. At the very moment that Debs and the BLF were working toward a more oppositional stance regarding management and greater cooperation with fellow brotherhoods, the Engineers slammed the door shut.[78]

With Debs's encouragement, BLF men excoriated the Engineers in the pages of the *Locomotive Firemen's Magazine*. Many writers took the BLE's amendment as a slap in the face, an action that consigned the BLF member to the status of "an animal belonging to the lower order," according to one contributor. The Engineers wished "to pat us on the head and tell us that we are good boys," fumed another.[79] More troubling was the way in which the BLE's policy affronted the principles of manliness that informed BLF membership. Debs attacked the Engineers for forcing newly promoted engineers "to apostatize, to strip themselves naked of independence, of self-respect, disown their brothers and trample upon oath and obligation that they may be eligible to membership in the Brotherhood of Locomotive Engineers." At issue was the BLE's exclusiveness, born of a worldview in which the prerogatives of skill defined the man and his worth, a perspective that came into conflict with the changing views of men like Debs: "We know of nothing more offensive than an aristocracy of labor, in which one toiler sets himself above another. . . . To our mind the beaded sweat on an honest laborer's brow is more resplendent than the diamonds in the crown of a king." In an editorial entitled "Manliness vs. Meanness," Debs equated the BLE's membership policy and its refusal to treat BLF members as equals with corporate blacklisting of union men. For the loyal BLF member, the Engineers' policy was nothing less than "an insult to his manliness."[80]

For their part, members of the Engineers argued that they had firemen's welfare at heart and tried to remind them that their long-term interests lay with the BLE.[81] The paternalistic and at-times condescending tone of engineers' responses, however, only aggravated the Firemen. "I belong to a school of runners that knew their places as firemen and kept them, and now make our firemen keep theirs," pointed out one engineer.[82] To be sure, some BLE members identified "the arrogance of the wealthy corporations" as responsible for the "bitter antagonism" between "the two 'B's'" and argued for "united efforts against this curse to our profession—'classification.'" Such a point of view reflected some division within the Engineers over the new membership policy and doubts about the ability of engineers to command the respect of managers on the basis of their skills. In the system of classification, they did not see harmonious relations with capital but rather evidence of management undercutting the standing of engineers as skilled workers.[83] Nevertheless, the majority of engineers refused to see their interests in common with those of firemen, much less form any alliances with them.

Rifts among all the brotherhoods came to a head in the Chicago, Burlington & Quincy (CB&Q) Railroad strike of 1888–89. By the late 1880s, even though the Firemen despised the Engineers' membership policies, members of both organizations had to agree that their interests were congruous on the issue of classification. Believing that the two trades were organically linked, BLF leaders argued that they must act in concert with the BLE when it declared its walkout. The strike, and a sympathetic boycott of CB&Q cars on connecting lines, failed as a result of management intransigence, scores of strikebreakers, and federal court orders enjoining neighboring railroads from refusing to handle Burlington traffic. Moreover, the Order of Railway Conductors (ORC), which had consistently followed its own separate course as a non-striking, benefit-oriented organization, refused to honor the strike, revealing both the order's ultraconservatism and a latent animosity between engineers and conductors. Conductors' chief C. S. Wheaton applauded the company's refusal to grant the BLE's "unjust" demands and advised ORC members to remain at their posts and even take the places of striking engineers. "This is not a fight between capital and labor, but between right and wrong, as all know the engineers are the best paid class of men on the railroad, and they are to-day receiving pay that is justly due the conductor," read an ORC circular, which went on to question the skill required of engineers before concluding that the "engineer has no interests that are identical with ours." The Engineers' journal labeled the Conductors "sycophants and traitors to every principle of manhood."[84] When Arthur unilaterally negotiated a settlement on behalf of the Engineers, however, it was Debs's turn to spill invective on the Engineers and encourage the idea of dual unionism.[85]

Part of the "Great Upheaval," in which unions that had emerged under conditions of economic expansion in the early 1880s clashed with employers in the latter part of the decade, the Burlington strike vividly demonstrated the limits of brotherhood unionism. As early as the mid-1880s, the conditions of labor scarcity that favored brotherhood unionism had begun to disappear, and intensifying rate competition drove the railroad system of classification. By the late 1880s and the early 1890s, the actions of railroad corporations to increase the supply of labor, together with the tapering off of railroad construction and a general slowdown in the national economy, produced a surplus of railroad labor. In those conditions, railroad management could ignore the brotherhoods. A successful strike depended on labor-market scarcity and no reserve pool of scab labor, or, failing that, a minimal solidarity among the ranks of railwaymen. The narrowness and exclusivity of the Engineers, however, not only undermined solidarity but also encouraged the vicious backbiting that characterized the strike. The Burlington's intransigence also signaled a new level of resistance to brotherhood unionism. CB&Q officers like Charles Elliot Perkins considered the brotherhoods' ideas a violation of natural laws of labor supply and demand, and viewed unions as bodies with little more to offer than interference with managerial prerogative. The engineers on the CB&Q, he wrote, had "been having their own way with the railroad managers, and the discipline in that branch of service ha[d] become exceedingly loose and inefficient." Writing during the heat of the Burlington strike, he thought that the only way to deal with such employees was "as if they were children," insisting "upon their behaving properly as the law requires."[86]

In the eyes of many brotherhood men, previous understandings of harmonious relations between workers and managers had broken down. "The arbitrary and tyrannical conduct of [General] Manager Stone of the C. B. & Q. Company has, in a large measure, I fear, destroyed that mutual good feeling and respect that existed previous to the present trouble, between railroad companies and our Brotherhood, the result of twenty-five years of conservatism on our part and the appreciation of it by railroad companies," lamented engineer E. Tinsley. He was particularly distressed to learn that "minor or petty officials [had] indulged in some ill-timed sneering at the request of our C. B. & Q. Brothers that they should be treated with courtesy." In chief Arthur's opinion, the strike was lamentable but unavoidable. Citing the "honorable and amicable adjustment" of differences on over a dozen railroads during the year in his 1888 annual convention address, he explained in each case (save that of the Burlington Railroad) that "the difficulty was between man and man, not between man and a demagogue."[87]

* * *

In the wake of the Burlington strike, the railroad brotherhoods lost a good deal of credibility in the eyes of a number of running-trades workers, particularly among those in the West. Rejecting craft-based organization, these men joined hands with workers from the shop crafts and formed the American Railway Union in 1893 with Eugene V. Debs as its head. Explicitly producerist in orientation, the ARU pursued a form of industrial action that would undertake strikes to the full extent of sympathetic action. In its inclusion of all grades of railroad labor, the ARU forthrightly embodied a broader spirit of fraternity and masculine identity based not in the prerogatives of skill, but rather in the broad idea that all men were equal and should be judged by their character, virtue, and effort in the workplace. In the view of these men, the brotherhoods' sharply drawn craft lines, attempts to control the labor supply, and vision of social harmony had become defunct. As Debs wrote in an 1894 letter to his friend Frank X. Hall, "The [BLF] is dead as are all the rest of the old orders so far as *protection* is concerned. All the old orders are dead by their own hands and in the graves of their own digging. . . . The A. R. U., I am happy to say, is coming nobly to the front. Its members are *men*, not boot-lickers."[88] Highlighting the impotence of the brotherhoods' conciliatory approach, the ARU's willingness to challenge capital may have represented a more confrontational style of manhood and a more compelling vision of social justice and fraternity to the thousands of converts drawn into the union. It appeared that the brotherhoods' golden age had come to an end.

But to focus on the brotherhoods' defeats during these years is to miss the significance of their unionism. It was not so much that brotherhood unionism represented a somehow-essentialized worldview of a privileged segment of the railroad labor force. Rather, organized in the shadow of the Civil War and coming to maturity during the volatile final third of the nineteenth century, brotherhood unionism reflected the efforts of skilled railroad labor to negotiate changing economic and ideological realities, as the emerging capitalist order and changes in the railroad workplace challenged the precepts of free-labor ideology. Partly idealistic and partly pragmatic, it sought to achieve material gains and curb capital's power in the workplace within a legal-political order firmly opposed to unionism. It did this by emphasizing the common identity held to exist among managers and workers as men. By the early 1890s, however, changes in the railroad labor market and workplace would force the brotherhoods to reconsider their rigidly craft-specific approach to unionism.

4

The Crisis of the 1890s and the Reordering of Railroad Labor Relations

The Pullman strike and boycott of 1894, one of the most significant episodes of nineteenth century railroad labor conflict, capped off over two decades of the most severe and sustained industrial warfare in U.S. history. Coming amid the 1893–97 depression, the nation's worst to date, it marked the pivot point of the 1890s crisis. That "crisis" came out of a quarter century of rapid socioeconomic development that had remade the northern United States from a largely agrarian- to an urban-industrial society. This period of development was so wracked by social and political unrest that amid the Pullman conflict, leading figures in business, government, and the labor movement questioned the viability of the old order.[1]

By the end of the 1890s, the outlines of a "new liberalism" had emerged, one that "broke from the nineteenth-century assumption of a beneficent proprietary individualism regulated by a self-adjusting competitive market," as Richard Schneirov has put it. Because the railroad industry figured centrally in the coming and playing out of the 1890s crisis, it was appropriate that one of the earliest expressions of the new liberalism in the realm of labor relations was in the Erdman Act of 1898, which provided for the voluntary mediation and arbitration of industrial disputes. Similar developments were under way in Europe and Australasia at century's end, where methods ranging from statist to private and associative emerged to manage labor conflict. The United States tended strongly to the latter, influenced in no small part by the actions of the federal judiciary. Even so, in its embodiment of a more collectivist alternative to the individualism of laissez-faire liberalism, the Erdman Act signaled two significant developments: the crumbling of nineteenth-century Victorian understandings of society, market, and state; and a beginning point of the "modern," twentieth-century liberal order defined by positive government and organizational regulation.[2]

Coming hard on brotherhood defeats in the late 1880s, the Pullman boycott challenged Gilded Age visions of social harmony and pushed a number of brotherhood leaders to reevaluate their approach to peaceful labor-capital relations. The Burlington strike of 1888–89 had made it clear that the brotherhoods' handling of labor relations could not succeed without favorable labor market conditions, sympathetic management, or some other mitigating factor. In the context of the crisis of 1894, no longer did it seem enough for labor and capital to mutually recognize and acknowledge their distinct but interconnected interests, and no longer did it seem plausible that railroad employees and employers could come together "as men" and sort out their differences. Rooted in the labor movement upsurge and conflicts of the mid-to-late 1880s, these realizations produced a new kind of unionism in the early 1890s. It was during these years, for instance, that the American Federation of Labor won control over the nation's trade union movement and that the AFL unions themselves began to demonstrate the innovations associated with the "new unionism," a phenomenon that had its counterpart in European labor movements during the same years.[3] Most visibly and dramatically, however, the American Railway Union captured the imagination and loyalty of hundreds of thousands of railroad workers throughout the nation and across the industry's hierarchy of jobs and skill. By comparison, the railroad brotherhoods' efforts at greater unity and concert of action through some form of federated association and their use of the boycott appeared to be mere halfway measures at best. At worst, they came across as a cynical and narrow-minded attempt on the part of union chiefs to further centralize and control running-trades unionism.[4]

This view, however, fails to appreciate the ways in which the brotherhoods' activity in the early 1890s fed into both the reordering of railroad labor relations sparked by the Pullman boycott and the wider Progressive Era reexamination of the relationships among society, market, and the state. Although the outcome was less than what federation's most ardent advocates envisioned (and boycotting was quashed by the federal courts), the result was a durable and adaptable institutional framework and organizational culture that promised to meet the railroad corporations on the scale that they demanded. It also saw the brotherhoods enter into formal political action through the pursuit of safety legislation and offer firm support for a permanent role for the state in railroad labor relations through government-sponsored arbitration. Moreover, with their already-established reputations for avoiding strikes, building contractual employment relationships, and disciplining the running-trades labor force, the brotherhoods' efforts garnered the attention of key figures in government, business, and an expanding network of middle-class reformers, all of whom shared aspects of the "new" liberal approach to class conflict. The brotherhoods' record persuaded these early progressives that they could be relied on as partners in stable railroad labor relations. Even so, these developments did not occur before the Pullman strike and boycott and judicial repression of unionism in the first half of the 1890s graphically demonstrated that unreasonable employers bore a portion of the blame for the era's class warfare; these developments also cast into high relief the brotherhoods' competency as labor organizations.[5]

The Pullman boycott and, before that, the brotherhoods' brushes with judicial authority led to the questioning of what passed for nineteenth-century American public labor relations policy—that is, the courts and judicial law. And the brotherhoods contributed both directly and indirectly to calls for alternative means for abating labor conflict. That alternative—government-facilitated collective bargaining with the mediation and arbitration of differences—took form over the course of a series of meetings, hearings, and conferences in the second half of 1894, and ultimately emerged in the Erdman Act of 1898. Altogether those proposals and the language in which they were presented amounted to a more arbitral and bureaucratic method of ordering railroad industrial relations, as well as an important statement of the emerging new liberalism.

The Beginnings of "New Unionism"

The railroad brotherhoods' experimentation contributed to the consolidation of what historians have called the "new unionism" during the late 1880s and early 1890s. Part of a wider stocktaking and redirection within the labor movement following the 1880s upheavals, the brotherhoods' efforts dovetailed with the more general trend of organized craft workers to distance themselves from the producerism of the Knights of Labor (KoL). With the decline of the KoL after 1886, craft workers reorganized under the banner of the American Federation of Labor and adopted a series of organizational and strategic innovations, which included attempts at organizing across craft-based lines, instituting higher dues, professionalizing union administration, controlling labor markets, and regulating product markets. Ideologically, these unions combined the proposition that they could be self-sustaining "business" entities with varying promises of industrial democracy. The full implications of this approach to unionism would play out over the first two decades of the twentieth century, but its basic contours were visible by 1893 in the nation's major metropolitan and industrial centers.[6]

The brotherhoods did not affiliate with the AFL, but they did prefigure important aspects of the new unionism during the 1880s. For years, of course, the brotherhoods had levied high dues and pioneered mutual benefits along with their efforts to control the railroad labor market. And as early as the mid-1880s, as the railroad labor market eroded, a number of the brotherhoods showed evidence of rethinking and broadening their approach to labor-capital relations. The Brotherhood of Locomotive Firemen dropped its no-strike pledge at their 1885 convention and made overtures to the Engineers. But the more dramatic shift occurred in the Order of Railway Conductors, infamous in labor circles for its identification with management and willingness to supply strikebreakers. By the middle of the 1880s, disaffected conductors, primarily in the West, were pushing the organization to adopt protective measures. The formation of a California-based rival union in 1888, along with the heated conditions of the late 1880s, precipitated a revolt within the order, resulting in the repeal of its antistrike clause and the election of Edgar E. Clark as grand chief conductor in 1890. Clark advocated judicious use of the strike, regulation of the labor market through trade agreements, and alliance building with the other railroad brotherhoods. Commenting on the union's new direction at the 1891 convention, he declared, "The Order is looked upon with more real and genuine respect by the railway managers of the country. The members of the Order feel more like free men."[7]

The experimentation that characterized the railroad brotherhoods from 1889 to 1893 principally took form in efforts to create some sort of federation among the brotherhoods. These movements grew out of the disaffection among western firemen, engineers, and switchmen generated by the Burlington strike's failure. Seeking ways to win the strike and boycott, opposition movements challenged national leadership to accept the federation of railroad employees across craft lines. In September 1890, engineers and conductors on several of the railroad systems operating out of Chicago met at Briggs House Hotel and adopted a plan to form a General Committee and institute a pledge to "stand by and support each other as other as far as the laws of our respective organizations will permit." Over the summer and fall of 1888, the Brotherhood of Locomotive Firemen and the Switchmen's Mutual Aid Association (SMAA), which had originated in Chicago's sprawling yards in 1877, adopted articles of confederation; in February 1889, officials of the Firemen, including Frank

Sargent and Eugene V. Debs, along with officers of the Brakemen, met with representatives from the Knights of Labor and the American Federation of Labor in Philadelphia for the purpose of creating stronger links with the labor movement beyond the railroad industry. Little came of the conference other than a circular calling for greater unity among organized labor. In the matter of federation, the plan adopted by the Firemen, Brakemen, and Switchmen differed markedly from the version pushed by western "radicals."[8]

As it took form in the Supreme Council of the United Orders of Railway Employees—the result of high-level meetings among the Firemen, Brakemen, and Switchmen in mid-1889—"federation" meant the coordination of brotherhood actions from the top-down (a formal affiliation of national unions), rather than from the bottom-up (as envisaged by western railroaders). Advocates of federating railroad employees at the level of the individual railroad or railroad system criticized the Supreme Council. T. P. O'Rourke, of Pocatello, Idaho, accurately characterized the Supreme Council as "an alliance of the grand officers of the orders connected with it." Such representation, in his view, "takes away from the Supreme Council all semblance of a Republican, or representative, system of government, and makes it entirely autocratic."[9] For brotherhood leaders, this was precisely the point; the attraction of the Supreme Council lay in its potential for centralizing authority, preventing strikes, and protecting their organizations, not to mention gaining control of the federation movement. In its first year, the Council moved to head off local-level or system-level federation movements on western railroads and intervened in and successfully resolved a series of strikes.[10]

These achievements seemed to promise that Council-style federation would be an effective instrument in bringing inter-brotherhood power to bear against centralized railroad corporations. By the late 1880s, railroads were merging into larger systems, and railroad managers were organizing themselves into associations such the American Railway Association (1885) and the General Managers' Association (GMA) (1886) for the handling of common issues in their product and labor markets. In August 1890, engineer W. W. Hall of Denver, Colorado, warned against failure to federate: "The claim that 'the B. of L. E., owing to its age, standing, and past achievements, is a sufficient guarantee of its ability to sustain its past greatness, independently of any and all odds,' is not a sage or well taken point, for it is evident that we are living in an age enthused with a spirit of centralization. Trusts and combinations in financial circles are becoming the order of the day the world over. Hence, organization and combination in labor circles must follow or they will be overridden and overpowered."[11]

Hall rejected the traditional brotherhood approach to labor-capital relations, a position shared by many western members of the Brotherhood of Locomotive Engineers, as well as by a majority of firemen, brakemen, and switchmen, in the aftermath of the Burlington strike. These circumstances encouraged those who wished to push federation to articulate a producerist vision of labor solidarity. Frank Walton, a fireman from Pocatello, Idaho, held up the Knights of Labor as an example of federation, citing their motto, "'An injury to one is the concern of all.'" Eugene V. Debs carried through this logic to conclusion: "We are in favor of the organization of all railroad employes and when organized, we are in favor of the federation of such organizations for mutual protection." With thoroughgoing organization and federation, argued Debs, railroad workers would "secure justice" and "railroad strikes would disappear from the land as if by a decree of Jehovah."[12] Expressions such as these revealed that even in its attenuated form in the Supreme Council, federation advocates saw potential for broader organization and action.

Engineer advocates of federation, however, even as embodied in the Supreme Council, stood in the minority. Opponents of federation remained faithful to the narrower, brotherhood, trade-unionist perspective, drawing on republican rhetoric to argue against "entangling alliances" with other segments of railroad labor. "We have been favored by the great majority of railroad managers for our conservatism," wrote an opponent under the signature of J. L. S. "Are we going to cast it aside?" Federation, he worried, "would excite suspicion and distrust" among management, jeopardizing the "harmony and friendship" prevailing on "numerous lines." The result could be disastrous, as John R. DeLancie of Chicago warned in August 1890: "Federation as now constituted is a combine that will be met sooner or later by a combine that will wipe it out like a roaring tornado, strewing devastation on all sides." Informing these arguments was the view that engineers' identity and interests were distinct from those of other railroad workers. J. L. S. put it simply: "If twenty-seven thousand engineers are to be but the peers of four or five thousand members of another Order, in a federated body, I, for one, do not fancy the change."[13] Sentiments like these brought condemnation from the Firemen. "Let one organization assume aristocratic superiority over another," wrote a correspondent to the *Locomotive Firemen's Magazine* in May 1889, "and an odious aristocracy of labor will be established, and workingmen will forever remain the slaves of the corporations."[14] Nevertheless, the BLE declined to join the Supreme Council. When a jurisdictional conflict born of craft-based tensions between the Trainmen and the Switchmen tore the

Supreme Council apart in 1891, the *Locomotive Engineers Monthly Journal* expressed relief at the brotherhood's abstention.[15]

A little over a year after the Supreme Council's demise, in December 1892, Frank Sargent and other brotherhood chiefs moved to construct a more flexible and durable form of federation. The "Cedar Rapids Plan" of "system federation" provided for more decentralized authority; further, it included procedures for handling grievances by making each individual railroad, or system of railroads, a complete and distinct unit of federation with its own federated grievance committee. The Cedar Rapids Plan effectively centralized the process for calling strikes, however, by requiring the consent of the federated brotherhoods' executive committees. It was "a conservative idea," wrote U.S. Labor Department analyst Samuel McCune Lindsay, intended to coordinate grievances and prevent "disastrous or ill-advised strikes." This was satisfactory enough for the Engineers, which adopted the plan at its 1894 convention.[16] In 1897, the Firemen, Trainmen, and Telegraphers attempted to push federation further into a formal, national organization, the Federation of American Railway Employees, which would have authority over the calling of strikes. This was too much for Peter M. Arthur, who was "not willing to delegate the power and authority to a conductor, a telegraph operator, a fireman, or a brakeman to say whether the engineers shall quit work or not." Without the full support of the BLE, the federation movement of the 1890s never realized its potential.[17]

The ignominious end of the Supreme Council—cast into relief by the formation and rapid rise of the American Railway Union a little over a year later in 1893—and the uneven results of the Cedar Rapids Plan appear to confirm the image of the brotherhoods, or at least their leadership, as rigid, narrow, and dysfunctional. In most interpretations, this portrayal serves to highlight the progressive nature of the American Railway Union (ARU).[18] Despite its shortcomings, the federation movement revealed serious efforts on the part of brotherhood leaders to build stable organizational structures capable of overcoming, or at least mitigating, jurisdictional animosities. It also aimed at meeting the larger and more centralized railroad corporations while moving closer to some kind of accord on the issues of grievances and industrial action on the part of running-trades workers. To be sure, the brotherhoods' federation efforts did not match the organizational unity of the amalgamation trend underway during the same years in industries like steel and construction. They nevertheless reflected a search for new organizational forms—pushed most vigorously by elements of the rank and file—and demonstrated a flexibility and capacity for change characteristic of the new unionism of the 1890s. Indeed, the federation movement fed into the Firemen's debate over affiliation with the AFL in 1896–97, and the system of federations and joint grievance committees persisted, providing the basis for the brotherhoods' "craft industrialism" of the early twentieth century.[19]

As the Gilded Age context that had both accommodated more personal, face-to-face railroad labor relations and informed respectable dissent disintegrated in the late 1880s, the brotherhoods sought other ways to improve the condition of railroaders. In addition to the federation movement, the brotherhoods began to pursue legislation at both the state and federal levels in the early 1890s.

Political Action and Railroad Safety

Federal regulation of railroad commerce and Gilded Age industrial warfare marked by judicial intervention led brotherhood leaders to an early understanding of industry's embeddedness in the political process. In light of the charters and lands granted to railroad corporations by state and federal governments, the influence of robber baron railroad leaders in the legislatures, the passage of state "Granger laws" to control railroad activities, the passage of the Interstate Commerce Act in 1887, the activities of state railroad commissions in the name of safety, and the use of injunctions by the courts to curb union strike and boycott activity, brotherhood men saw that government was deeply involved in almost every aspect of their industry, and that federal policies and actions vitally affected their unions. It was a short step for many to conclude that the brotherhoods' economic vision and strategy ought to be complemented by a political approach.[20] In the view of the Engineers' Charles H. Salmons, politics demanded railwaymen's collective attention: "Legislation in the interests of workingmen should interest us. The laws as we find them are pretty much on the side of the wealthy and against the best interests of the workers."[21]

The brotherhoods turned their attention to influencing state and national governments in matters of policy that affected railwaymen. Following the strategy of Samuel Gompers in the Cigar Makers' International Union during the 1880s (which he would expand with the AFL in the latter half of the 1890s), the brotherhoods adopted an approach that emphasized trade union and lobbying tactics as the central means for achieving political goals. As an institutional-political strategy, lobbying suited the brotherhoods. It allowed them to engage in political action yet remain independent of political parties, and to maintain the union as the primary vehicle through which workers could achieve goals unattainable through collective bargaining.[22]

Beginning in the late 1880s, the brotherhoods passed convention resolutions and established union bylaws encouraging brotherhood lodges to organize legislative boards for the purpose of formulating and supporting bills in state legislatures.[23] In the early 1890s, boards in several states organized legislative initiatives. These initiatives exploited a range of nonpartisan tactics such as petitions, lobbying, appearances before state legislative committees, and letters to political representatives. The boards called for laws against Pinkertons, blacklisting, and compulsory deductions from pay for company hospital plans. They voiced their support for bills modifying fellow-servant doctrine in employer liability cases and setting a minimum length of service before a company could hire or promote men to engineer or conductor. In the course of these legislative efforts, brotherhood men entered the political arena in an organized manner and learned a great deal about the political-legislative process. Brotherhood members discussed and debated legislative issues and formed institutional positions on them. They acted as lobbyists in state capitols, spoke with politicians from a range of political parties, and forged invaluable alliances with the men who wielded power in the political arena.[24] But the legislative issue that galvanized railroaders, pushed them to the federal level, and provided a bridge to middle-class reformers centered on workplace safety.

The movement for national legislation requiring railroads to adopt safety technology, like air brakes and the Janney automatic coupler, had its origins in the grim reality of workplace accidents and the concern that they elicited among the railroad brotherhoods and a network of Gilded Age reformers.[25] The problem lay not with passenger service, for the railroads had installed air brakes and automatic couplers soon after these technologies had demonstrated their viability in the late 1860s and early 1870s. In freight operations, however, where the frequent interchange of cars limited the ability of a firm to capture the full benefit of its investment, the diffusion of these technologies was much slower. By 1890, almost all passenger locomotives and cars had air brakes, but no more than half of freight locomotives and less than one-tenth of freight cars were so equipped, and only 3 percent of locomotives and 10 percent of freight cars were outfitted with automatic couplers.[26] Contemporaries attributed the railroads' reluctance to adopt safety appliances to the difficulties of diffusion as well as the modest cost to the corporation of brakemen deaths. The figures on workplace accidents compiled by state railroad commissions were enough to spark public debate on railroad safety.[27]

The concern of state railroad commissions led to state-level laws in the mid-1880s, but the limited effect of such laws on interstate commerce prompted reformers and the railroad brotherhoods to lobby for safety legislation on the national level.[28]

The mounting numbers of injured railwaymen and the movement of railroad corporations toward more "rationalized" procedures for dealing with injured employees prompted the brotherhoods' entry into political action on the safety issue. Through the 1870s, when railroads were more likely to be smaller affairs in which face-to-face relations prevailed, railway officials decided on assistance to the injured on an ad hoc basis, reflecting the possibility that railroad companies could be thought of as large families in which managers and workers shared in the burdens and rewards of the business.[29] By the late 1880s, however, railroads had become increasingly reluctant to hire or keep on even slightly impaired workers, claiming that such men were less efficient and had demonstrated their lack of competence by injuring themselves. At the same time, in an effort to reduce expenditures and evade liability, railroads began to institute relief departments, which often entailed mandatory employee participation and reflected a tendency to think of injured workers not as individuals but as "predictable costs of business." These departments did not operate on the basis of personal knowledge of employees' circumstances, and demonstrated a track record in which injured workers were less likely to receive compensation than in the earlier days of corporate relief. Yet railroads continued to hold employees personally responsible for their mishaps, even as they manipulated corporate welfare programs to foster employee loyalty and undermine railroad unionism.[30]

Brotherhood leaders recognized the contradictory nature of corporate policy and began working on preventing accidents. The effort led the brotherhoods into political action for legislation on state and national levels that would require the railroads to adopt air brakes and automatic couplers. Because it involved challenging employers in matters of technology and capital expenditure, and because it involved the very difficult matter of deploying technologies in a vast industrial enterprise on a national scale, the brotherhoods recognized that the issue lent itself more to a legislative than a collective bargaining approach. As the Brakemen's Edward F. O'Shea stated to the Interstate Commerce Commission (ICC) in 1889, "The only thing now necessary [for the adoption of safety appliances] is for the different companies to act together, which they will not do unless compelled by law." As early as the late 1860s and early 1870s, following their initial deployment on passenger trains, the Brotherhood of Locomotive Engineers supported the idea of air brakes and automatic couplers, and followed their development for freight service in the pages of its monthly journal. By the mid-1880s, the Brotherhood of Railroad Brakemen, the union whose members were most directly concerned, was calling on the public as well as state and federal legislatures to support legislation that would bring safer brakes and couplers to freight service.[31]

Lorenzo S. Coffin, farmer and former Iowa state railroad commissioner—who, as a passenger, witnessed firsthand an accident involving a link-and-pin coupling—emerged as leader of the coalition that achieved federal legislation. A humanitarian and Gilded Age reformer, Coffin lobbied the Iowa legislature to pass the Iowa Safety Appliance Act in 1890, and he crafted the bill that became a federal law in 1893 requiring the railroads to adopt safety appliances. In the course of his tireless lobbying, he galvanized the railroad brotherhoods into active support for safety legislation.[32] Writing hundreds of letters to the brotherhoods' journals, Coffin urged members to contact congressmen and senators in support of federal safety legislation and worked to eliminate divisions among the brotherhoods that might undermine the effort. In 1889 and in 1892, respectively, the Brotherhood of Railroad Brakemen and the Order of Railway Conductors appointed him their Washington lobbyist and representative in meetings with the U.S. Railroad Commissioners. Coffin's work yielded results. In 1889, the Brakemen organized a petition of approximately ten thousand brakemen for safety legislation and presented it to the Interstate Commerce Commission and Congress. The Engineers and the Firemen contributed to the lobbying effort through the pages of their monthly journals and by testifying at ICC and congressional hearings in support of safer couplers and brakes.[33] After years of pressure from citizens groups and the railroad brotherhoods, Congress passed the Safety Appliances Act in 1893, which required the installation of air brakes and automatic couplers on railroad equipment.[34]

A number of actors, ranging from Lorenzo Coffin to figures in the ICC and Congress to president Benjamin Harrison, played roles in the passage of the Safety Appliances Act, but the brotherhoods' role was also important. By lending their support, the railroad brotherhoods played an active part in creating legislation that initiated the use of the national state for workingmen's protection. The Switchmen's Mutual Aid Association, claiming that the bill passed only because of union support, labeled the Safety Appliance Act labor's first legislative triumph.[35] Indeed, the railroad safety movement signaled the beginning of the railroad brotherhoods' sustained activity in national-level politics. The campaign also marked the beginning of the brotherhoods' practice of maintaining permanent, salaried lobbyists in Washington. The Brotherhood of Locomotive Engineers' James F. Walsh represented the union before the ICC and went on to lobby Congress not just for the BLE but also, by 1894, jointly for the four train-service brotherhoods.[36] With the safety movement, the brotherhoods began to achieve in the realm of political action a unity of purpose and results that seemed to elude them in the industrial arena.

The railroad safety movement also marked the beginning of a transformation in the relationships among railroad corporations, workers, and the state. Through the 1880s, the railroad brotherhoods had presented themselves and their members as equal to managers and engaged with them in the common project of producing professional railroaders and maintaining stable labor relations. Brotherhood leaders had disavowed the strike as destructive and contrary to the interests of both labor and capital. With the common-law doctrines of fellow servant and implied contract, together with the hostility of the courts to organized labor, railwaymen had learned to be wary of state power. By the early 1890s, however, it had become clear that labor and management were anything but equal partners sharing common concern for running-trades workers' welfare. With the encouragement of reformers, railwaymen began to seek out the state and its regulatory power on the issue of safety. State actors, accordingly, began to expand their authority to control aspects of private enterprise with regard to workingmen's welfare, a harbinger of things to come after the turn of the century.[37] By the middle of the 1890s, the brotherhoods' lobbying efforts, their search for broader forms of organization and action, and their already-established reputation for winning contractual relationships with employers had begun to attract the attention of figures in government, business, and the middle class. The campaign for federal safety-appliance legislation went a long way toward making these connections and raising the brotherhoods' public profile as organizations dedicated not to industrial radicalism but to materially improving members' condition. The brotherhoods' record demonstrated that they could be relied on as partners in stable railroad labor relations, but not before the Pullman boycott and a series of bruising encounters with the federal courts cast into relief the brotherhoods' competency as labor organizations.

Boycotts and Encounters with the Courts

The brotherhoods' willingness to engage in broader forms of collective action perhaps made it inevitable that they would come into conflict with the federal judiciary. Since the beginning of the industry, the railroads' centrality to the nation's economic life and their embeddedness in the political process made it a certainty that any labor conflict that significantly disrupted commerce invited government intervention. Before the 1870s, constitutional restraints and the prevailing ideology of free labor kept the federal government relatively uninvolved in labor-capital relations. As the government became a permanent, if uneven, presence in railroad labor relations, the nature of the American state—one that from its inception had rejected centralized executive authority and administrative capacity—shaped the nature of that intervention. Thus the courts became the principal institution for regulating working-class organization under the common law doctrine of criminal conspiracy, and the federal judiciary assumed a dominant role in railroad labor relations through the end of the nineteenth century. In a position to make the common law the principal source of state policy, prone to seeing strikes as disorderly and as threats to the social order, and convinced that the public interest rested on the protection of the right to free contract within an unrestrained competitive market, federal judges made decisions that consistently favored employers and disadvantaged organized labor. During the late 1880s and early 1890s, judicial hostility to labor gathered force in a new and concerted manner against trade unionism.[38]

Over the late nineteenth century, the railroads were the first to experience the vehicle through which judges would intervene in labor disputes well into the twentieth century: the antistrike decree, or labor injunction. Beginning with the issuance of court orders against strikers in the Great Strike of 1877, federal judges expanded the scope of contempt proceedings in cases against the Knights of Labor in their strike against Jay Gould's Wabash Railroad in 1886. Also in 1886, the Supreme Court ruled that the railroad industry fell within federal responsibility under the Constitution's commerce clause, and the Interstate Commerce Commission Act of 1887 set the stage for the extension of federal jurisdiction over labor relations on interstate railroads. The 1888 Burlington strike furnished the occasion. The brotherhoods had remained more or less untouched by these developments until early in the strike, when the Engineers instituted a boycott of CB&Q cars on adjoining railroads. Federal judges issued injunctions, enjoining neighboring railroads from refusing to handle the Burlington's cars and forbidding the BLE to conduct secondary boycotts. The rulings behind the Burlington injunctions aimed to separate unions from boycotts and dissuade them from striking.[39]

The Engineers, however, were not deterred. Drawing the opposite conclusion from the strike's failure, the union's 1889 convention passed a rule making it a violation for a member to handle the property of a railroad on which a BLE strike was in effect. Because the rolling stock of a given railroad could be scattered around the country, the new rule (no. 12) effectively made secondary boycotts an automatic corollary of a decision to strike. As with use of the strike, rule no. 12 aimed less at expanding Brotherhood boycotts than in adding another weapon to the arsenal of the grand chief engineer in negotiations with railroad management. Nevertheless, in 1893 the rule brought the Engineers into conflict with the courts. In a case involving the Central of Georgia Railroad, in which the union applied for and won a writ of mandamus compelling the railroad to sign a contract with the brotherhood, a federal judge issued an obiter dictum declaring that railroad strikes and boycotts violated the ICC Act and the Sherman Antitrust Act of 1890 because of rule no. 12. In effect, the Engineers' efforts to broaden the scope of industrial action brought broader court action against it.[40]

The Engineers figured in several other federal cases that extended the scope of antilabor rulings. An 1893 strike and boycott against the Toledo, Ann Arbor & Northern Michigan Railroad resulted in an injunction and civil suit against Grand Chief Arthur. In issuing the injunction, justice William Howard Taft declared that workers did have a right to quit work if not in violation of contract, but that such a right did not extend to boycotts or sympathetic strikes, as under rule no. 12. He warned Arthur that "the existence and enforcement of rule 12 . . . make the whole brotherhood a criminal conspiracy against the laws of their country." In early 1894, as the depression brought on by the panic of November 1893 sent increasing numbers of railroads into receivership, a federal court in Wisconsin extended the logic of Taft's ruling when the receivers of the Northern Pacific Railroad went to court for an injunction against *potential* collective action in opposition to planned wage cuts. In issuing injunctions against the Engineers and other unions on the railroad, judge James C. Jenkins declared that strikes were conspiracies to extort the public; therefore, employees did not have "the right arbitrarily to quit service without regard to the necessities of that service." Building on the Sherman Antitrust Act, the theory and logic at work in court decisions in the early 1890s made railway strikes subject to injunctions on the basis that they illegally restrained trade.[41]

These antiunion rulings had an impact on the brotherhoods. Initially, they attempted to turn on its head the logic behind injunctions, reasoning that if the courts interfered in the relations between railroad employers and employees on behalf of the former, they must also do so for the latter. Such reasoning echoed the producerist view that governmental regulation of collective action ought to apply equally to capital as well as labor.[42] In April 1894, the Engineers' journal asked, "Why are not employers of workingmen who combine to improve the condition of the trade in which they are engaged by cutting wages and discharging men conspirators also? What we need and what the people demand are laws which operate against all classes alike." When the court-appointed receiver of the Cincinnati, Southern and East Tennessee, Virginia & Georgia Railroad announced wage cuts that spring, the brotherhoods jointly petitioned for an injunction to restrain him, arguing that the public welfare depended on adequate remuneration of railroad workers. In the District Court for the Southern District of Ohio, however, Justice Taft avoided the unions' argument, focusing instead on whether the receiver's action was justified. Finding the wage reduction "necessary," particularly in light of the deepening depression, Taft cut off this legal approach.[43] On the eve of the Pullman strike, then, the railroad brotherhoods found themselves increasingly hemmed in by the courts' legal web spun around the secondary boycott, the sympathy strike, and even the primary strike itself. Brotherhood journals denounced judicial discrimination against organized labor, joining with the broader late nineteenth century trade unionist outcry against the courts' use of the injunction and conspiracy doctrine.[44]

The brotherhoods and other trade unionists were not alone in their questioning of the legal doctrine underlying federal judges' use of the injunction in labor disputes. Since the 1880s, congressmen like George Tillman (D-S.C.), who chaired one of the numerous committees investigating the causes of the major strikes defining the years 1886–94, had begun to criticize judges for their pro-capitalist handling of criminal proceedings against strikers. They exposed the contradictions in the judicial theories informing the use of injunctions, which construed most forms of worker collective action against employers as violations of property rights. At the same time, they documented the conditions causing strikes, called for circumscribing private property rights and restraints on corporate power, upheld strikers' rights to bargain, and endorsed arbitration as a means of reconciling class action with the public interest. In so doing, these committees explored the possibilities of nonjudicial, more bureaucratic methods of administering the railroad industry, which would allow for "responsible collectivism in industrial relations," as Mary O. Furner has put it. The most comprehensive statement of these views came in the form of the legislative proposal that became the Arbitration Act of 1888, which might have provided the means for ordering railroad labor relations were it not for the dropping of compulsory arbitration in the face of employer and union opposition. In the resulting vacuum, the courts expanded the scope of the injunction and so helped set the stage for the nation's most dramatic labor conflict.[45]

The Pullman Boycott, the New Liberalism, and the Erdman Act of 1898

The Pullman strike and boycott had its origins in the long-term deflationary cycle that had plagued the U.S. economy since the 1870s and shaped conflicts over the supply of labor in the railroad operating crafts in the 1880s. Intensified by depression-induced wage cuts and layoffs in 1893, the strike at the Pullman works on Chicago's South Side grew out of long-running battles over hours, wages, and managerial attacks on skilled workers' control of the labor process. The strike became a nationwide conflict in June 1894 when the American Railway Union, under the leadership of Eugene V. Debs, declared a boycott on all railroads using Pullman sleeping cars.[46]

Escalating confrontation between labor and capital nationwide set the context for the Pullman boycott. With its roots in both the inclusive model of labor organization pioneered by the Knights of Labor, and the uneven results of the brotherhoods' federation movement, the American Railway Union embodied a style of unionism that embraced all grades of railroad workers and openly opposed the free market economy. Shop-craft workers composed the bulk of the union's membership, but large numbers of running-trades workers, particularly those in the West who had advocated the system model of federation, also joined. At the same time, during the early 1890s bituminous coal miners, textile workers, and waterfront workers also pursued broader forms of labor organization and undertook strikes that radiated outward from the city level to encompass entire geographical regions. In this context, the Pullman boycott drew the combined forces of capital—a coalition of twenty-four railroad corporations organized in the General Managers' Association—and government down on the heads of ARU leaders, strikers, and sympathizers. A federal court issued an injunction on July 2 declaring the boycott in violation of the Sherman Act, and one day later U.S. attorney general Richard Olney persuaded president Grover Cleveland to dispatch federal troops to Chicago, effectively crushing the strike.[47] These events led to the intensive questioning of the jurisprudential doctrines underpinning the federal antilabor injunction, as well as calls for more bureaucratic, arbitral alternatives for railroad labor relations.

The first meaningful statement of these views came in the report of the federal commission investigating the conflict, which Schneirov calls "a ringing manifesto of the new liberalism."[48] Appointed by President Cleveland in July 1894 both to investigate the causes of the Pullman strike and boycott and to propose means of avoiding such clashes, the U.S. Strike Commission heard testimony in August and September and issued its report in November 1894. Bearing the mark of its chair, commissioner of labor Carroll D. Wright, the report blamed the federal injunction and deployment of troops for the violence, condemned George Pullman's refusal to arbitrate, and declared that the GMA's collusive behavior in fixing prices and wages had violated the theory that the competitive market protected the public. It also made the point that such combination on the part of capital justly invited like combination on the part of labor. Nevertheless, it criticized the ARU for its inclusiveness of organization and its lack of safeguards, like "conservative leadership" and a public position against strikes except as a last resort. Significantly, it spoke approvingly of the trade union model of organization (read, railroad brotherhoods) and its "record of success both here and abroad," particularly its promotion of "conciliation, arbitration, conservatism, and responsibility in labor contentions and agreements." The report urged employers to recognize trade unions and called for collective bargaining under the auspices of a permanent federal commission empowered to both compel mediation and arbitration and issue binding awards. Wright premised the commission's recommendations on recognition of the fact that equitable contracts were impossible between powerful corporations and individual workers, and that in such circumstances the parties to arbitration must be collective bodies. The recommendations also reflected an understanding, then coalescing among intellectuals and liberal reformers, of society as composed of groups rather than individuals, and a view of trade unions as the legitimate and competent institutional embodiment of workers' interests.[49]

Wright's proposals were influenced by his firsthand observance of trade union competency as demonstrated by the railroad brotherhoods and the American Federation of Labor during the course of the Pullman boycott. During the boycott, the brotherhoods had encouraged members to take the places of sympathy strikers, an action that prevented the strike from spreading east. Rumor even had it that Stephen E. Wilkinson, Brotherhood of Railroad Trainmen (BRT) grand master, had shaved off his beard as a disguise to take up arms against the strikers. Moreover, in its immediate aftermath the brotherhoods' journals publicly criticized the ARU.[50] But it was at a high-level meeting of unionists, called by AFL president Samuel Gompers in Chicago as the strike was underway, that representatives of the brotherhoods first had the opportunity to respond to the boycott and set out their position.

Held at Briggs House Hotel on July 12 and 13, the meeting included presidents of the major AFL-affiliated unions, the AFL's executive committee, as well as Frank W. Arnold, grand secretary and treasurer of the Firemen, and Patrick H. Morrissey, first vice grand master of the Trainmen. The official purpose of the meeting was to consider what sort of support the trade unions would lend to the boycott. More broadly, the assembled representatives had to decide what would be their relationship to the ARU. After hearing from Eugene V. Debs, who had left the Firemen to become founder and president of the ARU, the conference issued a carefully worded statement expressing sympathy with the union's "vigorous protest against the gathering, growing forces of plutocratic power and corporation rule," but nevertheless declined to call a general strike in support of the boycott.[51]

The real significance of the Briggs House statement, however, lay in its defense of trade unionism as embodied in the AFL and the railroad brotherhoods. The document took pains to make clear that trade unionists were as "patriotic and law abiding as any other class of citizens," as demonstrated by their actions "in times of public need and public peril." "The trade union movement is one of reason, one of deliberation," the document stated. "It is democratic in principle and action, conservative in its demands and consistent in its efforts to secure them." It stood "as the protector of those who see the wrongs and injustice resultant of our present industrial system." The "railroad interests" represented the real threat to the public; in their disregard of the "laws to control them," "these corporations have given the greatest impetus to Anarchy and lawlessness." Thus, the statement closed with a call for trade unionists "to redeem this country from its present political and industrial misrule, to take it from the hands of plutocratic wreckers and place it in the hands of the common people." In distancing trade unionism from the ARU while aligning it with the public interest, the Briggs House statement earned the approval of the Strike Commission, which termed it "strong and temperate," an acknowledgement of labor's "responsibilities, the futility of strikes, and the appropriate remedies in this country for labor wrongs."[52]

In their testimony before the Strike Commission, brotherhood leaders confirmed their competency as well as their support for arbitration of labor disputes. Patrick Morrissey emphasized the "trades union principles" of the Brotherhood of Railroad Trainmen and his belief in "the separate and distinct organization of railroad men according to their separate grades or occupations," albeit federated "for common advancement and protection." Such "businesslike organization" had made his union successful and contributed to its reliability during the Pullman boycott. Morrissey stated that not only had the Trainmen not sanctioned the boycott, but it had instructed its members to "perform their regular duties and no others." As a remedy for strikes, Morrissey advocated arbitration under government ownership of the railroads, arguing that the public nature of the railroads under private ownership both opened up unions to judicial repression but also established the legitimacy of a measure that might otherwise be regarded as "socialistic." He thus anticipated Wright's conclusion that the railroads' importance to the public interest and special relationship to the state justified some form of government oversight, but that the legislature rather than the judiciary was the best venue. Still, Morrissey insisted on strong, businesslike labor organization as a necessary precondition for the success of arbitration, which should remain voluntary.[53] Appearing for the Conductors, Edgar Clark echoed many of Morrissey's points, especially in praising the brotherhoods' "trades union methods" and the arbitral means of adjusting differences.[54]

For Morrissey, Clark, and other brotherhood leaders, arbitration was an attractive idea in that it promised to validate the principle of collective bargaining and thus bestow on their unions a kind of legitimacy, indeed legal standing, that had previously eluded them. Middle-class reformers and some labor leaders had championed arbitration as a panacea for industrial disputes since the 1860s, reflecting a desire to restore social harmony. By the 1890s, with the growing realization and acceptance of class-based divisions in society, arbitration came to mean a voluntary procedure of adjusting differences between two organized and contending groups. Like most trade unionists, brotherhood leaders had believed in direct negotiation with employers as the best means of settling disputes; in light of the Burlington defeat and their rough handling by the courts, however, they came to see arbitration in a favorable light.[55] As the Engineers' journal editorialized in July 1894, if the courts decided that the peculiar public interest in the railroads required the service of employees, then the public ought to provide a means of settling disputes. Still, the means had to remain voluntary, for brotherhood men regarded arbitration as an extension of collective bargaining; compulsory arbitration would render that principle meaningless.[56] In the boycott's immediate aftermath, though, a number of proposals were introduced in Congress, including some calling for compulsory arbitration, and it was not at all clear what sort of means for settling disputes the state would adopt.[57]

To be sure, most corporation executives also opposed compulsory arbitration, and so when brotherhood representatives had the opportunity to state their views at the Chicago Civic Federation's (CCF) Congress on Industrial Conciliation and Arbitration in mid-November 1894, they contributed to a growing sentiment in favor of voluntary methods. The meeting was designed to give equal balance to the views of organized labor and corporate capital. Early in the Pullman strike, CCF members had attempted unsuccessfully to mediate the dispute between George Pullman and his employees. Frustrated and disturbed by widening class division and conflict, they called for a formal congress to debate and draft an arbitration bill. Convening during the same week that the Strike Commission released its report, the congress drew a carefully chosen array of labor leaders, industrialists, public figures, and reformers. As with the CCF, and its successor, the National Civic Federation (NCF), the congress embodied a new kind of politics as it aimed to serve as a medium of communication among organized groups representing different social classes, interests, and reform causes. The tone of the congress reflected the desire of its organizers to moderate social conflict by working out voluntary means of adjusting labor disputes in the court of public opinion. Although some trade unionists, like H. H. Garland, president of the Amalgamated Association of Iron, Steel, and Tin Workers, "seconded [Carroll] Wright's faith in the 'curative' powers of public sentiment," others, like Samuel Gompers, stressed labor organization and collective bargaining as a precondition for arbitration.[58]

If anything, the brotherhoods' contribution to the proceedings leaned moderately toward Wright's view, but with a twist. The Engineers' Peter Arthur represented the brotherhoods at the congress, but their sole speaker was Lorenzo Coffin, that concrete link between brotherhood unionism and Gilded Age reform, representing the Brotherhood of Railroad Trainmen. Coffin touched on the inappropriateness of judicial regulation of railroad labor relations and went on to emphasize the responsibility of the public to railroad workers, who, he stated, were public servants. As a solution to railroad labor conflict, he proposed institutionalizing the link between railroad wages and rates by empowering regulatory bodies to raise rates (if necessary) to cover living wages for railwaymen: "If what we now pay for freight and fare is not enough to meet the reasonable demand of this great army of employees so they can live . . . and to give a fair return to the capital invested, then let us be made to pay more." Coming from a former state railroad commissioner, Coffin's idea fit with the new liberalism, but it was unlikely to win serious consideration. As for disputes, he echoed the majority of the congress's speakers in conveying the brotherhoods' support for arbitration. In the end, as Furner has observed, conference speakers converged on the need for some alternative "to the individualistic language, concepts, and methods of the courts that reflected the technological and organizational realities of modern life." Thus, the conference called for national-level legislation incorporating the principle of voluntary arbitration in railroad industrial relations.[59]

The brotherhoods played both indirect and direct roles in shaping that legislation. Just as they had impressed Wright with their conservative competency, so too did they influence the Erdman Act's chief architect, Richard Olney. Even as he moved to crush the ARU boycott, the immensity of the conflict compelled him to reconsider the legal standing of unions, strikes, and the courts' attitudes toward these issues. In his rethinking, Olney was struck by what he regarded as the injustice of Judge Jenkins's 1893 Northern Pacific Railroad injunction and the perniciousness of his definition of strikes as illegal. Olney's views were further propelled by a September 1894 case in which the Brotherhood of Railroad Trainmen sought to enjoin the receivers of the Philadelphia & Reading Railroad from ordering employees to give up union membership as a condition of employment. The company had been imposing these "yellow-dog" contracts since the mid-1880s. After meeting with Stephen Wilkinson, and hearing the story of his role in the Pullman boycott, Olney decided to involve himself in the case.[60]

Olney drafted an amicus curiae brief in which he effectively set out a defense of brotherhood-style unionism. Taking direct issue with the logic informing the Reading's policy and Jenkins's decisions—that unions were illegal because they *might* provoke strikes—Olney drew attention to the "aims and purposes" of the BRT, which he found "laudable in the highest degree and as deserving the approbation and support of every good citizen." Olney conceded that the union did reserve the right to strike; he stressed, however, that its rules for the calling of strikes were "of an eminently conservative character," and that, moreover, primary strikes *were* legal. Accordingly, the case against unions as illegal, simply because they *sometimes* conducted strikes, was invalid. Echoing Carroll Wright, as well as the trade unionist view that both workers and employers must be treated equally by the state, Olney argued that if capital enjoyed the right to organize, so too should the employees of capital. Animating his line of reasoning were several pragmatic points: depriving employees of the right to organize did not necessarily obviate the possibility of strikes; unions improved the quality of service as a result of higher morale; and, under present industrial and social conditions, it was no longer possible for railroad employers to deal with employees "as so many isolated units." Unions like the brotherhoods were useful, necessary even, for adjusting "ever recurring controversies" developing between labor and capital. In other words, in a perspective suggestive of the new liberalism, labor unionism was inevitable, and so it was best to cultivate the right kind of unionism.[61]

Even though the judge in the case ignored Olney's brief and found for the receivers, Olney's arguments were indicative of changing views among a minority of judges and a growing number of elected government officials. As Melvyn Dubofsky has shown, the diffusion of ideas stressing the indeterminacy of life and mutability of society in the late nineteenth century encouraged a younger generation of academics, judges, and even corporate leaders to question the individualism of the Victorian era and to see worker organization, at least of the brotherhood variety, in a more positive light. By the mid-1890s, a nascent liberal jurisprudence had begun to develop, which allowed for collective action in the employment relationship. In 1893 a federal judge found that the BLE's rule no. 12 did not make the union illegal, and in 1894 justice John Marshall Harlan lifted Judge Jenkins's Northern Pacific injunction, employing logic that paralleled Olney's. Federal lawmakers also took on these new attitudes and, picking up where the congressional investigative labor committees of the 1880s had left off, began to challenge the judiciary's use of injunctions. Investigating the Jenkins injunction in the spring of 1894, and anticipating both Wright's and Olney's lines of thought, the House Judiciary Committee took issue with Jenkins's definitions of strikes as illegal and argued for the right of workers to organize. In recommending limits on the powers of federal judges to punish for contempt, the committee condemned Jenkins's action as "an oppressive exercise of the process of his court, an abuse of judicial power, and wrongful restraint upon said employés and the officers of said labor organizations."[62]

Catalyzed by the Pullman boycott, these strands of thought came together in legislation both calling for the voluntary arbitration of labor disputes and legitimating trade unionism as practiced by the railroad brotherhoods. Of the flurry of proposals, including one drafted by strike commissioners Carroll Wright and John D. Kernan at the request of the House Committee on Labor, only the bill drafted by Richard Olney received sustained attention. Selectively building on the Wright-Kernan bill, which he had been asked to critique, Olney proposed a combination of mediation and voluntary arbitration. In the event of a dispute, and at the request of either labor or management, the U.S. commissioner of labor and the chair of the Interstate Commerce Commission would be empowered to settle the dispute as mediators. If their efforts failed, the matter would go to arbitration before a three-member board, with each side choosing one arbitrator. These two, in turn, would choose a "neutral" chair. After hearing the cases of both sides, the panel would render a binding award that would stand for at least two years, enforceable by the courts.[63] In reviewing the bill, the House Committee on Labor consulted brotherhood leaders and adopted their suggestions, including protections to employees during the period of the arbitration award and restrictions on railroad receivers in wage-related matters.[64] These were the basic features of the legislation that made its way through Congress to become the Erdman Act of 1898.

The Erdman Act stood as a concrete expression of the new liberalism. In providing for federal mediation and arbitration of labor disputes, the act signaled what would be an ongoing and bureaucratic role for the state in railroad industrial relations. Moreover, as demanded by the public, it reflected an official acceptance of the role of organized groups of employers and workers for regulating the labor market relations of an industry in which the federal government had an established supervisory role. In reporting the bill, James H. Kyle, chair of the Senate Committee on Education and Labor, in language reminiscent of the Strike Commission's report, alluded to the Pullman strike and its disastrous consequences: "The necessity of the bill arises from the calamitous results, in the way of ill-considered strikes arising from the tyranny of capital or the unjust demands of labor organizations, whereby the business of the country is brought to a standstill and thousands of employees, with their helpless wives and children, are confronted with starvation."[65] It was incumbent on organized labor and corporate capital to peacefully manage industrial relations; to do so, and to prevent harm to consumers by these private interests, however, some sort of arbitration overseen by government was necessary.

Perhaps most important, state-sponsored mediation and arbitration functioned as a mechanism for legitimating the railroad brotherhoods and equalizing the bargaining relationship between labor and capital.[66] At numerous points in the congressional debate over the bills leading to the final act, lawmakers pointed out that the proposed legislation would mark the first time that unions of any sort would be legally recognized.[67] Such recognition, argued the bill's supporters, was necessary to place labor on a more equal footing with capital, which, in turn, was necessary for well-managed labor relations. In a letter supporting the bill, Interstate Commerce Commission chair Edward A. Mosley articulated this view: "With the corporations as employers on one side and the organizations of railway employees as the other, there will be a measure of equality of power and force which will surely bring about the essential requisites of friendly relations, respect, consideration and forbearance."[68] Arguments like Mosley's reflected the belief that the brotherhoods had legal personality. Such personality gave the brotherhoods the capacity not only to represent groups of workers but also to bind them and enforce contracts. With this capacity, the brotherhoods could be enlisted as agents of labor market management and of labor-management peace.[69] As Constantine J. Erdman, the bill's original sponsor in the House put it, "The purpose of the legislation is to treat the employees as incorporated organizations . . . and then it is apparent how readily and easily the [arbitration] judgment can be enforced."[70] Kyle put the issue in slightly different terms: the bill sought "to place labor on a more thorough business basis . . . It brings to labor organizations an opportunity for really perfecting their work and for cooperating with the managers of railroads in preventing strikes and violence."[71]

For brotherhood leaders, this feature of the bill held great attraction. To be sure, they made clear their disapproval of compulsory arbitration. And like other unionists, they worried about the power of government and the potential of the bill to infringe on the rights of workers to quit employment. Yet Patrick Morrissey, Edgar Clark, and the Firemen's William S. Carter saw more to be gained than lost, particularly in the bill's prohibiting the dismissal of an employee for union membership. In correspondence with Samuel Gompers, who opposed the bill, Carter admitted doubts about the effectiveness of voluntary arbitration; convinced "that there was nothing compulsory in the bill" and that violations of agreements would be punished only by recovery of damages in a court of law, however, he stood in favor of it. Carter pointed out that settlements reached by arbitration and enforced by the courts did subject unions to liability, but that the ability of unions to bring suit and recover damages from companies failing to abide by such agreements outweighed the risks: "I am one of those who believe that it is as necessary for the members of labor organizations to abide by the terms of the agreements as should the members of a corporation, and that the obligations should be mutual and equally binding on the one as on the other."[72]

Congressional debate over the Erdman bill reflected contrasting conceptions of property rights, individual rights, freedom of contract, and the relationship between state and society. As an outspoken critic of the bill, Gompers swung the AFL Executive Council into opposition and lobbied hard against it, citing its potential for involuntary servitude (resulting from court-enforced arbitration awards) and compulsory arbitration.[73] Congressional opponents charged that the bill threatened to "invade the liberty of laborers" with the specter of involuntary servitude. Others insisted that workers' liberty resided in freedom of contract, and that such freedom must not be abridged.[74] As Joseph G. Cannon put it, "A workingman who exercises the right of an

American freeman to say, 'I will not work longer,' may be imprisoned for contempt." Cannon, not exactly a friend of organized labor, also worried that the provision for contempt proceedings against individual members should a union strike within three months of an arbitration award was unlawful. Such views reflected the older Victorian order, which in the hands of the courts had stood as a barrier to unionization.[75]

For their part, the brotherhoods were willing to accept some limitation of individual liberty in return for the material benefits of arbitration.[76] To the critics of the bill, Carroll Wright replied, "Instead of contemplating involuntary servitude, the bill . . . places labor and capital on an equality as to the enforcement of contracts; and furthermore . . . it gives labor organizations a way to dignify their bodies in ways that have not been open to them heretofore." Others emphasized the necessity of railroad workers' collective action to secure their individual rights. Throughout, supporters pointed to the brotherhoods' backing of the measure, their dignity and reasonableness, and their recognition of a public interest in railroad labor peace.[77] Patrick Morrissey confirmed these impressions: "I believe that if the arbitration bill becomes a law we will have seen the end of strikes and labor disturbances on railways. The railway interests will be made better and the employees will have the assurance that their individual and collective rights will not be disregarded."[78] Underlying the arguments of Wright, Morrissey, and other supporters was a view that subordinated individual rights to collective rights, and so connected a measure of industrial democracy to a public interest in collective organization and action. Together with the brotherhoods' intensive lobbying, these arguments ultimately carried the bill into law.[79]

* * *

In public, brotherhood leaders attributed the favor of government officials to their historic work toward harmonious labor relations. "I think that we have convinced them by our work," testified Peter M. Arthur before the U.S. Industrial Commission in 1899, "that we are sincere and honest in our efforts to give to the railway companies a reliable, trustworthy class of men."[80] Privately, however, these men knew that it had taken the most severe labor crisis to date to convince their adversaries that their unions could be agents of industrial peace. In this context, the statement of Stuyvesant Fish, president of the Illinois Central Railroad, before the Industrial Commission, is noteworthy. He expressed his approval of "organized labor as exemplified by the Brotherhood of Locomotive Engineers, the Order of Railroad Conductors and like useful and honorable organizations of intelligent railroad men." He preferred the brotherhoods to "the lawless and disorganized bodies of outsiders who know nothing of, and care nothing for either the railroads or the high class of men whom they employ."[81] Remarks like Fish's persuaded William S. Carter, who took over editorship of the *Locomotive Firemen's Magazine* after Debs had left, that the ARU "taught railway corporations a useful lesson. It taught them that if corporations during times of distress could succeed in enforcing defeat upon the organized old brotherhoods they would also create a mob of unorganized workers who ignored law and order and entered into what came near being an insurrection."[82]

Carter's remarks reveal a good deal. The Pullman boycott, like the Great Strike of 1877, stood as a dramatic example of what angry workers could do—just the sort of thing that the brotherhoods had promised to prevent. The brotherhoods' survival arguably had less to do with their own strategy than with the more radical alternatives. To become the beneficiaries of the ARU's actions and the state's largesse, however, the brotherhoods had to offer something of substance. That substance came forward in their brand of new unionism, their avoidance of the boycott, and their efforts to provide the railroads with dependable men. The brotherhoods' conservative competency stimulated new liberal thinking; they became allies of respectable liberal reformers, as well as agents of progressive reform in their own right. What they shared with those reformers was the conviction that the unregulated free market, and the ideology of acquisitive individualism that justified it, actually stood at odds with the public interest and social harmony. Whereas the ARU challenged this order head-on and went down in defeat, the railroad brotherhoods carefully steered through the conflict to set out a strategy for class harmony centered on trade union organization and government-sponsored arbitration. In this way, the brotherhoods contributed to the discourse of arbitrative alternatives to railroad industrial relations, the framing and passing of the Erdman Act, and the coming of the twentieth-century liberal order.

The era of the 1890s thus opened up new opportunities for the railroad brotherhoods, but it also left its imprint on them. As the twentieth century got under way, and as they engaged with reformers in the construction of a new language of liberal reform, the brotherhoods as social and cultural institutions would look decidedly different than they had in the Gilded Age of the 1880s.

5

Progressive Era America and the Culture of the New Unionism

When he spoke at the Brotherhood of Locomotive Firemen's biennial convention in Chattanooga, Tennessee, on September 7, 1902, president Theodore Roosevelt did not just pay tribute to the union; he also warned the assembled delegates, "There is in modern life with the growth of civilization, with the growth of luxury a certain tendency to the softening of the national fiber [and a] . . . disuse of the rugged virtues which lie at the bed of manhood and fill professions like yours." He continued, "I feel that professions like yours have a tonic effect upon the whole body politic. It is a good thing that there should be a large body of our fellow citizens in whom the exercise of the old, old qualities of courage and daring resolution and unflinching willingness to meet danger. . . . A man is not going to be a fireman or an engineer or serve in any other capacity well on a railroad long unless he is a man." The Brotherhood of Locomotive Firemen, Roosevelt concluded, stood as an "object lesson in good American citizenship." The Firemen returned the compliment by making the president a grand honorary member of the lodge.[1]

Theodore Roosevelt's presence at the Firemen's convention reflected the railroad brotherhoods' rising power and influence, as well as the new liberal polity of the Progressive Era. To an unprecedented degree, Roosevelt as president made himself accessible to organized labor, particularly the brotherhoods. He spoke highly of the brotherhoods' leaders, and he invited them to dinner, conferred with them, and appointed them to federal bureaus and commissions, as he had with Frank Sargent. Perhaps it was TR's fascination with railroads and railroad men, or maybe it was the Republican leaning of the brotherhoods' leaders.[2] More likely it was the brotherhoods' conservatism that moved Roosevelt. Certainly, the brotherhoods' responsible trade unionism fit easily with his vision of labor-capital relations, one defined by collective bargaining and mediation by the state when necessary. Roosevelt may have timed his appearance to make this point, for at that moment he was engaged in brokering a settlement in the anthracite coal strike of 1902. Roosevelt's successful resolution of the conflict stood in stark contrast to the Cleveland administration's handling of the Pullman strike. It also reflected his conviction that the "public interest" could not be held hostage to labor-capital conflict, and that such conflict could and should be avoided through the intervention of government.[3]

The delegates welcomed Roosevelt's address, for it helped the brotherhoods and the labor movement overcome the public perception that they represented nothing more than a "special interest," selfishly looking after their own welfare to the detriment of the larger citizenry. As Michael Kazin has suggested, the political and industrial realities of the early twentieth century encouraged unionists to seek allies in what he calls the "counter-elite" of middle-class and upper-class progressives, both in and out of government. In an era in which the trade union movement stood as the principal expression of industrial discontent yet still had to contend with the continued enmity of most employers and the might of the state, labor leaders adopted a rhetoric aimed at deflecting hostility while enlisting the sympathy of progressives. For the brotherhoods, this rhetoric figured as a continuation of their Gilded Age strategies. But reforged in the crucible of the 1890s, and entering the vacuum created by the ARU's destruction, their language took on a neo-populist and producerist tone in its claim to speak for all Americans. To be sure, they pared this rhetoric of its rebelliousness; instead, they presented organized labor as made up of mobilized wage earners who simultaneously embodied the ideals of the patriotic producer and stood as defenders of Americans' citizenship rights.[4] In his speech, Roosevelt linked these elements and voiced the shifting center of discourse in and about the labor movement.

The changing rhetoric of union leaders involved pragmatic considerations, but it also figured as part of a larger process of cultural formation at the turn of the century. Numerous scholars have commented on the sense of cultural crisis associated with the end of the frontier and the rise of urbanization, immigration, and bureaucratic structures; these developments presented strong challenges to the gender ideologies, racial and ethnic categories, and fixed moral certainties of the Victorian era. The response of figures in the Protestant elite, like Theodore Roosevelt, was to vigorously build a renewed American society composed of men dedicated to action and national purpose.[5] Next to the soldier, perhaps no type of man fit TR's definition of the ideal American better than the railwayman, who embodied the perfect blend of discipline and independent spirit.[6] Roosevelt's view of railwaymen, however, did not entirely square with brotherhood men's changing understandings of manhood; the same forces causing him worry were at work within these unions. On the one hand, values associated with progressivism—the idea that individuals were part of a larger web of social relationships and the belief in organization and efficiency—were gaining in prominence. On the other, to paraphrase T. J. Jackson Lears, as the acids of modernity accompanying those values—creeping secularization, relativism, and bureaucratization—dissolved Victorian ideals, the brotherhoods' organizational culture lost some of its intensely fraternal quality, and the concept of manhood lost some of its relevance.[7]

As the culture of fraternalism began to wane within the brotherhoods, empire and mass immigration in the 1890s propelled the ideology and rhetoric of quasi-populist Americanism to the fore.[8] That Roosevelt, leader of the Rough Riders in the War of 1898, connected engineers and firemen to a renewed national citizenship was fitting, for he more than any other American stood as a symbol of manhood and nation restored through struggle for domination abroad.[9] With his words, TR conferred a good deal of legitimacy on railwaymen and connected them and their unions to a new American nationalism and reinvigorated white masculinity. Part of a larger shift in national identity and awareness also occurring in Europe during these years, the "new nationalism" emerged at precisely the same moment that the railroad brotherhoods and other trade unions were moving toward the "new unionism." These factors combined to produce a distinctive "labor patriotism" that linked defense of labor with expressions of working-class loyalty to the nation.[10] Events directly connected to the emergence of new unionism heightened "rights consciousness" and "rights talk," and fostered new attitudes about defense of the trade union and, more broadly, the labor community. With turmoil in railroad labor relations during the late 1880s and early 1890s and a rapidly growing unskilled immigrant working class, Americanism provided unionists both an interpretive framework to understand the larger transformations of the era and a language in which they could position themselves vis-à-vis potential allies and enemies.

The Practice and Culture of the New Unionism

In the early twentieth century, within the industrial relations regime established by the Erdman Act, the railroad brotherhoods continued to expand their organizational and tactical approaches to the business of unionism.

Anointed as respectable and legitimate, and unchallenged by competing union movements, the brotherhoods enjoyed a monopoly on the organization and representation of running-trades labor. The experience of working within the Erdman Act regime made them larger, more complex, and more "secular" organizations. One of the hallmarks of the new, business-oriented unionism was the dropping of the more overtly fraternal trappings that had defined brotherhood culture in the nineteenth century. As it evolved over the first two decades of the twentieth century, the railroad brotherhoods' approach to labor-capital relations accepted the permanence of class conflict, although leavened with support for progressive reform and cooperation with employers where possible and practical. By World War I, it mixed arguments that unions should be rational "business" propositions dedicated to raising the membership's standard of living with promises of industrial democracy.[11]

The most fundamental developments driving change within the railroad brotherhoods were perhaps the least dramatic. In the years after 1900, the brotherhoods not only recouped the membership losses that they had incurred during the economic depression and industrial conflicts of the 1890s, but they substantially increased in size as well. The Order of Railway Conductors, for instance, grew from a membership of a little over one thousand in 1880 to roughly twenty-five thousand in 1900 and over forty-nine thousand by 1913. The Brotherhood of Locomotive Engineers grew from approximately twenty thousand in 1886 to seventy-three thousand on the eve of U.S. entry into World War I. For its part, the Brotherhood of Locomotive Firemen grew from a membership of some fifteen thousand in 1885 to over thirty-six thousand in 1900 and eighty-six thousand in 1916. The Trainmen grew in like fashion.[12] As the brotherhoods increased in size of membership, so too did the extent and complexity of their written agreements with the railroad corporations expand. By 1902, the Engineers had secured agreements with 118 railroads, a figure that rose to 348 by 1916, which represented 100 percent of the major carriers. As they extended written contracts to more and more railroads, the length and content of these agreements expanded enormously, from less than one handwritten page in 1875 to almost one hundred typewritten pages by 1917.[13]

As the brotherhoods grew in size, their financial transactions expanded in volume and kind. The Conductors' expenditures, for example, rose from a mere $77 in 1870 to roughly $500,000 in 1913. From a relatively modest total of $120,000 in 1884, the Firemen's receipts rose to a little over $1 million in 1900 and to over $10 million in 1916.[14] The rest of the brotherhoods demonstrated similar patterns and rates of growth, but the Engineers also extended its financial holdings by creating and operating for-profit businesses. In 1909–10, the union built a thirteen-story skyscraper in Cleveland, Ohio, that housed its headquarters, paid for itself within ten years, established itself as a $3 million asset, and paved the way for the construction of a second building in 1925. In 1920, the Engineers entered into labor banking with the Brotherhood of Locomotive Engineers Cooperative Bank of Cleveland, capitalized at $1 million and maintaining a surplus of $1 million. Other banks followed in New York, Philadelphia, Boston, and Minneapolis. With these and other investments made under the direction of president Warren Stone, who succeeded Peter Arthur in 1903, the BLE's resources stood at $145 million at the time of Stone's death in 1925.[15] The brotherhoods' financial experiments reveal the increasing institutionalization and bureaucratic complexity of the brotherhoods; more important, they also suggest the new, even innovative, directions of brotherhood unionism in the twentieth century.

These developments fed the view that the brotherhoods needed to be run "rationally" and "efficiently" by "professional" leaders. And, indeed, as a result of expanding membership, swelling treasuries, expanding insurance and benefit programs, and diversifying financial activities—together with the extension of contractual relationships with management—leadership did become more professionalized after 1900. With more records to keep, larger funds to manage, increased time and resources required for the negotiation of contracts and adjustment of disputes, and additional services to provide, the brotherhoods steadily increased the number of national-level officers. As national brotherhood leaders served longer terms of office, the annual salaries that they earned increased proportionally, from $5,000 in 1900 to $10,000 in 1920 in the case of the Engineers grand master. (Such handsome remuneration outpaced that of other labor leaders, like James O'Connell of the International Association of Machinists, who received $1,500 a year, and even Samuel Gompers of the AFL, who drew only $2,100 in 1900.) Reflecting the need for greater administrative capacity, the brotherhoods also increased the numbers of vice presidents, organizers, general and system chairs, state legislative representatives, business agents, and Grand Lodge office staff. Various executive boards oversaw the activities of these officers. At the same time, shortly after 1900 these unions undertook measures to rationalize and streamline their bureaucracies. The growth of large administrative staffs and corps of organizers, as well as substantial financial compensation to officers, reflected the ongoing demands of running complex national unions and contributed to the image of brotherhood leaders as professional, career unionists.[16]

Changes in the organization of the railroad industry and developments in railroad industrialization also factored into the centralization of brotherhood organization and administration. The brotherhoods had been fairly centralized from their early days, but the degree of power vested in national officers increased after the turn of the century. Beginning with the reorganization of the General Managers' Association in 1893, railroad labor relations increasingly became a matter of national union leadership dealing with organized employers, a trend acknowledged and furthered with the passage of the Erdman Act in 1898. As mega-railroad systems emerged in the wake of the 1890s depression, the brotherhoods began to pursue coordinated bargaining movements, a tactic facilitated by the relatively high level of centralized authority among national-level leadership. The need to master increasingly complex agreements and the quasi-juridical procedures of mediation and arbitration, along with increased control over strike funds, relief funds, insurance portfolios, and investments in buildings and land, also reinforced the authority of upper-level leaders and stimulated their professionalization.[17] As was the case for unions in the construction, metalworking, and mining industries, post-1900 railroad labor relations shifted the locus of decision making within the brotherhoods away from membership meetings and toward the national officers; the latter became not simply emissaries of the workers but agents of an institution bound by contractual relationships to employers.[18]

The national brotherhood leaders of the early twentieth century were a fairly homogenous group. During these years a generational shift occurred at the level of national leadership, putting in place the men who would see the brotherhoods into the 1920s: Warren S. Stone for the Engineers in 1902, Austin B. Garretson for the Conductors in 1906, and in 1909 William S. Carter for the Firemen and William G. Lee for the Trainmen. These men, and their associates who served as executive officers during these years, were born between 1854 and 1882. As was true of the first generation of brotherhood leadership, they were predominantly American-born, largely of Anglo-Irish stock, Protestant or Catholic in religion, and disproportionately hailed from nonurban backgrounds. All had served roughly an average of ten years in the running trades, with many also working for shorter periods of time in nonrailroad factory or agricultural work. A small number had briefly owned or operated small businesses. Unlike first-generation union leadership, these men generally demonstrated a higher rate of educational attainment, with most completing a secondary school education and in a number of cases a year or two of university prior to union service. Lastly, those brothers who held national office did so earlier in their lives, spent longer periods of time moving up the union hierarchy, and held their highest offices longer on average than did the founders of their unions.[19]

The experiences and outlooks of these brotherhood leaders differed from those of their predecessors in ways that suggested their connections with new liberal reformers and their integration with a bureaucratically oriented state. Whereas the first generation of brotherhood leadership had to work hard simply to ensure union survival, these men had a world of expanded horizons open to them. Such exposure and contacts with figures of national political power led to the appointment of a number of brotherhood leaders into private business and government positions. Frank P. Sargent served on the U.S. Industrial Commission from 1898 through 1902, leaving the grand mastership of the Brotherhood of Locomotive Firemen for an appointment as U.S. Commissioner General of Immigration in 1902 (after declining an earlier offer of appointment as director of the Bureau of Engraving and Printing in 1900). Edgar E. Clark was appointed to the Anthracite Coal Strike Commission of 1902–3 and the Interstate Commerce Commission after that. During his tenure as ORC chief, Austin B. Garretson served on the U.S. Commission on Industrial Relations from 1912 to 1915, and William S. Carter took a leave of absence from the presidency of the Firemen to serve as head of the U.S. Railroad Administration's Division of Labor during the First World War. All the brotherhood chiefs held longtime memberships in the National Civic Federation, with Frank Sargent influencing Federation secretary Ralph Easley on labor-capital relations, and Warren Stone serving on the Federation's executive committee until 1925. Lastly, the Trainmen's Peter H. Morrissey headed the American Railway Employees and Investors' Association, an organization through which industry and union leaders lobbied for favorable ICC rulings. With the prominence that they enjoyed in the first decade of the twentieth century, it was not surprising that brotherhood chiefs came to prefer the title "railway labor executives."[20]

As the leadership, membership, and nature of the brotherhoods changed, brotherhood men less frequently referred to their organizations as "fraternities" of railwaymen and began to call for their unions to be run on more "businesslike" bases. Expressions of this view dated to the 1880s in connection with brotherhood insurance programs, particularly in the Engineers, and continued after the turn of the century.[21] Present in these statements was the old tension between the fraternal principles of charity and mutual aid, and the very real need to maintain insurance funds. Over the next decade or more, brotherhood members continued to argue over the merits of fraternally based insurance, the practice of uniform assessment rates, and the issue of old-age pensions. Nevertheless, the brotherhoods began to move toward more stringent medical examinations of insurance program members, the establishment of reserve funds designed to ensure long-term financial stability, and the diversification of insurance and pension offerings.[22]

Similarly, in the realm of labor relations, brotherhood spokesmen began to talk about dealing with management and the honoring of contracts less in terms of "manly" obligation and more as a matter of good "business practice." In his first convention address as the newly elected president of the Brotherhood of Railroad Trainmen in 1909, William G. Lee signaled a new tone: "Organization business must be conducted along the same lines and with the same regard for right that characterizes private business."[23] Such conduct, in the opinion of engineer D. J. Brown, had removed the prejudice of railroad officials against brotherhood representatives typical of the late nineteenth century: "The present satisfactory condition may be credited to the training that has come through organization. This training has fitted our men to do business with their employers in a businesslike manner."[24] Indeed, for brotherhood leaders of Lee's generation, railroad labor relations were no longer a matter of meeting with corporation executives on the common plane of manhood, as it had been during the expansionary days of the 1880s; although such a view asserted the essential equality of brotherhood officers and corporation officials, it also belied the essentially unequal terms of the relationship. By the 1910s, such "sentimental" notions had no place in "modern" railroad labor relations, for national brotherhood leaders regarded themselves as professionals, every bit the equal of the men they met across the bargaining table; they also considered the organizations that they represented to be as "legitimate," if not as powerful, as the corporations that they opposed.[25]

Changes in the brotherhoods' organizational cultures accompanied the emerging view of the union as a "business." The years 1906–9 were notable in this regard as the railroad brotherhoods revised the titles of grand lodge and subordinate lodge officers. "Grand masters" became "presidents," "grand" secretary treasurers became "general" secretary treasurers, and so forth.[26] Other unions had traveled this route. The International Association of Machinists had begun as the Order of United Machinists and Mechanical Engineers, and the Amalgamated Association of Iron, Steel, and Tin Workers had its origins in the Grand Forge of the United States, Sons of Vulcan.[27] The culture of fraternalism that had defined the railroad brotherhoods since their inception, particularly the ceremonial trappings, had become antiquated in the climate of "up-to-date" labor relations of the Progressive Era.

The shifting content of fraternal ritual in local lodges mirrored changes at the national level. During the 1890s, brotherhood leaders began to express concern over the "stale" nature of initiation rituals.[28] By century's end, it seemed that tired rituals performed in lackluster fashion resulted in low membership interest in lodge meetings. The timing is suggestive, for the apparent decline of interest coincided with the shift of the brotherhoods, particularly the Firemen and the Conductors, away from benevolence and toward more explicitly protective measures during the late 1880s and early 1890s. The wholesale revision of fraternal rituals by some of the brotherhoods figured as a cultural dimension of the new unionism.

The Brotherhood of Locomotive Firemen stood as a case in point. In 1894, the union charged its grand master and grand secretary treasurer with the task of devising a new, "fresher" initiation ritual "that can be made much more entertaining." Frank Sargent and Frank Arnold accepted the challenge, declaring, "We want to depart from the solemnities somewhat and introduce a little of the amusement of life, so as to make our meetings interesting. We have been too sedate in receiving candidates into our order. A little nonsense now and then has had a good effect upon mankind, and it would upon the character of our brotherhood."[29] What they produced included the conventional "illustrated scenes depicting the daily life of a fireman" and "robes for the adornment of the officers and members," as well as, in what seemed to be a departure, "certain accessories which can be used." The new ritual was introduced with great fanfare to a three-hundred-member audience at a March 1895 meeting of New York Lodge No. 149. The actual content of the ritual did not appear in their report, but something of its nature can be gleaned from the divided reception that it received. Although Sargent judged the ritual a success, it apparently possessed neither the dignity nor sacredness of the old ritual. "It has been characterized as 'Sargent and Arnold's traveling circus,'" he admitted.[30]

The new direction of these rituals became apparent over subsequent years as a practice known as "riding the goat" became a regular feature of initiations. In 1899, a fireman from Winslow, Arizona, described the experience, which involved a bucking hobbyhorse of some sort, as "the nearest to a combination of a Kincaid Stoker, a perpetual motion machine, and an airship. . . . The victim may weigh 200 pounds and pad his pants with his mother's bed quilt, but this goat certainly makes him lose all his right and knowledge to the law of gravity when he starts out to show him the ups and downs of a 'tallow-pot' existence."[31] After 1900, in addition to goat rides, lodges also put on burlesques and, as scattered evidence suggests, the use of devices to frighten the candidate. An Elmira, New York, BLF lodge, for instance, devised something called the "Mysterious Chair," which apparently surpassed "the old-time goat in effectiveness."[32] It is not clear what the Mysterious Chair actually did, but such innovations apparently went further than the Firemen's Grand Lodge deemed appropriate. Its 1910 convention raised concerns "that new members are injured and mistreated while being initiated," and the union revised its ritual to contain "positive instructions prohibiting during initiations the use of any electrical or other apparatus, contrivances or machines using electricity, blank cartridges or anything that is liable to be the cause of personal injury" or "mental shock."[33]

The apparent frivolousness of the new initiation rituals stood at odds with the serious business of "up-to-date" unionism. Yet the content and the calculus behind them were quite serious and indicative of the new unionism. If viewed in terms of what they were not—the quasi-religious rites of the 1870s and 1880s—they reflected a more "secular" organizational culture, one oriented more toward material achievement achieved through group organization than individual morality and rectitude. They even reflected a more "commercial" approach to the business of member loyalty, for although they did convey the "mysteries of the order," they seemed driven less by the need to impart uplifting truths than by the frank attempt to stimulate member interest. Indeed, brotherhood men apparently no longer saw ritual as sacred but rather as a commodity to be tweaked and marketed; in that respect, the revised rituals anticipated aspects of twentieth-century mass consumer culture. Surely, brotherhood leaders of these years must have understood that membership loyalty demanded more than a "business" approach to unionism. Accordingly, the new rituals in their entertainment capacity made good business sense. Such developments paralleled changes in the broader Masonic fraternal movement.[34] The new rituals also fit with the changing nature of railroad industrial relations in the 1890s. As the brotherhoods became more accepted by railroad managers in the wake of the Pullman boycott, and as the Erdman Act secured for them de facto legal standing, the need for secrecy and the rituals of periodic meetings lost some of their early necessity. Similarly, collective bargaining and the process of mediation and arbitration replaced the brotherhoods' earlier reliance on the commitment of individual members to enforce union rules and standards.[35] In such a setting, the older rituals became obsolete.

New Women . . . New Men?

If the shifting content of brotherhood culture reflected changes in the nature of railroad industrial relations, so too did it reflect changing understandings of masculinity and manhood. As historians have shown, the late nineteenth and early twentieth centuries represented a period of significant change in the social roles and gender norms for American women and men. Driven by changes in the material bases informing gender identity, these years witnessed the emergence of the "New Woman" and the decline of the self-conscious rhetoric of manhood characteristic of the Victorian era. A number of historians have pointed to the emergence of a "cult of masculinity" among middle-class men at the turn of the century as new forms of work, created by urbanization and the rise of bureaucratic structures, no longer provided men with a sense of economic independence and manly achievement. Gail Bederman, Elliot Gorn, and Michael Kimmel have discerned in the middle class a more aggressive, physically oriented style of manhood emphasizing self-realization through abundant experience, along with a corresponding shift in the language used to describe men. The older term "manly"—meaning adult, mature, responsible, the opposite of childlike—came to mean the opposite of all that was soft, feminine, or sentimental. "Being manly now meant being not womanly," as Gorn has put it. According to Bederman and Kimmel, *manhood*, defined by moral character, was replaced by *masculinity*, understood as a set of behavioral traits and attitudes that stood in contrast to *femininity*.[36]

Theodore Roosevelt's call for the "strenuous life," of course, stands as the quintessential expression of middle-class men's anxiety over the perceived emasculating effects of modern society, and it was no accident that Roosevelt held up railroad workers as examples of manly toughness and strength. In an 1894 letter to the English historian and author Charles Henry Pearson, TR argued that railroading was a "modern trade" that involved "the exercise of the manlier virtues to a degree that hardly any trade ever did formerly." Railroad men "practice a profession which beyond any other necessitates the exercise of hardihood, daring, self-reliance, and physical strength and endurance."[37]

Railwaymen and other industrial workers may have figured as examples of the "strenuous life" and thereby may have indirectly contributed to the middle-class reconstruction of manhood at the turn of the century, but the fact of the matter was that understandings of manhood in the brotherhoods were changing in ways not entirely consistent with Roosevelt's vision of workingmen. For one thing, in the wake of the 1890s crises it no longer seemed enough for labor and capital to recognize and acknowledge their distinct but interconnected interests, and it no longer seemed plausible that railroad employees and employers could come together "as men" and sort out their differences. The brotherhoods' new unionism and more "secular" culture manifested this understanding. As collective bargaining and the processes of mediation and arbitration replaced the brotherhoods' earlier reliance on the commitment of individual members to enforce union rules, union membership became less a matter of intense personal commitment and more a matter of routine necessity (hence, the need for more "entertaining" rituals). The contractualism of twentieth-century industrial relations did not render irrelevant the brotherhoods' nineteenth-century codes of honor, but it did enmesh them within bureaucratic structures that robbed them of the intense personal commitment that they had demanded. One marker of change was the declining use of manhood rhetoric and exhortations to personal morality in the pages of the brotherhoods' journals after 1900. The thrust of post–Erdman Act labor relations rendered increasingly anachronistic the florid, at-times sentimental, rhetoric of manhood, and instead fostered a style of masculinity less concerned with "manhood" in the Victorian sense of the term.

By the early twentieth century, the brotherhoods had won a real degree of predictability and control in areas like discipline, promotion, and grievances. At the same time, the brotherhoods had campaigned for the adoption of safety appliances, like the Janney automatic coupler and the air brake. Workplace safety and bureaucratic control over the work experience came at the expense of the "romance, adventure, and spontaneity of the work," to quote Walter Licht.[38] The wide-open, freewheeling days of the pioneering generation of railwaymen of the 1840s through the 1870s had fostered a fiercely independent and rough-and-tumble style of masculinity. In pressing for stability in the work experience and limits on the petty authority of local officials, the brotherhoods won for their members the right to be treated "as men"; in doing so, however, they inevitably narrowed the scope for the more exuberant expressions of masculinity that had informed running-trades work culture. Such an outcome was consistent with the brotherhoods' goal of taming railwaymen's rough masculinity and fostering a respectable manhood. Still, a sense of nostalgia for the "old days," before the workplace had became so rule-bound and before safety technology had taken some of the risk out of the work, suggested that for some members of the post-1900 generation manhood should have some basis in the risky and sometimes-rough side of railroad work.

The discomfort that some brotherhood men felt with regard to the implications of the changing nature of railroading for masculine identity appeared in the pages of the *Railroad Trainmen's Journal* and the *Railroad Trainman*. A "dialect" poem appearing in the *Trainmen's Journal* in 1904, for instance, captured generational differences and expressed mixed feelings over safety technology. The speaker, a veteran brakeman, addressed his younger counterparts. "Say, youse guys tink yer brakies. . . . Wy, wid all dis Janey system, maken couplins is a cinch, An' any kid could do it, er a woman, in a pinch." The narrowed scope for individual decision making on the road or in the yard that attended enhanced safety rules also challenged a traditional base of skilled railroader identity; for some, it suggested the unmanning of railwaymen. In a 1912 essay entitled "Brakemen of the Good Old Days," C. F. Carter observed that air brake inventor "Westinghouse has made railroading safer," but pointed out that "a few men have fond recollections of the old days of hardship and danger." In mock-scandalized tones, Carter bemoaned "these effeminate days" when a brakemen had become a "trainman," no longer did "any rawhiding," and was "so hedged and hectored with rules and regulations and special orders that he wouldn't dare kiss his wife good-bye without first consulting his Book of Rules to ascertain which arm he was expected to put around her waist while administering the salute." The old days, he concluded, were "simple and informal," with "the kind of railroading . . . to stir the blood of a mummy," while today there was "absolutely nothing left to keep up the interest." The illustration accompanying the essay depicted a too-tidy-looking brakeman in uniform, rule book in hand, as he kissed his wife.[39] Bound by rules and softened by technology, some brotherhood members worried that railroaders could no longer be men.

Shifting images and understandings of womanhood in the 1890s and early twentieth century heightened, and perhaps also drove, men's concerns. Most commonly associated with the image of the New Woman, these developments reflected changes in the American household and in the relationship of women to public life. By the late nineteenth century, the middle-class home had lost many of its productive functions and had become a site of consumption, albeit with homemakers in full control and bearing full responsibility for its well-being. At the same time, with rising standards of living and decreasing need for productive labor, daughters were more likely to attend school longer and complete a university education. By the 1870s and 1880s, women were also more likely to remain single and be active in the public sphere, either through involvement in an all-women's association or by employment in a profession dominated by women. In their settlement house and temperance work, respectively, Jane Addams and Frances Willard embodied the impulse of this generation to extend the values of the home to purify and uplift society, which formed one of the roots of progressive reform and the new liberalism. Combining Victorian virtues with an activist social role, the New Woman represented both a continuation of and challenge to prevailing gender ideology.[40]

The New Woman was a middle-class, if not an upper-class, phenomenon, but some of the social transformations that produced that image also touched the families of running-trades workers. With incomes approaching middle-class levels, engineers and conductors were able to afford some of the products that had previously been prepared at home and were increasingly characterizing middle-class life. Labor-saving technologies that remade urban middle-class households, such as indoor running water, oil- or coal-fired furnaces, and electrification, also came within reach of the upper strata of railroad workers. From the 1890s onward, the *Locomotive Engineers' Monthly Journal* carried advertisements for products like ready-made overalls, suits, and shoes; labor-saving devices like gas-fired stoves and automatic washing machines and wringers; home furnishings like couches, chairs, and "artistic" rugs; leisure goods like bicycles, phonographs, and pianos; and "luxury" items like diamonds.[41] Discussions of the problems and benefits of domestic help reflected a certain level of affluence (or at least an aspiration to affluence) and the higher standards of housekeeping that accompanied turn-of-the-century changes in the household.[42] Finally, as Ileen DeVault has found in her study of Pittsburgh in the late nineteenth and early twentieth centuries, the daughters of skilled workers like engineers and conductors demonstrated a high rate of educational achievement and social mobility, completing the kind of vocational training that positioned them to enter the "white-collar" clerical work opening up to women at the end of the nineteenth century. Although they did not receive the kind of university training associated with their wealthier counterparts, their "conspicuous employment" in terms of education, clothing, and prestige lent itself to the same kind of generational experiences as those of the New Woman.[43]

In the brotherhoods' journals these developments manifested themselves in discussions of women's intellectual and educational attainment. In this area, the *Locomotive Firemen's Magazine*'s Women's Department editor Ida A. Harper emerged as a leader. Shortly after she took over the department's editorship, Harper became a spokesman for women's achievement. In 1889, she signaled a change in editorial policy, replacing the lead article, which had tended to dwell on sentimental issues, with short, pithy comments on matters of interest to women. She also introduced several new subdepartments bearing the hallmark of the New Woman—"Education," "Temperance," "Industries,"

"Franchise," and "Domestic"—and warned correspondents that their letters would be published so long as they were brief and on a topic of general interest.[44] With the new editorial direction, Harper aimed to make the Woman's Department a source of serious reading and exchange for women. Across the 1890s, she wrote editorials and encouraged contributions on women's intellectual, artistic, and political potential.[45] In her writing, she joined Victorian standards of domesticity with modern notions of self-fulfillment. "My keenest regret," she wrote in 1893, "is that women do not live up to the best that they are capable of. The salvation of the world must come through its women, and there will be still a nobler race in the future than the past has seen."[46] The women's sections of the other brotherhood journals did not take such an outspoken position as did Harper, but they did include educational material for women readers. The Engineers' journal's Ladies Department, for instance, ran a monthly "Study Club."[47] Such content challenged the assumption among many men that women were intellectually and mentally inferior.

It was perhaps in their associational experiences, though, that the wives and daughters of running trades workers most closely approximated the activities defining the New Woman. The women's sections of the brotherhoods' journals, of course, were a direct result of women's organized presence within the brotherhoods. The auxiliaries were indicative of the all-female organizing of the era, which provided women with the experiences—learning from others, sharing female values, and defining and working toward common goals—that their middle-class counterparts found in the "clubwoman" movement. In their educational aspirations, the auxiliaries demonstrated the sort of pre-political domestic feminism that Karen J. Blair has identified in the literary women's clubs of the late nineteenth century. Like those involved in women's clubs, women in the brotherhoods' auxiliaries saw themselves as "ladies" and viewed the auxiliaries as vehicles for the attainment of ladyhood.[48]

At the same time, the advent of study clubs, both as "correspondence" through the journals and collectively in the monthly meetings of auxiliary lodges, served as an important first step for women who wished to improve their minds and status. The content of the auxiliaries' study programs closely resembled that of the literary clubs in their emphasis on literature, classical antiquity, history, and the Bible. And like the women's clubs, the auxiliaries interspersed their meetings with dramatic presentations and musical performances. Inasmuch as these activities reflected a striving for self-improvement, they were significant "in an era that defined ladies as selfless agents devoted to the well-being of others," as Blair has written.

The fact that brotherhood women were working class and striving for this goal, despite the fact that they most likely were following the lead of the middle-class clubs, adds to their significance. And when the auxiliaries began to introduce topics of current political relevance and feminist content, they took a step toward women's politicization, despite their admittedly circumscribed sense of social mission. Thus, the Engineers' journal's study club of March 1902 may have taken a provocative line with the topic, "Equal Rights for Women," and the question, "If taxation without representation caused the revolt of the Colonies in 1776, should not women in 1902 for the same cause rebel?"[49]

The auxiliaries may have had a circumscribed sense of mission compared to some of their middle-class counterparts, but it is important to remember that their raison d'être remained the supporting of the union by bringing female relations and families into closer contact. Viewed from the standpoint of class politics, this mission could be understood as something more than domestic feminism if the good work of the union delivered both economic justice to railroaders' families and the social conditions necessary for wives' "ladyhood." At the same time, by the turn of the century the letters of some auxiliary members suggested that they sought to transcend the inequality inherent in the domestic ideal. In 1903, Mrs. J. W. Beathard, of Knoxville, Tennessee, expressed the view that women ought to be able to organize on an equal basis: "Organizations are to be composed of women as well as men, and woman can enjoy the sociability of a lodge meeting as well as man." Lenore Herbert, writing to the *Railroad Trainmen's Journal*, put the matter more explicitly: "We want our brothers to feel we are of them, and for them in all their undertakings and that we will rise 'equal' to any emergency."[50] Intentionally or not, Herbert's use of "brothers" in place of "husbands" or "fathers" underscored her point and prefigured twentieth-century labor movement idiom. The issue of equality between women and men was nowhere more apparent, or contentious, than in the matter of women's suffrage. Like the women's clubs, the auxiliaries never made suffrage an organizational objective, and as organizations they remained silent on the subject.[51] Nevertheless, within the pages of the brotherhoods' journals, women and men discussed and debated the merits of the issue.

Support for women's suffrage first appeared in the late 1880s and early 1890s in the *Locomotive Firemen's Magazine* during Ida Harper's editorship of the Woman's Department. In her editorials she emphasized the principle of equal rights for women and the justice of enfranchising women, much in the tradition of the Civil War–era suffragists.[52] In January 1893, she approvingly printed the letter of a contributor that asked, "Why should women abstain from voting? Are they not men's equal in intelligence and education? No one with common sense will deny, that the virtues necessary to honest government are developed to the highest degree in the average woman of to-day."[53] Other pro-suffrage letters in the *Firemen's Magazine* and other brotherhood journals tended to follow the "expediency" line of argument, presenting women as morally superior to men and therefore a benefit to the nation through voting. Mrs. Alfred Eittreim, writing to the *Railroad Trainmen's Journal* in 1901, believed that it was "*just* for women [to] be allowed to vote." She went on to say that voting women would not neglect the home; rather, with the vote they would be in a position to do more good for the home. To make her case, she offered the example of men's alcohol consumption, its deleterious effects on the domestic sphere, and the temperance influence of women in states with women's suffrage.[54] Pro-suffrage advocates within the brotherhoods were well within the mainstream of suffrage thought, particularly the tendency to mix "justice" with "expediency" arguments (and the shift to the latter after 1890). And like the suffrage movement, the shift to "expediency" arguments represented a response to anti-suffrage sentiment within the brotherhoods.[55]

Anti-suffragists in the brotherhoods and their ladies' auxiliaries, as in the larger society, appear to have viewed suffrage as a threat to traditional beliefs. Including both women and men, suffrage opponents presented the sexes as fundamentally different, each with their separate sphere and each endowed with innate attributes. These sex roles, with women in the domestic and men in the public sphere, maintained the family as the basic unit of society. Women's suffrage, opponents argued, would destroy families and bring society into anarchy.[56] Arguments against suffrage connected closely with feelings of ambivalence about the New Woman. Critical commentary, which began to appear in brotherhood journals in the mid-1890s, centered on the New Woman's abandonment of traditional gender roles. Critics drew attention to the New Woman's neglect of domestic duties, whereas others dwelt on the unladylike behavior that they saw in women's political activism. Writing under the name of "Pansy," a contributor to the Engineers' journal in 1901 deprecated Carrie Nation's anti-saloon campaign in Kansas: "It seems to me that no good can come from such un-womanly proceedings . . . I think sometimes that perhaps women are progressing too fast, and it would be far better if they could be content to remain at home and rock the cradle awhile longer as the good old mothers used to do." The endpoint of such behavior was the "unsexing" of women, as a contributor to the *Trainmen's Journal* warned: "The new woman wants to retain all the privileges of her sex, and secure besides all those of a man; she wants to be a man and to remain a woman. She will fail to become a man, but she may succeed in ceasing to be a woman."[57]

If such blurring of womanhood bothered some brotherhood women and men, it certainly aroused anxiety in connection with manhood. Fear of role reversal had been a staple of anti-suffrage thought since the post–Civil War era, and it figured prominently in negative commentary on the New Woman. For brotherhood men, fears of women working at men's expense loomed large. The *Locomotive Firemen's Magazine* gave expression to this anxiety in 1896 when it ran a cartoon over the caption, "The New Woman Anno Domini 1896," in which a woman dressed in a man's suit returns home from work (she carries a tool box and lunch pail) to greet her husband, who is bearded, in a dress, a rolling pin in his hands, and a child tugging at his skirt. Scenes like this one were enough to raise the hackles of men, and more than a few women, concerned about the gender implications of the New Woman as well as the changing nature of railroad work. In the context of the 1890s depression, these concerns aroused serious concern. Among many trade unionists during these years, the "problem" of the New Woman was her propensity to be a workingwoman as much as her challenge to gender conventions.[58]

At times, brotherhood commentary on the New Woman seemed to simply equate her with the workingwoman. Like other organized craft workers, brotherhood men responded to the "problem" of workingwomen with mixed feelings. In the pages of the monthly journals, editors and correspondents acknowledged the real need of some women to work, and they called for wages and working conditions to keep them from undercutting male wage earners. Most commonly, though, they vehemently objected to women working in men's jobs or supporting families in place of their husbands. For the most part, they dismissed the possibility of organizing women workers, preferring instead to see unionized wages sufficient for men to support families as sole breadwinners.[59] With such arguments, brotherhood men and women revealed a desire to maintain a more traditional set of gender relations centered on female domesticity and male breadwinning. Even suffrage advocates and supporters of the New Woman agreed that this kind of social organization, in an updated form, was best for brotherhood families.

A New, Americanist Language

The new and more militant discourse on patriotism and nationalism that arose in the 1890s had its origins in the multiple social, economic, and political currents of the late nineteenth century. In the years after the Civil War, the heightened spirit of nationalism that had characterized the work of Reconstruction persisted in the idea of the nation as an organic whole, defined less in civic terms and more by sentiment and emotion. In the context of mass immigration beginning in the 1880s and the rise in racial violence and political disfranchisement of African Americans in the South in the 1890s, this organic and increasingly ethnic nationalism excluded African Americans and new immigrants. Coming through the crises of the 1890s, these strands merged into a new nationalism. This new outlook combined a vigorous defense of national interests abroad and the public interest at home through an activist state committed (in principle) to the idea of national citizenship and the opening of opportunity to the citizenry, although it was understood that opportunities should be maximized for the nation's "racial superiors."[60] The War of 1898 in Cuba and the Philippines completed this process by providing, in Amy Kaplan's words, "a final purgative battle" that completed national reunification on the basis of restored white manliness.[61]

The brotherhoods' Americanism emerged as part this new discourse, albeit with origins in the nineteenth-century language of labor republicanism and the conflicts that produced the new unionism.[62] Some brotherhood men shared the "producerist" critique of late nineteenth-century concentrations of wealth and power, while others downplayed republicanism's potentially radical social-political implications, preferring to see the corporation as a model of economic development and society as a moral hierarchy of unequal individuals. During the 1870s and 1880s, the vision of social harmony espoused by those tending to the latter vision held sway among the brotherhoods.[63] Over the second half of the 1880s, as this vision came under pressure, brotherhood republicanism and manhood rhetoric took on an oppositional quality. As early as 1885, Eugene V. Debs began sounding a more assertive note in his editorials.[64] Into the 1890s, as he moved away from the brotherhood approach to labor relations, he sprinkled his writing with references to "freedom," "liberty," and "independence," and likened oppressive employers to "czars." As the decade progressed, brotherhood men took a conservative view of republicanism—its functioning as a "civil religion" of nation worship and its potential to swathe social institutions in a kind of sacredness—and turned it into what Richard Schneirov calls "labor patriotism."[65]

The Chicago, Burlington & Quincy strike of 1888–89 marked a watershed in the emergence of labor patriotism in the Engineers and Firemen. Not only did the strike reveal the breakdown of previous understandings, but it also inspired in brotherhood men a new way of thinking about themselves, their families, and their unions: as a community under attack by unscrupulous employers. In its protracted nature and bitterness, the strike was unprecedented in brotherhood history. For the strikers, the Burlington's use of armed scabs, deputized employees, and Pinkertons signaled the corporation's determination to crush brotherhood unionism. Charles H. Salmons, the engineer chronicler of the strike, spoke of "the usurpation of state and municipal authority by the Burlington officials, with their deputy sheriffs and armed force of Pinkertons and scabs." The strike became nothing less than an industrial war in which defense of community against corporate aggression demanded courage and loyalty. Certainly, the violence that erupted after the arrival of scabs and Pinkertons suggested metaphors of invasion and battle. When striker George Watts was shot and killed while boarding an engine guarded by a deputized employee, the strike produced its first "hero." Other strikers similarly killed and injured became martyrs to labor's cause. Indeed, the Burlington strikers came to be regarded by mainstream unionists as "labor heroes" (the first such time the term was used, according to Schneirov) for their persistence against long odds, their loyalty to their unions, and their adherence to a code of conduct during the strike.[66]

The idea of labor as a community under attack found reinforcement in the brotherhoods' encounters with the courts. The Toledo, Ann Arbor & Northern Michigan Railroad case of 1893 and the Jenkins 1894 injunction of Northern Pacific workers convinced many brotherhood men that the courts intended to dismantle their unions and deprive them of their constitutional rights. In the opinion of the *Locomotive Engineers' Monthly Journal*, Judge Taft's ruling of railwaymen as "public agents" denied them the right to "resign their position," a basic citizenship right: "We believe the members of the B. of L. E. and B. of L. F. are what is termed free American citizens, whose loyalty to State has never been impeached, and we do not believe we can be deprived of the liberty vouchsafed to us by the constitution without due process of law." The following year, the *Journal* approvingly noted the findings of a congressional investigating committee, which found Judge Jenkins's injunction to be "an abuse of judicial power" that denied the "constitutional liberty" of workers.[67] Indeed, the committee regarded the injunction as "a clear command to render involuntary service" that not only violated the Thirteenth Amendment but effectively outlawed unions, denying labor a right of combination freely extended to capitalists. Trade unions were vital to workers' liberty, the committee argued. Thus, an order not to quit work was "an invasion of the rights of American citizens and contrary to the genius and freedom of American institutions."[68] The judicial repression of this era, one that lasted well into the twentieth century, convinced many in the labor movement that from their high office, judges were twisting the law and subverting the Constitution. Among brotherhood men, the rule by injunction heightened a sense of "rights" consciousness.[69]

The federation movement of the early 1890s inspired labor patriotism among brotherhood men and encouraged them to link their community to republican history and tradition. In the debate over the issue, some federation advocates identified the labor community as transcending brotherhood lines, and framed the matter as a battle between labor and capital. "'A house divided against itself cannot stand,'" wrote J. G. Cary, of Birmingham, Alabama,. "We are virtually divided. We are all laboring in one common field, and if an enemy attacks a brother across the way we are by a set of fixed rules and principles rendered powerless to assist him; and the forces and fortifications of our brothers are so weak that we stand only to mark their defeat, which greatly reduces our confidence in our own power to defeat them should they ever attack us." The tendency to invoke republican and American history—president Abraham Lincoln in Cary's case—would become characteristic of twentieth-century Americanism. "Our forefathers, in framing the constitution of our great nation, deemed it wise to provide for the organization of State governments . . . provided [their] laws do not conflict with the national government," wrote W. W. Hall. "Federation, as originally conceived, is based on the same principle of the several States and the general government." Perhaps it was natural for advocates like Hall to make the connection between union federation and the "genius" of American government, but for him the point was that federation would make brotherhood men "more potent in sustaining our just rights."[70]

"Rights talk" suggested that the vision of social harmony, the rhetoric of manhood, and the free-labor ideology that had sustained brotherhood unionism through the 1880s were waning among some brotherhood men by the mid-1890s. In the context of labor turmoil and apparently permanent class conflict, an emergent Americanism provided an alternative language with which to construct the labor community and its relationship to capital and the state. The Pullman strike, and the reconstruction of railroad industrial relations that followed, afforded the brotherhoods the opportunity to cast themselves on the side of the new liberals, who argued that harmony could be achieved only if labor and capital "accepted the higher claims and shared responsibilities of citizenship in a refurbished republic," in Shelton Stromquist's words. The new liberal thinking that went into the Erdman Act lent itself to both the collectivist tendency of labor patriotism and the strand of Americanism that in the Progressive Era would identify the interests of the people as opposed to economic concentration.[71] By the end of the 1890s, labor patriotism and Americanism were becoming defining features of the brotherhoods' new unionism, superseding but not entirely supplanting the fraternal idiom that had defined them since their beginnings.

As American nationalism entered its imperial phase with the War of 1898, brotherhood men began to draw closer associations among patriotic nationalism, labor patriotism, and unionism. If the crisis of the 1890s worked to separate the brotherhoods from their traditional cultural and ideological moorings, it also connected them with a new, more aggressive version of American nationalism. As a number of historians have observed, the combined impact of industrial unrest and mass immigration weakened the ability of republicanism and classical liberalism to sustain Americans' beliefs about national community. The response to this crisis took form in a patriotic boom during the 1890s, according to Stuart McConnell, as native-born middle-class patriotic groups led the way in the reconstruction of American nationalism centered on veneration of the national flag, public singing of "The Star-Spangled Banner," military drills, and other jingoistic displays as abstract symbols of national community and obligation. The level of abstraction in these patriotic rituals represented an attempt to describe a "nation" that had previously been understood through more immediate and concrete social experiences, such as town and family. The hallmarks of this new Americanism included, not necessarily consistently, the embracing of the federal state as the nation and a reimagining of the national community as broadly composed of the middle classes and native-born ethnicities. Unsurprisingly, the business community and the middle-class press excluded radical labor movements (as well as new immigrants) in the aftermath of events like Haymarket, Homestead, and Pullman.[72] In short, the patriotic boom, occurring during the same years as the new liberal reconstruction of railroad labor relations, both raised the stakes and offered an opportunity for the brotherhoods to redefine their relationship to the national state and to position their labor community within the national community.

Across the 1890s, the railroad brotherhoods promoted their patriotism and advanced their own versions of national loyalty. Patriotic iconography became conspicuous at social events and meetings, particularly references to and displays of the flag. Patriotic themes figured more prominently in the speeches of brotherhood officers, and the monthly journals began to run editorials on "Old Glory," "Independence Day," and the "Founding Fathers." The women's auxiliaries participated in these patriotic exercises by the addition of quasi-military marching drills.[73] Like other unionists, brotherhood men began participating in community-based patriotic demonstrations, replete with patriotic songs and nationalistic speeches by local politicians and clergy. The Brotherhood of Locomotive Engineers, for instance, participated in flag raisings, and many brotherhood lodges organized outings to cemeteries on Memorial Day, where they visited the graves of deceased members and placed flowers on their graves. The union even made observance of Memorial Day an official union duty by incorporating it into their constitution.[74] Labor Day celebrations offered particularly good opportunities for displays of patriotism, and brotherhood lodges entered floats bedecked with flags and red, white, and blue decorations. Whereas Labor Day had stood as labor's alternative to the Fourth of July through the 1880s, by the first decade of the twentieth century unions like the brotherhoods were explicitly linking their labor community with the national community.[75]

The War of 1898 injected a powerful jingoistic element into the patriotic boom and presented the brotherhoods with a critical national issue. In the lead-up to the war, the brotherhoods echoed mainstream sentiments by calling for recognition of the United States as a powerful nation, especially after the sinking of the battleship *Maine* in February 1898. *Locomotive Engineers' Monthly Journal* editor Charles H. Salmons spoke for others when he wrote, "The American people will stand behind [the president and Congress] and teach the world a lesson that the rights of America must be respected the world over." Salmons also approved of the U.S. intervention in Cuba, believing it "honorable."[76] In the war's aftermath, the brotherhoods joined in patriotic celebrations, the most notable of which occurred in October 1898 when Chicago brotherhood lodges organized a reception at the Chicago "Peace Jubilee." When president William McKinley addressed the assemblage at this union-hosted meeting, he recognized the loyalty and good citizenship of brotherhood men (and, by implication, honoring their "loyal" conduct during the Pullman boycott at the site of its occurrence): "The railroad men of the country have always been for the country, the railroad men of the country have always been for the flag of the country, and in every crisis of our national history, in war or in peace, the men from your great organizations have been loyal and faithful to every obligation." With his presence and words, McKinley confirmed at one of the highest levels what Patrick Morrissey had sworn earlier that year: "The man who is loyal to the principles of these organizations will never be disloyal to family or nation."[77]

Morrissey's comments hinted at the implications of empire and new nationalism for the changing definition of manhood. As Kaplan has written, empire helped refigure hierarchies of gender and race through a discourse of "recuperative heroism" central to the new nationalism. For middle-class men, imperial expansion and the militaristic exploits accompanying it provided another expression of the "strenuous life," by which some projected, if only vicariously, a bold, virile sense of masculinity.[78] Although the strenuous life had less application (or perhaps too much application) for industrial workers like railwaymen, the martial ideal of manhood that accompanied the patriotic boom and the war did have some resonance: if anything, railwaymen were more likely to serve in the military than were their middle-class counterparts. Journal editors like Charles Salmons commented approvingly on the railroad men "who talked little but acted well, and willingly assumed the guard of obligations of the soldier," while engineer "poet" Shandy Maguire offered paeans to "The Unheard-of Heroes" in uniform. Indeed, because military service entwined understandings of national obligation and loyalty—binding definitions of manhood to patriotism and service to the state—brotherhood leaders could be heard at union meetings stressing the allegiance of their followers in masculinist terms. In a 1901 address to a joint union meeting, entitled "Patriotism and True Manhood," Engineers third vice president Delos Everett explicitly joined manliness with loyalty to nation: "The true patriot is a man who loves his country, and true manhood represents courage, bravery, resolution and honor."[79]

In part, Everett's rhetorical exercise involved defining who was a "good" American—or, indeed, who was an American at all—in gendered and nationalist terms. The acquisition of overseas territories resulting from the war spurred this tendency, adding an explicitly racial dimension. In brotherhood journals, racial justifications and criticisms of empire invariably excluded the peoples of occupied territories from the national community, in addition to immigrants and people of color generally (while, of course, positioning brotherhood men and their families within it).

Beginning in the 1890s, the monthly journals began running a variety of articles, cartoons, and illustrations that emphasized the supposedly inferior, backward nature of colonized peoples. Especially in the years immediately following the war, journal editors typically led off monthly issues with photographic essays and travelogues of Cuba, the Philippines, Puerto Rico, Hawaii, and other foreign nations. In numerous articles, they contrasted American technology with the backward condition of "uncivilized" countries in Latin America, Africa, and the Pacific. The June 1901 issue of the *Locomotive Engineers' Monthly Journal*, for example, contained a photograph bearing the caption, "A Mexican Means of Transportation," depicting a woman sitting on a donkey. More subtle, but no less judgmental, articles like "Courtship as Practiced by Manila's 400" portrayed women in traditional and native dress and dwelt on the "exotic" nature of these peoples. An article on "Modern Mexico," with photos of ancient monuments, colonial churches, and peasant housing, suggested that the country was in fact anything but "modern" by American standards.[80] Although these pieces rarely involved any specific political comment, they helped build subtler attitudes toward "Other" peoples as legitimate subjects for the imposition of American "civilization." As the main source of information on those parts of the world under U.S. imperialist control, these publications reproduced the gaze of the colonizer and bolstered brotherhood men and their families' identification with the racial politics of colonialism.[81]

These racial justifications of empire, predicated on an often implicit contrasting of "savage" colonized peoples with "civilized" white Americans, enabled brotherhood men to draw on the category of race in a process of remaking national identity and manhood in ways that legitimized white racial superiority and male power. Linking whiteness with male supremacy was nothing new, but from the 1890s onward brotherhood journals more explicitly connected male power to race and the discourse of civilization through the publication of travelogues. Both the text and photographs contained in these pieces, particularly the way that they portrayed gender differences among foreign women and men, served to heighten the "uncivilized" nature of those peoples. Compared with the gender system of white Americans, which sharply distinguished between male and female and was associated with an "advanced" degree of "civilization," sexual-gender differences among peoples of other, more "savage," countries blurred: the women appeared less "womanly" and the men less "manly." For readers of brotherhood journals, these articles served to reinforce understandings of civilization as a racial and gendered concept. In the context of the popularized Darwinism of the late nineteenth century, civilization connoted the white-dominated, staunchly differentiated systems of industrialized western societies like the United States.[82]

Brotherhood views on the imperialist results of the War of 1898, as well as the Philippine War of 1899–1903, dovetailed with a longer-running discourse on immigration. From the 1870s onward, brotherhood men worried about competition with immigrants from southern and eastern Europe, Mexico, and Asia. Beginning in the 1890s, the statements on immigration in the monthly journals proliferated and took on a more strident and Americanist tone. In dozens of articles, editorials, and letters, journal editors and brotherhood members stressed the danger that unchecked immigration posed for American workers. The failure of immigrants to demand "white man's" wages, their inability to adopt an "American" standard of living, and their willingness to be exploited by ruthless capitalists against union labor would "pauperize" or "Russianize" native-born workingmen and their families. William S. Carter spoke for the vast majority of brotherhood men, and voiced the views of organized labor generally, when he concluded that the "average American workman is fully satisfied in his own mind, from practical experience, that he cannot successfully compete in wages, with the dark skinned races, and not even with some of his own color from other lands."[83] Carter's words were temperate compared with the allusions to moral excess, social marginality, and natural disaster that saturated brotherhood commentary on immigration well into the early twentieth century.[84]

Coming from a group of workers as well insulated from direct competition with new immigrants as the men of the running trades, such commentary may appear absurd. The timing of its outpouring, however, suggests that more was at play. On the one hand, as Eric Arnesen has suggested, in the context of disruptive economic change, complaints about new immigrants may have reflected fears about eroding working conditions and possible job loss in the railroad industry. Believing that they maintained a precarious hold on their political and economic autonomy, brotherhood men linked the changing composition of the American labor force to corporate attacks on their prerogatives as men and as citizens.[85] At the same time, the nativist sentiment in brotherhood journals coincided with the development of new unionism. In this view, nativism figured as an exercise in union building. Whether they really believed that they were under assault by immigrants is uncertain, but brotherhood members certainly expressed such sentiments. During the 1890s, when the brotherhoods were working toward an organizational response to defeats like the Burlington strike and challenges like the American Railway Union, when crises like the Pullman strike threatened the legitimacy of organized labor, and amid the reconstruction of nationalism, to inveigh against the immigrant threat was both to demonstrate union relevance and to construct common American identity. As was the case in other national unions at the time, the new unionism gained force from ideas about threats to the labor community; along with the figure of the scab, no threat loomed larger toward the end of the century than the specter of the new immigrant.[86]

* * *

The U.S. society that emerged from the 1890s was more racially conscious and segregated than it had been before, a result of imperialism, immigration, and the violent drive to white supremacy in the South. The labor movement played a part in these developments. It was during these years that the AFL recognized the International Association of Machinists, which admitted only whites, a move that paved the way for the admission of other unions barring black workers. The railroad brotherhoods had always barred black workers. But in the Firemen and Trainmen, southern members' outpouring of racist invective against black railwaymen would set these unions on a campaign for a new kind of segregation in the railroad industry—the complete elimination of all African Americans from the running trades. As with the brotherhoods' public pronouncements on immigration, racial occupational eviction would also be a process of union building. Nativism and racism stood as the new unionism's dark side, framing politics and objectives well into the twentieth century. Broadly, the cultural developments of the 1890s and early 1900s reshaped the brotherhoods. They became less fraternal and more secular, and the moralistic rhetoric of manhood waned as members and their wives explored the possibilities and problems of newer kinds of gender identity. They pursued "businesslike" approaches to union matters, as well as a more "hardheaded" approach to unionism pursued by a leadership chastened by the conflicts of the late 1880s and 1890s. Closer in their relationship to the national state than they had ever been before, they stood poised to work within the arbitrative system created by the Erdman Act and to win through political lobbying protective measures unobtainable through collective bargaining.

6

Craft Industrialism and the Arbitration System

"Beginning in 1898 a distinctly new period emerged," wrote Selig Perlman in the *History of Labour in the United States*.[1] With the excitement and novelty of the War of 1898 wearing off, the hardships and conflicts of the 1890s depression fading from memory, and a new century a little over a year away, Americans at the time had the feeling that the United States indeed was entering a new era. Careful observers also might have noticed other, perhaps less obvious, developments. Beginning with the war and continuing afterward, the national state, which had its modern origins in the Civil War, began a process of steady expansion in its size and administrative capacities as governmental bureaucracies grew and as the federal budget rose.[2] In the private sector, 1898 marked the quickening of the great merger movement as corporate leaders moved to consolidate industry. By 1904, over 1,800 companies disappeared into larger consolidations over half of which absorbed over 40 percent of their respective industries.[3] The railroad industry went through its own merger wave, concentrating into seven large mega-systems controlling over two-thirds of the nation's mileage. Within a matter of years, the growth of big business would bring the intervention of the federal government into new areas of the economy and an expanded regulatory role on the railroads.[4] Together with the passage of the Erdman Act in 1898, these developments signaled the centralization of power in the United States and the reordering of state and society, both of which shaped railroad labor relations during the Progressive Era.

These changes also had an impact on the railroad brotherhoods and the broader trade union movement, creating propitious conditions for growth and innovation. Like the American Federation of Labor (AFL), which shot ahead in membership from 280,000 members in 1898 to over 1.6 million by 1904, the brotherhoods increased in size and strength, almost doubling their membership over the same period of time and breaking the 200,000 mark. And like the AFL, which had secured its dominant position in the union movement, the brotherhoods stood practically unchallenged for the representation of running-trades labor. Indeed, with the disintegration of inclusive unions like the Knights of Labor and American Railway Union in the 1890s, trade unionism would dominate the early twentieth-century labor movement.[5] In France, the early twentieth century brought a period of syndicalist agitation, the rise of industrial unionism, and increased strike activity on the railways. But in England the picture more closely resembled developments in the United States. Despite calls for reform ranging from federation to amalgamation to industrial unionism, an updated form of craft unionism remained the dominant orientation, although by 1913 the National Railway Union was aspiring to become an industrial union for all railwaymen.[6]

In the United States, the new unionism of the 1890s fed into the burgeoning of unionism beyond the running trades as shop-craft and miscellaneous groups of railroad labor organized occupationally based unions and struggled toward federated strength. Despite its weakness until the World War I period, the very fact of unionism in these traditionally difficult-to-organize categories reflected the wider boom in union growth of these years. Both the brotherhoods and the nonoperating unions shared a "businesslike" approach to the work of unionism, combined with a sense of optimism and organizational innovation characteristic of the new unionism. To be sure, important differences remained in the patterns of brotherhood and shop-craft unionism. Nevertheless, in the AFL-affiliated shop-craft unions and the brotherhoods, the new unionism broadened into what Perlman calls "craft industrialism."[7]

The changes taking place in the railroad industry and its relationship to the state placed a premium on broader forms of industrial action. Along with its mediation and arbitration provisions, the de facto recognition and legitimacy that the Erdman Act conferred on the brotherhoods created an "opportunity structure" in the first decades of the twentieth century that permitted them to pursue coordinated, inter-brotherhood campaigns—"concerted movements"—for improvements in wages and working conditions. With their expanding industrial action, they contributed to a rising pattern of class conflict that swept the nation after 1909. Moreover, when the Firemen and the Trainmen turned their growing industrial power on black railwaymen and demanded their removal, the brotherhoods took the mediation and arbitration system in a direction not envisioned by its framers. And when successive concerted movements yielded awards that failed to satisfy the brotherhoods—and, in fact, pressed the railroads between the anvil of rate regulation and the hammer of state-mandated arbitration of labor disputes—tensions and weaknesses in the system reached a crisis point.

A New Century and Changing Conditions of Work

The organizational and industrial innovations in the railroad brotherhoods had a basis in the working conditions of running-trades workers in the new century. With a rising volume of traffic brought by the return to economic prosperity—about an 80 percent increase between 1900 and 1910—railroad companies worked their men and machines longer and more intensively.[8] To more efficiently use equipment and labor, trains became longer and heavier. In 1893, a train carried an average of 184 tons; by 1911, that load had increased to 383 tons. Per trainman, tons carried per mile increased from 638,635 in 1893 to 1,146,133 in 1911; train miles run per man increased from 5,589 in 1893 to 5,764 in 1911. The resulting productivity gains translated into an overall increase in tons carried per mile from 93.5 million in 1893 to over 250 million by 1911.[9] Although initiated on many roads after 1897, heavier trains did not become the norm throughout the industry until after 1905. "Since that time," wrote railroad economist William Z. Ripley in 1918, "the results achieved have been little short of stupendous. . . . Only one-fourth more train mileage transported three-fourths more freight."[10]

Advances in technology permitted the more intensive use of men and machines. The introduction of heavy steel rails accounted for the greatest gains. First used on the Pennsylvania Railroad in the 1860s, steel quickly became the favored material to construct rails (despite its higher cost over iron). By 1880, almost 30 percent of the nation's trackage was equipped with steel rails, and by 1890 that figure rose to 80 percent. After the turn of the century, virtually every rail used in the United States was made out of steel. Steel rails contributed to railway operations in two ways: they lasted much longer and bore much heavier loads without breaking, permitting railroad management to introduce longer, heavier trains pulled by larger, more-powerful engines. Over the period from 1870 to 1910, freight-car capacity more than tripled and motive power more than doubled as larger engines equipped with automatic coal stokers and oil-burning capability replaced the old "American" type 4–4–0. Beginning in the 1890s, locomotives like the ten-wheeled 4–6–0, the 2–8–0 "Consolidation," and the 4–4–2 "Atlantic," and twelve-wheelers like the 4–6–2 "Pacific" and, in 1904, the truly mammoth 0–6–6–0 "Mallet" (essentially, two locomotives mounted under one enormous boiler, so long that it had to be "articulated," or pivoted, to negotiate curves), came to dominate motive power in passenger and freight service. Altogether these developments yielded total factor productivity increases of over 15 percent between 1900 and 1910, a trend that continued on to 1917.[11]

From the standpoint of running-trades workers, however, increased productivity meant more demanding work, longer hours, and an unsafe work environment. Larger and longer trains required greater skill from engineers, as they had to nurse their steam and handle their brakes with greater care. Heavily loaded trains had to be coaxed over hills and around curves, and long trains had to be carefully started and stopped to avoid damage to couplings and cars. For conductors, longer trains meant more cars to check before departure—trains could be upward of a mile in length—and more potential repairs to make en route. And the clerical work increased in direct proportion to the number of cars.[12] Automatic stokers and oil-burning locomotives, necessary to the operation of the larger engines, made the lives of firemen easier by reducing their physical labor. The large locomotives—"battleships" in running-trades parlance—were not always oil burners, however, nor were they always equipped with automatic stokers. Moreover, the automatic stoker was no guarantee of an easy run. It still took physical labor to shovel coal down out of the tender and into the mouth of the device, and awkward or large chunks of coal could easily jam the works. In such instances, it was back to the old-fashioned method of hand firing these "man-killers." In a 1914 arbitration hearing, fireman William Ralston testified to shoveling twenty-five to twenty-eight tons of coal on his regular run on the Denver & Rio Grande Railroad. "I have to lay off occasionally because the work is so severe. I simply cannot stand it," he said.[13]

For brakemen, the introduction of safety appliances like air brakes and automatic couplers made their jobs safer and easier but also allowed management to make up longer trains using fewer workers. A freight brakeman writing to the *Railroad Trainmen's Journal* in 1905 explained the impact of these technologies on his work: "Twenty years ago, a full train consisted of thirty-five loads; today a full train consists of from seventy to ninety loads, and at times as high as ninety-five loaded cars in one train. Does any one think that seventy or ninety cars can be handled with the same amount of safety that thirty-five can? I say no, despite the modern safety appliance. Those appliances make it possible to handle such trains, but where they increase safety in one way they increase danger in another."[14] Especially on passenger runs, train masters sent out trains with one rather than two brakemen. Now that the brakeman's agility and skill were no longer necessary, management put a higher premium on courteous service. Brakemen had traditionally assisted the conductor in caring for passengers but earned reputations for less than "gentlemanly" conduct. Thus, managers began to introduce "train porters," or "porter-brakemen," who might perform some braking duties but whose main responsibilities involved emptying cuspidors, cleaning seats, looking after soap, and so forth. The fact that management hired African American men in these service positions, at a lower wage, added a racial dimension to the resentment that white brakemen felt at their displacement.[15]

Railroaders' most consistent grievance, though, centered on excessive and irregular hours of labor, which increased in direct proportion to the volume of traffic. Heavier, longer trains moved more slowly than shorter, lighter trains, and there were more trains competing for relatively limited track. Existing trackage and terminals became congested, and the process of assembling trains and moving them over the lines took more time.[16] "With the increase in speed and tonnage, notwithstanding the increased capacity of our engines, we were compelled to crowd them to their utmost," stated an engineer in 1905. "We were relieved of the physical labor of looking after the condition of our engines, but the mental labor connected with running them and getting our trains over the road increased enormously. . . . The increase in mental strain is piled on top of a great increase in physical strain . . . We are now continuously in the harness." Frank Sargent put it bitingly before the Industrial Commission in 1901: "The way business is now on the railroads, men are doing 9 and 10 days a week."[17] As they put in more hours, running-trades workers recognized that their wages per mile declined, not to mention the impact on their health and families.[18] To be sure, employers sometimes were willing to pay overtime to keep heavy trainloads and the efficiencies that they represented. "This gives the men more compensation," wrote Ripley, "but it still leaves them with long hours in service. Their right to relief is undeniable."[19]

The cost to mind and body increased markedly after 1898, for accident rates soared in the first decade of the twentieth century. Most dramatically, the higher density of traffic raised the chances of collisions. Traffic density, which rose about 5 percent between 1897 and 1907, increased the casualty rate about 12 percent. Peaking in 1907, worker casualty rates from collisions more than doubled their 1896 levels. Because the numbers of miles traveled and workers employed rose over this period, the actual numbers killed and injured rose even more dramatically. In 1897, 164 trainmen and 53 passengers were killed nationally, whereas in 1907, 572 workers and 214 passengers lost their lives in collisions.[20] Derailments also increased alarmingly after 1897, peaking around 1912. Behind the upsurge was an unfortunate combination of heavier trains and insufficiently heavy or defective rails, despite the railroads' increasing expenditures on roadbed and structures per mile of track nearly 40 percent between the 1890s and 1920s. Although it did not attract much public interest, locomotive and rolling stock safety figured as another area of concern to running-trades workers. If not maintained and operated properly, boilers could explode spectacularly. Between 1905 and 1909, boiler explosions killed 265 workers and injured 3,536. Less spectacular were accidents resulting from emptying of locomotive ash pans. A task that required the fireman to crawl underneath the engine, ash-pan cleaning resulted in injury or death as a result of being scalding from steam or crushed by an engine prematurely moved.[21]

Increased take-home pay proved chimerical as the early twentieth century heralded a steadily increasing cost of living. The same economic recovery that delivered increased business to the railroads reversed the deflationary cycle that had plagued the U.S. economy since the end of the Civil War. Beginning around 1900, the cost of living rose about 3 percent annually; by 1916, the cost of living in the United States was almost 50 percent over what it had been in 1898. Largely due to the efforts of their unions, railwaymen enjoyed a 40 percent increase in their money wages from 1898 to 1915, but this gain did not keep pace with the rising cost of living.[22] Brotherhood men were aware that their real wages declined as they worked harder and longer hours. In the monthly journals after 1900, articles, editorials, and correspondence regularly appeared under such titles as "Increased Wages and Increased Living Expenses," "The Race Between Wages and the Cost of Living," and "Going Up."[23] Correspondents pointed out that railwaymen were subject to the rising cost of living on two fronts: supporting their families but also themselves when they were held away from home.[24] The pressure to make ends meet, others argued, drove running-trades workers to take on more and longer hours than was healthy or safe. "The cost of living in the last few years has increased very much faster than our rate of pay," wrote Henry M. Reece, an engineer from Raleigh, North Carolina, in 1905, "and very many of us are trying to keep up our standard of living by making more miles than ever before." Writing a year later, a Montana engineer expressed his frustration: "Instead of patting the B. of L. E. on the back for being conservative, I say: 'Give us a little more pay and let us share a little of the prosperity that the bond-clippers are enjoying, for no engineer with ordinary intelligence will believe that by working eighteen or twenty hours a day pulling an overloaded freight train over the division, he is enjoying very remarkable prosperity.'"[25]

Members of the Firemen and Trainmen based in the South had another complaint: the presence of African Americans in their ranks. White brakemen and firemen had long resented their black counterparts, blaming them for a host of problems, including the organizational weakness of their unions in the region.[26] With their unions unable to protect them, white firemen and brakemen in the South endured harsher working conditions and lower wages than did white railroaders in other parts of the country. A southern delegate to the Firemen's 1896 convention complained, "Since the time of hiring [black] firemen the white fireman is constantly lectured and suspended; if he kicks, he is sent to some branch road at starvation wages, or entirely laid off."[27] Such treatment, combined with the mere presence of black brakemen and firemen, stood at odds with the efforts of brotherhood men to elevate the dignity of their crafts and led southern members of these unions to believe that they could not work and live as respectable white men. Heaping abuse on black railwaymen and African Americans generally, brotherhood men denounced their mental aptitude, morals, diligence, and bravery while insisting that white workers were in better every way.[28] In mild tones, given the nature of the discourse, BLF second vice grand master Timothy Shea placed the matter within the framework of the brotherhoods' traditional approach to railroad labor relations: "Whatever he can do and endure the white man can do . . . better. . . . If the railroad officials of the South . . . will make the position of locomotive fireman one for the white man exclusively . . . they will not have any difficulty in employing men . . . who are competent, capable and in every way . . . a profit to the company who employs him."[29]

Developments within and beyond the railroad industry influenced the timing of southern BLF and BRT members' complaints. In the last decade of the nineteenth and first decade of the twentieth centuries, changes in the railroad labor market considerably lengthened the time that firemen and brakemen spent before promotion to engineer or conductor. Whereas during the railroad expansion of the 1880s and early 1890s a fireman in the West might expect to advance to the engineer's side in little over a year's time, by the early twentieth century such short promotional periods were things of the past. A 1917 study showed that firemen on the Southern Pacific Railroad averaged eleven and one-quarter years, and many firemen on New England roads had been on locomotives since 1902 or earlier without taking examinations for positions as locomotive engineers. Testifying before arbitrators in 1914, Henry Rose of Escanaba, Michigan, believed that he had no hope of becoming an engineer within thirty or forty years' time.[30] Exacerbating the situation, southern railroads demanded greater effort from their white employees and had a readily available labor supply in lower-cost black workers with which to respond to increases in traffic.[31] Set against the dramatic rise in racial hatred and violence that swept the South at the turn of the century, white railwaymen's resentment found ready affirmation in the region-wide political disfranchisement and economic subordination of African Americans. In the context of ethnic nationalism and nativism at the turn of the century, African Americans appeared as a threat to the white labor community. "In the South," the *Railroad Brakemen's Journal* concluded ominously, "negro labor menaces white labor."[32]

The combination of corporate concentration, worsening working conditions, eroding cost of living, and the presence of black railwaymen led many brotherhood men to believe that their standing as craftsmen, citizens, and, indeed, as men was tenuous. In the early years of the twentieth century, they called on their unions to act.

Craft Industrialism, Collective Bargaining, and the Politics of Arbitration

The Erdman Act provided concrete means for the adjusting of labor disputes short of strikes, but at bottom the system operated on the assumption that workers and employers in the industry would conduct their relations through institutional representatives in the course of collective bargaining. In a series of concerted movements and arbitration rounds between 1899 and 1916, the brotherhoods and the railroads worked out the organizational, procedural, and institutional terms of the collective bargaining model that would define railroad labor relations until the World War I era.

Initially, though, it looked as if the Erdman Act would be doomed to a short life, for the first attempt to use its mediation provisions failed. In September 1898, the Brotherhood of Railroad Trainmen attempted to win wage increases and a ten-hour day from the railroads operating out of Pittsburgh. In June 1899, BRT chief Patrick H. Morrissey requested the mediatory efforts of ICC chair Martin A. Knapp and commissioner of labor Carroll D. Wright under the provisions of the Erdman Act. Pennsylvania Railroad president A. J. Cassatt, speaking for the railroads, declined mediation and arbitration, however, arguing that to consent to these procedures would be to abdicate the "vital prerogative of determining what [the company] can afford to employ its employees, and transfers that prerogative to a special transient committee of three arbitrators." Thus, although the BRT signaled its support of federal mediation and arbitration, Cassatt, viewing the matter as a test case, signaled that an important segment of railroad management had not accepted the principles of the act.[33] The incident also contained a number of elements that would be present in later mediation and arbitration cases, with one important difference: which party held the upper hand. Brotherhood leaders had witnessed the relationship between arbitration and economic power during the Pullman strike (the Pullman Company's refusal to arbitrate resided in its superior position relative to the strikers), and the railroads' rejection of mediation in 1899 reminded them of that lesson.[34] Nevertheless, the brotherhoods supported the act as much for its validation of collective bargaining as for the principle of arbitration, even if it had yet to be put into operation. Over the next several years, although it would be purely voluntary, that bargaining regime would work to the brotherhoods' advantage.

The system federation movement of the 1890s offered the brotherhoods a path to power. With the dissolution of the Federation of American Railway Employees in early 1900, the four brotherhoods, along with the Order of Railway Telegraphers, returned to system federation on the Cedar Rapids model in mid-1901. Like the Cedar Rapids Plan, brotherhood lodges on a given railroad system were to organize a federated, system-wide board of adjustment. The boards of adjustment consolidated the handling of grievances at the system level but centralized the calling of strikes with the chiefs of the federated organizations.[35] A key feature of federation was its correspondence in size and function to the reorganized railroad systems of the early twentieth century. Beginning with the Interstate Commerce Commission's grouping of the railroads on a regional basis, and followed by the organization and reorganization of the General Managers' Association, brotherhood men had observed the trend toward consolidation and centralization of power in the railroad industry. System federation facilitated the efficient handling of labor relations on the wider basis that the industry demanded. "It is intended to combine the good judgment of the men selected by the men on a system as their committeemen and representatives, as well as the judgment of the men who are entrusted with the administration of the affairs of the several organizations," wrote Edgar E. Clark in a 1901 editorial. "On the other hand, [it] is intended to build up strength for the organizations."[36]

Although Clark's reassuring tone aimed at stilling management worries about federation, it was not simply spin, for it reflected a vision of orderly railroad labor relations. *Railroad Trainmen's Journal* editor D. L. Cease offered a comprehensive statement of this vision, identifying the links among size, federation, and collective bargaining. He began by arguing that the fundamental purpose of trade unionism was to negotiate trade agreements or labor contracts. Given the scale of operations and degree of concentration in the railroad industry, collective agreements arrived at through collective bargaining was the only practical means of organizing labor relations. "Where such bargaining is the rule, stability of business is assured," he continued, because employees "organized into responsible associations" observed "the terms of the contract." Cease also pointed out that the "joint contract provides a way for the arbitration of disputed questions." System federation, he concluded, facilitated "in its most effective sense the plan of collective bargaining." He also added that it stood for industrial democracy, "the idea of representative government carried into everyday business." The idea's success depended, however, "on the responsibility and readiness of both parties to carry out the terms of the contract." Perhaps it was for these reasons that a contributor to the industry journal *Railway Age*, under the signature "General Manager," saw "no reason for opposing the proposed federation; on the contrary, I feel that it had better be encouraged."[37]

Railwaymen did not need management's encouragement, for system federations of brotherhood and shop-craft unions grew in number over the first decade of the twentieth century. By 1914, close to seventy system federations had been organized, each requiring a two-thirds membership vote.[38] Federation among the shop crafts had common origins with the running trades (in the ferment of the late 1880s and early 1890s) but ran directly through the Knights of Labor and the American Railway Union in railroad repair shops, as well as manufacturing establishments like Pullman's car-building works. Those shop-craft unions that survived the Pullman strike carried on the federation principle, organizing shop-craft federations on the Southern Railway system in 1908 and on the network of lines controlled by financier Edward H. Harriman in 1910. With its standard set of rules and wages, the Southern Railway federation set the model for those that followed, and moved the shop crafts to petition the AFL for the formation of a Railway Department. Chartered in 1909, the Railway Employees' Department became the expression of shop-craft industrialism. But due to divisions within the shops' ethnically and occupationally divided workforce, as well as intransigent corporate opposition, it never achieved the strength or industrial relations stability of the brotherhoods' system federations (or the regional associations that grew out of them).[39]

Driving the brotherhoods' brand of craft industrialism was the need to win wage advances to keep pace with the rising cost of living, as well as the difficulty that system federations encountered when pressing for wage advances and improvements in working conditions. The problem manifested in the federations' inability to standardize wages and working conditions, which varied tremendously across the nation. The situation reflected management's tenacious desire to maintain flexibility in determining wages and work rules. Standardization had been a principal objective of the brotherhoods since the 1880s, for it eliminated the ability of employers to deal with different groups of workers individually, paying each group as little as possible. Standardization also worked as a lever to gain wage increases, as the brotherhoods brought low-wage regions to the level of higher-wage regions. System federation promised to iron out differences within railroad systems, but it could not effectively counter the argument that a railroad could not pay wages higher than (or lower hours below) those of its competitors.

Accordingly, in June 1902 the Conductors and Trainmen organized the Western Association of General Committees along the lines of the ICC-designated western territory, making an integrated "super" committee of the unions' general chairs from each system. In January 1903, the association simultaneously presented demands, almost unanimously approved by rank-and-file vote, for higher wages, a shorter workday, and changes in work rules for the southwestern railroad systems operating out of St. Louis. When management balked at the prospect of negotiating on such a scale, the unions conducted strike votes. With the prospect of a regional strike on their hands, managers returned to the bargaining table and arrived at a compromise agreement, resulting in standardized wage schedules but no reduction of the working day. With the success of the Western Association, the two unions formed southern and eastern associations, corresponding to the geographical regions into which the ICC grouped the nation's railroads.[40]

Building on the system federations, the high-profile concerted movements that followed the Western Association's effort demonstrated a pattern of outwardly expanding collective action among the brotherhoods; they increasingly coordinated their wage and rules demands and presented them across wider sections of the industry and nation. The Brotherhood of Locomotive Engineers and Brotherhood of Locomotive Firemen separately followed the ORC/BRT example; due to the old jurisdictional conflicts that had divided them since the 1880s, however, they did not achieve the same kind of inter-brotherhood unity until 1913. Nevertheless, the Engineers' 1906 western concerted movement yielded higher, more standard wages, and the Firemen pursued concerted action with similar results after it organized its own regional associations in 1908. Although their craft industrialism differed in form, the brotherhoods' post-1902 wage campaigns suggest a continuity of purpose with the 1890s American Railway Union.[41]

The brotherhoods' concerted movements also had the effect of organizing railroad managers, who paralleled the employees' actions by forming regional bureaus. In 1902, the ORC/BRT Western Association's coordinated approach took managers by surprise, but when the Engineers presented the western railroads with uniform demands in 1906, they encountered an inter-railroad Conference Committee of Managers on the other side of the table.[42] And in 1907, when the Conductors and Trainmen organized their second concerted movement, presenting to the western railroads joint demands for a 15 percent wage increase and an eight-hour day, they encountered a Committee of Managers representing forty-two railroads prepared to submit the case to federal mediation. The case did go to mediation (conducted by Knapp and Wright's successor at the Bureau of Labor, Charles P. Neill, per Erdman Act procedure) after the unions had conducted strike votes. It was the first time since 1899 that either union or management had asked for state intervention, but this time it was the companies that made the request. The settlement favored the unions, but the affair signaled a change in railroad labor relations and a corresponding shift in attitude on the part of the railroads toward arbitrated settlement of labor disputes.[43]

From 1907 onward, the railroad brotherhoods mounted a succession of regionally based concerted movements, moving from west to east over time. Overall, between 1907 and 1913 there were sixty-one requests for assistance under the Erdman Act, the majority coming from management. Coming out of these proceedings, the brotherhoods won mediation and arbitration settlements that resulted in pay increases and improvements in work rules.[44]

Brotherhood successes resulted in part from their growing astuteness in dealing with railroad management and the federal government. Starting with the hard bargaining of their concerted movements, backing up demands with overwhelming strike votes if management refused to deal, the brotherhoods forced the convening of arbitration hearings at which they confronted arbitration panels with sophisticated arguments based on detailed research. In its 1912 arbitration with the eastern railroads, the BLE presented over eighty exhibits, including statements and statistical tables, blueprints and diagrams, rule books, timetables, and official bulletins.[45] They employed scholarly experts like Frank J. Warne, special agent for the U.S. Census Bureau and instructor at the University of Pennsylvania, and economist William Jett Lauck, trained by John R. Commons at the University of Wisconsin. In a 1913 arbitration case involving the ORC, the BRT, and a number of eastern railroads, Warne detailed figures relating to the increased volume of traffic, the financial condition of the railroads, injuries to trainmen, and the rising cost of living. The cost of Lauck's investigation and testimony for the Firemen in their 1913 arbitration ran upward of eighteen thousand dollars.[46]

The structure and practice of the arbitration proceedings exerted a seemingly inexorable upward pressure on wages and wage-related rules. In the first place, arbitration panels tended to arrive at compromise awards, "splitting the difference" between what the unions demanded and what management was prepared to concede. The resulting awards satisfied neither party entirely yet demonstrated an upward pattern over time. This tendency resulted in part from brotherhood demands for standardization. After the Western Association won its favorable settlement in 1907, eastern conductors won the same results in 1910. The maintenance of wage differentials among the various running trades, a standard brotherhood demand, also ratcheted wages up over time. When the eastern conductors and trainmen won their increase in 1910, eastern firemen and engineers demanded a wage increase to restore the differential that had been narrowed as a result of the conductor-trainmen award. And when eastern engineers won restoration of their differential in 1912, western engineers demanded the same in 1913. These arbitration processes "came together in a kind of double whiplash against the companies," according to Karen Orren.[47]

The pattern of government-sponsored mediation and arbitration suggested a shifting balance of power between union and management, one created by government intervention through arbitration. The circumstances of the post-Pullman era created an "opportunity structure" for the brotherhoods as it fostered a movement away from labor-management relations regulated by the courts and toward a regime of free collective bargaining defined by the federal legislature in the Erdman Act. By 1912, however, the situation also highlighted a problem in the state's arbitration machinery: its lack of connection to rate regulation, the other major form of government involvement in the railroad industry.[48]

Arbitration and Racial Occupational Eviction

Before tensions in the arbitration system fully appeared, the Brotherhood of Locomotive Firemen and Enginemen and the Brotherhood of Railroad Trainmen deployed their bargaining strength in an attempt to remove black firemen and brakemen from the running trades. Their actions against black railwaymen coincided with the reconstruction of railroad labor relations, the return to economic prosperity, and the rise in racial violence in the South at the turn of the century. Over the 1890s, brotherhood men moved beyond rhetorical gestures in the pages of their monthly journals to instances of violence against black running-trades workers and sporadic "race" strikes.[49] The increasingly hostile actions of southern brotherhood men fed into the federation movement as firemen and brakemen argued for greater inter-brotherhood unity to remove black workers. This racist agenda contributed to hard feelings, though, as the Engineers resisted the federation impulse and responded with only bland statements of support on the "race question."[50]

Dear as the race question was to southern brotherhood men, and despite the sympathy of national brotherhood leaders and members, it remained principally a southern issue in the BLF and BRT, subordinate to the national standardization of wages, hours, and work rules. It was also a question that did not lend itself to inter-brotherhood concerted action, as engineers and conductors did not share the concerns of their junior partners on this issue. Lastly, the Firemen and Trainmen in the South confronted companies with the will and resources to resist their demands. By 1907, however, the balance of power between the railroad corporations and the railroad brotherhoods had begun to shift. Concerted wage movements had demonstrated the efficacy of bargaining backed up by strike votes. The Firemen, in particular, had found that regionally coordinated action delivered results, even if they conducted it independently of the BLE. The success of western concerted movements encouraged the formation of a Southern Association of General Committees of the BRT and ORC in 1905 and a similar association of Firemen committees in 1908.[51] Developments on the Georgia Railroad drew the Firemen into the first nationally significant "race" strike and federal arbitration in 1909.

In April 1909, a long-simmering conflict between the Georgia Railroad and its white firemen burst into the open when management in the Atlanta yards replaced ten white assistant hostlers—workers who shifted engines around the yards—on the extra list with black workers. At issue was the use of seniority, which management had been observing strictly. Seniority systems had been one of the brotherhoods' key achievements during the 1880s, credited with curbing employer favoritism and discrimination; in a racially stratified labor force, however, black firemen, who were barred from advancing to engineer, accumulated seniority at the top of the firemen's list. Lower-paid, "non-promotable" black firemen took the most lucrative runs—the most expensive from the company's perspective—leaving younger white firemen "to take what is left by the negro," in the words of Firemen second vice president

Eugene A. Ball. Thus, the white strikers demanded the reinstatement of the displaced hostlers and the introduction of a dual seniority system that would allow "the oldest white fireman to stand first for passenger engines or runs."[52] The ensuing strike, marked by mob violence against trains manned by black firemen, brought the railroad to a halt and an appeal for federal mediation by the company. Arriving in Atlanta, Charles P. Neill encountered "a bitter race issue" that he described as "delicate and full of serious menace." With "extreme caution," lest the situation escalate into a full-blown race riot, he and Knapp mediated the dispute but without success.[53]

The ensuing arbitration did not yield the results that the union hoped for. During the proceedings, the Firemen's predictable and racist arguments for the removal of black firemen followed two lines: African Americans were not competent to work as firemen and therefore represented a threat to public safety, and the company's employment practices denied brotherhood firemen their rights as white men. Not only did the company's seniority policy keep the white firemen from earning "white men's wages," claimed the union, but it kept them from working in a "white man's job" and supporting their families at a level appropriate for their race. For its part, in racist and paternalist terms, the railroad's management testified to its confidence in the black employees: black men *were* suited to the semiskilled work of firing, and in fact, due to their physical strength and ability to stand high temperatures, were *better* suited than white men to the task of feeding the larger locomotives. Moreover, the general manager affirmed the company's economic stake in employing black workers as a lever to keep white wages down.[54] After six days of testimony, the three-member arbitration board ruled that the railroad could continue to employ black firemen and use its existing seniority system but had to pay blacks the same wages as whites.[55] Clinging to their racist logic and putting a positive spin on the outcome, Firemen officials reasoned that the stipulation requiring equal pay for black and white firemen would eliminate the financial incentive for employing African Americans. As it turned out, they were wrong.[56]

The Georgia "race" strike and arbitration differed from the brotherhoods' concerted movements of the era: it involved matters of region, race, and corporate power. It also developed spontaneously, arising out of the grievances of union members on a regional railroad, and involved less than one hundred workers. In contrast to the wage movements, which were meticulously planned "offensive" actions on a large scale, the Georgia strike was "defensive," a response to a managerial action. The national union did not initiate the strike, but rather had to decide whether to support the walkout. It did, viewing it as an opportunity to set a precedent for the rest of the region. The strike differed also in that it generated significant local support for the white firemen. Following close on the Atlanta race riot of 1906, it apparently did not take much for whites across northern Georgia to see the "injustice" of the company's policies "in a white man's country." For the arbitration board, the union's demands encroached on managerial prerogative. To the firemen's claim of black workers' incompetence, board member Hilary A. Herbert, former Alabama congressman and ex-secretary of the navy, stressed the lack of evidence. He also directly addressed the racial issue, accusing the union of attempting to "come down among us to stir up strife between the races." As a racial moderate, Herbert rejected the Firemen's white-supremacist claims: "If the negro is not competent to do the duties of fireman under the immediate supervision of a white engineer, what *is* he fit for?"[57] The Georgia strike demonstrated the unreliability of the strike as a weapon for the eviction of black railwaymen. It also established that arbitrators on federal boards were unlikely to agree with the brotherhoods' racist arguments. If anything, the board's equal-pay decision stood as a victory for the black firemen.

The Georgia strike marked the opening round of a longer-term struggle between white firemen and brakemen and southern railroads over the employment of black workers. In January 1911, management on the Cincinnati, New Orleans and Texas Pacific Railroad, the "Queen & Crescent," provoked a conflict—inadvertently or not—by assigning three black firemen, the most senior in the service, to the railroad's operating district running between Chattanooga and Oakdale, Tennessee. At issue were the same conflicting interpretations of seniority that had animated the Georgia strike. The Queen & Crescent's vice president interpreted it literally; to the road's white firemen, who interpreted "fireman" to mean "white" men eligible for promotion, management's action represented a "departure from all past practice, as well as a direct violation" of an existing agreement—and thus an attack on brotherhood unionism. In a unanimous vote of local Firemen lodges, 250 white firemen and about 100 white engineers struck on March 9, 1911. The Firemen played on the same themes that it had in Georgia in 1909. It explained the strike as an act self-defense, "due to the action of that company in subordinating white firemen to negro firemen, placing the latter on preferred runs and gradually displacing their white firemen with negroes." Over the course of the three-week work stoppage, strikers and sympathizers brought the railroad to a halt. The rural white communities along the division in Tennessee and Kentucky supported the strikers, shot at locomotive cabs along the route, and attacked train crews—white and black—who dared violate the strike.[58]

As with the Georgia strike, the Queen & Crescent strike went to arbitration. The Firemen demanded both the removal of black firemen from preferred runs and the acceptance of an amendment to the existing agreement stipulating that firemen "not eligible to become . . . engineers shall not be retained." Such a proposal would result in the dismissal of all black firemen. Management, however, would not accept either proposal. Federal arbitrators attempted a compromise, hoping to effect a means of managing this contentious issue through contractual stipulations defining the racial boundaries of employment. The percentage of black firemen would not exceed the percentage as of January 1, 1911, and black firemen would not be assigned to more than one-half of the passenger or preferred freight runs. The settlement did not make either party happy, but the union recognized that these two clauses would have the effect of contractually limiting the employment of black firemen.[59] In contrast to the Georgia strike decision, the Queen & Crescent award was detrimental to black railroaders, for it pointed the way toward their eventual removal.

The Firemen and the Trainmen concluded that contractual confinement of black railwaymen through collective bargaining rather than reactive "hate" strikes promised the most effective means for their eviction. These unions had good reason to reach this conclusion for, apart from the uneven results of arbitration, they had demonstrated that their regional concerted movements delivered results. Thus, in 1910 the Brotherhood of Railroad Trainmen launched a concerted movement against the Southern Railroad Association, the largest industry association in the South at the time, composed of a dozen key southern roads. The resulting agreement eliminated differences in pay scales between white and black workers and froze the percentage of black brakemen and yardmen at the percentage prevailing on January 1, 1910. An additional feature, barring the future promotion of black workers to positions as yardmen, promised to eliminate black workers from the yards over time. As black men in those jobs retired, they were to be replaced by "brakemen"—that is, white men.[60]

The Firemen paid attention to the Trainmen's negotiations and saw in their results a means of dealing with their own problems on southern railroads. Even as the Queen & Crescent strike wound down, the Firemen undertook concerted action against the Southern Railroad Association, demanding the reduction of black firemen to 30 percent of the firing workforce, in addition to pay increases and work-rule revisions. As with their concerted movements in other regions, they backed up their demands with an awesome strike vote. The controversy went to federal mediation. The arbitrators established separate seniority lists for blacks and whites and fixed the percentage of black firemen that could be employed on each of the Southern Railroad Association's operating divisions. For the overall system, the average maximum ratio of black to white firemen was set at 33 percent for passenger runs and 44 percent for freight runs. On divisions where the percentage of black firemen exceeded 50 percent, they were removed from preferred runs and whites were promoted in their place. The award also fixed a 30 percent differential between the wages of white and black firemen.[61]

Black firemen and brakemen did not acquiesce in their occupational eviction, as Eric Arnesen has shown. Over the course of the 1910s, groups of black railway workers attempted litigation against the Southern Railroad, contesting the contractual arrangements that limited their employment. Also during that decade, largely in response to the actions of the white brotherhoods, they organized local and regionally based unions, including the Colored Trainmen of America, the Colored Association of Railroad Employees, and the Interstate Association of Negro Trainmen. This last organization maintained chapters in over a dozen states and worked toward the creation of standard working conditions, uniform wage scales, and an end to racial discrimination against black railwaymen. It emphasized racial uplift, not class conflict, as its primary focus. The Railway Men's Benevolent Industrial Association (RMBIA), founded in 1915, distinguished itself in its goal of establishing a single federation of black railroaders. The RMBIA in particular lobbied politicians for legislation prohibiting discriminatory contracts, and initiated lawsuits over wages, job security, and working conditions. The RMBIA stood very much at odds with the white brotherhoods in its fight for black equality in railroad employment. It also stood at a serious disadvantage: it did not possess the kind of bargaining power or have the kind of access to the state, either through lobbying or arbitration, as did the brotherhoods.[62]

The state proved an ambiguous presence in the relationships among black and white workers and their employers, even as it contributed to the entrenchment of racial segregation in the South. Set up to contain labor conflict, it was not institutionally equipped to effectively handle questions of racial discrimination. It sided neither wholly with unions nor management. The decisions resulting from arbitration reflected the ad hoc nature of arbitration boards under the Erdman Act, yet over time they worked to the disadvantage of black railwaymen. The lesson for the Firemen and Trainmen at this point in their histories was that they could not depend on arbitration boards; rather, they had to rely on their own bargaining strength for the contractual eviction of black workers. From 1910 onward, the course of arbitration in their concerted movements confirmed this lesson.

Breakdown of the Arbitration System

From 1907 through 1915, brotherhood concerted movements involved the state more consistently and undeviatingly in railroad labor relations. Over that period of time, brotherhood leaders confronted a dilemma concerning the role of the state in the operation and regulation of railroad collective bargaining. On the one hand, by the early 1890s they had come to understand their inability to extend the sphere of collective bargaining, and so they turned to the state when the possibility of legislated mediation and arbitration arose. On the other hand, they were aware that in seeking such aid they rendered themselves vulnerable to a power over which they had little control. By 1915, circumstances would lead them to reject the state's arbitral role, which led to the breakdown of the arbitration system. Of the factors straining the system, such as rising living costs and the brotherhoods' growing power, it was the increasing federal regulation of railroad rates, the structural inadequacies of the arbitration process, and the disconnect between rate regulation and wage setting that posed the most acute problems.[63]

When the federal government first intervened in the railroad industry in 1887, it created the Interstate Commerce Commission and granted it limited powers of rate regulation but no authority over wage issues. The separation of commerce and labor into two areas of public policy became institutionalized with the passage of the arbitration statutes, first in 1888 and then again in 1898 and in 1913. The problems that this separation created became apparent after passage of the Hepburn Act in 1906. The commission's expanded regulatory capacity amplified the tendencies inherent in its case-by-case procedure, which failed to take into account labor costs and was inherently biased toward lower rates. In fact, shippers with favorable rates did not appeal to the commission. The Mann-Elkins Act of 1910 contributed to this pattern by requiring a waiting period for ICC investigation and hearings. The 1910 Eastern Freight case dramatically revealed both this dynamic as well as the ICC's susceptibility to shippers' pressure to keep rates down. In that case, and the ones that followed in 1914 and 1915, the railroads jointly sought rate increases on the grounds that labor costs had outstripped their ability to pay for improvements necessary to handle the rising volume of freight. In the hearing's adversarial setting, however, the burden of proof was on them. After taking in the argument of Louis D. Brandies, the progressive lawyer for the shippers, that labor costs could be reduced through scientific management, the commission denied the railroads' request. Thus, by 1910 the railroads were finding themselves squeezed between the ICC's downward pressure on rates and arbitration boards' upward pressure on labor costs.[64]

The ORC/BRT 1910 concerted movement on the eastern railroads proved a turning point in the course of arbitration politics. Up to then, the brotherhoods had concentrated on the ICC western region, which had historically been characterized by a relative undersupply of labor. There they had succeeded in standardizing and raising wages and, in many cases, shortening hours. In late 1909, the Conductors and Trainmen tackled the ICC eastern region through their Eastern Association. Relatively stronger than their western counterparts yet hemmed in on rates by the ICC, the eastern railroads refused to participate in joint negotiations. Undeterred, the two unions focused on the Baltimore & Ohio (B&O) Railroad as the one most likely to settle on favorable terms, which it did. They then proceeded to pick off the remaining railroads one at a time, threatening to strike unless the B&O settlement was accepted as the basis for an agreement. When the two brotherhoods got to the New York Central Railroad, management made a variety of arbitration proposals, including mediation and arbitration, both under the Erdman Act as well as outside of its framework. The unions refused these offers but finally agreed to submit the dispute to two private arbitrators (outside the Erdman Act framework). The arbitrators, Edgar E. Clark and Patrick H. Morrissey, were both former brotherhood chiefs (Clark was now an ICC member), and, in the brotherhoods' view, they issued a model statement.[65]

The brotherhoods and management responded differently to the award. On the one hand, unsurprisingly, Clark and Morrissey accepted the unions' arguments for standardization, shorter hours, and wage increases to keep pace with the cost of living. The resulting "Clark-Morrissey" award followed the contours of the B&O settlement in standardizing eastern wage rates and overtime pay for conductors and brakemen. In the view of the ORC and BRT, Clark and Morrissey—as former brotherhood men and experienced railroaders—had handed down an award so well worded that it was held up as a model for future arbitration settlements.[66] On the other hand, railroad management came to the conclusion that the arbitration system needed overhauling. Frederic A. Delano, president of the Wabash Railroad, spoke for the industry in a series of 1911 editorials in the *Railway Age Gazette*. He considered the complex interplay among rate making, wage paying, and dividend earning too important to be adjudicated by ad hoc panels in which the deciding voted essentially rested with the third, presumably neutral, arbitrator, who did not necessarily know anything about railroading. He proposed a permanent arbitration commission, staffed by specialists, with the authority to compel arbitration and to enforce awards. Moreover, Delano and other railway managers wanted an arbitration system that would institutionally link the issues of wages and freight rates.[67]

Delano's criticisms of the Erdman Act arbitration system and his calls for a permanent commission indicated that a significant shift had occurred in the attitudes of railroad management toward state involvement in labor relations and arbitration procedures. Up to 1902 or so, management had favored voluntary labor relations. Its most notable contribution to the debate over the Erdman bill, for example, had been a studied silence. Prior to passage of the Erdman and Hepburn acts, managers had been confident in their ability to meet and resist, if not defeat, organized labor's demands, secure in the knowledge that judicial regulation of labor relations limited unions' ability to wield collective action. When they had to concede wage gains and work-rule revisions, freedom to set rates enabled them to cover higher labor costs. By 1910, however, that situation had changed entirely. Legislative governance of railroad labor relations cleared the way for free collective bargaining, and expanded regulation of railroad commerce constrained managers' ability to meet higher costs.[68] In fact, according to a 1912 *Railway Age Gazette* poll, a majority of railway managers favored a permanent wage commission for the setting of wages and resolving of disputes. In short, the Hepburn and Mann-Elkins acts, as much as brotherhood power, pushed the railroads to accept state regulation of labor relations.[69] For their part, the brotherhoods' views on state involvement also shifted, but in the opposite direction. They had consistently disavowed strikes and repeatedly insisted on arbitration as the best means of resolving labor disputes. Although happy with the shelter from judicial regulation cleared by the Erdman Act, they began to resist arbitration when it conflicted with their bargaining power.[70]

By late 1911, the once-cordial relations between the brotherhoods and the railroads were becoming strained.[71] Labor–management tensions burst into the open as a result of the Engineers' 1912 eastern concerted movement. In that confrontation, the BLE encountered a group of railroads even more determined to resist their demands than had been the case with the ORC/BRT movement the previous year. But unlike the 1910 movement, the eastern railroads had organized into a general managers' association and collectively rebuffed the union. With both sides at an impasse, Knapp and Neill, in a move that departed from Erdman Act procedure, fashioned an agreement to arbitrate under a specially constituted seven-member board, one each for management and union and five neutrals representing the public. Morrissey, who had left the BRT in 1909, represented the union.[72]

The ensuing award, which came as a crushing disappointment to the Engineers, granted only modest raises and concessions regarding overtime, and denied the union's request for standardization.[73] That was only for starters, for in the union's view the substance of the award paled in comparison to the obiter dictum of the board's majority on the state of railroad arbitration generally. In the report, the board criticized arbitration under the Erdman Act for the settlement of disputes by compromise awards rather than through adjudication; it also highlighted the failure of this approach to protect the public from strikes. Noting the calamitous impact of a general rail strike, the report called for a national wage commission endowed with the kind of authority over railroad unions that the ICC exercised over the railroad companies. Echoing Frederic Delano's proposals, it suggested that a permanent commission regulating wages, linked with the commerce commission regulating rates and supported by statistical expertise, would establish "just" pay scales that balanced the interests of the employees, the railroads, and the public. In short, the report proposed to bring two vital areas of public policy into harmony by calling for both an end to free collective bargaining and a regime of compulsory arbitration. Read this way, the report advocated an expansion of state power. It stood as a more "statist" expression of the new liberalism, closer to the recommendations of the Pullman Strike Commission than the more voluntary system erected by the Erdman Act.[74]

The Engineers and the other brotherhoods reacted with dismay, and Morrissey issued a vigorous dissenting report. He protested the board's use of ICC statistics to compare the wages of eastern engineers with their western counterparts and insisted that compromise, rather than seeking a "just" wage, remained the best basis for settling disputes. But he reserved his strongest objection for the proposed wage commission. He agreed on the need for greater expertise in settling railroad labor disputes, larger arbitration boards, and the ability of federal officials to invoke mediation. He admitted the possibility of a permanent commission to collect statistical information. To empower such a commission with the authority to fix wages, however, amounted to compulsory arbitration, which "would shackle the rights of a large group of our citizens."[75] Commenting on the award, D. L. Cease focused on the relationship between railroad workers' rights and the public interest, arguing that subordinating workers' right to strike to the public's right to transportation made "a perpetual sacrifice" of railroaders. In practical terms, argued Cease, a wage-fixing commission "would be influenced by public opinion to the extent that wage increases would be impossible." Here was organized railroad labor's shift in thinking on arbitration spelled out. Brotherhood men like Cease and Morrissey still approved of voluntary arbitration; they argued that the system as it stood under the Erdman Act functioned well enough to protect the public from railway strikes. Nevertheless, the supremacy of the public interest, which they had upheld during debate on the Erdman bill and articulated in various National Civic Federation conferences, was decidedly muted. When push came to shove, they were not willing to submit railwaymen's interests to the higher claims of citizenship responsibilities implicit in both the report and, indeed, the new liberalism.[76]

The growing strain on the Erdman Act system derailed it entirely in 1913 when another concerted movement, this time conducted by the Conductors and Trainmen against the eastern railroads, led to another critical moment. In that instance, neither the brotherhoods nor management were prepared to arbitrate under the Erdman law; when the carriers' refusal of union demands resulted in a 95 percent vote in favor of quitting work, a regional rail strike loomed. Only the personal intervention of National Civic Federation chair Seth Low and president Woodrow Wilson averted the crisis.[77] The ensuing round of conferences and committee work resulted in a new arbitration law, the Newlands Act of 1913, but the manner in which it came about was highly significant.

By 1913, the brotherhoods' concerted movements had merged with a larger and deeper-running pattern of class conflict that seemed to many observers a return to the tumultuous days of the late nineteenth century. Following the sharp depression of 1907–8, and gaining momentum after 1909, a succession of strikes wracked a number of industrial sectors. A series of flash points riveted the nation's attention: McKees Rocks in 1909–10, the 1909 "uprising of the twenty thousand" in New York City, the 1910 bombing of the *Los Angeles Times* building, massive strikes of shop-craft workers organized in system federations against the Illinois Central Railroad and other Harriman-controlled lines in 1911, and in 1912 the Lawrence textile strike, closely followed by the Patterson silk workers' strike and strikes of miners from West Virginia to Colorado. The frequency of strikes, the violence, the participation of largely un- and semiskilled immigrant workers, and the involvement of the Industrial Workers of the World in several of the actions suggested that a new class war was erupting, one that threatened to bring down the structure of reform legislation and industrial conciliation that progressive reformers had worked for since the turn of the century.[78] Against this backdrop, the brotherhoods' concerted movements appear relatively tame. Nevertheless, at such a moment the prospect of a rail strike that could paralyze the eastern United States seemed dauntingly imminent.

Working his personal connections with railroad executives and the brotherhood chiefs, Seth Low persuaded the two sides to stay their actions while jointly drafting a new arbitration bill. In February 1913, a committee composed of NCF secretary Ralph Easley, NCF industrial mediation department chair Marcus A. Marks, and Low, along with several railroad presidents and the brotherhood chiefs, set to work. By the end of March, they had hammered out a draft bill providing for a permanent three-member board of mediation and conciliation.[79]

The moment for President Wilson's intervention came when the draft bill ran into opposition from Samuel Gompers and the secretary of the federal government's newly created Department of Labor, William B. Wilson, an ex-miner and AFL official. To turn aside bureaucratic competition over whether the labor department or an independent board should have jurisdiction over railroad labor disputes, the president convened a conference at the White House on July 14, attended by Wilson, congressional figures, and representatives of the NCF, the railroads, and the brotherhoods. The conference took on an urgent quality as the unions' general chairs converged on New York City to ratify the strike vote. Agreement among the contending parties paved the way for passage of the bill in Congress as an emergency measure two days later.[80] Still, it took ratification of the strike vote and Seth Low's influence to get the managers to agree to arbitrate the matter on the brotherhoods' terms. The press interpreted the railroads' capitulation as a complete triumph for the brotherhoods.[81]

The passage of the Newlands Act stood at the intersection of class conflict, labor relations, reform politics, and presidential-party politics. The rail crisis demanded action from both the National Civic Federation and the newly elected President Wilson. For Low and Easley, who by 1912 had become identified with a reform-oriented segment of the business community and the conservative wing of the labor movement, the dispute offered an opportunity to demonstrate the NCF's relevance at a critical moment in the Progressive Era. For Woodrow Wilson, who had become president only as a result of the unusual four-way nature of the 1912 election, the standoff not only presented a chance to show his willingness to act decisively in matters of domestic social conflict, but also to balance the contending claims of organized labor while securing its support. And for the brotherhoods, which had been involved in both the drafting of the bill and the process of seeing it through to law (not to mention forcing the railroads to submit the matter to arbitration), the affair demonstrated their influence and power.[82]

With its moments of crisis, presidential intervention, and emergency legislation, the events of 1913 also portended things to come. As an augmentation of the Erdman Act, the Newlands Act represented an expansion of legislative authority in railroad labor relations, but its results were mixed. The new law established a permanent Board of Mediation and Conciliation, empowered it to offer mediation services on its own initiative, and allowed for arbitration panels of three or six members, chosen in the same manner as under the Erdman Act. Mediation and arbitration, however, remained voluntary. With the permanent board enabling the state to intervene directly in railway labor disputes of its own accord, the act's architects hoped that "rational" mediation could avert future strike situations and controversial arbitration awards. Both the railroads and the brotherhoods hoped that the board, composed of figures versed in railroading, would demonstrate consistency and render awards based on the merits of cases rather than expediency or compromise.[83] Yet, as an extension of the existing system, arbitration conducted by the board resulted largely in the same disappointing results as under the Erdman Act and growing frustration on the part of brotherhood leaders and their membership.

By 1914, inspired by the example of shop-craft workers in their system federations and their bitter, ongoing conflicts with railroad management, running-trades workers were becoming involved in growing numbers of official and unofficial all-grades strikes. In early 1914, for instance, engineers, firemen, conductors, brakemen, and telegraphers walked off the job on the Delaware & Hudson Railroad over the unfair dismissal of employees. In March 1914, trainmen on the Pennsylvania Railroad's Monongahela Division went out in an illegal "wildcat" strike over the dismissal of a yard brakeman. Later that spring, Pennsylvania Railroad crews struck in sympathy with shopmen near Altoona and wildcat coal miners near California, Pennsylvania. Although these strikes were episodic affairs, they revealed the growing frustration of railwaymen over the nonwage issues of authoritarian management and its arbitrary use of discipline. They also demonstrated a noteworthy degree of unity among the various grades of train-service workers. And of concern to national brotherhood leadership was the development of insurgent, industrially oriented unionism—the Brotherhood of Federated Railway Employees—led by a dissident Firemen organizer for the purpose of assisting carmen, shopmen, clerks, and other unorganized Pennsylvania Railroad workers. By the summer of 1914, socialists were reporting talk among train service workers of "One Big Union" and a united drive to win the eight-hour day.[84]

The rising sense of injustice and impatience fueled calls within the four brotherhoods for closer cooperation and greater unity of action. The quickening of system-level federation in 1914 and 1915 demonstrated this desire, but what some brotherhood men had in mind was nothing less than national-level federation.[85] Such a federation would "make a stronger organization and augment the force which will be required to deal with the greater force on the opposite side of the desk," in the words of one BRT member. Or, as brakeman William H. Mathewson put it in 1913, "Let the BRT, ORC, BLE, B of LF & E cast aside their class prejudice and stand or fall together."[86]

As system-level cooperation increased, a more important development in inter-brotherhood unity occurred at the national level between the Brotherhood of Locomotive Engineers and the Brotherhood of Locomotive Firemen, which had yet to conduct a joint concerted movement. Conflicts over the promotion of firemen, as well as competing jurisdictional claims over membership, had continued into the twentieth century, flaring into open fights during the depressions of 1893–97 and 1906–7. The issue came to a climax during a series of strikes between 1907 and 1908, when the Firemen amended its name to include "Enginemen" (BLFE) to make explicit its claim on locomotive engineers once they had advanced from the fireman's side of the cab. After it became clear that the two unions could achieve only limited gains on their own, and with a change of leadership in the BLFE in 1908, the situation began to improve. The two unions met in Chicago in 1912 to resolve jurisdictional boundaries and disagreements over promotion. The resulting agreement committed the two unions to the joint conduct of negotiations with management. In the conference's aftermath, expressions in support of national-level federation, and even amalgamation, became more common. In an important 1913 editorial, the *Locomotive Firemen and Enginemen's Magazine* came out in favor of national-level federation as the only effective means of confronting organized employers and their influence over the arbitration machinery. As a result of these improved relations and the groundswell of sentiment in favor of united action, the top leadership of the four brotherhoods worked out a formal plan of cooperation in 1915.[87]

The immediate result of the Engineers and Firemen's rapprochement was the mounting of their first-ever joint concerted movement in 1914–15 for wage increases, shorter hours, and time-and-a-half overtime in the western territory. To date the largest of its kind, involving over fifty-five thousand railway employees, the campaign did not go according to plan. When the two unions presented their demands to the Conference Committee of Railway Managers for the western roads, the carriers countered with proposals of their own and the abrogation of existing schedules. Negotiations broke down in July when the Board of Mediation and Conciliation failed to bring the two sides to an agreement. The brotherhoods conducted strike votes in early August 1914. With war exploding in Europe, only Woodrow Wilson's personal plea to the managers' patriotism and "regard for the public welfare to make whatever sacrifice is necessary to avert a national disaster" prevented the strike.[88]

The ensuing arbitration proved another disappointment for the brotherhoods. The proceedings, which lasted several months, resulted in an award that fell short of brotherhood demands; the two union representatives on the arbitration panel refused to sign it, calling the award "unreasonable, unwarranted, reactionary, repugnant, disastrous." In a lengthy public statement that revealed the racial coding of industrial politics, they disputed the panel's findings and disavowed arbitration, asserting that "if allowed to flourish [it] will rapidly place the American wage earner in a condition similar to that of the Mexican peon." The Firemen's William S. Carter put the matter in equally harsh terms: "After years of experience under arbitration, I reached the conclusion: That the labor question is not arbitrable if the workingmen hope to secure justice in the results. I have discovered that anything that pertains to workingmen's wages or working conditions is purely a class question, a question on which there is an alignment hard and fast. The fact of the matter is . . . that arbitrators are necessarily selected from the master class, which either takes its profits from the labor of others or else is employed by corporations in the capacity of officer or attorney."[89] In the end, in April 1915, the two unions had to accept the award, but the series of events confirmed the brotherhoods' opposition to arbitration.[90] The *International Socialist Review* sardonically commented that the arbitration panel "accomplished something that we have failed to accomplish for ourselves by hard work in the past twenty years, that is, you have solidified all of the railroad men in spirit and this has been our greatest failing in the past."[91] The episode also served as a dress rehearsal for the events of 1916.

* * *

In the first decades of the twentieth century, the white workers of the running trades enjoyed a singular status as the only occupational group to enjoy mediation and arbitration agencies with well-defined statutory powers. By contrast, in 1907, managers on England's railways, under threat of labor conflict and pressure from government, formulated an informal and private conciliation scheme that excluded unions. In France, the state intervened in ways that encouraged decentralized, strike-prone unionism but not collective bargaining. In the United States, driven by conditions in the workplace and an inflationary economy, the brotherhoods pushed the boundaries of collective action and worked the Erdman arbitration statutes to their advantage. To be sure, American railroad workers exhibited lower rates of strike activity compared to their French counterparts. Nevertheless, they demonstrated both a willingness to use the *threat* of strikes and a degree of inter-brotherhood coordination that been rare in the nineteenth century, all of which was made possible by state intervention in railroad labor relations under the Erdman Act. By 1915, though, the brotherhoods were a different set of unions. For these reasons, Selig Perlman and Philip Taft entitled their chapter in the *History of Labor in the United States* on the brotherhoods during these years, "From Bargaining to Militancy."[92]

The Erdman Act helped foster the brotherhoods' craft industrialism, but it did so paradoxically. Created to forestall industrial-style, radical unionism, it permitted the railroad brotherhoods to move in that very direction. The brotherhoods' use of concerted movements and arbitration against black railwaymen also demonstrated the policy's unexpected outcomes. A "progressive" federal law facilitating the collective bargaining of the established brotherhoods seriously undermined the position of African American railroaders (and proved disastrous for them in the long run). Certainly, it complicated the already fraught relationships among black and white railroad workers and their employers. Yet in the pre–World War I years, despite the power that they effectively granted the brotherhoods in terms of workplace representation, the arbitration statutes did not prove consistently favorable to white railwaymen's aspirations. The changing intersection of workplace, economy, and government over time also produced shifting attitudes on the arbitral role of the state in railroad labor relations. As inflation ate away railroad workers' living standards, and as arbitration boards returned anemic awards, brotherhood members and leaders grew increasingly frustrated and militant. By the beginning of 1916, railroad managers generally favored arbitration, whereas the railroad brotherhoods had moved toward its complete rejection. Despite revision under the Newlands Act, the system appeared to be on the verge of collapse.

7

Political Action, Industrial Action, and the Making of the Liberal State

The election of Woodrow Wilson to the White House at the head of the Democratic Party in 1912 did not bode well for organized labor initially. Wilson, who in 1907 had written a "Credo" defending liberty of contract and declared his support of the open shop, campaigned on the basis of a decidedly less-interventionist government than most of his opponents. Wilson was a progressive who strove for a middle ground between Theodore Roosevelt—at the head of the Progressive Party (and to the left of him, Eugene V. Debs and the Socialists), whose "New Nationalism" envisioned an expanded use of the state—and William Howard Taft, the Republican candidate, who represented the older, laissez-faire order. With his "New Freedom," Wilson promised a return to conditions of economic competition and opportunity through a moderately expanded governmental presence.[1]

The New Freedom had a strong basis in Wilson's philosophical convictions as well as the political realities of the 1912 election. Yet those realities quickly changed and forced him to reconsider his relationship with organized labor and support an expanded role for government. The Democrats had won by a good margin in the electoral college but by only a plurality in the popular vote. Wilson polled fewer votes in victory than did William Jennings Bryan in defeat in 1908, and owed his election to the unusual four-way race. The results brought home to the Democrats that they needed labor's support if they were to win in the 1916 election. The American Federation of Labor had endorsed Wilson, but did so reluctantly, having favored Champ Clark of Missouri for the Democratic nomination. At the same time, during these years the progressive and socialist movements reached their peaks of popularity, as activists pressed for greater government responsibilities in diverse areas of society. Wilson responded to these pressures by opening his door to organized labor, slowly at first and then with alacrity. He supported, albeit unevenly, legislative initiatives that labor desired, created a Department of Labor, and helped form the U.S. Commission on Industrial Relations (USCIR) with progressive lawyer Frank Walsh as its chair. But it took a brotherhood-threatened rail strike of over 350,000 workers and a crisis moment in the late summer of 1916 to cement the reforged labor–Democratic Party alliance. The outcomes of that crisis were the Adamson Act, granting running-trades workers the eight-hour day, and a Democratic victory in November.[2]

The railroad brotherhoods stood at the center of these events. Although historical scholarship has focused on the American Federation of Labor and its assiduous cultivation of a political alliance with the Democrats, the brotherhoods had become involved in politics as well.[3] Circumstances had made necessary the development of a clear political strategy. Despite their growing strength, corporate consolidation and expansion of state bureaucracy had created a situation in which industrial action alone proved insufficient to win trade union goals. Accordingly, the brotherhoods built on their 1890s lobbying experience to pursue protective-labor and shorter-hours legislation in the next decade. At the same time, growing frustration with arbitration involved the brotherhoods directly in the legislative process with the Newlands Act, and ultimately led to the breakdown of the system. With the real possibility of U.S. entry into World War I, strains in the arbitration system and developments in national politics made 1916 a momentous year.

The Pursuit of Legislation

Beginning in the 1890s, the brotherhoods developed a two-fisted approach to political action, much like that of the American Federation of Labor: lobbying Congress for favorable legislation and encouraging brotherhood members to use their ballots wisely in state and national elections.[4]

Following their successful effort to win passage of the Safety Appliances Act in 1893, the brotherhoods paid attention to labor legislation in state and national legislatures and increased the number of their state-level legislative boards. They also cooperated with one another in maintaining joint legislative boards in several states. Beginning in 1894, they maintained a permanent "legislative representative" in Washington, D.C., who reported on congressional legislative activity, lobbied for labor-friendly bills, and made recommendations on legislative strategy. Altogether these moves reflected the maturing of the federation movement and recognition of the value of national-level lobbying. In the new century, the brotherhoods focused their political efforts on Congress, combining their nonpartisan stance with legislative lobbying and working closely with the American Federation of Labor on many issues. Like the AFL, they sought to accomplish legislatively what they could not achieve otherwise, but unlike the AFL's top leadership (and Samuel Gompers in particular), the brotherhoods were not rigidly antistatist. As the debate over the Erdman bill demonstrated, the brotherhoods could envision a positive role for government in workers' and trade unions' affairs, a view that shaped their major legislative goals.[5]

One of the early issues to draw brotherhood attention to the national legislative level was that of immigrant workers. Since the 1880s, along with their counterparts in the AFL unions, brotherhood members had expressed concern about the impact of unchecked immigration on the nation generally and on native-born workingmen specifically. As the immigration issue became politicized along racial-nativist lines in the 1890s, the brotherhoods joined other trade unions in calling for stringent forms of restriction.[6] In particular, they advocated nationally established literacy tests and endorsed the Lodge-Corliss immigration bill, first introduced in 1891.[7] In 1902, they joined the AFL-led fight for extension of the Chinese Exclusion Act of 1882.[8] Over the following years, the brotherhoods closely monitored congressional bills on immigration and the status of Asian workers and continued their support for literacy tests, taxes, and quotas (which were made national policy by federal legislation in 1917).[9]

A measure of the brotherhoods' national prominence in the immigration debate came in 1902 when President Roosevelt appointed as U.S. commissioner general of immigration the BLF's Frank Sargent. A supporter of restriction, with negative views of southern and southeastern European immigrants, Sargent embodied the brotherhood/trade union outlook on immigration at one of the highest levels of government and became one of Roosevelt's trusted advisers.[10] Despite the sustained attention that they gave to immigration, and the vituperative manner in which they opined on the relative worth and impact of immigrants, the brotherhoods allowed the AFL and Gompers, as labor's leading spokespeople on the issue, to take the lead in lobbying Congress. For the brotherhoods, immigration restriction figured largely as a matter of principle, symbolism, and positioning. Because limiting immigration was one of the few points on which the interests of organized labor and the federal government converged, calling for legislated restriction offered one way to extend brotherhood influence in the political mainstream.[11]

Another area that drew the brotherhoods into national-level politics concerned the welfare of running-trades workers, and no issue loomed larger than that of workplace safety. The brotherhoods had won landmark federal legislation with the Safety Appliances Act, but foot-dragging by the railroad companies provided an ongoing stimulus and rationale for legislative activity. The brotherhoods' lobbyist, Hugh R. Fuller, asserted the unions' rationale: "Our experience has been that if we desire appliances for our safety we have to come to Congress or go to a State legislature to accomplish anything. This is one of the things that we can not accomplish otherwise; we are not big enough or heavy enough through our organizations to make the railroads act in such matters. It takes the hand of Congress."[12] To force compliance, the brotherhoods monitored enforcement of the law, encouraged their members to report all instances of employer neglect, pursued the matter in the courts, and lobbied for amendments to the act. In 1901 and 1903, the brotherhoods' efforts produced laws enforcing stricter guidelines in the railroads' reporting of accidents, as well amendments to the 1893 act that clarified its intent and beefed up its enforcement. Additionally, the brotherhoods found an unexpected ally in the judiciary. In 1902 and 1904, federal appeals courts and the Supreme Court found railroad companies liable in suits in which employees had been injured and killed as a result of improper equipment.[13] Building on these successes, by 1915 the brotherhoods won legislation in four areas of concern: locomotive safety, signaling, shorter train lengths, and full crews.[14] The last of these served the double purpose of "making work" for railroaders by mandating full crews while legislatively evicting black railwaymen by requiring that crews be all-white.[15]

Closely related to workplace safety was the matter of working hours. From the 1890s onward, the brotherhoods had attempted to reduce the hours of service through collective bargaining and state-level legislation, but to little avail. In the next decade, however, the urgency of the matter increased with longer, heavier trains and mounting public concern over the rising collision toll.[16] In 1902, the Interstate Commerce Commission began calling attention to train accidents resulting from long working hours, and recommended legislation limiting train crews' hours of labor. Roosevelt also weighed in with his 1905 addresses to Congress, urging legislation to relieve railwaymen from the "strain, both mental and physical" of long hours of work, and thereby to ensure "the safety of all who travel by rail."[17] Working closely with the commission's Edward A. Moseley, the brotherhoods drafted bills limiting hours of service and had them introduced in both houses of Congress by allies senator Robert M. La Follette and congressman John J. Esch in 1906.

In congressional hearings, Fuller justified the bills as safety measures for the public and employees, but he also acknowledged that the unions sought to bring railwaymen's working lives under control and enable them more time at home. After all, Fuller added, home was "the proper place for a man to rest and to put in his spare time, both from a physical and a moral standpoint." With strong support from the ICC, Congress overrode management objections and passed the Hours of Service Act in January 1907. The first such law restricting the hours of nongovernmental employees, the act limited the maximum period of continuous duty of train crews to sixteen hours and empowered the ICC to conduct inspections in its enforcement.[18]

Running-trades workers welcomed safety and hours laws, but they knew that they remained vulnerable. Recognizing the impossibility of legislating an accident-free workplace, the brotherhoods complemented their drive for safety laws with support for employers' liability reform. The common-law doctrines of fellow servant and contributory negligence severely limited the chances of an injured employee recovering damages from a negligent employer. Since the late nineteenth century, the brotherhoods had closely followed judicial rulings elaborating exceptions to the fellow-servant doctrine; along with other trade unions, they called for a more liberalized law of workplace accidents. By the 1890s, based on fellow-servant or assumption-of-risk doctrines, states such as Iowa, Alabama, Ohio, and Massachusetts had passed laws limiting railroads' legal defenses in personal injury cases. Finding, as with safety laws, that reforms at the state level resulted in patchwork solutions that did little to help railwaymen engaged in interstate commerce, the brotherhoods focused their attention on the passage of a federal law.[19]

In championing liability legislation, the brotherhoods argued that the conditions of modern railroad operations made common-law doctrines archaic. "It is ridiculous," exclaimed Fuller during 1906 congressional hearings, "to expect a railroad employee to know all of the habits of those men who work upon the same line of railroad with him." Additionally, the very nature of railroad work made it all but impossible for a worker to avoid injury. Thus, it was unfair to hold an employee responsible for injuries under assumption of risk. Moreover, *someone* had to perform the vital, yet dangerous, work of moving the nation's goods and people, and employers bore some of the responsibility for this danger, particularly in cases where they were negligent in providing for the safety of employees. Bringing these elements together, the brotherhoods argued that railroad workers ought to stand on the same footing before the law as passengers, who for many years had won recovery in personal injury suits. In other words, railwaymen deserved protection like any other citizen. With the support of Roosevelt and progressive-minded congressmen, Congress passed the Employers' Liability Act in 1906, effectively abolishing defenses based on the doctrines of fellow servant and assumed risk that had shielded employers from liability.[20]

As the barriers to employers' liability fell, the rise in cases threatened to jam the courts, prompting the brotherhoods and a network of middle-class reformers to explore the possibility of workmen's compensation legislation. Workmen's compensation differed from employers' liability reform by taking the resolution of cases and the control of awards out of the courts and placing them in the hands of a governmental commission. Without assigning responsibility, commissions awarded compensation to injured workers or to the families of workers killed on the job. The approach reflected a view of workplace accidents as an inevitable cost of business that should be borne not by the individual employee, but rather by the employer (and, indirectly, the public). In these terms, workmen's compensation had obvious applicability to high-risk, quasi-public industries like the railroads.[21] Some members feared the loss of rights as defined by liability laws and harbored reservations about no-fault compensation. Edward Moseley helped to allay these misgivings with his belief that injured workmen deserved compensation in the same way that injured Civil War soldiers deserved pensions. The brotherhoods endorsed workmen's compensation, initiated introduction of the first federal-level compensation legislation in 1913, and supported the federal Workmen's Compensation Bill, which passed Congress in 1916.[22]

Brotherhood men welcomed the positive role of the state in workingmen's welfare, but remained chary of state authority in the form of the judiciary. The judicial repression of labor in the early twentieth century focused on AFL unions, but the brotherhoods were not beyond the heavy hand of the courts. Judicial hostility to labor continued as employers and judges used the Sherman Antitrust Act to break strikes and boycotts, most famously in the 1908 Danbury Hatters' case of *Loewe v. Lawler*. Employers and judges also stepped up the use of the injunction against strikes—over 1,600 were issued between 1900 and 1920 according to William Forbath. For these reasons, the AFL made anti-injunction legislation and amendment to the Sherman Act top priorities during these years.[23]

The brotherhoods avoided the kind of lawsuits that bedeviled the hatters, for they had learned their lesson about the boycott in the Toledo, Ann Arbor & Northern Michigan Railroad case of 1893 (see chapter 4). But the expanding industrial action that the brotherhoods had embarked on was certain to draw the injunction; in fact, it did so in the first concerted movement undertaken by the ORC/BRT Western Association of General Committees in 1902–3. As the unions took their strike votes, the Wabash Railroad went to judge Elmer B. Adams' District Court for the Eastern District of Missouri for an injunction on the grounds that the unions' actions amounted to conspiracy to restrain interstate commerce. It looked as though the brotherhoods had another Jenkins-style injunction on their hands until Adams heard brotherhood arguments and their stated willingness to submit the dispute to arbitration. Concluding that the employees had a right to strike, he dissolved the injunction. In the process, he contributed to the legitimacy of collective bargaining under the Erdman Act, even if it had not yet been used, and cleared the way for further concerted movements. Nevertheless, brotherhood men remained wary. "In this decision there is no new principle of law involved nor any addition conceded to the rights of citizens and employes as set forth in the Constitution," warned the *Railroad Trainmen's Journal*. "There is nothing to prevent Judge Adams, or any other jurist, from applying the same injunction privileges again and preventing men from exercising their rights as they have been acknowledged by the courts." The remedy was "that Congress pass a law that will prevent like use of the power of the courts in cases of this kind."[24]

The brotherhoods worked with the AFL for judicial reform, beginning in 1900 with the drafting and introduction of a congressional anti-injunction bill. The brotherhoods added their institutional weight to the effort. They took public positions on the progress of the various incarnations of the bill through committee, and Fuller testified before committees and personally met with key congressional figures. Brotherhood journals followed the up-and-down progress of the bill for the next fourteen years, urging local lodges and individual members to send letters and telegrams of support to their congressmen.[25]

The brotherhoods also worked with the AFL and the National Civic Federation to revise the Sherman Act. Their efforts focused on drafting and lobbying for the Hepburn bill in 1908, which exempted trade unions from antitrust laws, but the measure was defeated. Six years later, they pushed hard for union exemption from the bill that became the Clayton Antitrust Act of 1914, again without success. The brotherhoods came under few injunctions after the Wabash case, but the Supreme Court's decision in *Loewe v. Lawler*, forbidding *all* direct restraints of interstate trade—including boycotts, strikes, *and* union contracts—threatened the survival of collective bargaining and trade unionism. Moreover, the Supreme Court's 1908 decision in *Adair v. the United States*, which ruled as unconstitutional the Erdman Act's section prohibiting "yellow-dog" contracts, appeared as part of another general judicial assault on organized labor.[26]

By the early 1910s, brotherhood members could look back over the previous dozen or so years with some satisfaction. On the one hand, in those areas directly affecting railroaders' welfare, the brotherhoods' legislative record was impressive. They had wrung several pieces of protective-labor legislation from a Republican-dominated legislature—a lobbying record that compared favorably with that of the AFL's over the same period of time—and attained influence within Congress. Indeed, during these years, the brotherhoods won a degree of favor with the Roosevelt administration that, if anything, exceeded that enjoyed by Gompers and the AFL.[27] For their part, brotherhood leaders expressed admiration for President Roosevelt and supported him in his battles against the judiciary and an old guard, Republican-controlled Congress.[28]

Yet disappointment and apprehension tempered the brotherhoods' successes. The brotherhoods had gotten as far as they were likely to get in their legislative quest for shorter hours. In particular, the holy grail of the eight-hour day eluded both legislative and industrial approaches. As for judicial reform, the brotherhoods and the AFL had little to show for their hard work. After fourteen years of sustained effort, the most that they could achieve was a platitudinous and unenforceable line in the Clayton Act stating that labor was not a commodity.[29] By that point in time, however, it appeared to brotherhood men that it was the courts, rather than capital, that posed the gravest threat to trade unionism. Or, more precisely, it was the close connection that they perceived between the courts and the corporations—the corruption of politics—that posed the threat. Such thinking led brotherhood men to question the wisdom of lobbying as the best means of winning union goals.

Political Culture and the Wilsonian State

The successes and frustrations of legislative action pushed the railroad brotherhoods to reconsider their political strategies and their relationship to the national state. From the beginning of their legislative activity, the brotherhoods had remained nonpartisan, seeking to influence members of Congress regardless of party. When it came to electoral politics, the brotherhoods (like the AFL) simply encouraged their members to vote for those candidates who had demonstrated friendliness to labor. Between 1912 and 1916, however, as Julie Greene observes, the national state and American political culture underwent an important transformation. In response to growing class conflict and the rising popularity of the Progressive and Socialist parties, the Wilson administration became open to the idea of promoting trade unionism—what Martin J. Sklar terms "regulatory corporate liberalism," and Colin Davis describes as an "accommodative" state regarding organized labor.

These developments, and the rising class conflict driving them, combined to make questions of the state more central to American political culture and discourse.[30] They also helped propel the brotherhoods into partisan electoral politics on the side of the Democrats.

Typically, scholarly treatment of labor's political activism during the Progressive Era focuses on the American Federation of Labor. Beginning in the late 1890s, the Federation defined its nonpartisan political stance and legislative strategy under Samuel Gompers's leadership. By 1906, though, an employer counteroffensive, in the form of an open-shop drive sponsored by the National Association of Manufacturers (NAM), forced the AFL to enter electoral politics in a more formal way. It did so by working to elect trade unionists and "friends of labor" to the House of Representatives, most of whom turned out to be Democrats. The modest success of that effort encouraged the Federation to attempt a more ambitious partnership with the Democratic Party to elect William Jennings Bryan to the White House in 1908. That effort failed, causing an AFL retreat from mass political mobilization and prompting the Democratic Party to look beyond the Federation as a vehicle for an alliance with labor. The ideological and political distance between AFL leadership and the Democrats only increased with the election of Woodrow Wilson in 1912, as his administration's increasing willingness to use the state in a positive way to support social justice was something that the antistatist Gompers could not countenance.[31]

The brotherhoods, too, had developed a political program, one that shared a number of common origins and features with that of the AFL. Like the early AFL, the brotherhoods insisted on nonpartisanship in all aspects of their political activity, a policy that reflected the political loyalties of brotherhood members. As with most late nineteenth-century workers, railwaymen took a keen interest in politics. During this period of fierce party allegiance and high voter turnout, brotherhood men likely participated in electoral politics at a rate consistent with skilled workers as a whole.[32] Although data on their political affiliations is scant, the ethno-cultural makeup of running-trades workers as a group—native-born, Anglo-Protestant, and rurally reared—would have placed a majority of them in the Republican camp. This was true of national brotherhood leaders, who were predominantly Republican in their orientation. Such proclivities would have also placed them within the minority of overall workers, who tended toward the Democratic Party.[33] Still, southern brotherhood men were likely Democratic in sympathy, and anecdotal evidence suggests that in the West and across the Northeast, Republican affiliation was not uniform.[34] Given the intense nature of politics, brotherhood men probably thought about and discussed politics informally, as they often had a great deal of time on their hands as they readied their trains or waited on sidings. In these circumstances, with its potential for divisiveness, the railroad brotherhoods forbade discussion of politics (and religion) within the lodge, at conventions, and in the pages of the monthly journals.[35] The ban on political discussion did not mean, however, that the brotherhoods expected their members to refrain from political activity. In fact, when it came to electoral politics, the official brotherhood position was that voting was a matter of personal choice and local autonomy, with one broad caveat—that members not be slaves to the party system.

In the early years of the twentieth century, brotherhood leaders joined with Samuel Gompers in the view that successful political action must be joined with a revolt against the party politics.[36] Echoing Gompers, officials like *Railroad Trainmen's Journal*'s D. L. Cease expressed the view that political parties had conspired to steal from voters meaningful participation in the political system: "While we flatter ourselves that we really govern, we really haven't very much to do with the question. It is true we elect, but who plans the candidates and the platforms and the elections?"[37] The problems that organized labor faced, and the difficulties of working people generally, resulted from party control of government, Cease and others argued. Party politicians, once elected, either ignored their working-class constituencies or, worse, actively acted in the interests of capital. Such a view reflected the belief, prevalent in the early Progressive Era, that professional politicians and business had corrupted politics. The solution, reformers and brotherhood leaders argued, was reform of the political system along the lines of more direct democracy. In the first decade of the twentieth century, however, such reforms as the initiative, referendum, and recall had made only uneven progress across the nation.[38]

Brotherhood leaders and journal editors urged their followers to vote for the candidate rather than the party. "If voters would not hang quite so closely to party, but would select men for office who would be ready to repudiate a party measure for the interests of all of the people there would be some advantageous difference in legislative results," wrote Cease in 1904.[39] More pointedly, they reminded members to cast their ballots in the interests of themselves, their unions, and the labor movement as a whole. The Brotherhood of Railroad Trainmen, for instance, laid down very broad guidelines, encouraging every member to "take such political action as will more speedily bring him into and his organization the best results." With this policy, the union also promised to "remember its friends in every election and support them."[40] Charles H. Salmons, editor of the *Locomotive Engineers' Monthly Journal*, stated the idea as follows: "We trust every member of the order will keep himself sufficiently in touch with politics, national and state, to be in a condition to know what is best to do with his influence and his ballot in protecting the best interests of laboring men, and that his interest in the welfare of laboring men will be beyond party politics."[41]

Salmons's comments, published in the October 1906 issue of the Engineers' *Journal* in response to the AFL announcement of its political program, revealed both commonalities and differences between the BLE and the other brotherhoods on political action. Reiterating the Engineers' primary purpose as economic, and stressing the importance of keeping the union "free from entangling alliances and issues," Salmons insisted on keeping the BLE out of party politics: "Let us be a force in the purification of politics, in driving bad men out, putting good in, and in an effort to secure salutary laws for the benefit of laboring men; but let us do it as laboring men."[42] By contrast, D. L. Cease responded to the AFL announcement and queries from BRT members by dwelling on the similarities between the AFL's program and that of the BRT. Like the Federation, the Trainmen had solicited the views of political candidates on issues of concern to the union, published them, and encouraged members to vote in view of them, "rewarding them according to their work." Toward this end, Cease favored political discussion within the union, although confined to the issues and stopping short of partisanship: "We cannot understand just how an organization can carry on a legislative and political program without debating the questions in which it is interested." The Trainmen exercised a greater degree of coordination and planning in marshalling its members' votes than did the Engineers, but stopped short of campaigning for candidates as the AFL did in 1906.[43]

Political discussion, the degree to which members could engage in it, and the extent of brotherhood involvement in politics became issues of greater consequence after 1906. Motivated by some of the same factors driving the AFL's broadening political program, brotherhood men began to question the strict nonpartisanship of their unions and the exclusive focus on legislative action at the expense of electoral political participation. In the BRT some men favored more explicit instruction of the membership on voting. Others argued that deeper union involvement in politics was necessary to combat the well-financed NAM and a hostile judiciary. A. M. Douglas, agent for a Trainmen's lodge in Newark, New Jersey, argued for railroaders' direct involvement in politics in states that had passed initiative and referendum laws: "Organized labor can absolutely control the Legislature of New Jersey and the government of every leading city of the State if it will. The new primary law puts a tool in the hands of organized labor with which it may fashion the politics of the state."[44] Changing presidential administrations, combined with a downturn in the economy in 1907–8 (and persistent inflation thereafter), combined to make questions of political action more volatile than ever. The year 1912 proved to be especially fraught as Republican dominance showed signs of weakening, and the four-way presidential contest threw conventional political wisdom into doubt. An outpouring of sentiment for expanded political action in the pages of the *Locomotive Firemen and Enginemen's Magazine* indicated both the distance that the brotherhoods had traveled on the matter and the passion that it elicited among individual members.

The discourse in the *Magazine* from late 1911 through late 1912 revealed that brotherhood men were shifting from thinking in terms of a political strategy focused on influencing lawmakers to one that emphasized lawmaking itself through positive electoral action. Brotherhood men writing to the journal expressed a view that legislative lobbying alone was insufficient, for it had produced positive, but ultimately limited, results and at a high cost. "I agree that our legislative boards are doing much good for the Brotherhood," wrote a member of Lodge 103, "but much of this time and money is wasted because our pleadings fall upon deaf ears just because there are so few, if any, workingmen in the State Legislatures and national Congress."[45] The solution to the problem lay in the election of workingmen to Congress. "If the toilers were properly represented in our legislative bodies—if they were represented there by men from their own ranks, we would not need legislative boards," wrote C. C. Crawford.[46] Almost all correspondents agreed with "A Brother of Lodge 684," who insisted that open political discussion was essential to such action: "In the columns of our Magazine and in the columns of all other labor magazines the political questions must be fought out as well as in our Lodge rooms."[47] And some contributors, like R. A. Bryant, believed that with the spread of direct democracy through the initiative, referendum, and recall, the moment was right for such working-class electoral activity.[48]

A profound sense of discontent with the nation's economic and political systems animated this discourse. "We know there is something radically wrong," concluded J. S. Boyd in October 1912. In the view of many brotherhood men, much of what was "radically wrong" with the nation—unemployment, inflation, unequal distribution of wealth, and labor conflict—stemmed from the undemocratic nature of the political and industrial systems. "Politics are directly responsible for our industrial condition," wrote one correspondent.[49] For some, the problem was rooted in the loss of basic American freedoms. "We were all born with the same opportunity, and that has been taken away from us as though we had nothing to do but what the big interests bid us do," wrote a member from Lodge 449.[50] The implications were dire. "I fear that under the present working conditions, wages and high cost of living," worried another letter writer, "this country is fast approaching a revolution." Fireman Fred McCoy agreed, and saw the solution in politics: "Everything for the worker is wrong, and we will have to enter politics to make things right, but not the grafting, corrupt kind of politics the majority stands for. Labor will have to emancipate itself." "Vote as you strike," he advised, "and the world is yours."[51] Class consciousness, rights consciousness, militancy, and the sense that the welfare of working people, their organizations, and the nation depended on the immediate and concerted political action of unionists ran through the pages of the *Magazine* over the months leading up to the 1912 election. What is more, despite the belief that politics and government had become corrupted, there ran a corresponding conviction that government could be redeemed by labor's involvement and turned into a positive force for social justice.

The currents of thought in the Firemen, and to varying degrees in the other three brotherhoods, dovetailed with the willingness of the Wilson administration to use the federal government in the cause of social justice. Immediately after the election, the president-elect and Samuel Gompers initiated a relationship that would result in the admission of the AFL leader to the highest levels of policy making. This relationship and the creation of the Department of Labor, with William B. Wilson as its first secretary, gave organized labor cause to believe that it had won an unprecedented degree of political influence. According to Julie Greene, Wilson and congressional Democrats pursued this nascent labor policy in response to the sea change in politics. But Wilson's most important response to this change, one that would realign labor politics, was his appointment of progressive Frank W. Walsh (and others with labor sympathies) to the U.S. Commission on Industrial Relations. With three labor leaders as commissioners, including the Conductor's Austin B. Garretson, the USCIR took on a progressive, pro-labor agenda.[52]

Brotherhood men followed the activities of the commission, which in Walsh's hands became a crusade for social justice. From 1913 into 1915, it probed in exposé-like fashion into causes of labor unrest and generated tremendous publicity. Becoming a labor tribunal, the USCIR investigated the laboring conditions of unskilled and migrant labor, documented repressive company towns and scientific management practices, interrogated corporate villains like John D. Rockefeller Jr., and dug into the causes of flash points like the Ludlow Massacre and the Lawrence textile strike. The commission's uncompromising investigation, declared the *Magazine*, "is endorsed by every American citizen who believes in just government—who believes in human liberty—who is opposed to the destruction of the constitutional rights of working men." In the work of the USCIR, and in Walsh's rhetoric of industrial democracy, brotherhood men saw the promise of restored national democracy and a government purged of corruption. They approved of the commission's findings, for they had already discussed many of the same issues and identified solutions similar to those called for in its final report. That report, signed by Walsh and the pro-labor commissioners, identified the causes of labor unrest in the unequal distribution of wealth and income, unemployment, the denial of equal justice to working people, and the denial of the right to organize and collectively bargain. It decisively called for governmental action to cure these ills.[53]

In its findings and recommendations, the USCIR's final report reached out to workers excluded from the narrow ranks of the AFL and the railroad brotherhoods, and presented a radical analysis of industrial unrest.[54] That the brotherhoods applauded the report, and that it was signed off on by one of their own, suggests that they shared the commission's underlying assumptions; by 1915, they could look beyond their confines to the mass of unorganized labor and its role in the body politic. John F. McNamee, editor of the *Locomotive Firemen and Enginemen's Magazine*, called it "a fearless declaration of the truth as regards the evils of our industrial system."[55] Yet what the brotherhoods responded to most powerfully, located at the core of the commission's report and central to its solutions for workers' problems, was the vision of trade unionism and collective bargaining guaranteed by the state.[56] In the course of the USCIR's investigation, Walsh came to champion "the rapid extension of the principles of democracy to industry" as the solution to the nation's labor problem. The concept was not new. But Walsh's linking of industrial democracy to the right to join unions, and his connecting of this right to the nation's democratic heritage, gave industrial democracy mass appeal among progressives, trade unionists, and workers alike.[57]

The argument for industrial democracy embodied the view that the world of work had become as important as, and was intimately linked with, Americans' formal civil and political rights. Warren Stone elaborated on this idea in 1919, in words echoing the USCIR's final report: "We have a democratic form of government but an autocratic control of industry. We exist under government, but by industry we live. Under such a system the majority of a democracy can, through their government, enjoy only such rights as an autocracy in industry permits them to receive." Stone's logic was clear: industry had to be made to conform to democratic values; if democracy was appropriate in government, it was needed in industry. Indeed, democratizing industry and reconnecting Americans' working lives with their citizenship rights would go a long way toward solving the current crisis.[58] Thinking like this had been percolating in the brotherhoods for several years in the form of Americanist rhetoric that contrasted greediness and concentrated wealth as incompatible with American principles.[59] By 1915–16, John McNamee was both inveighing against the threat of "Rockerfellerism" to American liberties and calling for government regulation of industry and transportation, and Stone was calling for government regulation of railroad capitalization and securities.[60] Unlike Gompers and the AFL hierarchy, brotherhood men and their leaders welcomed the state as an agent of industrial democracy; industrial democracy was at bottom a state-centered argument, and the work of the USCIR helped to build support among brotherhood men for the Wilson administration.[61]

The USCIR's final report affirmed brotherhood thinking, both in its critique of American employers and in generating popular enthusiasm for state intervention in the cause of industrial democracy. Thus, when congressional opponents of the commission attempted to bury the final report, brotherhood lodges joined other trade unions in petitioning for its full publication, challenging Congress to advance "the happiness and well being and prosperity of the mass of our citizenship rather than [maintain] the ascendancy of our autocratic despotism." So taken was the brotherhoods' leadership with Walsh that after the commission adjourned in October 1915, they offered him a position as legal counsel. Walsh declined the offer, but the brotherhoods joined a network of trade unionists and reformers in supporting the Committee on Industrial Relations, which Walsh formed to carry on the commission's work.[62] Walsh and the committee, in turn, became supporters of the brotherhoods' drive the following year for an eight-hour day in the train service. By maintaining grassroots enthusiasm for the USCIR's final report and in pushing Congress to translate its recommendations into legislation, the committee's work would become central to Democratic politics as Wilson sought reelection in 1916. So too would the brotherhoods' eight-hour movement, as it created a moment of crisis calling for decisive presidential action.[63]

The Eight-Hour Movement, the Adamson Act, and the Election of 1916

In early 1916, as Woodrow Wilson and Democratic leaders surveyed the returns from the 1912 election, they understood that they had to convert their party from the standard of the New Freedom into a genuinely progressive party if they were to win the fall election. To do that, they needed to bring into the Democratic camp organized labor and various reform groups. Beginning in January, Wilson pushed, prodded, and berated a Democratic Congress into what Arthur S. Link has called "the most sweeping and significant progressive legislation in the history of the country up to that time." On January 28, he appointed Louis D. Brandeis to the Supreme Court and that summer forced passage of the Workmen's Compensation bill and the Keating-Owen Child Labor bill. Added to a revenue act providing for a progressive income tax, progressive legislation for rural Americans, and cooperation with business on tariff policy, these feats amounted to nothing less than an "astonishing metamorphosis in Democratic policies." Wilson's achievement bespoke his own political flexibility as well as the new zeal with which Democrats embraced the state as an agent of social justice. This policy orientation, though, did not accommodate the antistatist AFL very well; in fact, it reflected a different sort of Democratic-labor alliance, one that included the reformers associated with the Committee on Industrial Relations, socialists, the Women's Trade Union League, local trade unionists, and the railroad brotherhoods. And it was the railroad brotherhoods that crystallized this coalition with their eight-hour movement.[64]

The campaign for the eight-hour day in the train service merged the brotherhoods' widening industrial action with their deepening political sensibilities. On the face of it, the brotherhoods' disillusionment with the arbitration system by mid-1915 indicated their impatience with the record of state intervention in railroad labor relations. Yet brotherhood leaders were not opposed to government involvement per se. It was a question of what *kind* of involvement. In planning a national, all-brotherhood concerted movement during an election year with an incumbent president, and declaring that the issue was not subject to arbitration, brotherhood leaders must have known that governmental intervention was likely. Certainly, they could not have believed that the national state would permit a national railroad strike on the eve of possible U.S. entry into World War I. The question was what form would state intervention take. Given the direction of Wilsonian politics, they could be forgiven for thinking that government action would be executive and legislative rather than judicial, and that it would stop short of the heavy-handed policies that had characterized the nineteenth century. In short, the brotherhoods' drive for the eight-hour day was fundamentally *political.*

Shorter hours of service had been a brotherhood goal for many years. The Hours of Service Act of 1907 represented a positive step in curbing unrestricted hours of labor; as it required only eight hours' off-duty between sixteen-hour workdays, however, it hardly brought about an appreciable shortening of running-trades labor. Moreover, the act proved tricky to put into actual practice; crews routinely found themselves "stranded" in the middle of runs when the statutory sixteen-hour period ran out. In fact, the frequent delays resulting from heavy trains and congested rails almost guaranteed that certain runs could not be completed within sixteen hours. But to the aggravation of running-trades workers, management responded to the law by making up heavy trains that would reach their destinations just inside the sixteen-hour limit. Rather than shortening train crews' workdays, the law had the paradoxical effect of lengthening them in many instances. The railroad companies found it cheaper to work crews up to the statutory maximum than to make up a greater number of smaller, faster trains. Without punitive overtime, there existed no disincentive for this kind of practice.[65] It did not take long for brotherhood men at the local and divisional levels to begin discussing the eight-hour day.[66]

The hours problem also involved grievances on a range of issues. On the "work" side of the equation, railwaymen protested the increased length and pace of work. "In this enlightened age no man should be asked to work more than eight hours, and positively no more than ten," wrote A. M. Douglas in 1910. "There is no denying the fact that a majority of the frequent wrecks which are occurring at present are due to overworked crews, and if the various railway companies will not grant a shorter workday then it should be accomplished if possible by legislation." On the "household" or "consumption" side, railroad workers complained about the disruptive effects of running-trades work rhythms on family life. Adding to the intensity of the hours issue was the problem of rising living costs, which seemed to grow more acute after 1910. Douglas put it simply: "On the whole, neither the railroad man nor any other workman is receiving today wages in proportion to the ever increasing price of living."[67]

From mid-1915 into early 1916, brotherhood members aired their ideas in a series of local, system, and regional meetings that manifested a spirit and determination for unified action. At a June 27, 1915, joint meeting of Engineers and Firemen's lodges on the Boston & Maine Railroad, members expressed their support for "demands that would free [them] from a condition that is no better than slavery and place them in a condition where they could feel they were white men and entitled to treatment as such." Several hundred brotherhood men at a joint-union meeting in Birmingham, Alabama—lasting from September 18 to 21, and featuring "a mammoth barbecue at the fair grounds"—went "on record as heartily favoring" united action among the Big Four for the eight-hour day. At a joint-system meeting of BLE and BLFE men employed on the Chesapeake & Ohio Railroad in late October, a "spirit of genuine harmony, mutual good will and a desire for the closest possible co-operation between the organizations" prevailed. The round of meetings came to a climax at Boston's Faneuil Hall on October 31 when close to a thousand railroad workers gathered to demand of all the brotherhoods' executive officers "co-operation along the lines of a maximum eight-hour working day in all classes of train service." And the men were adamant that they would "never again submit to arbitration in any move for the increase of wages or betterment of conditions."[68]

At a series of high-level conferences over the fall of 1915, the brotherhoods' leaders agreed to work jointly for the eight-hour day and ironed out the details of a nationwide, all-brotherhood concerted movement. At a December 15 meeting in Chicago, executive committees representing the four unions formulated their plans and announced that the unions would jointly present a demand to fifty-two railroad companies for an eight-hour day, with punitive time-and-a-half overtime pay after eight hours or one hundred miles of service (whichever came first). They would submit their demands to the managers of these railroads by March 30, 1916, and the matter was not subject to arbitration.[69]

As soon as the railroad brotherhoods announced their intentions, both sides engaged in a fierce public relations war. The railroad corporations took the offensive, insisting that the brotherhoods' demands represented nothing more than a ploy to gain higher wages through the overtime that the eight-hour day would unavoidably bring, thereby resulting in higher shipping rates and even higher consumer prices. Working through a formally organized publicity bureau, the railroads swung the majority of major-circulation newspapers to their side and won the support of commercial clubs and chambers of commerce across the country. When the brotherhoods made clear their determination to resist arbitration, the railroads presented them as irresponsible and unpatriotic, prepared to thrust the nation into industrial conflict when it seemed that the country might be drawn into war in Europe. On the ground, the railroads bombarded their employees with arguments against the eight-hour campaign. They suggested that the brotherhoods were prepared to line the pockets of their members at the expense of the 1.5 million non-operating employees whose wages would be cut to afford the eight-hour day, and warned that a strike would result in a calamitous government takeover of the nation's railroad system. Two of these railroads, the Pennsylvania and the Santa Fe, resorted to intimidation and threats against running-trades workers to keep them from participating in the July strike vote.[70]

The employers' arguments succeeded in aligning the business community against the brotherhoods, which was little surprise, but they also had the potential to divide the brotherhoods from both the rest of the railroad labor force and the whole of the labor movement. Nevertheless, for many workers, progressives, and socialists, the brotherhoods' eight-hour campaign had come to symbolize the possibilities of strong, well-organized unionism in the service of a cause that all working people could identify with and benefit from. In the words of Samuel Gompers, in a letter to Warren Stone pledging the AFL's support, "a fundamental principle of freedom" was at stake.[71]

The brotherhoods responded to the corporate offensive with their own publicity bureau, joint "publicity" or "get-together" committees of railroad workers, and ladies' auxiliaries, all of which inundated communities with press releases, pamphlets, speakers, and public meetings. With the publicity bureau, the brotherhoods managed to get favorable coverage from a number of newspapers; with the auxiliaries and local committees organizing mass meetings, they generated grassroots support.[72] The meetings turned out to be high-profile events, contributing a "movement" momentum to the brotherhoods' campaign. Speaking at the March 19 mass meeting in Crestline, Ohio, governor Frank P. Willis declared the eight-hour movement "of great moment to the general public." The Rochester, Pennsylvania, meeting of March 26 "was the probably largest one of the kind ever held in the valley." And the mass meeting of April 30 in Richmond, Indiana, featured speeches by the former mayor of Indianapolis, the pastor of the First Christian Church of Richmond, and state judges and representatives, all of whom endorsed the brotherhoods' campaign.[73]

This multipronged effort emphasized the justness of the brotherhoods' cause. They dwelt on the role of overly long hours as a leading source of accidents, injuries, and poor health. As one brotherhood pamphlet put it, "Long Hours Cause Death." Other pamphlets and flyers explained how railwaymen's workload and productivity had steadily risen since the 1890s as a result of increased motive power and train lengths. Shorter hours made railwaymen's work lives safer; also, given the intensified nature of railroad work, they were "fair." Shorter hours also produced better rested, more highly motivated, efficient workers. As to the charge that the campaign merely cloaked a movement for a wage increase, brotherhood men did not deny that they were in need of wages to keep pace with the rising cost of living. Lastly, they refuted the railroads' contention that the eight-hour day would be too impractical and unprofitable to implement.[74] Brotherhood men acknowledged the difficulties of actually applying the eight-hour day in practice in railroading, but they insisted it was not impossible. In the yards, for instance, where trains were made up and switched, it was entirely feasible to employ crews on eight-hour shifts rather than for the standard ten hours. In road service, the men did not expect trains to necessarily complete their runs in eight hours, but they did intend to speed up the movement of slow, irregular freights by penalizing the railroads for time over eight hours.[75]

Brotherhood men and women also emphasized the qualitative improvements to life resulting from shorter hours. "Let us hope that all our railroad boys will get the eight-hour day, which will give them some time in which to think of the higher things of life, some time to devote to the pleasure of wife and children, many of whom are deprived of their companionship for long days at a time," wrote a member of a BLE ladies' auxiliary in June 1916. W. G. Canfield, a St. Louis engineer, believed that it would bring nothing less than "a new life; you will experience new pleasures, and it will not be necessary for you to lay off to see your family. The neighbors will know that you do come home for they will see you come. You will know that your conditions are better and will educate yourself to a higher standard of efficiency." Speaking at an Indianapolis publicity meeting, Clara Bradley, grand president of the BRT's Ladies' Auxiliary, suggested that the eight-hour day would also bring a new life to the wife of the running-trades worker, who bore the brunt of the family's domestic burdens "because of the many long hours [her husband] is compelled to be absent from his home."[76] Civic involvement also figured as an important benefit of the eight-hour day. For retired judge Charles J. Orbison, speaking at the Richmond, Indiana, mass meeting, the eight-hour day was necessary "because men have a duty to perform to the community." "It will make the laborer a better citizen. Better citizens make better nations and better government," announced the BLE in one of its official statements.[77]

Running through brotherhood statements, correspondence, and meetings was a republican-Americanist imagery that indicated a determined, militant spirit. Over the spring and summer of 1916, brotherhood men and officers declared their own solidarity, as well as their opposition to the "capitalist class" or "moneyed interests" that had "enslaved" them. A member of Firemen's Lodge 247, writing in April 1916, believed the railroads' publicity campaign against the brotherhoods threatened not only the brotherhoods, but also the entire republic: "All our forefathers bled and died for, all we hold dear is being taken from us. Washington and Jefferson started us right but we have drifted away from the original ideas of the founders of this republic. We exchanged a British king for a thousand of our own making . . . millions toil on in poverty . . . so that a few men can possess a billion or a few hundred million each. They are thus paving the way for the downfall of the republic." Organized railwaymen stood as a counter to such a threat, believed Ernest James Beutlele, agent for a Rahway, New Jersey, Trainmen's lodge: "We must stick together in our fight for the eight hour day, have strong courage, brave in our devotion to our principles of brotherhood, and fearless in this present struggle against the giant, capitalism, who is keeping us in slavery, working us long hours for a pay that is sufficient only for mere existence."[78]

With this kind of sentiment in the ranks, it was inevitable that Frank Walsh would be in demand for the campaign. He was flooded with invitations to speak at brotherhood rallies across the country on May 1, 1916. Walsh had to decline most of these requests, but he made a special effort to address the Brotherhood of Locomotive Firemen and Enginemen's June 1916 convention in Denver. There, Walsh reviewed the USCIR's findings, speaking to his conviction that "under no form of social organization can there be either political freedom or political democracy unless there is industrial democracy," and stressed the need for collective bargaining backed by federal legislation to secure the individual worker's independent citizenship. To thunderous applause, he endorsed the idea of a living wage that would enable workingmen and their families to live according to "American standards," as well as the right of free men to pursue "a healthy, clean pleasure in life" as a result of having to labor no more than eight hours a day. At numerous appearances across the country that summer, he endorsed the eight-hour day as an "inalienable right," part of a "fundamental democratic tide that is sweeping humanity." For railwaymen, it was their right "as workers and as American citizens." He credited the brotherhoods' campaign with advancing "the whole race, the building up of the family life, the strengthening of the state that goes to make so strong a nation, of independent and free people." Indeed, he declared, every American citizen "who hopes for an extension of democracy" was following the brotherhoods' efforts closely.[79]

Walsh's involvement in the railroad brotherhoods' eight-hour movement dovetailed with his work in reconstructing the labor-Democratic alliance.

With the formation of the Committee on Industrial Relations, Walsh and his colleagues had been working toward the goal of bringing labor into government, and with it the dawn of industrial democracy. At the same time, he had become concerned about both a string of events harmful to the labor movement and the drift of the nation toward involvement in European war. By early to mid-1916, Walsh perceived in the brotherhoods' cause the potential "to secure the reelection of Woodrow Wilson on a platform committing the Democratic Party to peace and to the defense of 'democracy' against 'privilege.'" As events in Europe increasingly portended war for the United States, and as the 1916 election neared, Wilson orchestrated the nation's preparedness campaign, but as he did so, he took care to shore up his support among progressives. The Democrats' adoption of a platform drawing on the recommendations of the USCIR rallied many socialists, progressives, and AFL activists to the party. Still, what Wilson needed, and what Walsh could deliver, was credibility on the political left. As the railroad crisis deepened in August, he summoned Walsh to the White House to advise him on the brotherhoods' eight-hour demand. For Walsh, the occasion was a chance to deliver that credibility and to confirm Wilson as a friend of labor.[80]

The railroad crisis offered Woodrow Wilson an opportunity to exercise decisive presidential leadership, demonstrate his newly minted progressive credentials, and prove his friendship to labor. With the nation on the brink of foreign war, the railroad crisis portended domestic catastrophe. After a long process of fruitless negotiations, by June it was clear that the railroad brotherhoods and railroad management stood at an impasse. In July, the brotherhoods conducted strike votes, with 94 percent of the brotherhoods' combined membership voting in favor of ceasing work, and set a national strike deadline for Labor Day, September 4, 1916. By early August, after the brotherhoods announced the results of their ballots, and after a halfhearted attempt at mediation, the two sides hunkered down for a strike. Facing the possibility of a national rail shutdown during his preparedness program and on the eve of the 1916 election, Wilson attempted personal mediation. In a series of conferences with the brotherhoods' leaders and the conference committee representing the railroads beginning August 14, Wilson offered a compromise solution. He proposed that the railroads accept the eight-hour day with the proviso that the overtime issue be postponed. He also held out a carrot in the form of a promise to urge the ICC to grant rate increases offsetting the effects of the resulting increase in labor costs. Although the unions indicated their openness to the president's plan, management rejected it outright and put forward their own counterproposals.

On August 28, the brotherhoods informed the six hundred division chairs they had called to Washington to debate the president's plan that strike orders had been set for September 4.[81]

On August 29, Wilson broke the deadlock. Going before a joint session of Congress, he outlined a complex and ambitious legislative solution. His proposal followed his earlier compromise package, but with some extras. Insisting on the justice of the brotherhoods' claim, he called on Congress to enact legislation mandating the basic eight-hour day on interstate railroads. His proposal also included provisions for reorganizing and enlarging the Interstate Commerce Commission, the establishment of a presidential commission to study the economic impact of the eight-hour day, amendments to the Newlands law prohibiting strikes and lockouts during the investigation of a railroad labor conflict, and the empowering of the president to take over and operate railroads, and draft train personnel "in case of military necessity."[82] The brotherhoods, the AFL, and the labor press excoriated the last two provisions and, together with Democratic "labor congressmen," made clear they would do all that they could to prevent their passage. Senator William C. Adamson, chair of the House Committee on Interstate and Foreign Commerce, convinced Wilson that only the eight-hour day with an investigative commission could pass before the strike deadline. On September 2, the Senate passed Adamson's pared-down bill by a 43–28 vote, the day after it had passed the House 239–56; the brotherhoods called off the strike.[83]

Both brotherhood and AFL leadership publicly expressed ambivalence at the eight-hour day won by legislative means. At the hearings conducted by the Senate Committee on Interstate Commerce on August 31, Samuel Gompers, hewing to his antistatist line, maintained his opposition to eight-hour laws for adult male workers. Still, not wanting to miss out on a historic moment, and agreeing that it was the only way to avoid the strike, he indicated his support of the law.[84] The brotherhoods' ambivalence, by contrast, reflected their uneven encounters with the state and their commitment to free collective bargaining. A. B. Garretson reiterated the brotherhoods' support of arbitration in principle, but maintained that it only worked "where there is mutual respect." When either party ceased in that respect, collective bargaining became impossible. In the present crisis, argued Garretson, the "greater power" of the brotherhood membership, aggravated by years of frustration, had made it difficult for them to bargain in the proper spirit. The same prevailed on the other side of the bargaining table. Only government intervention could end the deadlock. Provided that the legislation was satisfactory, the brotherhoods would accept a political solution.[85] There were a number of factors working to dispose the brotherhoods toward a legislative answer to the crisis. The brotherhoods' experience under the Erdman-Newlands industrial relations regime had not been wholly bad; in fact, overall it had been one of considerable gain. More important, though, was their considerable experience in winning favorable laws in Congress. Indeed, the ability of the brotherhoods, along with the AFL, to block the objectionable parts of the president's proposal reflected their political acumen and clout. In any event, the position into which Wilson had maneuvered them—either accept the eight-hour day by law or refuse it and lose all public support for their strike—left the brotherhoods little choice.

The Adamson Act in fact represented a huge victory for the railroad brotherhoods and labor generally. To be sure, the brotherhoods gave up their claim for time and a half overtime above eight hours' work. Moreover, the act applied only to running-trades workers, a minority of the railroad industry's labor force and an even smaller portion of the nation's overall workforce. Yet it reflected the profound discontent that had developed among running-trades workers and the power and success of their unions over the previous several years. Moreover, it proved to be an important precedent in securing the eight-hour day for nonoperating employees in the shops and stations during the ensuing war period.[86]

More immediately, the events of August-September 1916 transformed the emerging presidential campaign. Reformers welcomed the Adamson Act as a sign of government's capacity to ameliorate social injustice. Frank Walsh hailed it as nothing less than the dawning of a new era: "The year 1916 marks the beginning of the end of an industrial despotism which allows a few men to exercise autocratic control over the lives, mental aspirations and craving for happiness of countless producers." For Walsh, the government's actions, and the swell of working-class support for them, signaled the beginning of a "worldwide" movement for industrial democracy; more prosaically, it convinced him of the possibilities for advancing industrial democracy via the Democratic Party. Among working-class voters, Wilson became a hero. He had told Congress, "The eight-hour day now, undoubtedly, has the sanction of the judgment of society in its favor." With the Adamson Act the Democrats presented themselves as the party of labor, signaling their willingness to employ the government on behalf of workers' struggles for social justice. Of course, Republicans and conservatives took Wilson to task for surrendering the prerogatives of government to the unions.[87] For the railroad brotherhoods, the resolution to the eight-hour crisis and the presidential campaign that fall marked a watershed as they entered into electoral politics for the first time. For Wilson, the act completed his political strategy for 1916 and his party's alliance with organized labor.[88]

And a labor campaign it was. By late September, the Republican candidate, the conservative former Supreme Court justice Charles Evans Hughes, sought to turn the election by attacking Wilson on the issue of the Adamson Act and his "surrender" to union "blackmail." In a series of editorials, the *Locomotive Firemen and Enginemen's Magazine* set out the brotherhoods' position, identifying the Republicans as aligned "with the interests of the employers, and against the railroad employes," and Hughes as "repressive and uncompromisingly hostile" toward organized labor. Unabashedly partisan, and drawing on republican-Americanist rhetoric, it called on brotherhood men to defeat the Republican candidate, "to use their voting strength in the coming Presidential election in the interests of industrial freedom and for the preservation of their constitutional rights as citizens." In bold letters, the *Magazine* spelled it out: "This Means That All Train Service Employes Should Vote Against Charles E. Hughes . . . and That They Should Also Put Forth Their Best Efforts to Induce Every Other Voter They Can Influence To Vote Against Him."[89]

Across the country, the railroad brotherhoods mobilized local lodges and ladies' auxiliaries into a political machine behind President Wilson's reelection campaign. They turned their monthly journals into political campaign organs, circulated petitions, deployed organizers, carried on word-of-mouth efforts, and organized pro-Wilson meetings in a number of towns and cities. Trade unionists from across the labor movement worked for Wilson; Frank Walsh figured as the labor campaign's star attraction, but railroaders and their families were visible as well. The officers of the Woodrow Wilson League in Los Angeles, for example, were mostly from the brotherhoods' ladies' auxiliaries. In New York City, about a hundred railroad workers surrounded President Wilson's private car at Grand Central Station. When the president emerged to greet them, they called out, "Vote for Wilson, scratching Hughes; join the union, pay your dues!" and "Three cheers for the man who's for the eight-hour day!" In Toledo, Ohio, historically a Republican stronghold, party leaders attempted to organize a meeting among railroad men, with a BLE member who denounced the Adamson Act as the main event. At the meeting, however, as Julie Greene describes it, "a crowd of brotherhood men charged the stage, silenced the speaker, and then led all but a handful of the audience members to another hall, where they passed resolutions praising the president and his eight-hour legislation." At many of Hughes's campaign appearances, working-class audiences, some liberally dosed with railroad men, heckled the candidate and challenged him to declare his views on the Adamson Act. Traditionally, railroad workers had tended to vote Republican—three out of four of the Big Four's chiefs identified themselves as GOP men—but in 1916 they went for Wilson en masse.[90]

One more act was required, though, before the drama of 1916 was over. Immediately after passage of the Adamson Act, the railroads declared their intention to challenge its constitutionality. When the employers refused to abide by the law after January 1, 1917, the brotherhoods issued a strike order, setting March 17, 1917, as the deadline for compliance. Brotherhood of Railroad Trainmen chief W. G. Lee warned that "in this fight to the end," the brotherhoods' "strike vote is still in effect," and they would not hesitate to play "their strongest card." War with Germany was imminent, and it appeared that the nation had to face yet another rail crisis, despite a fast-tracked Supreme Court case, *Wilson v. New* regarding the Adamson Act's constitutionality. With time running out, the president appealed to the patriotism of the two sides: "It is now the duty of every patriotic man to bring matters of this sort to immediate accommodation. The safety of the country against manifest perils affecting its own peace and the peace of the whole world make accommodation absolutely imperative." On March 17, the brotherhoods agreed to postpone the strike forty-eight hours. The next day, after German submarines sank three American ships, and as a result of desperate mediation conducted by the Council of National Defense, the carriers capitulated. On March 19, in a five-to-four decision, the Supreme Court upheld the constitutionality of the law. The railroads argued that Congress had no power to regulate the relationship between employer and employee; the government argued that the Hours of Service Act provided sufficient precedent for intervening in such an emergency. The Court decided that although the relationship was primarily a private affair, the government had the power to act in a dispute in which the parties' failure to agree promised to result in "infinite injury to the public interest." The decision affirmed both Congress's right to regulate labor relations and its authority over interstate transportation.[91]

* * *

In helping to bring about *Wilson v. New*, the railroad brotherhoods played supporting, but crucial, roles in the larger story of American political development. According to Karen Orren, the case marked a historic turning point in a long-term transition from a labor relations regime based on common-law regulation of the workplace and enforced by the courts, to one of collective bargaining based on statute. With the Supreme Court's decision, the legislature extended its reach in the realm of railroad labor relations, an area of public policy historically governed by the judiciary. In so doing, it contributed an important component to the fully legislative polity defining the liberal state of the twentieth century. Insofar as the court decision resulted from the actions of the railroad brotherhoods—their widening scope of industrial action and their forays into legislative lobbying, both of which had the effect of forcing revision of the arbitration statutes and involving the executive branch directly in railroad labor relations—the brotherhoods served as catalytic agents in the development of a liberal polity in the United States.[92] Thus, although Gompers may have regarded the Clayton Act as having emancipated labor, engineer T. J. Mullen may have been more historically accurate in his view of the Adamson Act as a "Magna Charta," "a bill of rights" that would free railwaymen from "our railroad lords."[93]

Also of significance was the brotherhoods' part in the election of 1916. In the short term, they likely made the difference in delivering the labor vote to the Democrats and in returning Wilson to the White House. The president and the Democratic Party attached great meaning to the support of Walsh and organized labor. For reformers and those in the labor movement, such recognition suggested the possibilities for advancing labor's cause, as well as the cause of industrial democracy, through the Democrats and the national state. Over the longer haul, the brotherhoods' eight-hour drive, Wilson's intervention, and the presidential electoral campaign all brought together a process that had been some years in the making: the cementing of what would become an enduring, but not uncomplicated, alliance of labor and the Democratic Party, which would define American politics well into the twentieth century.[94]

For the railroad brotherhoods, the events of 1916 represented the capstone of a process that had been under way for over a decade. Not only had the brotherhoods risen to a place of unprecedented prominence and power, but they had become substantially different organizations than in the late nineteenth century. Aspects of their struggles epitomized the labor scene in 1916, as David Montgomery has suggested. First, the brotherhoods' approach to achieving their industrial and political goals was far more uncompromising than ever before, having more in common with the 1914–16 struggles of workers generally. Second, in their attitudes toward political action, the brotherhoods may have entered electoral campaign politics for the first time, but by no means did they view themselves as working exclusively through the Democratic Party. Rather, the brotherhoods took a broad view of the range of possibilities that political action offered. By early 1917, "leaders of the engineers, at least, were seriously discussing ways to ally with organized farmers and to enlist Walsh's coterie of reformers and publicists to woo popular support for the workers in their struggles against the railroad companies." From that point onward, the railroad brotherhoods began moving to the front of a labor-movement progressive bloc, which would figure prominently during World War I and the years beyond.[95]

Conclusion

Looking back on the events of 1916 and the passage of the Adamson Act, Edward Keating, editor of the progressive journal *Labor,* commented, "Perhaps no piece of legislation ever enacted by the American Congress has been more misrepresented."[1] He might have added that no piece of congressional legislation of such importance and controversy has received as little attention. Even though the act generated fierce partisan feelings in the 1916 election, contributed to voter realignment, fanned an increasingly partisan split between Democrats and Republicans on labor matters, and marked an important moment in the building of the liberal state, historians have given it relatively little consideration. Perhaps other pieces of Wilson-era progressive legislation like the Clayton Act overshadowed it. Or perhaps it got lost in the rush of events sweeping the United States into the First World War. As likely, though, such neglect has resulted from the fact that the railroad brotherhoods, not a fashionable group of unions to study over recent years, made it happen.

Brotherhood men and Americans at the time would have been surprised by this neglect, for the act influenced labor relations for years to come, and the brotherhoods continued as players in national-level politics through World War I and into the 1930s. In 1919 and 1920, they mounted an ambitious campaign (known as the "Plumb Plan") to continue wartime government control of the railroads into peacetime. Building on the successes and failures of that effort, they emerged as leading organizations in 1920s progressive politics. In 1922, they joined with the progressive unions of machinists, miners, clothing workers, and electricians, as well as sympathetic nonunion groups, to form the Conference for Progressive Political Action (CPPA). The CPPA adopted the program of what had become labor's postwar progressive bloc: nationalization of the railroads and mines, social welfare legislation, and an end to U.S. military intervention in the Caribbean and Central America. The CPPA stopped short of creating a new political party, choosing instead to continue the AFL-brotherhood approach to politics by electing pro-labor Democrats, Republicans, Farmer-Laborites, and Socialists to Congress. Building on their success in the 1922 congressional elections, the brotherhoods drew on their institutional strength and political experience to build a grassroots political machine behind the CPPA-endorsed independent campaign of Robert M. La Follette and Burton K. Wheeler in the 1924 presidential election. The La Follette-Wheeler campaign failed, but the brotherhoods remained active in politics throughout the decade.[2]

In the industrial arena, the brotherhoods continued to influence the course of national labor relations policy. Into the 1920s, representing one of the few strongly unionized segments of industry in the wake of postwar reaction against organized labor, the brotherhoods continued to push the railroads in the interests of their members. That they hung on to work rules and slowed the erosion of wages must be regarded as an achievement in light of the general reverses of the labor movement during the 1920s. Another measure of the brotherhoods' presence during these years related to their lobbying efforts and railroad labor legislation. The failure of the Plumb Plan campaign resulted in the passage of the Transportation Act of 1920, a cumbersome and objectionable piece of legislative machinery that constrained the railroad unions' organizational autonomy. As they worked to deliver friendly, progressive men to Congress, the brotherhoods worked for revision of the Transportation Act, succeeding in 1926 with the Railway Labor Act. The legislation guaranteed workers' rights to choose their bargaining representatives, obliged employers to negotiate with those representatives, and regulated the associational freedom of unions. Amended in 1934 to outlaw "yellow-dog" contracts and to enable the employees of a craft to determine the sole bargaining agent of that craft, the Railway Labor Act governs railroad labor relations to this day. As the centerpiece of 1920s Republican labor policy, the act set an important precedent for the National Labor Relations Act of 1935, the keystone of New Deal—and twentieth-century—labor policy.[3]

Lastly, and as something of a coda, the brotherhoods played a role in New Deal welfare legislation with their involvement in the drafting and passage of the Railroad Retirement Act in 1934. The Retirement Act was significant in its own right, marking a key moment in a decades-long transformation of retirement into social security. But the debates and constitutional tests surrounding its passage also gave formal sanction to the ideology of social security, paving the way for the Social Security Act of 1935. The railroad brotherhoods, therefore, played a minor yet important role in the construction of the welfare state. In this regard, the brotherhoods are notable not only in their own right, but also serve as a concrete link between the political activism of the Progressive Era and the New Deal.[4]

The railroad brotherhoods' successes, however, came as nothing less than a disaster for black railwaymen. Throughout the 1910s and 1920s, the Firemen and Trainmen continued their efforts to drive black workers from their jobs, but with only limited results. Government control of the railroads during the First World War enhanced the ability of these unions to marginalize black workers, but it also provided those workers access to the higher authority of the federal government. With the return of the railroads to private ownership, members of the BRT and BLFE resorted to a series of unauthorized, racially motivated strikes and, in the early 1930s, vigilante-style terrorism against black train workers up and down the Mississippi River Valley. Yet it was the passage of the Railway Labor Act, and its 1934 amendment providing for a single union elected by a majority of workers to represent a given craft (thereby preventing employers from pitting one union against another), that proved most devastating. Because whites constituted the majority in the operating crafts, the provision deprived black railwaymen of effective representation, killing many of their independent unions and clearing the way for the brotherhoods to contractually eliminate them.[5]

The railroad brotherhoods' historical record—for good and ill—suggests something of their significance, as well as the significance of skilled railwaymen generally. As a starting point, this story highlights the importance of skilled workers for the American economy, the labor movement, and labor politics. As with skilled workers in other sectors, railwaymen remained indispensable to the maturing industrial economy well into the twentieth century. In contrast to the deskilling or "homogenization of labor" that occurred in the mass-production industries, railroad managers found it difficult to separate conception from execution in the railroad running trades.[6] They had to rely on the skills of engineers, conductors, firemen, and brakemen to move the trains. Motive power and carrying capacity increased in size, and safety and labor-saving technology made the lives of brakemen and firemen safer and easier over time. But it was only with the technological and organizational changes following the Second World War that management succeeded in breaking the hold of running-trades unions over train operation. Trains that would have required a crew of a half dozen a hundred years ago can be run today with two or three men using electronic and computerized systems of operation and control.

This story also offers insight to the nature and distinctiveness of skilled railroad workers and their organizations. Like their European counterparts, American running-trades workers earned wages and developed a sense of privilege and exclusivity that placed them within the "labor aristocracy," as Eric Hobsbawm has defined it. Such status, however, did not necessarily entail a simple ideological embourgeoisement, as critics sometimes suggest. Both European and American railroaders aspired to respectability, and through trade unions they worked toward that goal collectively as well as individually. Unionism was *necessary* to the privileged status of skilled workers. Membership in a union signaled working-class identity and reflected the realities of working-class life. Similarly, railwaymen's political attitudes and narrow union strategies did not signal an essential conservatism. In the first instance, the brotherhoods represented an important tradition of sustained working-class activism; in the second instance, compared to what? Were laborers and unskilled workers inherently more radical? Not really. The Knights of Labor and the American Railway Union represented broader, more inclusive expressions of union organization in the nineteenth century, a tradition carried out in the more militant, if not revolutionary, Industrial Workers of the World in the twentieth century. But in both Europe and the United States, skilled workers formed the core of labor movements across both centuries, and in France and the United States they stood at the forefront of strike activity. To be sure, skilled railwaymen in the railroad brotherhoods did not aim at the overthrow of capitalism. Rather, as in Howard Kimeldorf's formulation, brotherhood unionism represented a kind of a "business syndicalism" embodying "the struggle of ordinary working men and women to extract some greater measure of comfort and security from a capitalist system that regularly withheld both."[7]

The brotherhoods' story, then, should also help to dispel the stereotyped view of skilled workers as simply the "aristocrats of labor." It was more complicated, for skilled workers like railwaymen occupied a contradictory class position. They stood "in-between" white-collar workers and lower-level managers (who were increasing their earnings and social status by the second decade of the twentieth century) and the manual working class of laborers, domestics, and machine operators (many of them recent immigrants or black). Skilled workers could identify "upward" or "downward," and they could adopt "exclusivist" or "laborist" outlooks. From their vantage points, not only were they in a position to understand the workings of the nation's political economy and its production of class inequality, but they were also in a strategic position to act against it. They could use their institutional strength to act on behalf of both the wider mass of wage earners and, through political action and reform, the general public. Or they could draw on the stable forms of trade unionism that they had developed to look after themselves. Many aspired to upward mobility, seeking greater remunerative rewards and social status in business or government service. This contradictory, "bifocal gaze," in Andrew Dawson's words, characterized the outlook of running-trades workers and the actions of their unions.[8]

Historical circumstances largely determined whether skilled workers identified up or down or whether they pursued more or less exclusive union strategies. It is worth remembering that the Brotherhood of Locomotive Engineers started out as a fairly militant striking union until it was beaten back in a series of early clashes with railroad management in the mid-1860s. Those early experiences led to the ouster of the union's assertive first leadership and its replacement with one that was much more cautious and conservative. It was also at that moment that the BLE made the decision to emphasize benefit work over industrial action. Over the next four decades, brotherhood men articulated a range of opinion on union relations with the railroad corporations. If brotherhood leadership and a majority of members agreed on a vision of harmonious relations, a minority held dissenting views and saw the merits of broader forms of union organization and action. Factors like the railroad labor market, the industry's segmented job hierarchy, the power of the railroad corporations, and the larger legal-political order's hostility to unionism help explain the brotherhoods' exclusivist trade unionism. They also help to explain the changing nature of brotherhood unionism over time. As the structure of railroad industrial relations, the political environment, and matters of culture and national identity changed in the early twentieth century, so too did brotherhood unionism. The brotherhoods may not have become inclusive industrial unions by the era of World War I, but they did become more industrially militant and politically engaged. Compared to their European counterparts, the brotherhoods figure as part of a spectrum of union organization and strategy. In France after 1900, railroad unionism took a decidedly inclusive and syndicalist turn, whereas in Britain, despite calls for more inclusive organizational forms, railroad unionism remained largely craft-based. But in those instances, as in the United States, context and circumstance shaped outcome.

The significance of the railroad brotherhoods resides in how they provide a window onto larger issues of class and gender, unionism and the labor movement, and politics and society, as well as in the impact they had on their times. The history of the railroad brotherhoods illustrates the ways in which the class experience is lived through gender and how gender can shape collective action.[9] As did European unions, the brotherhoods built on, incorporated, and modified the masculine identities and cultures formed in the workplace and household. Like their European counterparts, they drew on workplace experiences and refashioned elements of the dominant culture to their working-class ends. These elements came together in the brotherhoods' fraternal culture and reworking of hegemonic masculinity. Free-labor ideology, the American tradition of republicanism, and the racial order—all of which, in theory at least, asserted the equality of white men—gave brotherhood expressions of manhood a decidedly American cast. Articulated and elaborated in their work culture, fraternal culture, and language of harmonious social relations, understandings of manhood shaped the brotherhoods as all-male associations. By the same token, approaching the brotherhoods as all-male associations casts these dynamics into relief while shedding light on the role of fraternalism in the nineteenth-century U.S. labor movement.

Nevertheless, women mattered to these all-male associations. Through the women's auxiliaries, wives, mothers, and sisters played significant roles in the life of the union, demonstrating that unions were neither entirely homosocial nor exclusively masculinist. Even more important, attention to this fact highlights the relational nature of gender, both between men and women and among the household, workplace, and union. Unions like the brotherhoods may have formed and remained principally oriented toward producing institutional support systems for men's interests, but insofar as men's interests encompassed the household and as women recognized their own interests in the union, that orientation did not go uncontested. In the United States, the unique circumstances of running-trades work and its impact on the household fostered a particular set of gender relations and identities, distinguishing railway families from other working- and middle-class families. Railroad workers' wives developed the auxiliaries into vehicles for the expression and realization of their own interests. Nevertheless, women's interests in the brotherhoods remained largely wedded to and circumscribed by the ideal of the male breadwinner and the family wage.[10]

The history of the railroad brotherhoods also illustrates the pervasive influence of race on working-class life. As with many facets of American life, race was deeply embedded in the social relations of railroading and the communities in which railroaders lived. Together with gender, it functioned as a primary category of identity, shaping the class experience. Indeed, gender and racial solidarities buttressed brotherhood men's sense of class identity and solidarity, a dynamic that became clear in the early twentieth century as brotherhood men articulated their class concerns in an Americanist language of empire, race, and nation. Institutionalized in unions like the railroad brotherhoods, whiteness and racist attitudes toward nonwhite peoples had historical consequences, the most significant of which has been racial inequality and its centrality to the history of the U.S. working class. Employers created and maintained racially segregated labor markets and racialized divisions of labor, but white workers, organized in unions, made these walls of inequality their own. They derived material benefits from these inequalities, and their sense of manhood, citizenship, and nationalism depended on the subordination and exclusion of black workers—the racial "Other." This was by no means a peculiarly American phenomenon, for Europeans also experienced empire and constructed the colonial "Other" in racial terms. But the American experience had its own nature and features due to the historical proximity of slavery, the legacy of the Civil War, and the circumstances under which the United States became a colonial empire in its own right.[11]

The railroad brotherhoods' historical record in matters of race calls into question the very legitimacy of organized labor. Indeed, neoliberal scholars seize on unions' efforts to monopolize jobs for white male workers as evidence of their illegitimacy as inefficiency-producing job cartels. Yet the doctrinaire economic analysis that these critics employ too easily dismisses the cultural and political worlds of workers and their unions, reducing them to caricature.[12] Unions like the brotherhoods *did* work to control the labor market and raise the price of their members' labor. In the age of corporate capitalism and growing class inequality, that was the very point of a union, as Carroll D. Wright explained in 1894. But "bread-and-butter" issues alone do not animate unions and member loyalty. Unions share a basic commitment to protecting their members from arbitrary, unfair treatment by employers, and that is just what the brotherhoods did in creating safer, more equitable workplaces through collective bargaining and legislative lobbying. Unions also foster civic activity, and the brotherhoods engaged in politics and encouraged the political participation of their members. To paraphrase Robert Zieger, the problem with unions like the railroad brotherhoods was not that they attempted to regulate the labor market, but rather that that they discriminated with their regulatory power.[13] And to understand the sources and dynamics of the attitudes and beliefs driving the use of union power demands attention to matters of culture and politics.

"Received" cultural forms and the larger legal-political order shaped the railroad brotherhoods. These unions came into being in the latter third of the nineteenth century to meet the needs of men and their families in the running trades. Railwaymen's work cultures and customary practices of mutual aid, elaborated into institutional form, shaped the brotherhoods' pattern of unionism. Nineteenth-century brotherhood organizers borrowed from the tradition of Masonic fraternalism because it was readily available as an organizing frame. Together, these elements combined to produce the brotherhoods' distinctive fraternal/mutual aid logic, one that fostered deep commitments on the part of members and met the needs of their families. Such an approach made sense within the context of the Victorian moral-legal-political order of the late nineteenth century, and it informed the brotherhoods' approach to labor-capital relations in the Gilded Age. From the 1870s onward, the railroad brotherhoods' fraternal craft culture exhibited elements of individualism and collectivism, as well as exclusivity and solidarity, particularly in its emphasis on moral edification. The brotherhoods' approach to uplift and relations with employers reflected the producerist view that skilled workers deserved both the fruits of their labor and standing as respectable citizens as fundamental moral principles. Such a view derived from the antebellum legacy of artisanal culture, the Victorian ethos of acquisitive individualism, and the political economy of nineteenth-century laissez-faire capitalism.

During the 1890s, brotherhood men, along with organized skilled workers both in the United States and Europe, refashioned their organizational cultures, structures, and strategies with an emphasis on durability and adaptability. The more pragmatic—and arguably less idealistic, where individual perfectibility and social harmony were concerned—new unionism of the early twentieth century was more political and spoke in the language of Americanism, simultaneously positioning itself broadly as for the people and narrowly as serving primarily the interests of brotherhood members and their families. Either way, it accepted bigness in the economy, workers' collective action, and the need to regulate both. To be sure, enough brotherhood men had viewed the large-scale nature of the railroad corporation as inevitable to open the door for support of government intervention for the greater social good. They accepted that competitive capitalism in the railroad industry did not work efficiently either in the product market or in labor relations. This view, a hallmark of the new liberalism, nevertheless contained real limits, for in its envisioning of the broader body politic it excluded those who did not meet the standards of citizenship and respectability by which brotherhood men defined themselves. Thus, insofar as the brotherhoods contributed to the new liberalism through their industrial and political action, one root of the limited liberal state in America may have resided in the complex and contradictory world of skilled workers and the powerful, yet often narrow, forms of unionism that they built.[14]

In this connection, the brotherhoods both offer insight into the process of policy making and state formation that took place at the turn of the century and figure as active agents in that process. As historically conservative and narrowly focused, at least in the conventional view, the brotherhoods at first appear unlikely candidates in this story. Nevertheless, as both "passive" and "active" agents, the brotherhoods influenced labor relations legislation and the direction of the liberal state at crucial moments. That the brotherhoods had little stated intention of playing this historical role only adds complexity to the state-building process. The brotherhoods' interactions with state policy produced unexpected outcomes, highlighting the historical specificity and contingency of policy making demonstrated by scholars of the "new institutionalism." Attention to the role of the brotherhoods in shaping railroad labor policy also sheds light on the often-murky relationship between state and society, and the ways in which organized pressure groups make their interests and desires known.[15] Viewing the railroad brotherhoods in this way illuminates the intricate, historically specific relationships among workers, unions, management, and the state.

During the period under study in this book, the railroad brotherhoods grew from their origins as quasi-fraternal benefit associations to become the most powerful set of unions in the land, commanding the attention of ordinary railroad workers and U.S. presidents alike. Their pattern of growth, change, and influence demands discarding older views of trade unions as being narrow and apolitical. Unions like the brotherhoods demonstrated rich cultures and flexible strategies. The brotherhoods did not reach beyond their own crafts, they rejected ethnic groups other than those that had historically dominated the running trades, and they perpetuated some of the worst tendencies of the U.S. labor movement, but their memberships developed changing and multifaceted ideological beliefs and political attachments. These dynamics caused tension within and among these unions. But they also reflected a diversity of experience and opinion, and they demonstrated an ability to command member loyalty, an acumen for political engagement, and a flexibility and capacity for change that has often gone unappreciated in the history of trade unionism.

The history of the railroad brotherhoods may have relevance and applicability today. As some scholars have argued, the brotherhoods' mutual aid logic can serve as a model for the current labor movement in its struggles to win new members and retain current ones within a hostile political climate.[16] The railroad brotherhoods, unexpectedly maybe, can contribute to a useable past, even as negative examples where the shortcomings of trade unionism and its racial practices are concerned. At the least, understanding the brotherhoods' culture and approach to unionism helps us make sense of these organizations and the circumstances that produced them. Until we know more about the successes and failures, strong points and shortcomings, of unions like the railroad brotherhoods, we will not fully comprehend the history of American labor.

Notes

Introduction. Reconsidering the Railroad Brotherhoods

1. *Locomotive Firemen's Magazine* 33 (October 1902), 547–56 (hereafter *LFM*); *New York Times,* September 9, 1902; Edmund Morris, *Theodore Rex* (New York: HarperCollins, 2001), 18–19, 44–45.

2. Eric Rauchway, *Murdering McKinley: The Making of Theodore Roosevelt's America* (New York: Hill and Wang, 2003), x–xiii, 3, 14–20, 86–96 166–74.

3. Bruno Ramirez, *When Workers Fight: The Politics of Industrial Relations in the Progressive Era, 1898–1916* (Westport, Conn.: Greenwood Press, 1978), 33–45; Michael McGerr, *A Fierce Discontent: The Rise and Fall of the Progressive Movement in America* (New York: Oxford University Press, 2003), 118–25; Morris, *Theodore Rex,* 144–69.

4. *New York Times,* September 9, 1902.

5. I am using the term "responsible unionism" less in the sense elaborated by Ruth O'Brien (as a legal theory of union standing and accountability), and more as Mary Furner uses it (to describe unions as a responsible presence in a system of industrial relations). See Ruth O'Brien, *Workers' Paradox: The Republican Origins of New Deal Labor Policy, 1886–1935* (Chapel Hill: University of North Carolina Press, 1998), 1–18, 39–62; Mary O. Furner, "The Republican Tradition and the New Liberalism: Social Investigation, State Building, and Social Learning in the Gilded Age," in Michael J. Lacey and Mary O. Furner, eds., *The State and Social Investigation in Britain and the United States* (Cambridge: Cambridge University Press, 1993), 201–13.

6. See David Montgomery, *The Fall of the House of Labor: The Workplace, the State, and American Labor Activism, 1865–1925* (Cambridge: Cambridge University Press, 1987), 399–404; Karen Orren, *Belated Feudalism: Labor, the Law, and Liberal Development in the United States* (Cambridge: Cambridge University Press, 1991), 4, 19–20, 29–30, 210–11.

7. Montgomery, *Fall of the House of Labor,* 365–66; Eric Arnesen, *Brotherhoods of Color: Black Railroad Workers and the Struggle for Equality* (Cambridge: Harvard University Press, 2001), 28–41; Howard Kimeldorf, *Battling for American Labor: Wobblies, Craft Workers, and the Making of the Union Movement* (Berkeley and Los Angeles: University of California Press, 1999), 2.

8. See Selig Perlman, *A Theory of the Labor Movement* (New York: Macmillan, 1928; repr., New York: Augustus M. Kelley, 1949). See also Howard Kimeldorf's discussion of the "proletarian conservatism" thesis in *Battling for American Labor,* 7–11.

9. John R. Commons et al., *History of Labour in the United States,* vol. 2 (New York: Macmillan, 1921), 63–68, 309–10; Selig Perlman, *A History of Trade Unionism in the United States* (New York: Macmillan, 1922; repr., New York: Augustus M. Kelley, 1949), 6, 131, 154–55, 162–76, 182–207. Gompers quoted in Michael Kazin, *Barons of Labor: The San Francisco Building Trades and Union Power in the Progressive Era* (Urbana: University of Illinois Press, 1987), 3. See Kimeldorf, *Battling for American Labor,* 2–4, for this assessment of scholarly opinion.

10. See David Brody, "The Old Labor History and the New: In Search of an American Working Class," *Labor History* 20 (1979): 111–26. More recent work in labor history has contributed to a more nuanced picture of craft unionism, particularly concerning its organizational cultures, diverse memberships, flexible strategies, political engagement, and relations with the state. See, for example, Kazin, *Barons of Labor*; Dorothy Sue Cobble, *Dishing It Out: Waitresses and Their Unions in the Twentieth Century* (Urbana: University of Illinois Press, 1991); Christopher Tomlins, "AFL Unions in the 1930s: Their Performance in Historical Perspective," *Journal of American History* 65 (March 1979): 1021–42; Julie Greene, *Pure and Simple Politics: The American Federation of Labor and Political Activism, 1881–1917* (Cambridge: Cambridge University Press, 1998); Victoria C. Hattam, *Labor Visions and State Power: The Origins of Business Unionism in the United States* (Princeton: Princeton University Press, 1993).

11. See Shelton Stromquist, *A Generation of Boomers: The Pattern of Railroad Labor Conflict in Nineteenth-Century America* (Urbana: University of Illinois Press, 1987). See also Shelton Stromquist, "'Our Rights as Workingmen': Class Traditions and Collective Action in a Nineteenth-Century Railroad Town, Hornellsville, N.Y., 1869–82," in David O. Stowell, ed., *The Great Strikes of 1877* (Urbana: University of Illinois Press, 2008), 55–75.

12. For this assessment of the "new" labor history, see Cobble, *Dishing It Out,* 7.

13. For a sampling of the debates over the English "aristocracy of labor," see E. J. Hobsbawm, "The Labour Aristocracy in Nineteenth-Century Britain," in Hobsbawm, ed., *Labouring Men: Studies in the History of Labour* (London: Weidenfeld and Nicolson, 1964); E. J. Hobsbawm, "The Labour Aristocracy Reconsidered," in Hobsbawm, ed., *Worlds of Labour: Further Essays in the History of Labour* (London: Weidenfeld and Nicolson, 1984); Geoffrey Crossick, "The Labour Aristocracy and Its Values: A Study of Mid-Victorian Kentish London," *Victorian Studies* 19 (March 1976): 301–28;

Robert Q. Gray, *The Labour Aristocracy in Nineteenth-Century Britain, c. 1850–1900* (London: Macmillan, 1981).

14. On class boundaries and contradictory class locations, see Erik Olin Wright, *Class, Crisis, and the State* (London: New Left Books, 1978), 61–65, 75–78. On the contradictory location and outlook of skilled workers, see Andrew Dawson, "The Parameters of Craft Consciousness: The Social Outlook of the Skilled Worker, 1890–1920," in Dirk Hoerder, ed., *American Labor and Immigration History, 1877–1920s: Recent European Research* (Urbana: University of Illinois Press, 1983), 137–39. Michael Kazin highlights the ambivalent status and outlook of skilled carpenters in his *Barons of Labor.*

15. For an analysis emphasizing the "homegrown" populist dimension of American workers' attitudes and values over Marxian class-consciousness, see Michael Kazin, *The Populist Persuasion: An American History,* rev. ed. (Ithaca: Cornell University Press, 1998), 49–78.

16. See Kimeldorf, *Battling for American Labor,* 3–5, 11–20; Kazin, *Barons of Labor,* 4.

17. See Ava Baron, ed., *Work Engendered: Toward a New History of American Labor* (Ithaca: Cornell University Press, 1991).

18. See Nick Salvatore, *Eugene V. Debs: Citizen and Socialist* (Urbana: University of Illinois Press, 1982); Gregory L. Kaster, "Labor's True Man: Organised Workingmen and the Language of Manliness in the USA, 1827–1877," *Gender and History* 13 (April 2001): 24–64; Stephen H. Norwood, *Strikebreaking and Intimidation: Mercenaries and Masculinity in Twentieth-Century America* (Chapel Hill: University of North Carolina Press, 2002); and essays in Baron, *Work Engendered.*

19. See, for example, David R. Roediger, *The Wages of Whiteness: Race and the Making of the American Working Class* (New York: Verso, 1991); David Roediger, "Race and the Working-Class Past in the United States: Multiple Identities and the Future of Labor History," *International Review of Social History* 38 (1993): 127–43; Eric Arnesen, "Whiteness and the Historians' Imagination," *International Labor and Working-Class History* 60 (Fall 2001): 3–32, and Responses and Arnesen Reply, 33–92; Peter Kolchin, "Whiteness Studies: The New History of Race in America," *Journal of American History* 89 (June 2002): 154–73.

20. Gail Bederman, *Manliness and Civilization: A Cultural History of Gender and Race in the United States, 1880–1917* (Chicago: University of Chicago Press, 1995), 7–8. See also Joan Wallach Scott, "Gender: A Useful Category of Historical Analysis," in Scott, ed., *Gender and the Politics of History* (New York: Columbia University Press, 1988), 28–50.

21. Evelyn Brooks Higginbotham, "African-American Women's History and the Metalanguage of Race," in Joan Wallach Scott, ed., *Feminism and History* (Oxford: Oxford University Press, 1996), 183–208; Barbara J. Fields, "Ideology and Race in American History," in J. Morgan Kousser and James McPherson, eds., *Region, Race, and Reconstruction: Essays in Honor of C. Vann Woodward* (New York: Oxford Uni-

versity Press, 1982), 151–54, 160–62. See also Roediger, *The Wages of Whiteness*; Barbara J. Fields, "Whiteness, Racism, and Identity," *International Labor and Working-Class History* 60 (Fall 2001): 48–52; Eric Foner, "Response to Eric Arnesen," *International Labor and Working-Class History* 60 (Fall 2001): 58–59.

22. Rose M. Brewer, "Theorizing Race, Class and Gender: The New Scholarship of Black Feminist Intellectuals and Black Women's Labor," in Stanlie M. James and Abenia P. A. Busia, eds., *Theorizing Black Feminisms: The Visionary Pragmatism of Black Women* (New York: Routledge, 1993), 16–17.

23. Daniel Nelson, *Divided We Stand: American Workers and the Struggle for Black Equality* (Princeton: Princeton University Press, 2001), 293–94.

24. For a sampling of the literature on black workers, white workers, and the labor movement, see Herbert Hill, "Race, Ethnicity, and Organized Labor: The Opposition to Affirmative Action," *New Politics* 1 (Winter 1987): 31–82; Herbert Hill, "The Problem of Race in American Labor History," *Reviews in American History* 24 (June 1996): 189–208; Eric Arnesen, "Up from Exclusion: Black and White Workers, Race, and the State of Labor History," *Reviews in American History* 26 (March 1998): 146–74; Robert H. Zieger, *For Jobs and Freedom: Race and Labor in America Since 1865* (Lexington: University Press of Kentucky, 2007).

25. See Nelson, *Divided We Stand*, xxxi–xxxii.

26. Roediger, "Race and the Working-Class Past," 134.

27. See Ava Baron, "Gender and Labor History: Learning from the Past, Looking to the Future," in Baron, ed., *Work Engendered: Toward a New History of American Labor* (Ithaca: Cornell University Press, 1991), 3; Colleen A. Dunlavy, *Politics and Industrialization: Early Railroads in the United States and Prussia* (Princeton: Princeton University Press, 1994), 5–11; Jonathan Zeitlin, "From Labor History to the History of Industrial Relations," *Economic History Review* 2 (1987): 159–60; Meg Jacobs and Julian E. Zelizer, "The Democratic Experiment: New Directions in American Political History," in Meg Jacobs, William J. Novak, and Julian E. Zelizer, eds., *The Democratic Experiment: New Directions in American Political History* (Princeton: Princeton University Press, 2003), 4–6. The phrase "un-Commons" is Baron's.

28. See Gerald Friedman, *State-Making and Labor Movements: France and the United States, 1876–1914* (Ithaca: Cornell University Press, 1998), 13–14, 21, 302–3; William E. Forbath, *Law and the Shaping of the American Labor Movement* (Cambridge: Harvard University Press, 1991), 1–9; Hattam, *Labor Visions and State Power,* 11–21; Greene, *Pure and Simple Politics,* 9.

29. Walter Licht, *Working for the Railroad: The Organization of Work in the Nineteenth Century* (Princeton: Princeton University Press, 1983); Stromquist, *A Generation of Boomers.* James Ducker, *Men of the Steel Rails: Workers on the Atchison, Topeka, and Santa Fe, 1869–1900* (Lincoln: University of Nebraska Press, 1983), is a rich portrayal of the lives of railwaymen on a single railroad, with attention paid to the railroad brotherhoods. Documenting the workplace experiences and union histories of African American railwaymen, Eric Arnesen's *Brotherhoods of Color* has

shifted our understanding of railroad unionism and the relationship of unionism to civil rights.

30. See George Rogers Taylor, *The Transportation Revolution, 1815–1860* (New York: Rinehart, 1951); Barbara Young Welke, *Recasting American Liberty: Gender, Race, Law, and the Railroad Revolution, 1865–1920* (New York: Cambridge University Press), 2001.

31. Commons et al., *History of Labour*, vol. 2, 13–15, 62; Stromquist, *A Generation of Boomers*, 48–99. In 1889 the Brotherhood of Railroad Brakemen renamed itself the Brotherhood of Railroad Trainmen (BRT), and in 1907 the Brotherhood of Locomotive Firemen became the Brotherhood of Locomotive Firemen and Enginemen (BLFE).

32. See Eric Foner, *Reconstruction: America's Unfinished Revolution, 1863–1877* (New York: Harper and Row, 1988); David Gordon, Richard Edwards, and Michael Reich, *Segmented Work, Divided Workers: The Historical Transformation of the United States* (New York: Cambridge University Press, 1982); Richard Schneirov, Shelton Stromquist, and Nick Salvatore, eds., *The Pullman Strike and the Crisis of the 1890s: Essays on Labor and Politics* (Urbana: University of Illinois Press, 1999); Martin J. Sklar, *The Corporate Reconstruction of American Capitalism, 1890–1916* (New York: Cambridge University Press, 1988).

Chapter 1. Workplace and Household Life in the Running Trades

1. Chauncey Del French, *Railroadman* (New York: Macmillan, 1938), 60–61, 81–83, 86–87, 96, 101–4.

2. Lance E. Davis et al., *American Economic Growth: An Economist's History of the United States* (New York: Harper and Row, 1972), 493, 500–505; Alfred Chandler Jr., *The Visible Hand: The Managerial Revolution in American Business* (Cambridge: Harvard University Press, 1977), 88, 159–85.

3. Licht, *Working for the Railroad*, 31–33; Mark Aldrich, *Safety First: Technology, Labor, and Business in the Building of American Work Safety, 1870–1939* (Baltimore: Johns Hopkins University Press, 1997), 15.

4. Licht, *Working for the Railroad*, 34–35; U.S. Department of Commerce, Bureau of the Census, *Historical Statistics of the Population of the United States: Colonial Times to 1970* (Washington, D.C.: Government Printing Office, 1975), 139, 740.

5. Chandler, *The Visible Hand*, 94–109; Licht, *Working for the Railroad*, 23; Dunlavy, *Politics and Industrialization*, 16–17, 33, 146; Margot B. Stein, *The Social Origins of a Labor Elite: French Engine-Drivers, 1837–1917* (New York: Garland Publishing, 1987), 68–71, 79–84.

6. Frank McKenna, "Victorian Railway Workers," *History Workshop Journal* 1 (Spring 1976): 42–47.

7. Licht, *Working for the Railroad*, 33; Montgomery, *Fall of the House of Labor*, 66–81.

8. Licht, *Working for the Railroad,* 33–34, 215; Colin J. Davis, *Power at Odds: The 1922 National Shopmen's Strike* (Urbana: University of Illinois Press, 1997), 21–23.

9. See Licht, *Working for the Railroad,* 221–23; Stein, *The Social Origins of a Labor Elite,* 201, 417–20; McKenna, "Victorian Railway Workers," 27.

10. See Licht, *Working for the Railroad,* 67–69, 214–16, 224–25; Arnesen, *Brotherhoods of Color,* 24–27.

11. Licht, *Working for the Railroad,* 153, 288; Stein, *The Social Origins of a Labor Elite,* 424–25; Stromquist, *A Generation of Boomers,* 122, 131–32.

12. Licht, *Working for the Railroad,* 153; Russell L. Johnson, *Warriors into Workers: The Civil War and the Formation of Urban-Industrial Society in a Northern City* (New York: Fordham University Press, 2003), 9, 12, 104, 146–47, 317–22.

13. Reed C. Richardson, *The Locomotive Engineer, 1863–1963: A Century of Railway Labor Relations and Work Rules* (Ann Arbor: University of Michigan, 1963), 93–94; B. B. Adams, "The Every-Day Life of Railroad Men," in Thomas Curtis Clarke et al., *The American Railway: Its Construction, Development, and Appliances* (New York: Scribner's, 1889), 402–3.

14. Brotherhood of Locomotive Firemen and Enginemen, *Feeding the Iron Hog: The Life and Work of a Locomotive Fireman* (Cleveland: Brotherhood of Locomotive Firemen and Enginemen, 1927), 19–20; Richardson, *The Locomotive Engineer,* 103.

15. W. Fred Cottrell, *The Railroader* (Stanford: Stanford University Press), 18; Adams, "The Every-Day Life of Railroad Men," 398–99; U.S. Congress, House of Representatives, *Report of the Eight-Hour Commission,* Appendix VII, "Employment Conditions in Train and Yard Service Under the Eight-Hour Law," by Victor S. Clark, H. doc. 690, 65th Cong., 2d sess. (1918), 384–85.

16. Charles Clark, "The Railroad Safety Movement in the United States: Origins and Development, 1869–1893" (PhD diss., University of Illinois–Urbana, 1966), 14–26.

17. Licht, *Working for the Railroad,* 126–30; U.S. Bureau of Labor Statistics, *Railway Employees in the United States, Bulletin No. 37,* by Samuel M'Cune Lindsay (Washington, D.C.: Government Printing Office, 1901), 1038–40; U.S. Commissioner of Labor, *Fifth Annual Report of the Commissioner of Labor, 1889: Railroad Labor* (Washington, D.C.: Government Printing Office, 1890), 140, 143–44; Perlman, *History of Trade Unionism,* 181.

18. Marla Hughes, "Social Relations in a Railroad Town: The Locomotive Engineers, Locomotive Firemen, and Switchmen of Galesburg, Illinois, and the Burlington Strike" (PhD diss., University of Maryland, 1996), 155; Stromquist, *A Generation of Boomers,* 106–7; Hobsbawm, "The Labour Aristocracy," 273, 292.

19. U.S. Commissioner of Labor, *Fifth Annual Report,* 163–65; U.S. Bureau of Labor Statistics, *Railway Employees in the United States,* 1036, 1046; U.S. House of Representatives, "Employment Conditions," 402–3; *Locomotive Engineers' Monthly Journal* 3 (November 1869), 487.

20. Licht, *Working for the Railroad,* 164–74; U.S. Commissioner of Labor, *Fifth Annual Report,* 82, 122, 108, 126, 136, 139.

21. Richardson, *The Locomotive Engineer,* 112; Stromquist, *A Generation of Boomers,* 116–17, 119–20.

22. U.S. Commissioner of Labor, *Fifth Annual Report,* 82, 122, 108, 126, 136, 139; U.S. House of Representatives, "Employment Conditions," 382–83, 393–94.

23. McKenna, "Victorian Railway Workers," 48; U.S. Industrial Commission, *Report of the Industrial Commission on Labor Organizations, Labor Disputes and Arbitration, and on Railway Labor,* vol. 17 (Washington, D.C.: Government Printing Office, 1901), 848.

24. See Amy G. Richter, *Home on the Rails: Women, the Railroad, and the Rise of Public Domesticity* (Chapel Hill: University of North Carolina Press, 2005), 149–52.

25. Licht, *Working for the Railroad,* 190–94; McKenna, "Victorian Railway Workers," 51–52.

26. Aldrich, *Safety First,* 15; Gunther Peck, "Manly Gambles: The Politics of Risk on the Comstock Lode, 1860–1880," *Journal of Social History* 26, no. 4 (Summer 1993): 718n20.

27. Illinois Bureau of Labor Statistics, *Biennial Report of the Bureau of Labor Statistics of Illinois* (Springfield: Illinois State Journal Co., State Printers,, 1908), 74, 13, 156, 17.

28. Aldrich, *Safety First,* 17–25; Robert Wiebe, *Self-Rule: A Cultural History of American Democracy* (Chicago: University of Chicago Press, 1995), 94–95.

29. Licht, *Working for the Railroad,* 194–96; Fred L. Feick, *The Life of Railway Men* (Chicago: H. O. Shepard, 1905), 27–31; U.S. Commissioner of Labor, *Fifth Annual Report,* 42.

30. U.S. House of Representatives, "Employment Conditions," 387; French, *Railroadman,* 15.

31. Richardson, *The Locomotive Engineer,* 98–99.

32. Mark Rosenfeld, "'She Was a Hard Life': Work, Family, Community, Politics, and Ideology in the Railway Ward of a Central Ontario Town, 1900–1960" (PhD diss., York University, 1990), 148–50, 155–62; Elizabeth Jameson, *All That Glitters: Class, Conflict, and Community in Cripple Creek* (Urbana: University of Illinois Press, 1998), 115.

33. Ducker, *Men of the Steel Rails,* 72–73. Walter Licht, in *Working for the Railroad,* found that close to 60 percent of railwaymen living in Philadelphia in 1880, and 80 percent of a sample of Illinois Central Railroad employees in 1900, were married. See Licht, *Working for the Railroad,* 226n45.

34. Kansas Bureau of Labor and Industrial Statistics, *Sixth Annual Report of the Bureau of Labor and Industrial Statistics* (Topeka, 1891), 120; Kansas Bureau of Labor and Industrial Statistics, *Sixteenth Annual Report of the Bureau of Labor and Industrial Statistics* (Topeka, 1901), 22, 24, 28, 30.

35. Ileen A. DeVault, *Sons and Daughters of Labor: Class and Clerical Work in Turn-of-the-Century Pittsburgh* (Ithaca: Cornell University Press, 1990), 102–3; Stein, *The Social Origins of a Labor Elite,* 429–30; Jameson, *All That Glitters,* 121.

36. Licht, *Working for the Railroad,* 226n45; Ducker, *Men of the Steel Rails,* 72–73; Illinois Bureau of Labor Statistics, *Second Biennial Report of the Bureau of Labor Statistics of Illinois* (Springfield, 1884), 270–75, 261–63, 257, 308–9.

37. Illinois Bureau of Labor Statistics, *Second Biennial Report,* 270–75, 261–63, 257.

38. Stromquist, *Generation of Boomers,* 107, 116; Hughes, "Social Relations in a Railroad Town," 157–58.

39. Rosenfeld, "'She Was a Hard Life,'" 149.

40. Jeanne Boydston, *Home and Work: Housework, Wages, and the Ideology of Labor in the Early Republic* (New York: Oxford University Press, 1990), 134–37.

41. Rosenfeld, "'She Was a Hard Life,'" 158–59.

42. Stein, *The Social Origins of a Labor Elite,* 213–14, 219, 225–27; Rosenfeld, "'She Was a Hard Life,'" 149, 159.

43. Boydston, *Home and Work,* 82–83; Rosenfeld, "'She Was a Hard Life,'" 165–66; *Locomotive Firemen and Enginemen's Magazine* 46 (January 1909), 116 (hereafter *LFEM*).

44. Ducker, *Men of the Steel Rails,* 81–83; Stein, *The Social Origins of a Labor Elite,* 219, 225–26. *Emporia Gazette* quoted in Ducker, *Men of the Steel Rails,* 80–81.

45. Ducker, *Men of the Steel Rails,* 129–30; *LFEM* 46 (January 1909), 116.

46. See letters from "May," *LFM* 14 (October 1890), 885; "Ruby," *LFM* 15 (February 1891), 130; *Railroad Brakemen's Journal* 9 (May 1892), 419 (hereafter *RBJ*).

47. Sam Speas, as told to Margaret Coel, *Goin' Railroading: A Century on the Colorado High Iron* (Boulder, Colo.: Pruett Publishing, 1985), 60.

48. Rosenfeld, "'She Was a Hard Life,'" 187–91, 162; Boydston, *Home and Work,* 91–92; *LFEM* 46 (January 1909), 116.

49. Jameson, *All That Glitters,* 118, 121–22. See, for example, *LFM* 26 (January 1899), 57.

50. John Tosh, "What Should Historians Do with Masculinity? Reflections on Nineteenth-Century Britain," *History Workshop Journal* 38 (1994): 185; Rosenfeld, "'She Was a Hard Life,'" 155. Engineer's son quoted in Rosenfeld, "'She Was a Hard Life,'" 155. See also Barbara Welter, "The Cult of True Womanhood: 1820–1860," *American Quarterly* 18 (Summer 1966): 151–74.

51. Rosenfeld, "'She Was a Hard Life,'" 208–14.

52. See Jameson, *All That Glitters,* 121.

53. David Montgomery, "Workers' Control of Machine Production in the Nineteenth Century," in Montgomery, ed., *Workers' Control in the United States* (Cambridge: Cambridge University Press, 1979), 13–15; Susan Porter Benson, "'The Customers Ain't God': The Work Culture of Department-Store Saleswomen," in Michael J. Frisch and Daniel J. Walkowitz, eds., *Working-Class America: Essays on Labor, Community, and American Society* (Urbana: University of Illinois Press, 1983), 184–85; Richardson, *The Locomotive Engineer,* 102–3; David Montgomery, *Citizen Worker: The Experience of Workers in the United States with Democracy and the Free Market During the Nineteenth Century* (Cambridge: Cambridge University Press, 1993), 44–51; Stromquist, "'Our Collective Rights,'" 69; Licht, *Working for the Railroad,* 123.

54. Licht, *Working for the Railroad,* 80; McKenna, "Victorian Railway Workers," 27–31; Stein, *The Social Origins of a Labor Elite,* 84–86; Andy Friedman, "Responsible Autonomy Versus Direct Control over the Labour Process," *Capital and Class* 1 (Spring 1977): 47–48, 51–53.

55. Licht, *Working for the Railroad,* 87, 93, 122–24. Compared to English railways, however, discipline on American railroads appears to have been neither as rigid nor as combined with the kind of paternal welfarism characteristic of railroad companies in England. See McKenna, "Victorian Railway Workers," 31–41.

56. Frederick Gamst, "The Railroad Apprentice and the 'Rules': Historic Roots and Contemporary Practices," in Michael W. Coy, ed., *Apprenticeship: From Theory to Method and Back Again* (Albany: State University of New York Press, 1989), 70–71; Licht, *Working for the Railroad,* 89–93.

57. Gamst, "The Railroad Apprentice and the 'Rules,'" 66, 73.

58. Licht, *Working for the Railroad,* 93, 98–100; French, *Railroadman,* 153–55.

59. Montgomery, "Workers' Control," 13–15.

60. Michael Kimmel, *Manhood in America: A Cultural History* (New York: The Free Press, 1996), 16, 28–30.

61. On the Union army as an industrial workplace, see Johnson, *Warriors into Workers,* 145–91.

62. Gamst, "The Railroad Apprentice and the 'Rules,'" 72; Samuel B. Bacharach, Peter A. Bamberger, and William J. Sonnenstuhl, *Mutual Aid and Union Renewal: Cycles of Logics of Action* (Ithaca: Cornell University Press, 2001), 61.

63. Licht, *Working for the Railroad,* 232–35; Ramon F. Adams, *The Language of the Railroader* (Norman: Oklahoma University Press, 1977), 20–21, 27, 36, 50, 55, 74, 115, 141.

64. Rosenfeld, "'She Was a Hard Life,'" 101–2; Licht, *Working for the Railroad,* 233.

65. *LFM* 14 (June 1890), 555; *LFM* 22 (May 1897), 335.

66. Licht, *Working for the Railroad,* 233–34.

67. McKenna, "Victorian Railway Workers," 42; Adams, *The Language of the Railroader,* 144; Hobsbawm, "The Labour Aristocracy Reconsidered," 236. Costa quoted in Rosenfeld, "'She Was a Hard Life,'" 104.

68. Roediger, *The Wages of Whiteness.*

69. Arnesen, *Brotherhoods of Color,* 32–33; *LFM* (September 1887), 516.

70. See Robin D. G. Kelley, "'We Are Not What We Seem': Rethinking Black Working-Class Opposition in the Jim Crow South," *Journal of American History* 80 (June 1993): 100–101; Roediger, "Race and the Working-Class Past," 135–37.

71. Roediger, "Race and the Working-Class Past," 136–37; Adams, *The Language of the Railroader,* 14, 105; Coel, *Goin' Railroading,* 10.

72. Ducker, *Men of the Steel Rails,* 59. On middle-class attitudes toward manual labor, see Jonathan Glickstein, *Concepts of Free Labor in Antebellum America* (New Haven: Yale University Press, 1991), 9–10, 14–16.

73. See Salvatore, *Eugene V. Debs,* 46; Montgomery, "Workers' Control," 13.

74. See Paul Willis, "Shop-Floor Culture, Masculinity, and the Wage Form," in John

Clarke, Charles Crichter, and Richard Johnson, eds., *Working Class Cultures: Studies in History and Theory* (New York: St. Martin's Press, 1979), 188–89, 196; Rosenfeld, "'She Was a Hard Life,'" 105–10, 270.

75. Herbert Hamblen, *The General Manager's Story: Old-Time Reminiscences of Railroading in the United States* (New York: Macmillan, 1898; repr., Upper Saddle River, N.J.: Gregg Press, 1970), 232–33.

76. Frances Clarke, "'Honorable Scars': Northern Amputees and the Meaning of Civil War Injuries," in Paul A. Cimbala and Randall M. Miller, eds., *Union Soldiers and the Northern Homefront: Wartime Experiences, Postwar Adjustments* (New York: Fordham University Press, 2002), 379; Elliot J. Gorn, *The Manly Art: Bare-Knuckle Prize Fighting in America* (Ithaca: Cornell University Press, 1986), 160–61; David W. Blight, "No Desperate Hero: Manhood and Freedom in a Union Soldier's Experience," in Blight, ed., *Beyond the Battlefield: Race, Memory, and the American Civil War* (Amherst: University of Massachusetts Press, 2002), 60–62.

77. *RBJ* 3 (March 1886), 6; John Williams-Searle, "Courting Risk: Disability, Masculinity, and Liability on Iowa's Railroads, 1868–1900," *Annals of Iowa* 58 (Winter 1999): 41–45.

78. Clarke, "'Honorable Scars,'" 362–68, 379, 389; Drew Gilpin Faust, *This Republic of Suffering: Death and the American Civil War* (New York: Knopf, 2008), xi–xiii.

79. Licht, *Working for the Railroad,* 236–38; French, *Railroadman,* 11–12.

80. CB&Q official quoted in Paul V. Black, "Employee Alcoholism on the Burlington Railroad, 1876–1902," *Journal of the West* 17, no. 4 (1978): 6.

81. "Clinton M. Graham," in Stuart Leuthner, ed., *The Railroaders* (New York: Random House, 1983), 57.

82. Bacharach, Bamberger, and Sonnenstuhl, *Mutual Aid and Union Renewal,* 56–60, 75–76; French, *Railroadman,* 11–12. *Locomotive Engineers' Monthly Journal* (hereafter *LEMJ*) quoted in Licht, *Working for the Railroad,* 238.

83. French, *Railroadman,* 11–12, 157–58.

84. Black, "Employee Alcoholism on the Burlington Railroad," 3, 6–7; French, *Railroadman,* 81–83, 86–87, 96, 101–4.

85. Richardson, *The Locomotive Engineer,* 106–9, 118–19; Licht, *Working for the Railroad,* 69–70; Commons et al., *History of Labour,* vol. 2, 13–15.

86. Stromquist, "'Our Collective Rights,'" 58–59, 66–69.

Chapter 2. Victorian America and the Brotherhoods' Fraternal Culture

1. Order of Railway Conductors, *Ritual for the Use of Subordinate Divisions of the Order of Railway Conductors* (Cedar Rapids, Iowa: n.p., 1911), 7–12, Order of Railway Conductors and Brakemen Archives, 5148 (hereafter ORC Archives), Kheel Center for Labor-Management Documentation and Archives, Martin P. Catherwood Library, Cornell University (hereafter Kheel Center).

2. See Mary Ann Clawson, *Constructing Brotherhood: Class, Gender, and Fraternal-*

ism (Princeton: Princeton University Press, 1989), 4–5, 136–37; Lynn Dumenil, *Free Masonry and American Culture, 1880–1930* (Princeton: Princeton University Press, 1984), 31–111.

3. David T. Beito, *From Mutual Aid to the Welfare State: Fraternal Societies and Social Services, 1890–1967* (Chapel Hill: University of North Carolina Press, 2000), 1–2, 5–16.

4. Alan Derickson, *Workers' Health, Workers' Democracy: The Western Miners' Struggle, 1891–1925* (Ithaca: Cornell University Press, 1989), xi–xii; James B. Kennedy, *Beneficiary Features of American Trade Unions* (Baltimore: Johns Hopkins University Press, 1908), 7–83; U.S. Department of Labor, Bureau of Labor Statistics, *Beneficial Activities of American Trade Unions, Bulletin No. 465* (Washington, D.C.: Government Printing Office, 1928), 45–84.

5. Bacharach, Bamberger, and Sonnenstuhl, *Mutual Aid and Union Renewal*, 7–8; Robert Franklin Hoxie, *Trade Unionism in the United States* (New York: D. Appleton, 1920), 47.

6. See Brian Greenberg, *Worker and Community: Response to Industrialization in a Nineteenth-Century American City, Albany, New York, 1850–1884* (Albany: State University of New York Press, 1985), 97–99.

7. Melvyn Dubofsky, "The Federal Judiciary, Free Labor, and Equal Rights," in Richard Schneirov, Shelton Stromquist, and Nick Salvatore, eds., *The Pullman Strike and the Crisis of the 1890s: Essays on Labor and Politics* (Urbana: University of Illinois Press, 1999), 167.

8. See Tosh, "What Should Historians Do with Masculinity?" 186; Clawson, *Constructing Brotherhood*, 14–15, 30, 146, 248-49; Sidney Tarrow, *Power in Movement: Social Movements, Collective Action, and Politics* (Cambridge: Cambridge University Press, 1994), 21–22.

9. John Fabian Witt, *The Accidental Republic: Crippled Workingmen, Destitute Widows, and the Remaking of American Law* (Cambridge: Harvard University Press, 2004), 71–73, 76.

10. Ibid., 77–79; George James Stevenson, "The Brotherhood of Locomotive Engineers and Its Leaders, 1863–1920" (PhD diss., Vanderbilt University, 1954), 93–97; Kennedy, *Beneficiary Features of American Trade Unions*, 19–27.

11. U.S. Department of Labor, Bureau of Labor Statistics, *Brotherhood Relief and Insurance of Railway Employees, Bulletin No. 17*, by Emory R. Johnson (Washington, D.C.: Government Printing Office, 1898), 587.

12. Drew Gilpin Faust, "The Civil War Soldier and the Art of Dying," *Journal of Southern History* 67 (February 2001): 3–6; Faust, *This Republic of Suffering*, xi–xiv; Clarke, "'Honorable Scars,'" 362; Theda Skocpol, *Protecting Soldiers and Mothers: The Politics of Social Policy in the United States* (Cambridge: Harvard University Press, 1992), 149–51; Witt, *The Accidental Republic*, 23–24.

13. Derickson, *Workers' Health, Workers' Democracy*, 61–62; Vivian A. Rotman Zelizer, *Morals and Markets: The Development of Life Insurance in the United States*

(New York: Columbia University Press, 1979), 43–46, 91–93; Dumenil, *Free Masonry and American Culture,* 103–4.

14. Brotherhood of Railroad Brakemen, *Constitution and By-Laws of the Brotherhood of Railroad Brakemen* (Galesburg, Ill., 1886), 2.

15. *Firemen's Magazine* 1 (December 1876), 29 (hereafter *FM*); *LFM* 22 (January 1897), 23.

16. See Kennedy, *Beneficiary Features of American Trade Unions,* 27–28.

17. See Order of Railway Conductors, *Constitution* [1868], in *Proceedings of the Grand Division of the Order of Railway Conductors, from Organization to the Eighteenth Session, Inclusive, 1868–1885* (Cedar Rapids, Iowa, 1888), 21; Brotherhood of Locomotive Engineers, *Constitution and By-Laws of the Grand International Brotherhood of Locomotive Engineers* (Cleveland, 1885), 25.

18. Brotherhood of Railroad Trainmen, Division No. 191, Minute Book, vol. 1, February 7, 1886, October 6, 1889, April 29, 1887, August 1891, October 11, 1891, vol. 2, June 19, 1892, vol. 4, March 26, 1916, Brotherhood of Railroad Trainmen, A. W. Gardner Lodge No. 191, Records, State Historical Society of Wisconsin (hereafter BRT 191, Minute Book).

19. U.S. Interstate Commerce Commission, "Relations Existing Between Railway Corporations and Their Employes," in *Sixth Annual Report, 1892* (Washington, D.C.: Government Printing Office, 1893), 328–29.

20. See Brotherhood of Railroad Trainmen, Division No. 177, Minutes, February 14, 1886, April 14, 1886, August 22, 1886, Brotherhood of Railroad Trainmen, Lodge No. 177, Records, box 1, folder 1, State Historical Society of Wisconsin, Madison, Wisconsin (hereafter BRT 177, Records).

21. See U.S. Bureau of Labor Statistics, *Brotherhood Relief and Insurance,* 577–79.

22. See Brotherhood of Railroad Trainmen, Lodge No. 164, Utica, New York, *Mutual Aid Fund By-Laws* (Utica, N.Y.: n.p., 1901), 4; BRT 191, Minute Book, vol. 4, February 26, 1911.

23. Brotherhood of Railroad Brakemen, *Constitution* (1886), 28.

24. See Brotherhood of Railroad Trainmen, Moosic Tunnel Lodge No. 93, Minute Book, January 14, 1894, Kheel Center (hereafter BRT 93).

25. *Railroad Trainmen's Journal* (hereafter *RTJ*) 8 (May 1891), 248–49; Derickson, *Workers' Health, Workers' Democracy,* 69–70.

26. Brotherhood of Locomotive Engineers, *Constitution* [1885], 57–58; U.S. Bureau of Labor Statistics, *Brotherhood Relief and Insurance,* 564–65.

27. *RTJ* 12 (March 1895), 362, 458.

28. BRT 191, Minute Book, vol. 2, June 19, 1892.

29. See Brotherhood of Locomotive Engineers, Simpson Division No. 210, Minutes, August 4, 1901, Brotherhood of Locomotive Engineers, Simpson Division No. 210, Records, box 314, folder 26, The Southern Labor Archives, William Russell Pullen Library, Georgia State University, Atlanta, Georgia (hereafter BLE 210, Records).

30. Derickson, *Workers' Health, Workers' Democracy,* 77–79; *LFM* 23 (November 1897), 444–45.

31. Witt, *Accidental Republic*, 72, 88–89; Jameson, *All That Glitters*, 93.

32. David I. Kertzer, *Ritual, Politics, and Power* (New Haven: Yale University Press, 1988), 15–16.

33. Stevenson, "The Brotherhood of Locomotive Engineers and Its Leaders," 35–36; Richardson, *The Locomotive Engineer*, 125–28; Edwin C. Robbins, *Railway Conductors: A Study in Organized Labor* (New York: Columbia University Studies in Social Sciences, 1914), 25–30.

34. Order of Railway Conductors, *Constitution* [1881], 467.

35. See *Order of Railway Conductors, Catalogue No. 28, Illustrated and Descriptive Price List Supplies and Regalia, Manufactured by The Henderson-Ames Co., Kalamazoo, Mich.*, ORC Archives.

36. Order of Railway Conductors, *Ritual*, 5–6, 15–16.

37. Brotherhood of Locomotive Firemen and Enginemen, *Ritual of the Brotherhood of Locomotive Firemen and Enginemen* (n.p.: 1920), 7–14, 27–28, 47–51, Brotherhood of Locomotive Firemen and Enginemen Archives, 5141, Kheel Center.

38. Allan Pinkerton, *Strikers, Communists, Tramps, and Detectives* (New York: G. W. Carlton, 1878; repr., New York: Arno Press, 1969), 125–29.

39. See Order of Railway Conductors, *Ritual*, 7–12; Robert E. Weir, *Beyond Labor's Veil: The Culture of the Knights of Labor* (University Park: Pennsylvania State University Press, 1996), 26.

40. Pinkerton, *Strikers, Communists, Tramps, and Detectives*, 120–25. To be sure, Pinkerton may have embellished this account for dramatic purpose.

41. See E. J. Hobsbawm, "Ritual in Social Movements," in Hobsbawm, ed., *Primitive Rebels: Studies in Archaic Forms of Social Movement in the 19th and 20th Centuries* (New York: Praeger, 1963), 150–74; Clawson, *Constructing Brotherhood*, 180–81, 196–97.

42. Brotherhood of Railway Carmen, *Subordinate Lodge Ritual* (n.p., n.d.), 8–19. The conductor's wagon is held at the Kheel Center. The description of its use comes from a personal conversation with Kheel Center director Richard Strassberg.

43. Mark C. Carnes, *Secret Ritual and Manhood in Victorian America* (New Haven: Yale University Press, 1989), 3.

44. *LFEM* 58 (April 1915), 475; Salvatore, *Eugene V. Debs*, 26.

45. Brotherhood of Locomotive Firemen and Enginemen, *Ritual*, 39–46.

46. See *RBJ* 3 (March 1886), 50; *RTJ* 12 (May 1895), 482; *LFM* 13 (February 1889), 190.

47. Dumenil, *Free Masonry and American Culture*, 39; Hobsbawm, "Ritual in Social Movements," 159.

48. Stevenson, "The Brotherhood of Locomotive Engineers and Its Leaders," 31–33, 39; *LEMJ* 39 (January 1905), 80.

49. See Hobsbawm, "Ritual in Social Movements," 150–53.

50. Dumenil, *Free Masonry and American Culture*, 37–38, 73; Weir, *Beyond Labor's Veil*, 28, 30, 35; Clawson, *Constructing Brotherhood*, 42, 258.

51. See Jameson, *All That Glitters*, 117–18; Welter, "The Cult of True Womanhood,"

151–74; Anthony Rotundo, *American Manhood: Transformations in Masculinity from the Revolution to the Modern Era* (New York: Basic Books, 1993), 10–30; Clarke, "'Honorable Scars,'" 366–67, 391–94.

52. Thomas Winter, *Making Men, Making Class: The YMCA and Workingmen, 1877–1920* (Chicago: University of Chicago Press, 2002), 48; Clarke, "'Honorable Scars,'" 362; Earl J. Hess, *Liberty, Virtue, and Progress: Northerners and Their War for the Union,* 2d ed. (New York: Fordham University Press, 1997), 4–17. On hegemonic masculinity, see R. W. Connell, *Masculinities,* 2d ed. (Cambridge: Polity Press, 2005), 76–81.

53. Anne C. Rose, *Victorian Americans and the Civil War* (Cambridge: Cambridge University Press, 1992), 4–5, 19, 69–70, 235–42; Blight, "No Desperate Hero," 60–62; Faust, *This Republic of Suffering,* xiii, 5; Clarke, "'Honorable Scars,'" 366–68, 392–94; David W. Blight, "Healing and Memory: Battlefields and the Problems of Civil War Memory," in Blight, ed., *Beyond the Battlefield: Race, Memory, and the American Civil War* (Amherst: University of Massachusetts Press, 2002), 178.

54. Winter, *Making Men, Making Class,* 48; Kimmel, *Manhood in America,* 13–43.

55. John Fabian Witt, "The Transformation of Work and the Law of Workplace Accidents, 1842–1910," *The Yale Law Journal* 5 (March 1998): 1470–71. Sayre quoted in Witt, "The Transformation of Work," 1471n20.

56. Kaster, "Labor's True Man," 25, 27–30, 34; Salvatore, *Eugene V. Debs,* 23–55; *FM* 33 (May 1885), 283–85; David W. Blight, "'For Something Beyond the Battlefield': Frederick Douglass and the Struggle for the Memory of the Civil War," in Blight, ed., *Beyond the Battlefield: Race, Memory, and the American Civil War* (Amherst: University of Massachusetts Press, 2002), 99, 103; Blight, "No Desperate Hero," 71; *LFM* 13 (June 1889), 546.

57. Kaster, "Labor's True Man," 35; *LFM* 13 (June 1889), 546–47; *LFM* 17 (August 1893), 714; *LFM* 13 (March 1889), 208.

58. *LEMJ* 22 (September 1888), 803; *LFM* 15 (May 1891), 452; Kaster, "Labor's True Man," 29.

59. See Winter, *Making Men, Making Class,* 65; Salvatore, *Eugene V. Debs,* 22–30; Clawson, *Constructing Brotherhood,* 42.

60. *Engineers' Monthly Journal* 10 (July 1876), 308.

61. See Brotherhood of Locomotive Firemen and Enginemen, *Ritual,* 22; Order of Railway Conductors, *Ritual,* 9–10.

62. *LFM* 25 (August 1898), 217–18.

63. *LEMJ* 20 (December 1886), 875; *LEMJ* 24 (November 1890), 861; *LEMJ* 36 (August 1902), 535.

64. Kaster, "Labor's True Man," 35–38.

65. Ibid., 37; Clawson, *Constructing Brotherhood,* 129–30.

66. Brotherhood of Locomotive Firemen, *Constitution of the Brotherhood of Locomotive Firemen* (Terre Haute, Ind., 1888), 41, 42.

67. See Arnesen, *Brotherhoods of Color,* 28–30; Nelson, *Divided We Stand,* xxvi–xxvii.

68. *LFM* 21 (July 1896), 64–65; *LFM* 22 (February 1897), 111–16.

69. *LFM* 22 (April 1897), 261–62; *LFM* 33 (September 1902), 430–31; *LFM* 33 (September 1902), 428.

70. Arnesen, *Brotherhoods of Color,* 30.

71. *LFM* 22 (February 1897), 126; *LFM* 33 (September 1902), 429.

72. Blight, "'For Something Beyond the Battlefield,'" 98–99; Bruce Collins, "Confederate Identity and the Southern Myth Since the Civil War," in Susan-Mary Grant and Peter J. Parish, eds., *Legacy of Disunion: The Enduring Legacy of the American Civil War* (Baton Rouge: Louisiana State University Press, 2003), 31–32; Dumenil, *Free Masonry and American Culture,* 101–2.

73. *LFM* 21 (September 1896), 248–49; *LFM* 33 (September 1902), 431; *LFM* 33 (September 1902), 436.

74. Wiebe, *Self-Rule,* 86–111.

75. *LFM* 33 (September 1902), 436; *LFM* 33 (September 1902), 427; *LFM* 31 (July 1901), 155; *LFM* 24 (March 1898), 318–19; *RTJ* 17 (June 1900), 508; *RTJ* 17 (April 1900), 222.

76. Kaster, "Labor's True Man," 45–46.

77. Ibid., 43–47.

78. *LFM* 13 (August 1889), 731; *LFM* 14 (February 1890), 138; *LFM* 14 (April 1890), 325.

79. See Tarrow, *Power in Movement,* 21–22.

80. Clawson, *Constructing Brotherhood,* 179–80, 185–95.

81. See Susan Levine, "Workers' Wives: Gender, Class, and Consumerism in the 1920s United States," *Gender and History* 3 (Spring 1991): 47; Melinda Chateauvert, *Marching Together: The Women of the Brotherhood of Sleeping Car Porters* (Urbana: University of Illinois Press, 1998), 71.

82. See Levine, "Workers' Wives," 48.

83. *LFM* 20 (May 1896), 353; *LFM* 30 (February 1901), 277; *LFEM* 48 (June 1910), 855; Memorial to Georgia M. Sargent (1912) in Grand Lodge, Ladies Society of the Brotherhood of Locomotive Firemen and Enginemen, Records, box 2, folder 2, Kheel Center (hereafter BLFLS Records).

84. *LEMJ* 25 (February 1891), 135–36.

85. U.S. Bureau of Labor Statistics, *Brotherhood Relief and Insurance,* 585–86.

86. Ladies Perseverance Lodge, Oneonta, New York, Minute Book, May 26, 1906, June 2, 1906, July 18, 1906, August 1, 1906, August 15, 1906, in Brotherhood of Railroad Trainmen Lodge No. 96, Records, Kheel Center (hereafter Ladies Perseverance Lodge); *Constitution and General Laws of the Ladies' Society of the Brotherhood of Locomotive Firemen* (Boone, Iowa: Boone Blank Book Co., 1904) in BLFLS Records, box 1, folder 1.

87. BLE Ladies Auxiliary and ORC auxiliary statements quoted in U.S. Bureau of Labor Statistics, *Brotherhood Relief and Insurance,* 585–86.

88. Rosenfeld, "'She Was a Hard Life,'" 199–200; *LEMJ* 35 (January 1901), 46; *LFM* 13 (June 1889) 535.

89. *LEMJ* 36 (April 1902), 244.

90. *LEMJ* 26 (March 1892), 237.

91. Clawson, *Constructing Brotherhood,* 200–201; *LFM* 15 (May 1891), 460.

92. *Journal of Proceedings of the First Biennial Convention of the Ladies' Society, B. L. of F.,* BLFLS Records, box 1, folder 1; *RTJ* 18 (December 1901), 1009–1010; BRT 191, Minute Book, vol. 4, October 12, 1913.

93. See, for example, Elizabeth Faue, "Paths of Unionization: Community, Bureaucracy, and Gender in the Minneapolis Labor Movement of the 1930s," in Ava Baron, ed., *Work Engendered: Toward a New History of American Labor* (Ithaca: Cornell University Press, 1991), 296–319.

94. See Levine, "Workers' Wives," 48–51, 59–60; Chateauvert, *Marching Together*; Paula Pfeffer, "The Women Behind the Union: Halena Wilson, Rosina Tucker, and the Ladies' Auxiliary to the Brotherhood of Sleeping Car Porters," *Labor History* 36 (Fall 1995): 557–78.

95. *LFM* 15 (March 1891), 227; *LEMJ* 25 (May 1891), 433.

96. *LFM* 14 (January 1890), 32; *LFM* 23 (September 1897), 232–33.

97. See Susan Levine, *Labor's True Woman: Carpet Weavers, Industrialization, and Labor Reform in the Gilded Age* (Philadelphia: Temple University Press, 1984), 121–27.

98. See Nancy Cott, *The Bonds of Womanhood: "Woman's Sphere" in New England, 1780–1835* (New Haven: Yale University Press, 1977), 64–70; *Engineers' Monthly Journal* 10 (June 1876), 260; *LEMJ* 24 (February 1890), 87.

99. *LFM* 21 (October 1896), 277; *LEMJ* 19 (October 1885), 608.

100. *LEMJ* 25 (May 1891), 433; *LFM* 15 (January 1891), 39.

101. *LFM* 16 (September 1892), 799–800; Levine, "Workers' Wives," 60.

102. *LFM* 14 (June 1890), 527.

103. *LFM* 14 (July 1890), 692; *LFM* 14 (October 1890), 885, 888–89.

104. *RBJ* (March 1886), 43–44; BRT 191, Minute Book, vol. 1, October 30, 1887.

105. See Wiebe, *Self-Rule,* 90–91.

106. *LFM* 17 (March 1893), 253; *FM* 1 (December 1876), 24.

107. Montgomery, "Workers' Control," 16.

Chapter 3. Free-Labor Ideology and Labor Relations in the Gilded Age

1. *RBJ* 3 (March 1886), 31–32.

2. Shelton Stromquist, *Reinventing "The People": The Progressive Movement, the Class Problem, and the Origins of Modern Liberalism* (Urbana: University of Illinois Press, 2006), 4–5; Dubofsky, "The Federal Judiciary," 160–62, 169; Furner, "The Republican Tradition and the New Liberalism," 174; Greenberg, *Worker and Community,* 1–2, 5.

3. See Salvatore, *Eugene V. Debs,* 23–24.

4. Leon Fink, "Labor, Liberty, and the Law: Trade Unionism and the Problem of the American Constitutional Order," *Journal of American History* 74 (December 1987): 909–10.

5. See David Howell, *Respectable Radicals: Studies in the Politics of Railway Trade Unionism* (Aldershot: Ashgate, 1999); Sonya O. Rose, "Respectable Men, Disorderly Others: The Language of Gender and the Lancashire Weavers' Strike of 1878 in Britain," *Gender and History* 5 (Autumn 1993): 382–97; Eugenio F. Biagini, "British Trade Unions and Popular Political Economy, 1860–1880," *Historical Journal* 30 (December 1987): 811–40.

6. See Jerome Toner, *The Closed Shop* (Washington, D.C.: American Council on Public Affairs, 1942), 16, 58–92. On union control of the of labor supply, see Cobble, *Dishing It Out*, 138–39.

7. David O. Stowell, "Introduction," in Stowell, ed., *The Great Strikes of 1877* (Urbana: University of Illinois Press, 2008), 2–8.

8. Foner, *Reconstruction*, 29–30, 460–62, 475–78, 512–15; Witt, *The Accidental Republic*, 33–34; Montgomery, "Workers' Control," 20; Montgomery, *Fall of the House of Labor*, 22–44.

9. Stromquist, "'Our Collective Rights,'" 58–70; Stromquist, *Generation of Boomers*, 25–44, 60; Licht, *Working for the Railroad*, 245–64.

10. See Davis et al., *American Economic Growth*, 510–12; Melvyn Dubofsky, "Technological Change and American Worker Movements, 1870–1970," in Joel Cohen and Stuart Bruchey, eds., *Technology, the Economy, and Society: The American Experience* (Boulder: University of Colorado Press, 1987), 165, 177–80.

11. Stein, *The Social Origins of a Labor Elite*, 387; Chandler, *The Visible Hand*, 107; Charles Elliot Perkins, "Memorandum on Organization to Thomas J. Potter," May 22, 1882, in Thomas C. Cochran, *Railroad Leaders, 1845–1890: The Business Mind in Action* (New York: Russell and Russell, 1965), 93, 435–36.

12. Witt, *The Accidental Republic*, 34–35; Cochran, *Railroad Leaders*, 173–75, 182, 344; Licht, *Working for the Railroad*, 27, 111–24, 269–70.

13. Simon Cordery, *British Friendly Societies, 1750–1914* (Basingstoke: Palgrave Macmillan, 2003), 6; Richard Price, *Labour in British Society: An Interpretative History* (London: Croom Helm, 1986), 127; Howell, *Respectable Radicals*, 6–7; Stein, *The Social Origins of a Labor Elite*, 275–82, 329–31. On respectability as idiom and tactic, see Cordery, *British Friendly Societies*, chap. 4.

14. See David Montgomery and Marcel van der Linden, eds., *August Sartorius von Weltershausen: The Workers' Movement in the United States, 1879–1885* (Cambridge: Cambridge University Press, 1998), 197–98.

15. Richardson, *The Locomotive Engineer*, 138–39; Montgomery, "Workers' Control," 15–18; Sanford Jacoby, *Employing Bureaucracy: Managers, Unions, and the Transformation of Work in American Industry, 1900–1945* (New York: Columbia University Press, 1985), 24.

16. Licht, *Working for the Railroad*, 133–34.

17. *LEMJ* 37 (March 1903), 167.

18. Stevenson, "The Brotherhood of Locomotive Engineers and Its Leaders," 44–52. Quoted in Toner, *The Closed Shop*, 93–94.

19. *LEMJ* 14 (November 1880), 502–3; *FM* 8 (November 1884), 617; *FM* 8 (May 1884), 280; Brotherhood of Locomotive Firemen, *Proceedings* [1876], in *Journal of Proceedings of the First Twelve Annual Conventions of the Brotherhood of Locomotive Firemen: From 1874 to 1885, Inclusive* (Terre Haute, Ind., 1885), 6.

20. See Stevenson, "The Brotherhood of Locomotive Engineers and Its Leaders," 165–69.

21. Salvatore, *Eugene V. Debs,* 29, 32; Hattam, *Labor Visions and State Power,* 134–37. Debs quoted in Salvatore, *Eugene V. Debs,* 36.

22. Salvatore, *Eugene V. Debs,* 24–25; Richard Schneirov, "Labor and the New Liberalism in the Wake of the Pullman Strike," in Richard Schneirov, Shelton Stromquist, and Nick Salvatore, eds., *The Pullman Strike and the Crisis of the 1890s: Essays on Labor and Politics* (Urbana: University of Illinois Press, 1999), 209; Fink, "Labor, Liberty, and the Law," 914–15.

23. Kaster, "Labor's True Man," 46.

24. *FM* 4 (August 1880), 273; *RBJ* (March 1886), 31-32.

25. Biagini, "British Trade Unions and Popular Political Economy," 114; Kaster, "Labor's True Man," 48; Bruce Laurie, *Artisans into Workers: Labor in Nineteenth-Century America* (Urbana: University of Illinois Press, 1997), 176–77, 198–99.

26. Rose, "Respectable Men, Disorderly Others," 383, 385–86; Warren R. Van Tine, *The Making of the Labor Bureaucrat: Union Leadership in the United States, 1870–1920* (Amherst: University of Massachusetts Press, 1973), 1–31.

27. *FM* 3 (January 1879), 17.

28. "To T. J. Potter, Gen Mgr, CB&Q Railroad, from committee," July 1, 1881, Papers Concerning Employees, 33 1870 3.6, Burlington Archives, Newberry Library, Chicago; Petition of Switch Engineers, Chicago, n.d., Pennsylvania Railroad Archives, Operating Department, box 1261, folder 14, Hagley Museum and Library, Wilmington, Delaware.

29. Richardson, *The Locomotive Engineer,* 141–42.

30. Ibid., 136–39; Stevenson, "The Brotherhood of Locomotive Engineers and Its Leaders," 56–68.

31. *LFEM* 123 (July 1947), 17; Salvatore, *Eugene V. Debs,* 355–56n50.

32. Stevenson, "The Brotherhood of Locomotive Engineers and Its Leaders," 58, 74, 80–81, 111–20.

33. Brotherhood of Locomotive Firemen, *Proceedings* [1876], 7; *RBJ* (March 1886), 30–31.

34. See Sidney Webb and Beatrice Webb, *The History of Trade Unionism* (London: Longmans, Green, 1894; repr., New York: Augustus M. Kelley, 1965), 160.

35. *FM* 5 (June 1881), 169.

36. Salvatore, *Eugene V. Debs,* 37.

37. Salvatore, *Eugene V. Debs,* 23, 48–49; Montgomery, *Beyond Equality,* 204–5.

38. *Engineers' Monthly Journal* 8 (September 1874), 77–78; *LEMJ* 12 (January 1888), 34–35.

39. *FM* 6 (January 1882), 16.

40. Brotherhood of Locomotive Firemen, *Proceedings* [1876], 7.

41. *LEMJ* 35 (January 1901), 49–50; *LEMJ* 35 (March 1901), 187.

42. *LFM* 20 (June 1896), 465–66; *LFM* 26 (January 1899), 107; *LFEM* 45 (February 1908), 192.

43. *LFEM* 46 (January 1909), 6.

44. See *LFM* 27 (August 1899), 179; *LFM* 32 (February 1902), 156–62.

45. Brotherhood of Locomotive Firemen, *Proceedings* [1876], 7.

46. See *RBJ* 3 (March 1886), 28.

47. Ibid.; *LFM* 17 (January 1893), 53–55; C. S. Wheaton to Chief Conductors, Secretaries and Brothers, n.d., ORC Archives, box 2, folder 5. See also *LFM* 14 (June 1890), 495.

48. See Salvatore, *Eugene V. Debs,* 23; Tosh, "What Should Historians Do with Masculinity?" 185–86.

49. *LFM* 13 (January 1889), 17–18; *LFM* 14 (November 1890), 997.

50. *FM* 6 (March 1882), 128.

51. *FM* 6 (January 1882), 16; *FM* 8 (May 1884), 277.

52. *FM* 6 (January 1882), 16; *LFM* 15 (July 1891), 634–35.

53. *FM* 3 (January 1879), 17-18; U.S. Commissioner of Labor, *Fifth Annual Report,* 38.

54. Brotherhood of Locomotive Engineers, *Constitution* [1885], 33; recommendation card, Brotherhood of Locomotive Firemen and Enginemen Archives, 5141, Box 4, Kheel Center.

55. Salvatore, *Eugene V. Debs,* 30–31.

56. "To the Officers and Members of All Divisions of the B. L. E. on Southern System," April 1, 1901, BLE 210, Records, box 311, folder 2.

57. Brotherhood of Locomotive Engineers, *Constitution* [1885], 21; BRT 93, Minute Book, December 24, 1893; Salvatore, *Eugene V. Debs,* 31.

58. U.S. Interstate Commerce Commission, "Relations Existing Between Railway Corporations and Their Employes," in *Third Annual Report, 1889* (Washington, D.C.: Government Printing Office, 1890), 387.

59. Brotherhood of Locomotive Firemen, *Proceedings* [1882], 14–15; *RBJ* 3 (March 1886), 27; *LFM* 15 (August 1891), 725–26.

60. Winter, *Making Men, Making Class,* 54–58. Vorhees and Colby quoted in Winter, *Making Men, Making Class,* 54–55, 57.

61. Salvatore, *Eugene V. Debs,* 37.

62. *FM* 5 (February 1881), 169; *FM* 4 (May 1880), 347–48.

63. *LEMJ* 19 (October 1885), 608. Depew quoted in Stevenson, "The Brotherhood of Locomotive Engineers and Its Leaders," 172–73.

64. Ducker, *Men of the Steel Rails,* 133.

65. See *LEMJ* 20 (February 1886), 83; *LEMJ* 20 (July 1886), 467; Eugene V. Debs to Homer E. Sargent, March 11, 1881, in J. Robert Constantine, ed., *Letters of Eugene V. Debs,* vol. 1, *1874–1912* (Urbana: University of Illinois Press, 1990), 13–14; Eugene V.

Debs and Frank W. Arnold to Thomas Fletcher Oakes, March 1, 1881, in Constantine, *Letters of Eugene V. Debs,* vol. 1, 17–18; Licht, *Working for the Railroad,* 264.

66. Richardson, *The Locomotive Engineer,* 196–97, 284–85.

67. See Kimeldorf, *Battling for American Labor,* 16; Jacoby, *Employing Bureaucracy,* 30.

68. Stevenson, "The Brotherhood of Locomotive Engineers and Its Leaders," 178–80.

69. Richard Schneirov, *Labor and Urban Politics: Class Conflict and the Origins of Modern Liberalism in Chicago, 1864–97* (Urbana: University of Illinois Press, 1998), 311–12; Stromquist, *Generation of Boomers,* 54–57, 12–13, 122–23.

70. Stromquist, *Generation of Boomers,* 56–58, 101–3, 120–23, 138–40. Similarly, in Britain over the 1880s and 1890s managerial efforts to rationalize the work process while scaling back paternal welfare commitments sparked labor conflict on the nation's railroads, culminating in the famous Taff Vale Railroad strike of 1900. See Price, *Labour in British Society,* 121–27.

71. Stromquist, *Generation of Boomers,* 32; Schneirov, *Labor and Urban Politics,* 193.

72. Stromquist, *Generation of Boomers,* 59–60, 122.

73. Ibid., 132–36; *LEMJ* 19 (October 1885), 595–96.

74. Stromquist, *Generation of Boomers,* 58–59; *LFM* 13 (March 1889), 195.

75. Salvatore, *Eugene V. Debs,* 57–58; *LFM* 13 (January 1889), 38, 52; *LFM* 13 (March 1889), 233.

76. Salvatore, *Eugene V. Debs,* 59–64; Hughes, "Social Relations in a Railroad Town," 127–28.

77. *FM* 9 (March 1885), 159; *LFM* 15 (August 1891), 725–26.

78. Salvatore, *Eugene V. Debs,* 56–58; Stevenson, "The Brotherhood of Locomotive Engineers and Its Leaders," 184–85; *LFEM* 123 (July 1947), 23.

79. *LFM* 10 (July 1886), 419; *FM* 9 (July 1885), 425.

80. *LFM* 13 (March 1889), 195; *LFM* 13 (January 1889), 40; *LFM* 13 (June 1889), 546; Hughes, "Social Relations in a Railroad Town," 113–14.

81. See *LEMJ* 20 (June 1886), 386–88, 394–97.

82. *LEMJ* 20 (September 1886), 634.

83. *LEMJ* 20 (September 1886), 635–36. See also *LEMJ* 20 (October 1886), 713–14.

84. Donald L. McMurry, *The Great Burlington Strike of 1888: A Case History of Industrial Relations* (Cambridge: Harvard University Press, 1956), 90–140; *LEMJ* 23 (May 1889), 420, 421.

85. Stromquist, *Generation of Boomers,* 59–60, 135–36, 211–14; Salvatore, *Eugene V. Debs,* 73–77.

86. Cochran, *Railroad Leaders,* 179–80; Charles Elliot Perkins to Frank S. Bond, March 23, 1888, in Cochran, *Railroad Leaders,* 447.

87. *LEMJ* 22 (July 1888), 605; *LEMJ* 22 (November 1888), 1011, 1012.

88. Stromquist, *Generation of Boomers,* 81–84 ; Eugene V. Debs to Frank X. Holl, November 28, 1894, in Constantine, *Letters of Eugene V. Debs,* vol. 1, 78–79.

Chapter 4. The Crisis of the 1890s and the Reordering of Railroad Labor Relations

1. Richard Schneirov, Shelton Stromquist, and Nick Salvatore, "Introduction," in Schneirov, Stromquist, and Salvatore, eds., *The Pullman Strike and the Crisis of the 1890s* (Urbana: University of Illinois Press, 1999), 1–6.

2. Richard Schneirov, "Labor and the New Liberalism in the Wake of the Pullman Strike," Schneirov, Stromquist, and Salvatore, eds., *The Pullman Strike and the Crisis of the 1890s* (Urbana: University of Illinois Press, 1999), 205–6; Melvyn Dubofsky, "The Federal Judiciary," 173; Furner, "The Republican Tradition and the New Liberalism," 175, 216.

3. Schneirov, "Labor and the New Liberalism," 208; Leo Wolman, *The Growth of American Trade Unions, 1820–1923* (New York: National Bureau of Economic Research, 1924), 29–31; E. J. Hobsbawm, "The New Unionism in Perspective," in Hobsbawm, ed., *Worlds of Labour: Further Essays in the History of Labour* (London: Weidenfeld and Nicolson, 1984), 152–75; Howell, *Respectable Radicals,* 6; Stein, *The Social Origins of a Labor Elite,* 280–81.

4. See Stromquist, *Generation of Boomers,* 69–79.

5. See Schneirov, "Labor and the New Liberalism," 209; Schneirov, *Labor and Urban Politics,* 321–22.

6. Laurie, *Artisans into Workers,* 198–99; Schneirov, *Labor and Urban Politics,* 307–22; Schneirov, "Labor and the New Liberalism," 208–9.

7. Robbins, *Railway Conductors,* 22–24, 60–61; Donald L. McMurry, "Federation of the Railroad Brotherhoods, 1889–1894," *Industrial and Labor Relations Review* 7 (October 1953): 80; U.S. Bureau of Labor Statistics, *Brotherhood Relief and Insurance of Railway Employees,* 556–57; Order of Railway Conductors, *Proceedings of the Order of Railway Conductors* (St. Louis, 1891), 8–9.

8. Stromquist, *Generation of Boomers,* 69–73; Stevenson, "The Brotherhood of Locomotive Engineers and Its Leaders," 201–2; Hughes, "Social Relations in a Railroad Town," 134; "Minutes of union meeting of engineers and conductors of the Brotherhood of Locomotive Engineers and Order of Railway Conductors held at Briggs House, Chicago, September 21, 1890," ORC Archives, box 2, folder "Grand Chief Conductor Clark, 1890–1906"; "A Report of a Circular Issued by the Unity Conference Held at Bingham House, Philadelphia," July 11, 1889, in Stuart B. Kaufman, ed., *The Samuel Gompers Papers,* vol. 2, *The Early Years of the American Federation of Labor, 1887–90* (Urbana: University of Illinois Press, 1987), 218–20.

9. *LFM* 15 (March 1891), 251.

10. Stromquist, *Generation of Boomers,* 73–75; McMurry, "Federation of the Railroad Brotherhoods," 77–83; *LFM* 14 (August 1890), 708.

11. *LEMJ* 24 (August 1890), 598. See also *LEMJ* 24 (May 1890), 357; *LEMJ* 24 (September 1890), 698–99; *LEMJ* 24 (December 1890), 921–23; *LFM* 14 (January 1890), 12–13; *LFM* 14 (April 1890), 328; *LFM* 15 (May 1891), 406.

12. *LFM* 14 (January 1890), 12; *LFM* 14 (April 1890), 329–30.

13. *LEMJ* 24 (May 1890), 346; *LEMJ* 24 (August 1891), 716; *LEMJ* 24 (August 1890), 597. See also *LEMJ* 24 (April 1891), 330.

14. *LFM* (May 1889), 424.

15. *LEMJ* 25 (August 1891), 754–55; McMurry, "Federation of the Railroad Brotherhoods," 83–86.

16. Stromquist, *Generation of Boomers*, 77–78; McMurry, "Federation of the Railroad Brotherhoods," 88; U.S. Bureau of Labor Statistics, *Railway Employees in the United States*, 1101–6.

17. Robbins, *Railway Conductors*, 50–51; Order of Railway Conductors, *Proceedings of the Order of Railway Conductors* (Atlanta, 1895), 79–80; *LFM* 24 (April 1898), 397–99; *LFM* 25 (July 1898), 89–90; Richardson, *The Locomotive Engineer*, 295–97; P. M. Arthur, testimony, U.S. Industrial Commission, *Report of the Industrial Commission on Transportation*, vol. 4 (Washington, D.C.: Government Printing Office, 1900), 122; John R. Commons et al., *History of Labor in the United States*, vol. 4 (New York: Macmillan, 1935), 375; Stevenson, "The Brotherhood of Locomotive Engineers and Its Leaders," 228–30. See also *LFM* 25 (July 1898), 89–90.

18. See Stromquist, *Generation of Boomers*, 73–79.

19. U.S. Bureau of Labor Statistics, *Railway Employees in the United States*, 1103; Schneirov, *Labor and Urban Politics*, 309; Perlman, *History of Trade Unionism*, 130–33; Perlman, "Upheaval and Reorganization," in Commons et al., *History of Labour*, vol. 2, 535–37.

20. Melvyn Dubofsky, "Abortive Reform: The Wilson Administration and Organized Labor, 1913–1920," in James E. Cronin and Carmen Sirianni, eds., *Work, Community, and Power: The Experience of Labor in Europe and America, 1900–1925* (Philadelphia: Temple University Press, 1983), 200–2; Richardson, *The Locomotive Engineer*, 271.

21. *LEMJ* 25 (November 1891), 1003–4.

22. Greene, *Pure and Simple Politics*, 55–57. On the AFL's nonpartisan lobbying, see Greene, *Pure and Simple Politics*, 65–70, 80–82.

23. Richardson, *The Locomotive Engineer*, 271–72.

24. Greene, *Pure and Simple Politics*, 57; Ducker, *Men of the Steel Rails*, 89–96; *LEMJ* 24 (May 1890), 378–79; *LEMJ* 25 (May 1891), 423; *LEMJ* 25 (October 1891), 917–28; *LFM* 16 (June 1892), 547–38; *LFM* 17 (January 1893), 95–96; *RBJ* 17 (January 1894), 22–23.

25. It appears that state railroad commissioners concerned about the industry's appalling accident rate were the first public figures to raise questions about safer technology. See Aldrich, *Safety First*, 32.

26. Ibid., 28–29; Clark, "The Railroad Safety Movement," 319–52; Steven W. Usselman, "Air Brakes for Freight Trains: Technological Innovation in the American Railroad Industry, 1869–1900," *Business History Review* 58 (Spring 1984): 31–32.

27. Aldrich, *Safety First*, 29–32; Williams-Searle, "Courting Risk," 65.

28. Clark, "The Railroad Safety Movement," 243–77; Usselman, "Air Brakes for Freight Trains," 47.

29. Licht, *Working for the Railroad,* 201–4, 205.

30. Williams-Searle, "Courting Risk," 52–60; Licht, *Working for the Railroad,* 209–11.

31. Clark, "The Railroad Safety Movement," 166–68, 174. O'Shea quoted in Clark, "The Railroad Safety Movement," 163.

32. Clark, "The Railroad Safety Movement," 283–90; Aldrich, *Safety First,* 33–35.

33. Clark, "The Railroad Safety Movement," 174–75, 308–9. See *LEMJ* 23 (December 1889), 985–88 (by Coffin); *LEMJ* 25 (December 1891), 1147–48; *LEMJ* 26 (February 1892), 160–62; ICC, *Third Annual Report, 1889,* 312–37; U.S. Congress, House of Representatives, *Safety of Railway Employes and the Traveling Public,* H. Rpt. 1678, 52d Cong. 1st sess., 1892, 1–2; U.S. Congress, Senate, Committee on Interstate Commerce, S. Rpt. 1049, 52d Cong. 1st sess., 1892, 56–70.

34. Williams-Searle, "Courting Risk," 66–67.

35. Clark, "The Railroad Safety Movement," 187, 311–12; *Switchmen's Journal* 7 (March 1893), 806.

36. Richardson, *The Locomotive Engineer,* 271–72.

37. Williams-Searle, "Courting Risk," 67.

38. Melvyn Dubofsky, *The State and Labor in Modern America* (Chapel Hill: University of North Carolina Press, 1994), 6–7, 15; Stephen Skowronek, *Building A New American State: The Expansion of National Administrative Capacities, 1877–1920* (Cambridge: Cambridge University Press, 1982), 47–55; Hattam, *Labor Visions and State Power,* 11, 15, 30–75; Forbath, *Law and the Shaping of the American Labor Movement,* 25–36.

39. Dubofsky, *The State and Labor,* 14–15; Forbath, *Law and the Shaping of the American Labor Movement,* 66–69; Gerald Eggert, *Railroad Labor Disputes: The Beginnings of Federal Strike Policy* (Ann Arbor: University of Michigan Press, 1967), 83–90.

40. Stevenson, "The Brotherhood of Locomotive Engineers and Its Leaders," 209–11; Dubofsky, *The State and Labor,* 20, 25.

41. Dubofsky, *The State and Labor,* 26–27; Stevenson, "The Brotherhood of Locomotive Engineers and Its Leaders," 211–15, 218–20; Forbath, *Law and the Shaping of the American Labor Movement,* 70–71; *LEMJ* 27 (May 1893), 454–56. Taft quoted in Forbath, *Law and the Shaping of the American Labor Movement,* 70; Jenkins quoted in Dubofsky, *The State and Labor,* 26.

42. Hattam, *Labor Visions and State Power,* 19–20.

43. *LEMJ* 28 (April 1894), 360; *LEMJ* 28 (July 1894), 612–16.

44. Forbath, *Law and the Shaping of the American Labor Movement,* 77; Hattam, *Labor Visions and State Power,* 20, 133, 139–45. See *LEMJ* 29 (August 1895), 717–19; *LFM* 18 (March 1894), 275–77; *LFM* 23 (November 1897), 386; P. M. Arthur, testimony, U.S. Industrial Commission, *Report,* vol. 4, 119–20.

45. Furner, "The Republican Tradition and the New Liberalism," 201–13.

46. Susan Eleanor Hirsch, *After the Strike: A Century of Labor Struggle at Pullman* (Urbana: University of Illinois Press, 2003), 25–36.

47. Schneirov, Stromquist, and Salvatore, "Introduction," 7–9; David Montgomery, "Epilogue: The Pullman Strike and the Making of Modern America," in Schneirov, Stromquist, and Salvatore, eds., *The Pullman Strike and the Crisis of the 1890s* (Urbana: University of Illinois Press, 1999), 234–38; Stromquist, *Generation of Boomers,* 91–92.

48. Schneirov, *Labor and Urban Politics,* 341.

49. U.S. Strike Commission, *Report on the Chicago Strike of June–July, 1894* (Washington, D.C.: Government Printing Office, 1895), xxiii–xxxi, xlvi–lvi (quote on xxviii); Furner, "The Republican Tradition and the New Liberalism," 213–14.

50. Schneirov, Stromquist, and Salvatore, "Introduction," 8; Gerald Eggert, *Richard Olney: Evolution of a Statesman* (University Park: Pennsylvania State University Press, 1974), 156.

51. Shelton Stromquist, "The Crisis of 1894 and the Legacies of Producerism," in Schneirov, Stromquist, Salvatore, eds., *The Pullman Strike and the Crisis of the 1890s* (Urbana: University of Illinois Press, 1999), 189–92; "A Statement Issued by the Conference of Representatives of Labor Organizations Meeting at Briggs House, Chicago," July 13, 1894, in Stuart B. Kaufman and Peter J. Albert, eds., *The Samuel Gompers Papers,* vol. 3, *Unrest and Depression, 1891–94* (Urbana: University of Illinois Press, 1989), 536–37.

52. "A Statement Issued by the Conference of Representatives of Labor Organizations Meeting at Briggs House, Chicago," 537–38; U.S. Strike Commission, *Report on the Chicago Strike of June–July, 1894,* xl–xli.

53. P. H. Morrissey, testimony, U.S. Strike Commission, *Report on the Chicago Strike of June–July, 1894,* 181–84; Furner, "The Republican Tradition and the New Liberalism," 213.

54. Edgar E. Clark, testimony, U.S. Strike Commission, *Report on the Chicago Strike of June–July, 1894,* 186–87.

55. Schneirov, "Labor and the New Liberalism," 210; Furner, "The Republican Tradition and the New Liberalism," 198–205; Perlman, *History of Trade Unionism,* 144–45. On the brotherhoods' attitudes toward arbitration, see *LEMJ* 28 (July 1894), 635–36; *LFM* 18 (February 1894), 135–39; Titus S. Ingraham, testimony, in ICC, *Sixth Annual Report,* 328–29.

56. *LEMJ* 28 (July 1894), 638.

57. Elwin Wilbur Sigmund, "Federal Laws Concerning Railroad Labor Disputes: A Legislative and Legal History, 1877–1934" (PhD diss., University of Illinois, 1961), 25–26.

58. Schneirov, "Labor and the New Liberalism," 209, 211; Schneirov, *Labor and Urban Politics,* 334–35; Stromquist, *Reinventing "The People,"* 52–53.

59. *Congress of Industrial Conciliation and Arbitration Arranged Under the Auspices of the Industrial Committee of the Civic Federation, Held at Chicago, Tues-*

day and Wednesday, November 13 and 14, 1894 (Chicago: Civic Federation of Chicago, 1895), 26–28; Furner, "The Republican Tradition and the New Liberalism," 215–17.

60. Eggert, *Richard Olney*, 153–56.

61. Ibid., 156–58; Hattam, *Labor Visions and State Power*, 133; Sigmund, "Federal Laws Concerning Railroad Labor Disputes," 26–27. Quotes are from Olney's brief, which is reprinted in U.S. Congress, Senate, A Compilation of Documents Relating to Injunctions in Conspiracy Cases Together with Arguments and Decision of the Court in Case of "Commonwealth v. Hunt," 4 Metcalf, Etc., S. doc. 190, 57th Cong., 1st sess. (1902), 36–40.

62. Dubofsky, "Federal Judiciary," 169–72; Forbath, *Law and the Shaping of the American Labor Movement*, 72–73; U.S. Congress, House of Representatives, Judiciary Committee, *Receivership of the Northern Pacific Railroad Company*, House Report No. 1049, 53d Cong., 2d sess. (1894), 17–19.

63. Leonard A. Lecht, *Experience Under Railway Labor Legislation* (New York: Columbia University Press, 1955), 16–18; U.S. Department of Labor, Bureau of Labor Statistics, *Mediation and Arbitration of Railway Labor Disputes in the United States*, Bulletin No. 98., by Charles P. Neill (Washington, D.C.: Government Printing Office, 1912), 6–20.

64. U.S. Congress, House of Representatives, *Carriers Engaged in Interstate Commerce*, House Report No. 1754, 53d Cong. 3d sess. (1895), 1–4; *Congressional Record*, 53d Cong., 3d sess. (1895), 2793.

65. U.S. Congress, Senate, *Carriers Engaged in Interstate Commerce and Their Employees*, Senate Report No. 591, 55th Cong. 2d sess. (1898), 1.

66. Furner, "The Republican Tradition and the New Liberalism," 217.

67. *Congressional Record*, 55th Cong., 2d sess. (1898), 4640, 4647–48; Edward Mosley to E. E. Clark, February 11, 1898, ORC Archives, box 2, folder "Grand Chief Conductor Clark, 1890–1906," Kheel Center.

68. U.S. Congress, Senate, *Carriers Engaged in Interstate Commerce and Their Employees*, 2. See also *Congressional Record*, 53d Cong., 3d sess. (1895), 2793.

69. Christopher Tomlins, *The State and the Unions: Labor Relations, Law, and the Organized Labor Movement in America, 1880–1960* (Cambridge: Cambridge University Press, 1985), 84–86.

70. *Congressional Record*, 53d Cong., 3d sess. (1895), 2790, 2795, quote 2790.

71. U.S. Congress, Senate, *Carriers Engaged in Interstate Commerce and Their Employees*, 4.

72. Stevenson, "The Brotherhood of Locomotive Engineers and Its Leaders," 293–95; William S. Carter to Samuel Gompers, July 22 and August 4, 1896, American Federation of Labor, Records, State Historical Society of Wisconsin, box 45, folder 10.

73. Samuel Gompers to Frank Sargent, January 28, 1897, in Stuart B. Kaufman, Peter J. Albert, and Grace Palladino, eds., *The Samuel Gompers Papers*, vol. 4, *A National Labor Movement Takes Shape, 1895–98* (Urbana: University of Illinois Press,

1991), 292–94; Ralston and Siddons to Samuel Gompers, January 23, 1897, American Federation of Labor, Records, box 45, folder 10; Edward Mosley to E. E. Clark, May 14, 1898, ORC Archives, box 2, folder "Grand Chief Conductor Clark, 1890–1906," Kheel Center.

74. *Congressional Record,* 53d Cong., 3d sess. (1895), 2793, 2799; *Congressional Record,* 54th Cong., 2d sess. (1897), 2388–89.

75. *Congressional Record,* 53d Cong., 3d sess. (1895), 2789–90, 2794–95.

76. Tomlins, *The State and the Unions,* 85.

77. *Congressional Record,* 54th Cong., 2d sess. (1897), 2388; *Congressional Record,* 53d Cong., 3d sess. (1895), 2790–93; *Congressional Record,* 55th Cong., 2d sess. (1898), 4639.

78. U.S. Congress, Senate, *Carriers Engaged in Interstate Commerce and Their Employees,* 3.

79. Furner, "The Republican Tradition and the New Liberalism," 218; Order of Railway Conductors, *Proceedings* (1895), 23–25; *LFM* 20 (May 1896), 326–29; *LFM* 22 (February 1897), 81; *LEMJ* 32 (August 1898), 531–33; reports of H. F. Hynes in "History of National Legislation Relating to Labor Arbitration, 49–57 Congresses, 1886–1902," and reports of H. R. Fuller, March 8, 1897 and August 22, 1898, in "Report of the National Legislative Representative, 54–58 Congresses," typescript volumes, n.d., Brotherhood of Railroad Trainmen Archives, 5149, Kheel Center, box 187.

80. P. M. Arthur, testimony, U.S. Industrial Commission, *Report,* vol. 4, 117.

81. Stuyvesant Fish, testimony, U.S. Industrial Commission, *Report,* vol. 4, 324. See also comments of Samuel Callaway, president, New York Central and Hudson Railroad, U.S. Industrial Commission, *Report,* vol. 4, 221–22.

82. *LFM* 30 (June 1901), 987.

Chapter 5. Progressive Era America and the Culture of the New Unionism

1. *LFM* 33 (October 1902), 547–56; *New York Times,* September 9, 1902.

2. See Theodore Roosevelt, *Letters,* vol. 3, vol. 4, ed. Elting E. Morison and John M. Blum (Cambridge: Harvard University Press, 1951–54), 616–17, 876–80.

3. McGerr, *A Fierce Discontent,* 118–25; Morris, *Theodore Rex,* 144–69.

4. Kazin, *The Populist Persuasion,* 52–56.

5. See T. J. Jackson Lears, *No Place of Grace: Antimodernism and the Transformation of American Culture, 1880–1920* (New York: Pantheon Books, 1981), 3–58; Bederman, *Manliness and Civilization,* 11–15, 177–215; Winter, *Making Men, Making Class,* 1.

6. See Theodore Roosevelt, *Letters and Speeches,* ed. Louis Auchincloss (New York: Library of America, 2004), 57–58.

7. Lears, *No Place of Grace,* 107–17.

8. Historians have amply demonstrated the ways in which imperialist expansion shaped domestic political culture and identity. See, for example, Bederman, *Manliness*

and Civilization; Amy Kaplan and Donald E. Pease, eds., *Cultures of United States Imperialism* (Durham: Duke University Press, 1993).

9. On Roosevelt and the connections among imperialism, masculinity, and nationalism, see Amy Kaplan, "Black and Blue on San Juan Hill," in Amy Kaplan and Donald E. Pease, eds., *Cultures of United States Imperialism* (Durham: Duke University Press, 1993), 219–36.

10. On the new nationalism, see Eric J. Hobsbawm, *Nations and Nationalism Since 1780: Programme, Myth, Reality,* 2d ed. (Cambridge: Cambridge University Press, 1992), 101–30. The term "labor patriotism" is Schneirov's, but I have added to it the positive link with nationalism. See Schneirov, *Labor and Urban Politics,* 319–20.

11. Hattam, *Labor Visions and State Power,* 137–38; Schneirov, "Labor and the New Liberalism," 208; Stevenson, "The Brotherhood of Locomotive Engineers and Its Leaders," 242.

12. Robbins, *Railway Conductors,* 18; Richardson, *The Locomotive Engineer,* 259; *LFEM* 123 (July 1947), 23, 25, 30, 31.

13. Richardson, *The Locomotive Engineer,* 196–97, 285; U.S. Congress, House of Representatives, *Report of the Eight-Hour Commission,*" Appendix VI, "Railway Wage Schedules and Agreements," by William Z. Ripley, H. Doc. 690, 65th Cong., 2d sess., 1918, 352–65.

14. Robbins, *Railway Conductors,* 19–20; *LFEM* 123 (July 1947), 23, 25, 30, 31, 37.

15. Van Tine, *The Making of the Labor Bureaucrat,* 25; Stevenson, "The Brotherhood of Locomotive Engineers and Its Leaders," 246; Jon R. Huibregste, "A New Type of Capitalist: The Brotherhood of Locomotive Engineers' Financial Scheme, 1920–1927," *New England Journal of History* 56 (Fall 1999): 36–49.

16. Van Tine, *The Making of the Labor Bureaucrat,* 143, 146–47, 152; Montgomery, *Fall of the House of Labor,* 276; Richardson, *The Locomotive Engineer,* 270; Stevenson, "The Brotherhood of Locomotive Engineers and Its Leaders," 239, 315–18, 323–26; Robbins, *Railway Conductors,* 29–30; Joel Seidman, *The Brotherhood of Railroad Trainmen: The Internal Life of a National Union* (Chicago: University of Chicago Press, 1962), 5, 51–65, 122–58.

17. Van Tine, *The Making of the Labor Bureaucrat,* 113–14, 152–55; Seidman, *The Brotherhood of Railroad Trainmen,* 5, 68–96.

18. See David Montgomery, "Industrial Democracy or Democracy in Industry? The Theory and Practice of the Labor Movement," in Nelson Lichtenstein and Howell John Harris, eds., *Industrial Democracy in America: The Ambiguous Promise* (Cambridge: Cambridge University Press, 1993), 31–32.

19. Van Tine, *The Making of the Labor Bureaucrat,* 18–19, 21, 23, 29–30; Seidman, *The Brotherhood of Railroad Trainmen,* 68; Robbins, *Railway Conductors,* 165; Gary M. Fink, ed., *Biographical Dictionary of American Labor* (Westport, Conn.: Greenwood Press, 1984), 146, 187, 242–43, 321, 348, 462, 487, 501, 531–32, 583; *LEMJ* 40 (August

1906), 711; *LFEM* 123 (July 1947), 17–24, 26, 28, 36–37; *Railroad Trainman* 26 (January 1909), 3–7 (hereafter *RT*).

20. Van Tine, *The Making of the Labor Bureaucrat*, 17, 26–27, 79, 175–78; Fink, ed., *Biographical Dictionary*, 146, 187, 501; Morris, *Theodore Rex*, 167–69; *LFEM* 123 (July 1947), 26, 28; Marguerite Green, *The National Civic Federation and the American Labor Movement, 1900–1925* (Washington, D.C.: Catholic University Press, 1956), 14, 224; Montgomery, *Fall of the House of Labor*, 366; *RT* 26 (January 1909), 89–90.

21. See *LEMJ* 37 (January 1903), 32; *LEMJ* 36 (April 1902), 232–33.

22. Robbins, *Railway Conductors*, 139–42; U.S. Bureau of Labor Statistics, *Beneficial Activities of American Trade Unions*, 189–99; *LFEM* 60 (June 1916), 654.

23. *RT* 26 (June 1909), 506.

24. *LEMJ* 37 (March 1903), 167.

25. See *RT* 26 (May 1909), 369, 371; Van Tine, *The Making of the Labor Bureaucrat*, 51; Stevenson, "The Brotherhood of Locomotive Engineers and Its Leaders," 11–12.

26. Robbins, *Railway Conductors*, 165; *LFEM* 60 (June 1916), 654; *RT* 26 (April 1909), 346; *RT* 26 (July 1909), 611.

27. Clawson, *Constructing Brotherhood*, 137.

28. See *LFM* 19 (April 1895), 352–53; Brotherhood of Locomotive Firemen, *Journal of Proceedings of the Third Biennial Convention* (Terre Haute, Ind., 1892), 109.

29. Brotherhood of Locomotive Firemen, *Journal of Proceedings of the Fourth Biennial Convention* (Terre Haute, Ind., 1894), 246.

30. Brotherhood of Locomotive Firemen, "Grand Master's Report," in *Journal of Proceedings of the Fifth Biennial Convention* (Peoria, Ill., 1896), 60–61, 67.

31. *LFM* 26 (January 1899), 140.

32. *LFM* 22 (January 1897), 54; *LFEM* 46 (April 1909), 598.

33. Brotherhood of Locomotive Firemen and Enginemen, *Proceedings of the Twelfth Biennial Convention* (St. Paul, Minn., n.p., 1910), 225, 550.

34. See Clawson, *Constructing Brotherhood*, 212–13, 230–32.

35. See Montgomery, "Industrial Democracy or Democracy in Industry?" 32.

36. Gorn, *The Manly Art*, 192–93; Bederman, *Manliness and Civilization*, 17–19, 170–215; Kimmel, *Manhood in America*, 117–20, 181–88.

37. Roosevelt, *Letters and Speeches*, 57–58.

38. Licht, *Working for the Railroad*, 296.

39. *RTJ* 21 (September 1904), 684; *RT* 26 (October 1909), 846–52.

40. Nancy Woloch, *Women and the American Experience: A Concise History* (New York: McGraw-Hill, 1996), 168–70.

41. The more expensive of these items were available on installment plans, some aimed specifically at railroad men. See advertising sections at end of *RTJ* 20 (1903); *LEMJ* 41 (1906); and *RT* 26 (1909).

42. *LEMJ* 35 (May 1901), 298; *LEMJ* 38 (June 1904), 409–10; *LFM* 18 (January 1894), 43; *LFM* 29 (December 1899), 629–31.

43. DeVault, *Sons and Daughters of Labor*, 102–3.

44. *LFM* 13 (February 1889), 125.

45. See *LFM* 16 (May 1892), 428; *LFM* 18 (April 1894), 380–81; *LFM* 21 (December 1896), 429; *LFM* 22 (January 1897), 24–25.

46. *LFM* 17 (March 1893), 219.

47. *LEMJ* 35 (April 1901), 242.

48. Woloch, *Women and the American Experience,* 184; Karen J. Blair, *The Clubwoman as Feminist: True Womanhood Redefined, 1868–1914* (New York: Holmes and Meier, 1980), 1–2, 4, 57–58.

49. Blair, *The Clubwoman as Feminist,* 58; *LEMJ* 36 (March 1902), 173; Woloch, *Women and the American Experience,* 187–88.

50. *RTJ* 20 (April 1903), 257; *RTJ* 20 (March 1903), 178.

51. Blair, *The Clubwoman as Feminist,* 111.

52. *LFM* 13 (June 1889), 519; *LFM* 17 (April 1893), 317–19; *LFM* 18 (March 1894), 282–85.

53. *LFM* 17 (January 1893), 84–85.

54. *RTJ* 18 (January 1901), 37

55. Woloch, *Women and the American Experience,* 217, 219; Sara Evans, *Born for Liberty: A History of Women in America* (New York: The Free Press, 1989), 153; Eileen Kraditor, *Ideas of the Woman Suffrage Movement, 1890–1920* (New York: Columbia University Press, 1965), 43–62.

56. Kraditor, *Ideas of the Woman Suffrage Movement,* 15–28, 103–4; Woloch, *Women and the American Experience,* 217–18. On the range of anti-suffrage arguments, see *RTJ* 18 (February 1901), 128; *RTJ* 18 (January 1901), 36; *RTJ* 18 (January 1901), 43; *RTJ* 18 (February 1901), 124–25; *RTJ* 18 (February 1901), 142–43; *RTJ* 18 (March 1901), 215–17; *RTJ* 18 (June 1901), 476–78.

57. *LFM* 25 (December 1898), 600–601; *LEMJ* 35 (March 1901), 172; *RTJ* 18 (September 1901), 738.

58. *LFM* 21 (August 1896), 134. See also *LFM* 20 (January 1896), 30.

59. See Alice Kessler-Harris, "Where Are the Organized Women Workers?" *Feminist Studies* 3 (Fall 1975): 94–100.

60. See John Bodnar, "The Attractions of Patriotism," in John Bodnar, ed., *Bonds of Affection: Americans Define Their Patriotism* (Princeton: Princeton University Press, 1996), 8–9; Gary Gerstle, *American Crucible: Race and Nation in the Twentieth Century* (Princeton: Princeton University Press, 2001), 4–5; Reynolds J. Scott-Childress, "Introduction," in Childress, ed., *Race and the Production of Modern American Nationalism* (New York: Garland Publishing, 1999), x–xi.

61. Kaplan, "Black and Blue on San Juan Hill," 219.

62. See Paul Krause, *The Battle for Homestead, 1880–1892: Politics, Culture, and Steel* (Pittsburgh: University of Pittsburgh Press, 1992), 8–9.

63. Hughes, "Social Relations in a Railroad Town," 118–19, 134; *Engineers' Monthly Journal* 13 (July 1879), 315–17.

64. *LFM* 9 (March 1885), 159.

65. *LFM* 14 (April 1890), 325–27; *LEMJ* 24 (January 1890), 37–38; *LEMJ* 24 (March 1890), 197–98. On this conservative use of republicanism, see Leon Fink, "Looking Backward: Reflections on Workers' Culture and Certain Conceptual Dilemmas Within Labor History," in J. Carroll Moody and Alice Kessler-Harris, eds., *Perspectives on American Labor History: The Problems of Synthesis* (DeKalb: Northern Illinois University Press, 1989), 12; Schneirov, *Labor and Urban Politics,* 319–20.

66. McMurry, *The Great Burlington Strike of 1888,* 175–80, 185–88; C. H. Salmons, *The Burlington Strike* (Aurora, Ill.: Bunnell and Ward, 1889), 69, 231, 232–41; Schneirov, *Labor and Urban Politics,* 319.

67. *LEMJ* 27 (May 1893), 454–56; *LEMJ* 28 (July 1894), 638.

68. Furner, "The Republican Tradition and the New Liberalism," 213; *LEMJ* 28 (July 1894), 638–39. Senate committee quoted in Furner, "The Republican Tradition and the New Liberalism," 213.

69. Kazin, *The Populist Persuasion,* 64–65; Hendrik Hartog, "The Constitution of Aspiration and 'The Rights That Belong to Us All,'" *Journal of American History* 74 (December 1987): 1013–34. See also *LFM* 20 (February 1896), 105.

70. *LFM* 14 (September 1890), 816; *LEMJ* 24 (August 1890), 598. On organized labor's use of Americanist language in the twentieth century, see Gary Gerstle, *Working-Class Americanism: The Politics of Labor in a Textile City, 1914–1960* (Cambridge: Cambridge University Press, 1989), 153–95.

71. Stromquist, "The Crisis of 1894," 179; Kazin, *The Populist Persuasion,* 49–52.

72. Stuart McConnell, "Reading the Flag: A Reconsideration of the Patriotic Cults of the 1890s," in John Bodnar, ed., *Bonds of Affection: Americans Define Their Patriotism* (Princeton: Princeton University Press, 1996), 103–6, 110–13, 116–18; Andrew Neather, "Labor Republicanism, Race, and Popular Patriotism in the Era of Empire, 1890–1914," in John Bodnar, ed., *Bonds of Affection: Americans Define Their Patriotism* (Princeton: Princeton University Press, 1996), 89–93.

73. See *LEMJ* 32 (May 1898), 347; *LEMJ* 38 (July 1904), 470; *LEMJ* 41 (July 1907), 599; *Locomotive Engineers' Journal* 44 (July 1910), 593 (hereafter *LEJ*); *LFEM* 44 (May 1908), 729–30.

74. Neather, "Labor Republicanism," 97–98; *LEMJ,* 35 (November 1901), 675; Brotherhood of Locomotive Engineers, *Constitution and Statutes of the Grand International Brotherhood of Locomotive Engineers* (n.p., 1918), 53.

75. Michael Kazin and Steven J. Ross, "America's Labor Day: The Dilemma of a Workers' Celebration," *Journal of American History* 78 (March 1992): 1303–4; Neather, "Labor Republicanism," 92; Schneirov, *Labor and Urban Politics,* 319.

76. *LEMJ* 32 (March 1898), 213; *LEMJ* 32 (May 1898), 346.

77. *New York Times,* October 3, 1898; *New York Times,* October 21, 1898; *LFM* 25 (July 1898), 93–95.

78. Kaplan, "Black and Blue on San Juan Hill," 219; Kimmel, *Manhood in America,* 111–12; Gorn, *The Manly Art,* 193.

79. *LEMJ* 32 (August 1898), 563; *LEMJ* 32 (September 1898), 611; *LEMJ* 35 (January 1901), 55–56.

80. *LEMJ* 35 (June 1901), 365; *LEMJ* 35 (September 1901), 539.

81. Neather, "Labor Republicanism," 96–97.

82. Bederman, *Manliness and Civilization,* 20–22, 25.

83. *Engineers' Monthly Journal* 10 (September 1876), 403; *LEMJ* 31 (February 1897), 148–49; *LFM* 24 (March 1898), 319.

84. Arnesen, *Brotherhoods of Color,* 31.

85. Ibid.

86. See Catherine Collomp, "Unions, Civics, and National Identity: Organized Labor's Reaction to Immigration," *Labor History* 29 (Fall 1988): 462–68; Schneirov, *Labor and Urban Politics,* 319.

Chapter 6. Craft Industrialism and the Arbitration System

1. Perlman, "Upheaval and Reorganization," in Commons et al., *History of Labour,* vol. 2, 521.

2. See Skowronek, *Building a New American State,* 165–76.

3. Naomi R. Lamoreaux, *The Great Merger Movement in American Business, 1895–1904* (Cambridge: Cambridge University Press, 1985), 1–5.

4. Chandler, *The Visible Hand,* 171–75, 332; Albro Martin, *Enterprise Denied: The Origins of the Decline of American Railroads, 1897–1917* (New York: Columbia University Press, 1971), 98–102, 173–93.

5. Perlman, "Upheaval and Reorganization," in Commons et al., *History of Labour,* vol. 2, 522–23, 535–37; Wolman, *The Growth of American Trade Unions,* 55.

6. Friedman, *State-Making and Labor Movements,* 220, 243–44; Stein, *The Social Origins of a Labor Elite,* 316–96; Hobsbawm, "Artisans and Labour Aristocrats?" 268–69; Howell, *Respectable Radicals,* 12–13. In Europe and the United States, a tension had always existed in railway unionism between craft exclusiveness and broader forms of organization. See Stromquist, *A Generation of Boomers*; Howell, *Respectable Radicals,* 6–10; Stein, *The Social Origins of a Labor Elite,* 246, 280–82.

7. Davis, *Power at Odds,* 26–27; Perlman, *History of Trade Unionism,* 180, 221–25.

8. See Christopher Clark, "The Railroad Safety Problem in the United States, 1900–1930," *Transport History* 7, no. 2 (1974): 100; *Arbitration Between the Eastern Railroads and the Order of Railway Conductors and Brotherhood of Railroad Trainmen* (New York: Law Reporting Co., 1913), 122–97, 167–69, 175.

9. Figures cited in *Arbitration Between the Eastern Railroads and the Order of Railway Conductors and Brotherhood of Railroad Trainmen.*

10. U.S. House of Representatives, "Railway Wage Schedules and Agreements," 289; U.S. House of Representatives, "Employment Conditions," 406.

11. Martin, *Enterprise Denied,* 65–71, 76–78, 94–95; Davis et al., *American Economic Growth,* 508.

12. U.S. House of Representatives, "Employment Conditions," 405–7.

13. Brotherhood of Locomotive Firemen and Enginemen, *Feeding the Iron Hog,* 16–18; U.S. House of Representatives, "Employment Conditions," 386; *Chicago Tribune,* December 19, 1914, news clipping in Records of the National Mediation Board, Record Group 13, Entry 18, box 29, folder 10, National Archives and Records Administration, Washington, D.C. (hereafter NMB).

14. *RTJ* 22 (February 1905), 115–16.

15. Ducker, *Men of the Steel Rails,* 120–21; Richter, *Home on the Rails,* 115–16.

16. U.S. House of Representatives, "Railway Wage Schedules," 289; U.S. House of Representatives, "Employment Conditions," 407–8.

17. "The Engineer's Side of It," in Leon Stein and Philip Taft, eds., *Workers Speak: Self Portraits* (New York: Arno and the New York Times, 1971), 113; F. P. Sargent, testimony, U.S. Industrial Commission, *Report,* vol. 4, 86–87.

18. *LEMJ* 36 (September 1902), 584.

19. U.S. House of Representatives, "Employment Conditions," 406; U.S. House of Representatives, "Railway Wage Schedules," 289.

20. Aldrich, *Safety First,* 168–71, 177–78; Clark, "The Railroad Safety Problem," 98–101; U.S. Congress, Senate, *Casualties Due to Excessive Hours of Labor, Etc.,* S. doc. 406. 59th Cong., 1st sess. (1906), 2–4; *RT* 27 (April 1910), 300–303.

21. Aldrich, *Safety First,* 179–85.

22. Paul H. Douglas, *Real Wages in the United States, 1890–1926* (New York: Houghton Mifflin, 1930), 60–61, 166–69; John R. Commons et al., *History of Labour in the United States,* vol. 3 (New York: Macmillan, 1935), 56–61.

23. *LFM* 34 (March 1903), 328–40; *RT* 26 (January 1909), 34–35; *RT* 31 (January 1914), 94–96.

24. *LFEM* 46 (May 1909), 745; *LFEM* 58 (February 1915), 224–25.

25. *LEMJ* 39 (January 1905), 47; *LEMJ* 40 (March 1906), 222.

26. Arnesen, *Brotherhoods of Color,* 25–26, 32; *LFEM* 60 (June 1916), 679–82.

27. Brotherhood of Locomotive Firemen, *Journal of Proceedings* [1896], 14.

28. See *LFM* (March 1896), 224; *LFM* 22 (January 1897), 58; *RTJ* 17 (June 1900), 506.

29. Brotherhood of Locomotive Firemen, *Proceedings of the Tenth Biennial Convention* (Milwaukee: S. E. Tate & Co., 1906), 19–20.

30. See Stromquist, *Generation of Boomers,* 122, 131–32; U.S. House of Representatives, "Employment Conditions," 390–91; *Chicago American,* December 18, 1914, news clipping in NMB, Entry 18, box 29, folder 10.

31. Arnesen, *Brotherhoods of Color,* 24–25.

32. *RTJ* 16 (September 1899), 880.

33. Lecht, *Experience Under Railway Labor Legislation,* 18–19; Peter H. Morrissey to Martin A. Knapp and Carroll D. Wright, June 21, 1899, and A. J. Cassatt to Knapp and Wright, July 15, 1899, both in NMB, Entry 2, box 1, folder 1.

34. See Clarence E. Wunderlin, *Visions of a New Industrial Order: Social Science*

and Labor Theory in America's Progressive Era (New York: Columbia University Press, 1992), 61.

35. Richardson, *The Locomotive Engineer,* 296–98; U.S. Industrial Commission, *Report,* vol. 17, 852–57; *LFM* 28 (March 1900), 241–43; *RTJ* 18 (August 1901), 670–71.

36. Orren, *Belated Feudalism,* 180n57; *RTJ* 18 (December 1901), 969.

37. *RT* 26 (January 1909), 87–88; *RTJ* 18 (December 1901), 972.

38. See Robbins, *Railway Conductors,* 166–69; *RTJ* 18 (August 1901), 670.

39. Davis, *Power at Odds,* 27; Hirsch, *After the Strike,* 23–24, 62–64; Perlman, *History of Trade Unionism,* 224–25.

40. Robbins, *Railway Conductors,* 61–63; J. Noble Stockett, *Arbitral Determination of Railway Wages* (Boston: Houghton Mifflin, 1918), 1–8, 12–15; Brotherhood of Railroad Trainmen, *Report of the Grand Master,* in *Proceedings of the Seventh Biennial Convention* (n.p., 1905), 11–13, 54–55; Brotherhood of Railroad Trainmen, *Report of Grand Master P. H. Morrissey,* in *Proceedings of the Ninth Biennial Convention* (n.p., 1909), 13–14.

41. Commons et al., *History of Labour,* vol. 4, 379; Lecht, *Experience Under Railway Labor Legislation,* 20; Orren, *Belated Feudalism,* 180.

42. Stevenson, "The Brotherhood of Locomotive Engineers and Its Leaders," 239, 315–18, 323–26.

43. Commons et al., *History of Labor,* vol. 4, 376–77; Lecht, *Experience Under Railway Labor Legislation,* 20; U.S. Bureau of Labor Statistics, *Mediation and Arbitration of Railway Labor Disputes,* 44–45; Brotherhood of Railroad Trainmen, *Report of Committee on Reports of Grand Lodge Officers,* in *Proceedings of the Eighth Biennial Convention* (n.p., 1907), 14–18.

44. Lecht, *Experience Under Railway Labor Legislation,* 19–25; Orren, *Belated Feudalism,* 193.

45. *Report of the Board of Arbitration in the Matter of the Controversy Between the Eastern Railroads and the Brotherhood of Locomotive Engineers, November 2, 1912* (Washington, D.C.: Published Under the Direction of the Secretary to the Board, n.d.), 10.

46. *Arbitration Between the Eastern Railroads and the Order of Railway Conductors and Brotherhood of Railroad Trainmen,* 122–97, 199–316; *Proceedings, Arbitration Between the Eastern Railroads and the Brotherhood of Locomotive Firemen and Enginemen* (New York, 1913), 21–115, 582–604, 605–1021.

47. Stockett, *Arbitral Determination of Railway Wages,* xii–xxi, 8–12; Orren, *Belated Feudalism,* 193–94.

48. Orren, *Belated Feudalism,* 191.

49. Arnesen, *Brotherhoods of Color,* 34–36; *LFM* 14 (December 1890), 1095–95.

50. See Brotherhood of Locomotive Firemen, *Journal of Proceedings* [1892], 330–31; Brotherhood of Locomotive Firemen, *Grand Lodge Proceedings of the Sixth Biennial Convention* (Peoria, Ill., 1898), 17; Brotherhood of Railroad Trainmen, *Proceedings of the Sixth Annual Convention* (Galesburg, Ill., 1889), 59.

51. Brotherhood of Railroad Trainmen, *Report of the Grand Master,* in *Proceedings of the Seventh Biennial Convention* (n.p., 1905), 54–55; *LFEM* 55 (June 1913), 830–31.

52. Arnesen, *Brotherhoods of Color,* 36–37; *LFEM* 47 (August 1909), 261–62; *LFEM* 47 (August 1909), 284–85; "Arbitration Proceeding, Georgia Railroad, and Its Employees," typescript in Special Collections Department, University of Georgia Library, Athens, Georgia, 479–83, 492–94, 485–86, 23–24.

53. John Michael Matthews, "The Georgia 'Race Strike' of 1909," *Journal of Southern History* 40 (November 1974): 613–23; Charles P. Neill to Bureau of Labor, May 26, 1909, NMB, Entry 2, box 4, folder 20.

54. "Arbitration Proceedings," 14–19, 80–84, 479–501, 482–83, 489, 517, 626–29, 792–93.

55. Ibid., 813–16; Hugh B. Hammett, "Labor and Race: The Georgia Railroad Strike of 1909," *Labor History* 16 (Fall 1975): 480.

56. *Atlanta Constitution,* June 30, 1909; *Atlanta Journal,* June 30, 1909; *LFEM* (August 1909), 267; Arnesen, *Brotherhoods of Color,* 37.

57. Herbert quoted in Hammett, "Labor and Race," 480–81; Arnesen, *Brotherhoods of Color,* 37.

58. Arnesen, *Brotherhoods of Color,* 37–38; *LFEM* 50 (April 1911), 519–20; W. S. Carter to Martin A. Knapp, March 12, 1911, NMB, Entry 2, box 6, folder 42.

59. Arnesen, *Brotherhoods of Color,* 38; *LFEM* 50 (May 1911), 655–57.

60. Arnesen, *Brotherhoods of Color,* 39; Atlantic Coast Line Railroad Company, *Revised Schedule of Wages, Rules, and Regulations for Trainmen and Yardmen,* effective October 1st, 1912 (pp. 16–17); "Memorandum," Atlantic Coast Line Railroad, August 8, 1914; and Val Fitzpatrick to Martin A. Knapp, August 10, 1914, all in NMB, Entry 18, box 6, folder 42.

61. Arnesen, *Brotherhoods of Color,* 37–38; "Memo" (pp. 7–9), NMB, Entry 18, box 7, folder 44.

62. See J. Frazier Glenn to Charles P. Neal, March 22, 1912, Charles P. Neal to J. Frazier Glenn, April 1, 1912, NMB, Entry 18, box 7, folder 44; Arnesen, *Brotherhoods of Color,* 59–62.

63. See Tomlins, *The State and the Unions,* 95; Perlman, *History of Trade Unionism,* 182–83.

64. Orren, *Belated Feudalism,* 182–86, 191–96; Martin, *Enterprise Denied,* 123–28; Montgomery, *Fall of the House of Labor,* 367.

65. Lecht, *Experience Under Railway Labor Legislation,* 20–21; Commons et al., *History of Labour,* vol. 4, 377; "Memorandum relating to demands of conductors and trainmen, Baltimore & Ohio Railroad, as presented December 28, 1909," NMB, Entry 2, box 5, folder 28.

66. Lecht, *Experience Under Railway Labor Legislation,* 21; Robbins, *Railway Conductors,* 74–75.

67. *Railway Age Gazette* 50 (April 7, 1911), 825–26 (hereafter *RAG*); *RAG* 50 (May 12, 1911), 1096–1100; *RAG* 50 (June 2, 1911), 1235–36; U.S. Department of Labor, Bureau

of Labor Statistics, *Use of Federal Power in Settlement of Railway Labor Disputes, Bulletin No. 303,* by Clyde Olin Fisher (Washington, D.C.: Government Printing Office, 1922), 43–44.

68. Orren, *Belated Feudalism,* 191; U.S. Bureau of Labor Statistics, *Use of Federal Power in Settlement of Railway Labor Disputes,* 44–45; Lecht, *Experience Under Railway Labor Legislation,* 26.

69. *RAG* 53 (December 27, 1912), 1247–50.

70. Lecht, *Experience Under Railway Labor Legislation,* 23.

71. One indicator of shifting orientation in the brotherhoods came at the Trainmen's 1909 convention when delegates repudiated the American Railroad Employees and Investors' Association. This action led to Patrick Morrissey's departure from the union. See Montgomery, *Fall of the House of Labor,* 366.

72. Lecht, *Experience Under Railway Labor Legislation,* 21–22; U.S. Bureau of Labor Statistics, *Use of Federal Power in Settlement of Railway Labor Disputes,* 45.

73. Stevenson, "The Brotherhood of Locomotive Engineers and Its Leaders," 337–39.

74. *RAG* 53 (November 29, 1912), 1022–23, 1039–43; *Report of the Board of Arbitration,* 9–15, 21–24, 47, 79–122; Sigmund, "Federal Laws Concerning Railroad Labor Disputes," 52.

75. *Report of the Board of Arbitration,* 111–23, quote 123.

76. *RT* 30 (January 1913), 86–87; address of Frank P. Sargent in *Industrial Conciliation: Report of the Proceedings of the Conference Held Under the Auspices of the National Civic Federation, December 16 and 17, 1901* (New York: G. P. Putnam's Sons, 1902), 48–58; E. E. Clark, "Conferences and Agreements of Railway Conductors," paper presented at the Chicago Conference, December 17–18, 1900, in *Industrial Conciliation,* 217–222.

77. Lecht, *Experience Under Railway Labor Legislation,* 25; Sigmund, "Federal Laws Concerning Railroad Labor Disputes," 56; U.S. Bureau of Labor Statistics, *Use of Federal Power in Settlement of Railway Labor Disputes,* 47–48; Green, *The National Civic Federation and the American Labor Movement,* 224–25.

78. Stromquist, *Reinventing "The People,"* 166–69.

79. Green, *The National Civic Federation and the American Labor Movement,* 224–25; Ralph Easley to Warren Stone, March 4, 1913, National Civic Federation, Records, New York Public Library, box 426, folder 4 (hereafter NCF Records); W. S. Carter to Martin A. Knapp and G. W. W. Hanger, March 7, 1913, Seth Low to Knapp, May 10, 1913, NMB, Entry 14, box 4, folder 1.

80. Green, *The National Civic Federation and the American Labor Movement,* 226–32; Seth Low to Martin A. Knapp, June 10, 1913, NMB, Entry 14, box 4, folder 1; *New York Times,* June 21, July 11, and July 12, 1913.

81. A. B. Garretson and W. G. Lee to U.S. Board of Mediation and Conciliation, July 24, 1913, NMB, box 38, folder 71, part 1; Seth Low to Elisha Lee, July 17, 1913, NCF Records, box 201, folder 2; *New York Times,* July 27, 1913.

82. Stromquist, *Reinventing "The People,"* 99, 166–67; W. C. Adamson to Seth Low, June 16, 1913, NMB, Entry 14, box 1 folder 1; "Report on National Legislation, Sixty-third Congress, Joint Legislative Bureau," 64–65, in NMB, Entry 26, box 8.

83. Lecht, *Experience Under Railway Labor Legislation,* 25–26.

84. Montgomery, *Fall of the House of Labor,* 367; Stevenson, "The Brotherhood of Locomotive Engineers and Its Leaders," 340, 352; *RT* 31 (February 1914), 163–66; *RT* 31 (March 1914), 257–58; *RT* 31 (May 1914), 429–40; *RT* 31 (September 1914), 837–41.

85. See *RT* 31 (August 1914), 718–20; *RT* 31 (October 1914), 930; *RT* 32 (January 1915), 86–89; *RT* 32 (June 1915), 564–65.

86. *RT* 29 (February 1912), 142–43; *RT* 30 (February 1913), 152.

87. Stevenson, "The Brotherhood of Locomotive Engineers and Its Leaders," 230–34, 247–65; Commons et al., *History of Labor,* vol. 4, 379–80; *LFEM* 54 (March 1913), 278–79.

88. Stevenson, "The Brotherhood of Locomotive Engineers and Its Leaders," 340–42; Philip S. Foner, *History of the Labor Movement in the United States,* vol. 6, *On the Eve of America's Entry into World War I, 1915–1916* (New York: International Publishers, 1982), 146–47. Wilson quoted in Foner, *History of the Labor Movement in the United States,* 147.

89. *International Socialist Review* 15 (June 1915), 710–11 (hereafter *ISR*); Carter quoted in U.S. Bureau of Labor Statistics, *Use of Federal Power in Settlement of Railway Labor Disputes,* 54.

90. Stevenson, "The Brotherhood of Locomotive Engineers and Its Leaders," 342–45; Foner, *History of the Labor Movement in the United States,* 147–48; *ISR* 15 (June 1915), 710–11. Wilson quoted in Foner, *History of the Labor Movement in the United States,* 147.

91. *ISR* 16 (July 1915), 15; *ISR* 16 (August 1915), 98.

92. Price, *Labour in British Society,* 127; Friedman, *State-Making and Labor Movements,* 220, 237–45; Commons et al., *History of Labor,* vol. 4, 374–85.

Chapter 7. Political Action, Industrial Action, and the Making of the Liberal State

1. Arthur S. Link, *Woodrow Wilson and the Progressive Era, 1910–1917* (New York: Harper and Row, 1954), 21–22; Dubofsky, *The State and Labor,* 52–53.

2. Dubofsky, *The State and Labor,* 53–54; Greene, *Pure and Simple Politics,* 242; Link, *Woodrow Wilson and the Progressive Era,* 22–24, 69–70.

3. See Greene, *Pure and Simple Politics,* 107–214.

4. See Greene, *Pure and Simple Politics,* 56–57, 80–81.

5. Richardson, *The Locomotive Engineer,* 272; Thomas W. White, "A History of Railroad Workers in the Pacific Northwest, 1883–1934" (PhD diss., University of Washington, 1981), 130; Greene, *Pure and Simple Politics,* 80–82, 93–94; reports of H. R. Fuller in "Report of the National Legislative Representative."

6. See Gwendolyn Mink, *Old Labor and New Immigrants in American Political Development: Union, Party, and State, 1875–1920* (Ithaca: Cornell University Press, 1986), 124, 128n29, 132; *LEMJ* 24 (September 1890), 706–7; *LEMJ* 25 (March 1891), 263–64; *LEMJ* 26 (February 1892): 165–66; *LEMJ* 27 (July 1893), 651.

7. See *LEMJ* 30 (December 1896), 1071–72; *LEMJ* 31 (April 1897), 338–41; *LFM* 22 (February 1897), 80.

8. See *RTJ* 19 (May 1902), 391–92; *LFM* 34 (January 1903) 65–66; reports of H. R. Fuller, July 14, 1902 and May 6, 1904, in "Report of the National Legislative Representative."

9. See *RTJ* 23 (August 1906), 725–27; *LFEM* 57 (October 1914), 474; *LEJ* 50 (April 1916), 356.

10. Fink, *Biographical Dictionary,* 501; Roosevelt, *Letters,* vol. 3, 332, 539, 607; vol. 4, 892; vol. 5, 285, 413.

11. Collomp, "Unions, Civics, and National Identity," 452–54, 458–68.

12. U.S. Congress, Senate, *Safety Appliances, Automatic Ashpans: Hearing Before a Subcommittee of the Committee on Interstate Commerce, United States Senate* (Washington, D.C.: Government Printing Office, 1908), 3, 23.

13. Aldrich, *Safety First,* 35–36; Clark, "The Railroad Safety Problem," 103–5, 112–13; E. E. Clark to J. K. Richards, acting attorney general, January 13, 1903, and Philander Knox, attorney general, to E. E. Clark, January 30, 1903, both in ORC Archives, box 2, folder: Grand Chief Conductor Clark, 1890–1906; *RTJ* 18 (April 1901), 328–3; *LFM* 25 (August 1903), 280–303; reports of H. R. Fuller, June 11, 1900, March 11, 1901, July 14, 1902, and March 12, 1903, in "Report of the National Legislative Representative."

14. Aldrich, *Safety First,* 183–86; *RTJ* 23 (January 1906), 84–86; *LFEM* 54 (November 1913), 698–70; *LEJ* 49 (December 1915), 1176–78; *RTJ* 24 (June 1907), 550–51; *RT* 29 (June 1912), 531–34.

15. Arnesen, *Brotherhoods of Color,* 38–39.

16. Commons et al., *History of Labour,* vol. 3, 548–49, 662–64; U.S. House of Representatives, "Railway Wage Schedules," 289.

17. Aldrich, *Safety First,* 171; U.S. Congress, House of Representatives, *Hearing Before Committee on Interstate and Foreign Commerce House of Representatives on the Bills HR 4438, HR 16676, and HR 18671, to Limit the Hours of Service of Railroad Employees* (Washington, D.C.: Government Printing Office, 1906), 4–8; Dubofsky, *The State and Labor,* 44.

18. Aldrich, *Safety First,* 171–72; U.S. House of Representatives, *Hearing Before Committee on Interstate and Foreign Commerce House of Representatives,* 8, 13–16.

19. Witt, *Accidental Republic,* 67; reports of H. R. Fuller, March 9, 1899, March 12, 1903, May 6, 1904, and March 8, 1905, in "Report of the National Legislative Representative."

20. *RTJ* 23 (June 1906), 535; U.S. Congress, Senate, *Liability of Employers: Hearings Before the Committee on Interstate Commerce, United States Senate* (Washington, D.C.: Government Printing Office, 1906), 48–50, 69–72; Witt, *Accidental Republic,* 67;

Dubofsky, *The State and Labor,* 44; report of H. R. Fuller, March 9, 1899, in "Report of the National Legislative Representative."

21. Edward D. Berkowitz, *Disabled Policy: America's Programs for the Handicapped: A Twentieth Century Fund Report* (Cambridge: Cambridge University Press, 1987), 15–21.

22. Witt, *Accidental Republic,* 146–47, 149; *LEJ* 46 (July 1912), 705–6; *LFEM* 53 (August 1912), 229–31; *RT* 30 (August 1913), 734–46; U.S. Congress, House of Representatives, *Workmen's Compensation: Hearings Before a Subcommittee of the Committee on Interstate and Foreign Commerce of the House of Representatives* (Washington, D.C.: Government Printing Office, 1914), 17–18, 23; *RT* 29 (December 1912), 1103–4.

23. Greene, *Pure and Simple Politics,* 83–85; Forbath, *Law and the Shaping of the American Labor Movement,* 193.

24. Sigmund, "Federal Laws Concerning Railroad Labor Disputes," 35–36; *RTJ* 19 (May 1902), 403–4; *RTJ* 20 (May 1903), 385–98.

25. See reports of H. R. Fuller, June 11, 1900, March 11, 1901, July 14, 1902, March 12, 1903, May 6, 1904, and March 8, 1905, in "Report of the National Legislative Representative"; *RTJ* 19 (May 1902), 321–23, 379–82, 391–92; *RTJ* 21 (February 1904), 135–36; *RTJ* 21 (April 1904), 278–81; *LEMJ* 40 (March 1906), 253–54; *RT* 27 (December 1910), 1011; *RT* 30 (July 1913), 653; U.S. Congress, Senate, A Compilation of Documents Relating to Injunctions in Conspiracy Cases, 34–35.

26. Commons et al., *History of Labour,* vol. 2, 530–31; Sklar, *The Corporate Reconstruction of American Capitalism,* 223–26, 331; Brotherhood of Railroad Trainmen, *Report of Grand Master,* in *Proceedings of the Ninth Biennial Convention,* 24.

27. Roosevelt, *Letters,* vol. 6, 992; *LEMJ* 36 (February 1902), 115; *RT* 25 (June 1908), 516.

28. *LFEM* 44 (March 1908), 378–79; *LFEM* 44 (April 1908), 533; *RTJ* 18 (November 1901), 954; *RTJ* 21 (January 1904), 45–47.

29. On the AFL's experience with lobbying Congress, see Greene, *Pure and Simple Politics,* 93–104.

30. Greene, *Pure and Simple Politics,* 242; Sklar, *The Corporate Reconstruction of American Capitalism,* 324–32, 383–84, 401–30; Davis, *Power at Odds,* 31–32; Dubofsky, "Abortive Reform," 199–200.

31. Greene, *Pure and Simple Politics,* 71–214.

32. Ibid., 48; Richard L. McCormick, "The Party Period and Public Policy: An Exploratory Hypothesis," in McCormick, ed., *The Party Period and Public Policy: American Politics from the Age of Jackson to the Progressive Era* (New York: Oxford University Press, 1986), 222–23.

33. Dubofsky, "Abortive Reform," 200; Licht, *Working for the Railroad,* 231; Stevenson, "The Brotherhood of Locomotive Engineers and Its Leaders," 271–72.

34. Ducker, *Men of the Steel Rails,* 87–101.

35. See Brotherhood of Locomotive Engineers, *Constitution* [1902], 29.

36. Greene, *Pure and Simple Politics,* 66–67.

37. *RTJ* 18 (March 1901), 244.

38. Richard L. McCormick, "The Discovery That Business Corrupts Politics: A Reappraisal of the Origins of Progressivism," in McCormick, ed., *The Party Period and Public Policy: American Politics from the Age of Jackson to the Progressive Era* (New York: Oxford University Press, 1986), 326–48; *RTJ* 18 (May 1901), 410–12; *RTJ* 20 (February 1903), 88–94.

39. *RTJ* 21 (March 1904), 150.

40. *LEMJ* 30 (April 1896), 294–95; *LEMJ* 32 (September 1898), 619–20; *LFM* 21 (October 1896), 266; Brotherhood of Railroad Trainmen, *Proceedings of the Fifth Biennial Convention* (Cleveland, 1901), 64–65.

41. *LEMJ* 40 (October 1906), 896.

42. Ibid., 896–97.

43. *RTJ* 23 (June 1906), 523–25; *RTJ* 23 (September 1906), 828–29.

44. *RTJ* 24 (February 1907), 140–41; *RT* 25 (June 1908), 496–97; *RT* 25 (July 1908), 598.

45. *LFEM* 53 (October 1912), 521.

46. *LFEM* 52 (April 1912), 538. See also *LFEM* 53 (July 1912), 104; *LFEM* 53 (October 1912), 529.

47. *LFEM* 52 (March 1912), 397. See also *LFEM* 52 (March 1912), 394; *LFEM* 52 (April 1912), 538, 546; *LFEM* 53 (October 1912), 529.

48. *LFEM* 52 (April 1912), 684.

49. *LFEM* 53 (October 1912), 530; *LFEM* 52 (March 1912), 394. See also *LFEM* 52 (March 1912), 397; *LFEM* 53 (July 1912), 104, 105.

50. *LFEM* 53 (October 1912), 529.

51. *LFEM* 52 (April 1912), 546; *LFEM* 53 (July 1912), 104; *LFEM* 52 (February 1912), 275.

52. Greene, *Pure and Simple Politics,* 243–46, 249.

53. Ibid., 250–51; *LFEM* 59 (July 1915), 46.

54. Greene, *Pure and Simple Politics,* 251–53.

55. *LFEM* 59 (October 1915), 462.

56. *LEJ* 50 (January 1916), 81; *LFEM* 61 (August 1916), 170–74.

57. Joseph A. McCartin, *Labor's Great War: The Struggle for Industrial Democracy and the Origins of Modern American Labor Relations, 1912–1921* (Chapel Hill: University of North Carolina Press, 1997), 18–28; U.S. Commission on Industrial Relations, *Final Report and Testimony Submitted to Congress by the Commission on Industrial Relations,* S. doc. 415, 64th Cong., 1st sess. (1916), 17.

58. U.S. Congress, House, Committee on Interstate and Foreign Commerce, *Hearings: Return of Railroad to Private Ownership,* 66th Cong., 1st sess. (1919), 4380; Howell John Harris, "Industrial Democracy and Liberal Capitalism, 1890–1925," in Nelson Lichtenstein and Howell John Harris, eds., *Industrial Democracy in America: The Ambiguous Promise* (Cambridge: Cambridge University Press, 1993), 49–50.

59. See Joseph A. McCartin, "'An American Feeling': Workers, Managers, and the

Struggle over Industrial Democracy in the World War I Era," in Nelson Lichtenstein and Howell John Harris, eds., *Industrial Democracy in America: The Ambiguous Promise* (Cambridge: Cambridge University Press, 1993), 72–74; *LFEM* 44 (March 1908), 378–79; *LFEM* 44 (April 1908), 533; *LEJ* 46 (May 1912), 492; *RT* 29 (July 1912), 597.

60. *LFEM* 59 (December 1915), 702–4; *LFEM* 60 (February 1916), 192–97; *LEJ* 48 (December 1915), 1193.

61. Greene, *Pure and Simple Politics,* 255–56; Harris, "Industrial Democracy," 49.

62. McCartin, *Labor's Great War,* 19, 30; Montgomery, *Fall of the House of Labor,* 360–61; *LEJ* 49 (May 1915), 425; *LFEM* 56 (May 1914), 604–5; *LFEM* 59 (October 1915), 462–64; *LFEM* 60 (March 1916), 319–20; *LEJ* 50 (May 1916), 441.

63. Greene, *Pure and Simple Politics,* 253–55.

64. Link, *Woodrow Wilson and the Progressive Era,* 192–96; 224–30, quotes 224, 229; Greene, *Pure and Simple Politics,* 256–57.

65. Stevenson, "The Brotherhood of Locomotive Engineers and Its Leaders," 319–22; Richardson, *The Locomotive Engineer,* 251–52; U.S. House of Representatives, "Railway Wage Schedules," 289, 299–304; "Grand Lodge, Brotherhood of Railroad Trainmen," *RT* 28 (October 1911), 761–62.

66. See *RTJ* 24 (July 1907), 624–25; *RT* 27 (March 1910), 223–25; *RT* 29 (January 1912), 73; Brotherhood of Railroad Trainmen, *Proceedings* [1909], 107–8; *LEJ* 45 (November 1911), 958–59; *LEJ* 46 (January 1912), 44; *LEJ* 48 (September 1914), 804–6; *LFEM* 55 (October 1913), 587; U.S. House of Representatives, "Railway Wage Schedules," 299–300.

67. *RT* 27 (February 1910), 132.

68. *LFEM* 59 (September 1915), 355; *LFEM* 59 (November 1915), 594–95; *LFEM* 59 (December 1915), 721; *LFEM* 59 (December 1915), 729–30. The last quote appears in Montgomery, *Fall of the House of Labor,* 368.

69. Stevenson, "The Brotherhood of Locomotive Engineers and Its Leaders," 352–55; Montgomery, *Fall of the House of Labor,* 368; David R. Roediger and Philip S. Foner, *Our Own Time: A History of American Labor and the Working Day* (Westport, Conn.: Greenwood Press, 1989), 195–96; Brotherhood of Railroad Trainmen, *Proceedings of the First Triennial Convention* (Detroit, 1916), 11–18, 105.

70. Roediger and Foner, *Our Own Time,* 196; Foner, *History of the Labor Movement in the United States,* 150–55, 159–61; Stevenson, "The Brotherhood of Locomotive Engineers and Its Leaders," 355–58, 365–66; *LFEM* 60 (August 1916), 190–93; *New York Times,* April 7, 1916 and July 7, 1916; M. O. Mather to all members, March 4, 1916 and H. M. Carson to S. C. Long, April 29, 1916, both in Personnel Department, Pennsylvania Railroad Archives, box 988.

71. Roediger and Foner, *Our Own Time,* 196; Foner, *History of the Labor Movement in the United States,* 162–63; *New York Times,* January 30, 1916; Samuel Gompers to Warren Stone, August 2, 1916, in Peter J. Albert and Grace Palladino, eds., *The Samuel Gompers Papers,* vol. 9, *The American Federation of Labor at the Height of Progressivism, 1913–17* (Urbana: University of Illinois Press, 2003), 463.

72. Montgomery, *Fall of the House of Labor,* 368; *LFEM* 60 (March 1916), 350; *LFEM* 60 (April 1916), 459–60; *LFEM* 60 (May 1916), 571–72; *RT* 33 (March 1916), 171–73.

73. *LFEM* 60 (May 1916), 578–81; *LFEM* 60 (May 1916), 599–600; *LFEM* 60 (June 1916), 701–3

74. Roediger and Foner, *Our Own Time,* 196; Foner, *History of the Labor Movement in the United States,* 151–52; *RT* 33 (January 1916), 3–5; *LFEM* 60 (March 1916), 333–36; *LFEM* 60 (June 1916), 632–38; *LFEM* 60 (May 1916), 575–78; *RT* 33 (March 1916), 229–31; *RT* 33 (April 1916), 312; *RT* 33 (May 1916), 397–400.

75. Stevenson, "The Brotherhood of Locomotive Engineers and Its Leaders," 358–60; Foner, *History of the Labor Movement in the United States,* 153–54; *RT* 33 (March 1916), 167–72; *RT* 33 (April 1916), 332–35.

76. *LEJ* 50 (June 1916), 505; *LEJ* 50 (January 1916), 206; *LFEM* 61 (September 1916), 306–7.

77. *LFEM* 60 (June 1916), 703; *LEJ* 50 (May 1916), 429.

78. *LFEM* 60 (April 1916), 473; *RT* 33 (August 1916), 689.

79. Montgomery, *Fall of the House of Labor,* 368; *LFEM* 61 (August 1916), 170–75; letters to Walsh from brotherhoods lodges, *Pittsburgh Leader,* May 1, 1916, and *New York Call,* May 12, 1916, news clippings, all in Frank Walsh Papers, Personal Scrapbooks, vol. 42, New York Public Library.

80. Montgomery, *Fall of the House of Labor,* 361–65; McCartin, *Labor's Great War,* 33–35; Greene, *Pure and Simple Politics,* 258.

81. Roediger and Foner, *Our Own Time,* 196–97; Martin, *Enterprise Denied,* 317–35; Statement of Conference Committee of the Railways, June 15, 1916; "Statement of Stone, Lee, and Garretson," n.d.; W. L. Chambers to Woodrow Wilson, August 9, 1916; Martin A. Knapp to Woodrow Wilson, August 13, 1916; Chambers to J. T. Tumulty, August 13, 1916; Chambers to Knapp, August 14, 1916; Chambers to Knapp, August 18, 1916; and Chambers to Wilson, August 18, 1916, all in NMB, box 38, folder 71, part 1.

82. Roediger and Foner, *Our Own Time,* 197–98.

83. Ibid., 198; Foner, *History of the Labor Movement in the United States,* 176–83.

84. Roediger and Foner, *Our Own Time,* 195, 198; Foner, *History of the Labor Movement in the United States,* 177–79; U.S. Congress, Senate, *Threatened Strike of Railway Employees: Hearing Before the Committee on Interstate Commerce United State Senate,* S. doc. 549, 64th Cong., 1st sess. (1916), 24–25.

85. U.S. Congress, Senate, *Threatened Strike of Railway Employees,* 24–25, 32–33, 42–58, 143–45.

86. See William Z. Ripley, "The Railroad Eight Hour Law," *The American Review of Reviews,* 391, news clipping, n.d., in NMB, Entry 18, box 16, folder 6; Roediger and Foner, *Our Own Time,* 198.

87. Foner, *History of the Labor Movement in the United States,* 183–84; McCartin, *Labor's Great War,* 34; Greene, *Pure and Simple Politics,* 258–60. Walsh quoted in Foner, *History of the Labor Movement in the United States,* 184. The Wilson quote is from Montgomery, *Fall of the House of Labor,* 368.

88. Dubofsky, *The State and Labor,* 60.

89. Greene, *Pure and Simple Politics,* 262, 267–68; *LFEM* 61 (October 1916), 389; *LFEM* 61 (November 1916), 505.

90. Greene, *Pure and Simple Politics,* 262, 266; Foner, *History of the Labor Movement in the United States,* 228–29; Montgomery, *Fall of the House of Labor,* 369; *LFEM* 60 (December 1916), 576–77; *LFEM* 60 (December 1916), 586–89. Quoted passages are from Greene, *Pure and Simple Politics,* 262.

91. Roediger and Foner, *Our Own Time,* 198–99; Link, *Woodrow Wilson and the Progressive Era,* 237n33; Orren, *Belated Feudalism,* 196–97; U.S. Congress, Senate, *Eight-Hour Workday for Railway Employees: Opinion of the Supreme Court of the United States in the Case of Francis M. Wilson . . . vs. Alexander New and Henry C. Ferris,* S. doc. 20, 65th Cong., 1st sess. (1917), 6–10, quote 7.

92. Orren, *Belated Feudalism,* 19–20.

93. *LEJ* 50 (May 1916), 397.

94. Greene, *Pure and Simple Politics,* 272; McCartin, *Labor's Great War,* 35–36.

95. Montgomery, *Fall of the House of Labor,* 369.

Conclusion

1. Edward Keating to Louis W. Cunningham, March 30, 1923, Keating Files, *Labor* Papers, Kheel Center, box 3, folder 1.

2. Montgomery, *The Fall of the House of Labor,* 406–7, 420, 434–37; Robert H. Zieger, *Republicans and Labor, 1919–1929* (Lexington: University of Kentucky Press, 1969), 172–89; Erik Olssen, "The Making of a Political Machine: The Railroad Unions Enter Politics," *Labor History* 19 (Summer 1978): 273–96.

3. Zieger, *Republicans and Labor,* 190–215; O'Brien, *Workers' Paradox,* 8–9, 15–17.

4. William Graebner, *A History of Retirement: The Meaning and Function of an American Institution, 1885–1978* (New Haven: Yale University Press, 1980), 156–63.

5. Arnesen, *Brotherhoods of Color,* 48–73, 116–28.

6. See Gordon, Edwards, and Reich, *Segmented Work, Divided Workers,* 112–53.

7. McKenna, "Victorian Railway Workers," 42, 66–67; Hobsbawm, "The Labour Aristocracy," 275; Crossick, "The Labour Aristocracy and Its Values," 306–10; Hobsbawm, "The Labour Aristocracy Reconsidered," 221–23, 239–45; Friedman, *State-Making and Labor Movements,* 229; Kimeldorf, *Battling for American Labor,* 158.

8. Wright, *Class, Crisis, and the State,* 63; Dawson, "The Parameters of Craft Consciousness," 139, 142. I am indebted to Michael Kazin for this argument. See Kazin, *Barons of Labor,* 278–79.

9. Baron, "Gender and Labor History," 25–26, 29–32.

10. See Kessler-Harris, "Treating the Male as 'Other,'" 194; Tosh, "What Should Historians Do with Masculinity?" 183.

11. See Roediger, "Race and the Working-Class Past," 133–34; Bederman, *Manliness and Civilization,* 20–23; Nelson, *Divided We Stand,* 288, 293–94; Kolchin, "Whiteness Studies," 160, 170–71.

12. David E. Bernstein, *Only One Place of Redress: African Americans, Labor Relations, and the Courts from Reconstruction to the New Deal* (Durham: Duke University Press, 2001); Paul D. Moreno, *Black Americans and Organized Labor* (Baton Rouge: Louisiana State University Press, 2006).

13. See Zieger, *For Jobs and Freedom,* 4–7.

14. See Dawson, "The Parameters of Craft Consciousness," 139–47.

15. See Jacobs and Zelizer, "The Democratic Experiment," 4–6.

16. See Cobble, *Dishing It Out,* 7; Bacharach, Bamberger, and Sonnenstuhl, *Mutual Aid and Union Renewal,* 1–21, 55–91.

Index

PAUL MICHEL TAILLON is a senior lecturer in the History Department at the University of Auckland, New Zealand.

THE WORKING CLASS IN AMERICAN HISTORY

Worker City, Company Town: Iron and Cotton-Worker Protest in Troy and Cohoes, New York, 1855–84 *Daniel J. Walkowitz*

Life, Work, and Rebellion in the Coal Fields: The Southern West Virginia Miners, 1880–1922 *David Alan Corbin*

Women and American Socialism, 1870–1920 *Mari Jo Buhle*

Lives of Their Own: Blacks, Italians, and Poles in Pittsburgh, 1900–1960 *John Bodnar, Roger Simon, and Michael P. Weber*

Working-Class America: Essays on Labor, Community, and American Society *Edited by Michael H. Frisch and Daniel J. Walkowitz*

Eugene V. Debs: Citizen and Socialist *Nick Salvatore*

American Labor and Immigration History, 1877–1920s: Recent European Research *Edited by Dirk Hoerder*

Workingmen's Democracy: The Knights of Labor and American Politics *Leon Fink*

The Electrical Workers: A History of Labor at General Electric and Westinghouse, 1923–60 *Ronald W. Schatz*

The Mechanics of Baltimore: Workers and Politics in the Age of Revolution, 1763–1812 *Charles G. Steffen*

The Practice of Solidarity: American Hat Finishers in the Nineteenth Century *David Bensman*

The Labor History Reader *Edited by Daniel J. Leab*

Solidarity and Fragmentation: Working People and Class Consciousness in Detroit, 1875–1900 *Richard Oestreicher*

Counter Cultures: Saleswomen, Managers, and Customers in American Department Stores, 1890–1940 *Susan Porter Benson*

The New England Working Class and the New Labor History *Edited by Herbert G. Gutman and Donald H. Bell*

Labor Leaders in America *Edited by Melvyn Dubofsky and Warren Van Tine*

Barons of Labor: The San Francisco Building Trades and Union Power in the Progressive Era *Michael Kazin*

Gender at Work: The Dynamics of Job Segregation by Sex during World War II *Ruth Milkman*

Once a Cigar Maker: Men, Women, and Work Culture in American Cigar Factories, 1900–1919 *Patricia A. Cooper*

A Generation of Boomers: The Pattern of Railroad Labor Conflict in Nineteenth-Century America *Shelton Stromquist*

Work and Community in the Jungle: Chicago's Packinghouse Workers, 1894–1922 *James R. Barrett*

Workers, Managers, and Welfare Capitalism: The Shoeworkers and Tanners of Endicott Johnson, 1890–1950 *Gerald Zahavi*

Men, Women, and Work: Class, Gender, and Protest in the New England Shoe Industry, 1780–1910 *Mary Blewett*

Workers on the Waterfront: Seamen, Longshoremen, and Unionism in the 1930s *Bruce Nelson*
German Workers in Chicago: A Documentary History of Working-Class Culture from 1850 to World War I *Edited by Hartmut Keil and John B. Jentz*
On the Line: Essays in the History of Auto Work *Edited by Nelson Lichtenstein and Stephen Meyer III*
Labor's Flaming Youth: Telephone Operators and Worker Militancy, 1878–1923 *Stephen H. Norwood*
Another Civil War: Labor, Capital, and the State in the Anthracite Regions of Pennsylvania, 1840–68 *Grace Palladino*
Coal, Class, and Color: Blacks in Southern West Virginia, 1915–32 *Joe William Trotter, Jr.*
For Democracy, Workers, and God: Labor Song-Poems and Labor Protest, 1865–95 *Clark D. Halker*
Dishing It Out: Waitresses and Their Unions in the Twentieth Century *Dorothy Sue Cobble*
The Spirit of 1848: German Immigrants, Labor Conflict, and the Coming of the Civil War *Bruce Levine*
Working Women of Collar City: Gender, Class, and Community in Troy, New York, 1864–86 *Carole Turbin*
Southern Labor and Black Civil Rights: Organizing Memphis Workers *Michael K. Honey*
Radicals of the Worst Sort: Laboring Women in Lawrence, Massachusetts, 1860–1912 *Ardis Cameron*
Producers, Proletarians, and Politicians: Workers and Party Politics in Evansville and New Albany, Indiana, 1850–87 *Lawrence M. Lipin*
The New Left and Labor in the 1960s *Peter B. Levy*
The Making of Western Labor Radicalism: Denver's Organized Workers, 1878–1905 *David Brundage*
In Search of the Working Class: Essays in American Labor History and Political Culture *Leon Fink*
Lawyers against Labor: From Individual Rights to Corporate Liberalism *Daniel R. Ernst*
"We Are All Leaders": The Alternative Unionism of the Early 1930s *Edited by Staughton Lynd*
The Female Economy: The Millinery and Dressmaking Trades, 1860–1930 *Wendy Gamber*
"Negro and White, Unite and Fight!": A Social History of Industrial Unionism in Meatpacking, 1930–90 *Roger Horowitz*
Power at Odds: The 1922 National Railroad Shopmen's Strike *Colin J. Davis*
The Common Ground of Womanhood: Class, Gender, and Working Girls' Clubs, 1884–1928 *Priscilla Murolo*
Marching Together: Women of the Brotherhood of Sleeping Car Porters *Melinda Chateauvert*

Down on the Killing Floor: Black and White Workers in Chicago's Packinghouses, 1904–54 *Rick Halpern*

Labor and Urban Politics: Class Conflict and the Origins of Modern Liberalism in Chicago, 1864–97 *Richard Schneirov*

All That Glitters: Class, Conflict, and Community in Cripple Creek *Elizabeth Jameson*

Waterfront Workers: New Perspectives on Race and Class *Edited by Calvin Winslow*

Labor Histories: Class, Politics, and the Working-Class Experience *Edited by Eric Arnesen, Julie Greene, and Bruce Laurie*

The Pullman Strike and the Crisis of the 1890s: Essays on Labor and Politics *Edited by Richard Schneirov, Shelton Stromquist, and Nick Salvatore*

AlabamaNorth: African-American Migrants, Community, and Working-Class Activism in Cleveland, 1914–45 *Kimberley L. Phillips*

Imagining Internationalism in American and British Labor, 1939–49 *Victor Silverman*

William Z. Foster and the Tragedy of American Radicalism *James R. Barrett*

Colliers across the Sea: A Comparative Study of Class Formation in Scotland and the American Midwest, 1830–1924 *John H. M. Laslett*

"Rights, Not Roses": Unions and the Rise of Working-Class Feminism, 1945–80 *Dennis A. Deslippe*

Testing the New Deal: The General Textile Strike of 1934 in the American South *Janet Irons*

Hard Work: The Making of Labor History *Melvyn Dubofsky*

Southern Workers and the Search for Community: Spartanburg County, South Carolina *G. C. Waldrep III*

We Shall Be All: A History of the Industrial Workers of the World (abridged edition) *Melvyn Dubofsky, ed. Joseph A. McCartin*

Race, Class, and Power in the Alabama Coalfields, 1908–21 *Brian Kelly*

Duquesne and the Rise of Steel Unionism *James D. Rose*

Anaconda: Labor, Community, and Culture in Montana's Smelter City *Laurie Mercier*

Bridgeport's Socialist New Deal, 1915–36 *Cecelia Bucki*

Indispensable Outcasts: Hobo Workers and Community in the American Midwest, 1880–1930 *Frank Tobias Higbie*

After the Strike: A Century of Labor Struggle at Pullman *Susan Eleanor Hirsch*

Corruption and Reform in the Teamsters Union *David Witwer*

Waterfront Revolts: New York and London Dockworkers, 1946–61 *Colin J. Davis*

Black Workers' Struggle for Equality in Birmingham *Horace Huntley and David Montgomery*

The Tribe of Black Ulysses: African American Men in the Industrial South *William P. Jones*

City of Clerks: Office and Sales Workers in Philadelphia, 1870–1920 *Jerome P. Bjelopera*

Reinventing "The People": The Progressive Movement, the Class Problem, and the Origins of Modern Liberalism *Shelton Stromquist*

Radical Unionism in the Midwest, 1900–1950 *Rosemary Feurer*

Gendering Labor History *Alice Kessler-Harris*
James P. Cannon and the Origins of the American Revolutionary Left, 1890–1928 *Bryan D. Palmer*
Glass Towns: Industry, Labor, and Political Economy in Appalachia, 1890–1930s *Ken Fones-Wolf*
Workers and the Wild: Conservation, Consumerism, and Labor in Oregon, 1910–30 *Lawrence M. Lipin*
Wobblies on the Waterfront: Interracial Unionism in Progressive-Era Philadelphia *Peter Cole*
Red Chicago: American Communism at Its Grassroots, 1928–35 *Randi Storch*
Labor's Cold War: Local Politics in a Global Context *Edited by Shelton Stromquist*
Bessie Abramowitz Hillman and the Making of the Amalgamated Clothing Workers of America *Karen Pastorello*
The Great Strikes of 1877 *Edited by David O. Stowell*
Union-Free America: Workers and Antiunion Culture *Lawrence Richards*
Race against Liberalism: Black Workers and the UAW in Detroit *David M. Lewis-Colman*
Teachers and Reform: Chicago Public Education, 1929–70 *John F. Lyons*
Upheaval in the Quiet Zone: 1199/SEIU and the Politics of Healthcare Unionism *Leon Fink and Brian Greenberg*
Shadow of the Racketeer: Scandal in Organized Labor *David Witwer*
Sweet Tyranny: Migrant Labor, Industrial Agriculture, and Imperial Politics *Kathleen Mapes*
Staley: The Fight for a New American Labor Movement *Steven K. Ashby and C. J. Hawking*
On the Ground: Labor Struggles in the American Airline Industry *Liesl Miller Orenic*
NAFTA and Labor in North America *Norman Caulfield*
Making Capitalism Safe: Work Safety and Health Regulation in America, 1880–1940 *Donald W. Rogers*
Good, Reliable, White Men: Railroad Brotherhoods, 1877–1917 *Paul Michel Taillon*

The University of Illinois Press
is a founding member of the
Association of American University Presses.

Composed in 10.5/13 Adobe Minion Pro
by Celia Shapland
at the University of Illinois Press
Manufactured by Cushing-Malloy, Inc.

University of Illinois Press
1325 South Oak Street
Champaign, IL 61820-6903
www.press.uillinois.edu